Greenhill Books

A History of the Art of War in the Middle Ages
Volume Two: 1278-1485AD

Other Books by Sir Charles Oman
published by Greenhill Books

The Art of War in the Sixteenth Century

The Great Revolt of 1381

Wellington's Army
(Napoleonic Library No.4)

Studies in the Napoleonic Wars
(Napoleonic Library No.6)

A History of
The Art of War
in the
Middle Ages
Volume Two: 1278-1485 AD

SIR CHARLES OMAN

Greenhill Books, London
Presidio Press, California

This edition of *The Art of War in the Middle Ages,*
*Volume Two: 1278-1485*AD first published 1991
by Greenhill Books, Lionel Leventhal Limited,
Park House, 1 Russell Gardens, London NW11 9NN

and

Presidio Press
31 Pamaron Way, Novato, Ca.94949, U.S.A.

Copyright C.W.C. Oman, 1924
This edition © The Trustees of the Estate of C.W.C. Oman,
1991

British Library Cataloguing in Publication Data
Oman, Charles 1860-1946
The art of war in the Middle Ages.
1. Military operations, history
I. Title
355.02

ISBN 1-85367-105-3 Volume Two
ISBN 1-85367-100-2 Volume One

Library of Congress Cataloguing in Publication Data available

Publishing History
A *History of the Art of War in the Middle Ages* originates with
Oman's Lothian Prize Essay of 1884, which was published as
The Art of War in the Middle Ages in 1885 (Blackwells,
134 pages). The work was expanded and a new edition
as *A History of the Art of War* was published in 1898
(Methuen, 667 pages). In 1924 a revised edition, expanded
to two volumes, was published. This edition reproduces the
1924 edition (Methuen) and is complete and unabridged.

Printed by Billing & Sons Limited, Worcester

TABLE OF CONTENTS

BOOK VII

ARMS, FORTIFICATION, AND SIEGECRAFT (1100–1300)

CHAPTER I.—ARMS AND ARMOUR (1100–1300)

CHAPTER II.—FORTIFICATION (1100–1300)

CHAPTER III.—SIEGECRAFT (1100–1300)

BOOK VIII

ENGLAND, WALES, AND SCOTLAND (1296–1333)— DEVELOPMENT OF THE LONGBOW

CHAPTER I.—EDWARD I AND HIS WELSH WARS (1277–1295)— DEVELOPMENT OF THE LONGBOW

CHAPTER II.—ENGLAND AND SCOTLAND (1296–1328)— FALKIRK AND BANNOCKBURN

CHAPTER III.—CONTINUATION OF THE SCOTTISH WAR : FIRST COMBINATION OF ARCHERY AND DISMOUNTED CAVALRY— DUPPLIN AND HALIDON HILL

BOOK IX

THE LONGBOW IN FRANCE AND SPAIN (1337–1396)

CHAPTER I.—COMMENCEMENT OF THE HUNDRED YEARS' WAR : THE ARMIES OF EDWARD III.

BOOK X

GUNPOWDER AND CANNON (1250–1450)

BOOK XI

THE SWISS

BOOK XII

ITALY IN THE FOURTEENTH AND FIFTEENTH CENTURIES—THE CONDOTTIERI

BOOK XIII

EASTERN EUROPE AND THE NEAR EAST (1230–1500)

CHAPTER I.—EASTERN EUROPE AND THE TARTARS

PAGES

Genghiz Khan and his Conquests—Mongol Arms and Armies—Their Tactics and Strategy—Russia and Poland in the Thirteenth Century—Battle of the Kalka (1224)—Batu conquers North Russia (1238–9)—Sack of Kief (1240)—Poland invaded, Battle of Liegnitz (1241)—Hungary invaded, Battle of the Sajo (1241)—The Mongols turn back—Consequences of the Invasions 315–335

CHAPTER II.—SOUTH-EASTERN EUROPE AND THE OTTOMAN TURKS (1300–1500)

Rise of the Ottoman Turks—Othman and Orkhan—Orkhan as State-builder—The Turkish Feudal System—Decay of the Byzantine and Serbian Empires allows the Ottoman to cross into Europe (1355)—Career of Murad I.—The Janissaries—Destruction of Serbia and Bulgaria—The Battle of Nicopolis (1396)—The Battle of Angora (1402)—Career of Murad II.—His Opponents Huniades and Scanderbeg—Second Battle of Kossovo (1448)—Mahomet II. and the Siege of Constantinople(1453)—The Turks checked by Hungary till 1521 . 336–360

CHAPTER III.—EASTERN EUROPE AND THE HUSSITES (1420–1440)

Tactical Importance of the Hussite Wars—John Zisca and his System of War—The *Wagenburg*—Its Origin and Object—Causes of the Successes of the Hussites—Their Limitations—Battle of Lipan (1434). 361–370

BOOK XIV

WESTERN EUROPE IN THE FIFTEENTH CENTURY

CHAPTER I.—FRANCE AND ENGLAND (1400–1422)—AGINCOURT

France and England in 1413—Changes in Arms and Armour in the Early Fifteenth Century—Roosebeke and Shrewsbury Field—Henry V. invades France—Battle of Agincourt (1415)—Strategy and Conquests of Henry V.—His Plan of subduing France—Its Difficulties . . 373–389

TABLE OF MAPS, PLANS, AND ILLUSTRATIONS

xi

BOOK VII

ARMS, FORTIFICATION, AND SIEGECRAFT

1100–1300

CHAPTER I

ARMS AND ARMOUR (1100–1300) [1]

IN the fifth chapter of our Third Book we described the development of knightly armour down to the end of the eleventh century, when it consisted of the conical helmet furnished with a nasal, of a long mail-shirt with or without a coif to cover the head and neck, and occasionally of guards for the legs (*ocreae bainbergae*).[2] We must now make clear the stages by which this comparatively simple equipment gradually passed into the heavy and complicated plate armour of the fourteenth century.

For some time after the Norman Conquest the improvement of armour progressed very slowly. Before the end of the eleventh century the short broad sleeves of the mail-shirt had been lengthened so as to reach the wrist, and made more closely-fitting. The Great Seal of William II. displays the change very clearly when compared with that of his father.[3] But, with the exception of this single alteration, there is practically no variation in armour till the third quarter of the twelfth century. In the time of Henry II. the fully-equipped knight was armed exactly as had been his great-grandfather who served under the Red King. It is astonishing to find that sixty years of contact with the East had affected European arms so little, but it is not till the end of the century that modifications in equipment to which we can ascribe a crusading origin make much progress. The long warfare with the Turks and Byzantines did, as we have shown on an earlier page,

[1] The periods in the history of armour do not coincide with those in the history of tactics. This chapter should be read in connection with that on fourteenth century armour.

[2] Only a very few of the personages in the Bayeux Tapestry wear leg armour. Duke William, however, generally shows it : probably only chiefs and wealthy barons were so equipped.

[3] Cf. the two Great Seals of the two Williams in Plate XVII.

have some effect in inducing Europe to esteem the horse-bowman.[1] He was, however, seldom seen in very great numbers, save in Hungarian armies, and the Magyars had been archers from the first. We never find him assuming such importance in the West as the " Turcopoles " of the military orders and the Kingdom of Jerusalem had in the Levant. It is probable that the surcoat was borrowed from the Byzantines, whose cavalry had been wont to wear it as early as the ninth century.[2] But it is only at the very end of the twelfth century that we find this light over-garment growing common : of the English monarchs John is the first who is represented as regularly wearing it.

It is also probable that the great development of the use of quilted protections for the body came from the East, where the Saracens had long been acquainted with them. The *wambais* or *gambeson*, which grows common in Europe in the twelfth century, was a defence of this sort, composed of layers of cloth, tow, rags, or suchlike substances,[3] quilted on to a foundation of canvas or leather, and then covered with an outer coat of linen, cloth, or silk. The knightly class took to wearing gambesons under their mail-shirts as an additional protection for the body, while infantry and the poorer sort of horsemen wore them as their sole defence. They are well known to Wace, who mentions them repeatedly as worn by Normans at Hastings.[4] The great Assize of Arms of Henry II. orders that " burgenses et tota communa liberorum hominum " are to wear " wambais et capellet ferri," as opposed to the knights who bear " loricas cassides, et clypeos." [5] One of the forms of the gambeson, the acton (hacqueton), shows its Oriental origin by its name, derived from the Arabic *al-qutun*. It was so called because the quilting was stuffed with cotton. Students of the third Crusade will remember that Saladin gave to Richard Coeur de Lion " unum *alcottonem* satis levem, nullo spiculo penetrabilem "

---

[1] It must be remembered that Europe was acquainted with the Magyar horse-archer long before the Crusades. There is a horse-archer in the Bayeux Tapestry among the three Normans who in its last group are represented as pursuing the flying English. So the idea was not absolutely new.

[2] See vol. i. pp. 187, 188.

[3] The gambeson (wambasia) is defined in a thirteenth-century document (Hewitt, i. 127) as "tunica spissa ex lino et stuppa, vel e veteribus pannis, consuta."

[4] "Plusors orent vestu gambais" (*R. de Rou*, 12811).

[5] Assize of Arms in Stubbs' *Charters*, p. 154.

SEALS OF WILLIAM I. AND WILLIAM II.

SEALS OF RICHARD I. AND HENRY III.

as a specimen of the best Eastern armour.   The *perpunctum* (*pourpoint*) was another name for one of the many varieties of the gambeson.

By the middle of the twelfth century it would seem that a distinction had been established between *lorica* and *albergellus*, the two forms of the mail-shirt—the former being the newer and more complete form with the coif, the latter the old byrnie without that extra protection.   Hence, in the Assize of Arms of Henry II. mentioned above, while the knights and all having chattels to the value of more than sixteen marks wear the *lorica* and *cassis*, persons owning between sixteen and ten marks are only expected to provide themselves with a hauberk and steel cap (" albergel et capellet ferri ").[1]

It is only at the end of the twelfth century that serious changes in the character of the knightly equipment begin.   The helm is the first part of the panoply to be affected : abandoning the conical shape, it begins sometimes to be flattened at the top, though it still retains the nasal and leaves the face exposed. Such a shape may be seen in the figures of knights in the well-known Life of St. Guthlac in the British Museum.[2]   Very shortly after this modification in headgear began, a more complete one follows,—the nasal expands into a covering for the whole of the face, leaving only the eyes exposed.   Thus is produced the pot-helmet or casque, whose earliest form we see on the second Great Seal of Richard I.[3]   This is the first headpiece concealing the whole head which had been used since classical times.   It was enormously heavy, so much so that it was often made to come down on to the shoulders, so as to relieve the neck from as much weight as possible.   In the figure of King Richard the casque is filled with a movable vizor with two long slits for the eyes, which can be lifted at need.   But the prevailing form in the thirteenth century was a helm without vizor, but having eyeholes, and below them a group of circular or square openings for breathing, such as is displayed on the Great Seal of Henry III.[4]   This very heavy and cumbrous headpiece lasted throughout the thirteenth century, retaining generally its original flat-topped shape ; but it is occasionally found with a conical summit like a sugar loaf.[5]   Owing to its weight, it was assumed only the moment before the battle : at

---

[1] Assize of Arms in Stubbs' *Charters*, p. 154.   [2] Harleian Roll, x.
[3] See Plate XVIII. Fig. A.   [4] See Plate XVIII. Fig. B.   [5] See Plate XIX. Fig. C.

the Marchfeld we are told how the cry, " Helms on ! " ran down Rudolf's ranks when the Bohemians came in sight. At Taglia-cozzo the knights of Charles of Anjou removed their helms during the short interval between the discomfiture of Conradin's corps and the reappearance of Henry of Castile upon the field. A knight whose helm had been knocked awry so that the eye-slits no longer came opposite the eyes was in a most helpless condition. We are told of Guy of Montfort at Tagliacozzo that he got his helmet battered aside, and consequently laid about him like a blind man, and wounded his friend Alard of St. Valery, who came to set it straight for him.[1] It must be remembered that this head-dress was by no means universally worn. Many knights disliked it on account of its weight, and preferred to wear the older and simpler mail coif. This we see on the effigy of William Longsword [1227], as also in the much later battle scene on Plate xx.

The pot-helm of the thirteenth century was not unfrequently adorned with various sorts of ornaments, a thing which had not been seen since the crested Frankish helm was superseded by the plain helm with nasal three centuries before. Richard I. on his second Great Seal wears a large fan-shaped ornament. The Count of Boulogne at Bouvines had crowned his helm with two large horns of whalebone : [2] even more complicated addi-tions to the headpiece are sometimes seen.

These were probably assumed not only for decorative pur-poses, but to identify their wearers, who, since the face was com-pletely covered by the pot-helm, could no longer be recognised by their friends. For the same reason, the surcoat, instead of being left plain, was now embroidered with the coat-of-arms of the bearer. Heraldry had begun to come in about the middle of the twelfth century,[3] but it was not till its end that all members of the knightly class assumed regular armorial bearings. Richard I. is the first king who displays the three golden lions on a red ground, which have become the arms of England.

About the same time that the pot-helm and the armorial

[1] Primatus in Bouquet, xxiii. 35.
[2] *Philippeis*, xi. 232 :
  " Cornua conus agit superasque eduxit in auras
    E costis assumpta nigris quas faucis in antro
    Branchia balenae Britici colit incola ponti."
[3] The Great Seal of Philip of Flanders (1161) is one of the first on which definitely heraldic bearings as opposed to mere ornamental designs are to be found displayed.

surcoat came into fashion, the shield was very considerably
reduced in its dimensions. The knight was now so well protected by his body armour that it had become less necessary to
him. In the thirteenth century it was no longer kite-shaped,
but triangular : all through that age it steadily diminished in
size, till by 1300 it was comparatively insignificant, and could no
longer be used (as it had been for many ages) to carry a wounded
knight, or to convey a corpse.

It will be easily seen that the knights who fought at Bouvines
or Mansourah were very different in outward appearance from
their ancestors of the early twelfth century. The closed pot-
helmet and the surcoat, together with the small shield, presented
a totally different appearance from the nasal-helmet, the un-
covered hauberk, and the long kite-shaped shield. But beneath
these outward trappings the main body armour was not very
much altered. The mail-shirt and its coif were still the universal
wear, though they had been rendered more effective for defence
by improved gambesons or actons worn beneath. All accounts
agree that the armour of 1200 discharged its purpose very
well : it will be remembered how thoroughly the Franks at
Tiberias were protected by their mail against the Turkish arrows,[1]
and how even the gambesons of the foot-soldiery proved impenetrable at Arsouf.[2] Guillaume le Breton remarks in his
account of Bouvines how much the battles of his own day differed
from those of antiquity. Formerly men fell by the ten thousand,
now the slaughter was comparatively slight—

> "Corpora tot coriis, tot gambesonibus armant."

The same author shows us that already a further form of protection for the breast was coming into use : under the gambeson
some knights were beginning to wear a thin plate of iron. When
William des Barres and Richard Coeur de Lion tilted against
each other—

> "Utraque per clipeos ad corpora fraxinus ibat,
> Gambesumque audax forat, et thoraca trilicem
> Disjicit : ardenti nimium prorumpere tandem
> *Vix obstat ferro fabricata patena recocto*
> Qua bene munierat pectus sibi cautus uterque."[3]

This first hint of plate armour differs entirely from its later
development, in that it was worn *beneath* and not *above* the rest
of the panoply.

[1] See vol. i. p. 331.   [2] See vol. i. p. 309.   [3] *Philippeis*, iii.

As the manufacture of chain mail was perfected, it was found possible to use it in more delicate sizes for the protection of the hands and feet. Mail mittens consisting of a thumb and a single covering for the other four fingers came in with the thirteenth century : the effigy of William Longsword in the nave of Salisbury Cathedral displays them very well.[1] They were fixed to the sleeves of the mail-shirt, but there was left in the palm of the hand an opening like that of a modern glove, but larger, through which the wearer could draw out his hand, leaving the mitten dangling at his wrist. It was only at the end of the century that the art of the smith advanced so far as to provide separate openings for each finger, and so to turn the mitten into a glove.

Leg coverings were much improved at the same time : in the twelfth century they had generally guarded the outer side of the leg, being laced together and leaving the inner part, which touched the saddle, unprotected. In the thirteenth century they became continuous and complete coverings for the limb, which came up to the hips and were joined there to the inner side of the mail-shirt, which overlapped them. At Bouvines, when Reginald of Boulogne had been thrown from his horse, one of the French sergeants endeavoured to thrust him through under the skirts of his hauberk, but failed because the leg mail and the shirt were firmly secured together.

The beginnings of plate armour applied *above* the rest of the panoply appear about the middle of the thirteenth century. At first they were used only for exposed parts, such as the elbows, knee-caps, and shins, small plates being here fixed over the mail. Somewhat later the cuirass of plate commences to appear. It was no more than an iron covering for the breast, not guarding the armpit or the neck, and, though it weighed down the wearer considerably, gave him no very complete protection. The reader will remember how ill the German knights at Benevento (1266) fared, in spite of their breastplates, when contending with the French knights, who still wore mail-shirts alone. The development of plate armour is really a matter of the fourteenth century — the thirteenth saw no more than its commencement.

Typical figures from the end of the thirteenth century may serve to show the modest nature of these first beginnings of

[1] See Fig. A of Plate XIX.

THIRTEENTH-CENTURY ARMOUR

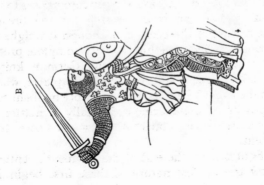

plate armour. In the battle-piece from the celebrated *Lives of the Two Offas*[1] in the British Museum (Plate xx.), King Offa himself wears defences for his knees and greaves of plate strapped above his chain-mail hose   One of the defeated enemies, who is receiving a spear-thrust in the throat, has a vizor of plate curiously fitted on to the front of his chain-mail coif—a composite head-dress much less common than either the plain coif or the massive pot-helm. The effigy of William de Durfort, from the cloisters of the Annunziata at Florence (1289) (Plate XIX. B), gives decidedly more plate than the representation of King Offa. He is protected to the thigh, and not merely to the knee, by highly-ornamented plates girt on above his mail. It will be noticed that his mail gloves have fingers, and not merely the mitten-like divisions between thumb and fingers shown by Offa and his knights as well as by the figures of the early part of the thirteenth century.

[1] Nero. D. i.

CHAPTER II

FORTIFICATION (1100–1300)

IN the third, fourth, and sixth chapters of our Third Book
we indicated the causes which led to the rehabilitation
of military architecture in the West after nearly five centuries
of neglect. Under the stress of the concentric attack from
Viking, Magyar, and Saracen, which was at its worst between
850 and 950, all the peoples of Latin Christendom had been
compelled to avail themselves, to the best of their power, of the
resources of fortification. Hence came the patching up of
countless Roman walls in every region between England and
Apulia ; hence, too, the erection of the palisaded *burhs* and
burgs of Edward the Elder and Henry of Saxony, and the
fencing in of the innumerable private strongholds of the feudal
aristocracy of Europe.

Down to the eleventh century it is not too much to say
that stonework was the exception, and palisaded earthworks
the general rule, in all places where Roman works were
not already in existence. Where the ancient enceinte was
susceptible of repair, it was of course utilised by the tenth-
century builder, *e.g.* at London or Chester. On the Continent
(though not on this side of the Channel) there were a certain
number of great towns which had preserved a continuous
existence as fortresses since the fall of the Western Empire,
whose walls needed only to be kept in good order, not to be
rebuilt : such were Rome, Verona, Narbonne, and Carcassonne.
But such cases were exceptional. Even of the old Roman towns
many had been so repeatedly destroyed that their original
walls were too far gone for repair, and the tenth-century
builder had practically to start afresh in the task of fortification.
Often we find mere ditches and palisades surrounding what had
once been a city, possessing a regular Roman enceinte. The

THIRTEENTH-CENTURY ARMOUR

new works might coincide with the lines of the old, or they
might enclose a greater or a lesser space. At Lincoln, for
example, the Anglo-Danish city stretched much farther down the
hillside towards the Witham than the Roman walls had done.
At York, on the other hand, the tenth-century city occupied
less ground than the ancient Eboracum. But both were alike
in that they were now defended only by earthworks and stakes,
not by solid masonry. Asser explains the storm of York by
the Danes in 867 by the fact that " non enim tunc adhuc
illa civitas firmos et stabilitos muros illis temporibus habebat." [1]

Of the centres of urban life in Western Christendom,
therefore, some were guarded with stone walls, many more by
ditch and palisade, while perhaps most numerous of all were
those which were dominated by a royal, episcopal, or baronial
stronghold, but were not themselves girt with any complete ring
of defence. On the Continent especially, counts and bishops
were often jealous of allowing the townsmen to fortify themselves, and preferred to make them rely on a place of refuge
which was in the hands of their feudal lord. In time of war the
population were able to retire into their master's palisaded
mound or walled castle. In time of peace the fortress dominated the town and kept the burghers in obedience. During
the tenth and the first half of the eleventh century these
seigneurial fortresses were, as a rule, mere moated mounds ;
the stone castle was a rarity. Castle-building was not, indeed,
unknown in much earlier ages. In the second half of the sixth
century, Venantius Fortunatus describes Nicetius, Bishop of
Trier, as building a real stone fortress to dominate the ancient
city below him. [2] But the art of building had actually retrograded
between 550 and 800, and it was long before stone castles came
into general use. They were both too expensive for the
ninth- or tenth-century count or bishop's purse, and too hard of
construction for his master-builder. Instead, rocky fastnesses
were strengthened with cuttings and ditches, or, where rocks

[1] Asser, § 27.
[2] " Hic vir apostolicus Nicetius, arva peragrans
  Condidit optatum pastor ovile gregi.
  Turribus incinxit terdenis undique collem,
  Praebuit hanc fabricam, quo nemus ante fuit.

 . . . . . .

  Turris ab adverso quae constitit obvia clivo
  Sanctorum locus est, arma tenenda viris."

did not abound naturally, hillocks or artificial mounds were trenched and palisaded. *Motte* (mound) seems to have been the general name for these structures among the Romance-speaking races. In England the private fortress did not exist till the coming of the Normans. The *burhs* of Alfred and Edward the Elder were not castles but walled enclosures, some guarding old settlements—of all sizes from London downward—some new, but destined to become great towns; others with no future before them, and doomed to early oblivion. They were never residential strongholds of individual magnates.

The character of the continental " motte " is well expressed in a passage from the *Acta Sanctorum*, describing the life of St. John, Bishop of Terouanne in Flanders, who died in 1130. It is worth quoting at full length.[1]

" Bishop John had in the town of Merchem a mansion where he could abide with his retinue, while perambulating his diocese. Beside the court of the church there was a stronghold, which we might call a castle or a *municipium*.[2] It was a lofty structure, built, according to the local custom, by the lord of that town many years before. For the rich and noble of that region, being much given to feuds and bloodshed, fortify themselves in order to protect themselves from their foes, and by these strongholds subdue their equals and oppress their inferiors. They heap up a mound as high as they are able, and dig round it as broad a ditch as they can excavate, hollowing it out to a very considerable depth. Round the summit of the mound they construct a palisade of timber, to act as a wall; it is most firmly compacted together, with towers set in it at intervals in a circle as best can be arranged. Inside the palisade they erect a house, or rather a citadel,[3] which looks down on the whole neighbourhood. No one can enter the place save by a bridge, which starts from the outer edge of the ditch and is carried on piers, built two or three together gradually rising in height, so that it reaches the flat space on top of the mound and comes in opposite the gate of the

---

[1] I owe my knowledge of this most interesting description to Mr. G. T. Clark's *Mediæval Military Architecture*. Though some of his theories are out of date, his collections of facts remain invaluable.

[2] What did the author, John of Colmieu, intend by a *municipium*? Certainly not a "corporate town"; but probably a "burg," taking the word *municipium* straight from *munire*, to fortify.

[3] *Arx*.

palisade. . . . The bishop returned to the stronghold with his retinue after holding a confirmation, in order to change his vestments, for he was next proposing to consecrate a cemetery. As he was coming down again from his abode, with no small crowd before and behind him, and had reached the middle of the bridge, some thirty-five feet or more above the level of the ditch, the structure gave way—no doubt owing to the illwill of our Old Enemy [Satan]. The bridge fell, and all the crowd upon it: beams, planks, and supports came down with a fearful crash. So great was the cloud of dust which rose up above the ruin, that no one could see exactly what had happened."

The description of this Flemish mound-fortress might serve for that of countless tenth- and eleventh-century strongholds in the Low Countries, France, and Germany. But in England the Anglo-Saxon magnates had no such private fortresses. They dwelt in halls such as we may see represented in the Bayeux Tapestry, where Harold Godwineson is shown feasting his friends at Bosham. The picture shows a two-storied building, more probably of timber than of stone, with pillared vaults below and living-rooms above. There is no indication of any external defences—probably a hedged enclosure sufficed. The first private strongholds seen on this side of the Channel were erected in the reign of Edward the Confessor by some of his Norman satellites. They were so strange to the Anglo-Saxon chronicler that he uses the foreign word " castle " to define them. One is recorded as having been put up on the Welsh border, perhaps at Ewyas Harold, by Osbern Pentecost, another by one Robert at Clavering in Essex : possibly there were one or two others.[1] But the thegnhood had not begun to copy the device, and Orderic Vitalis is undoubtedly right when he remarks that the easy subjection of England by William the Conqueror was in no small degree due to the fact that "there were practically no fortresses ' such as the French call *castella* ' in the land, wherefore the English, though warlike and courageous, proved too feeble to withstand their enemies." [2]

The Normans were essentially castle-builders, but it must not be supposed that already before the Conquest they had introduced stone fortresses : the mound, ditched and timbered, such as we see it in the Bayeux Tapestry, was the type of Duke

[1] See Round in *Feudal England*, p. 190.   [2] Orderic, iii. 14.

William's castles.   His barons were provided with nothing
better, for it is a mistake to suppose that the stone castle was
prevalent everywhere on the Continent by the year 1066.
William himself, though a great builder, was only able to
erect a very limited number of castles of the type of the Tower
of London.   Domesday Book mentions forty-nine castles as
existing in 1086 ; and of these, thirty-three at least were on
sites which had been previously occupied by Saxon strongholds.
Twenty-eight of these thirty-three are built on artificial mounds.
But when the buildings of those which still survive are in-
vestigated, the large majority of them are found to be of Norman
work, but of a date distinctly later than the Conqueror—of
the time of Henry I. and Stephen.   As it is incredible that one
Norman keep should have been removed merely to make
way for another of the same type, slightly modified, we are
driven to the conclusion that nearly all of William's castles
were merely timbered *mottes*.   The masonry was added half a
century later.[1]

Historical evidence bears out this conclusion, for we know
that many of William's " castles " were constructed in a few
months—a time wholly insufficient for the building of stone
works.   The castle of York, for example, he ordered to be
built during the summer of 1068.   It was finished and
garrisoned by 500 men.   But in March 1069 the Northum-
brians rose in revolt and besieged it.   William returned to
relieve it, and supplemented it by the erection of a second
castle on the opposite bank of the river.   This structure was
completed in *eight days*.[2]   But in September 1069 the natives
rose again, aided by the Danes, stormed the castles, and
demolished them by burning them with fire.   Obviously such
hastily - constructed works, capable of being burned down,
cannot possibly have been composed of masonry, and must
have been palisaded mound and ditch fortresses, not keeps of
the later Norman style.   Such undoubtedly were the large
majority of William's strongholds.

But there were also a small number of true stone castles

[1] See excellent deductions on this point in Hamilton-Thompson's *Military
Architecture in England*, pp. 37-45, and in Mrs. Armitage's *Early Norman Castles
of the British Isles*.

[2] Orderic Vitalis, 512 D : "Rex autem dies octo in urbe morans, alterum
praesidium condidit, et Gulielmum comitem Osberni filium ad custodiendum
reliquit."

erected in the Conqueror's day, either in places where no earlier
fortifications existed, or where an important town or region
needed to be held down by a citadel of exceptional strength.
The Tower of London may serve for an example : it rises to a
height of ninety feet, and consists of an enormous quadrangular
keep (a hundred and seven feet by a hundred and eighteen),
built of rubble rudely coursed, and with a very large proportion
of mortar to the stone. Only the windows, quoins, and pilaster
strips were of ashlar. The individual stones are not very large,
so that the loss of a certain amount of them by the attacks
of an enemy using the bore (*terebrus*) [1] would not have been
very dangerous to the stability of the fabric. The walls are
fifteen feet thick in the basement storey, thirteen in the first,
between ten and eleven in the second and third. The entrance
was probably on the south side on the first floor level ; there
was also a small postern on the same stage. These entries
were at a considerable distance above the ground, and could
only be reached through some sort of a fore-building, which
disappeared when the original keep was surrounded by outer
walls, on which the main stress of the defence fell. A vertical
wall within the tower divides it into a smaller eastern and
a larger western half ; each of these halves, again, is sub-
divided into chambers. The gloomy basement served as a
storehouse ; the first floor, hardly less gloomy, must have been
intended for habitation, perhaps as guardrooms for the garrison,
as it is fitted with chimney flues. The second floor contains the
large Chapel of St. John and the banqueting-chamber ; the
third, or " state floor," comprises the council-room and the
king's apartments. There are, of course, other smaller rooms
in each stage. The largest individual spaces of the chambers
(excluding the vast storeroom in the basement, which measures
ninety-one feet by thirty-five) are those in the western half,
of which several are ninety feet long : the chapel is forty feet
by thirty-one. The main access from floor to floor is given by
a spiral staircase, eleven feet in diameter, contained in the
north-eastern angle of the keep, which is curved out into a
turret for the purpose ; there are also smaller spiral staircases
contrived in the thickness of the wall.

In the Conqueror's time this vast quadrangular building stood
by its own strength : any outer defences which existed must

[1] See vol. i. p. 133.

have been unimportant ; they amounted to no more than the usual ditch, mound, and palisade. It was not till William had been dead some years that his son the Red King set to work to surround the keep with a wall of masonry : it was an extensive and expensive undertaking, so that " the shires which with their work belonged to London suffered great detriment by reason of the wall, and of the king's hall-work which was being wrought at Westminster." [1]

The strength of such a structure as the Tower of London lay in the extraordinary solidity of its construction. Against walls fifteen or twenty feet thick the feeble siege-artillery of the day beat without perceptible effect. With no woodwork to be set on fire, and no openings near the ground to be battered in, it had an almost endless capacity for passive resistance. Even a small garrison could hold out as long as its provisions lasted. Mining was perhaps the device which had most hope of success against such a stronghold ; [2] but if the castle was provided with a deep ditch, or if it stood on rocky ground, mining even was of no avail. There remained the laborious expedient of demolishing the lower parts of the walls by the bore, worked under the shelter of a penthouse. If the ditch was shallow enough to be filled, and a " cat " could be brought close to the foot of the tower, this method might have some faint hope of success. Before brattices [3] or bastions were invented, there was no means by which the missiles of the besieged could adequately command the ground immediately below the wall. The loopholes were very small, and did not permit of vertical fire, so that the only way by which the garrison could get at the engineers of the besieger was by leaning over the battlements at the top of the tower. Here they would be exposed to the fire of the military engines and archers of the enemy, who were brought up to protect the men working under the shelter of the " cat." Hence something might be done by the method of demolishing the lower stages of the walls ; but the process was always slow, laborious, and exceedingly costly in the matter of

[1] A.S. Chronicle, *sub anno* 1097.
[2] The classical instance of the success of a mine against a Norman keep is the capture of Rochester by King John in 1215. He succeeded in bringing down a corner of the building.
[3] The brattice was a hoarding of woodwork projecting outside the stonework of the tower, being supported on beams fixed in the wall, or on corbels built into it. From holes in its floor it commanded the ground at the foot of the tower.

human lives. Unless pressed for time, a good commander would generally prefer to work by starvation, the one form of attack which the keep was wholly unable to withstand. It will be noted that the defenders had no facilities for annoying the besiegers by sorties ; the entrance of their stronghold was narrow, visible, and high above the ground. A force could only issue from it slowly, and when checked would have the greatest difficulty in returning to their fastness. Hence the defender seldom wasted his men in endeavouring to attack the assailant : the only occasion on which he would be likely to essay it would be when military machines were doing such damage that they must be at all costs destroyed.

The square stone-keep, however, was rare in King William's own day, though the keeps of Colchester and Richmond Castles date along with the Tower of London : the great castle-building age of the Normans was the twelfth century, to which belong such splendid examples as the keeps of Rochester (built before 1140), Dover (built *circ.* 1160), Portchester, Castle Heding-ham, and Norwich. In all of them the square keep, even if originally the main or only fortification, became in time part of a system of outer works. Sometimes it was isolated in the middle of a " bailey" or outer enclosure, at others it was in-corporated in the outer defences of the castle considered as a whole ; still more frequently it was not left in the outermost ring, but became the innermost refuge forming part of the interior ward. It was the shape and character of the site which dictated the ultimate destiny of the keep.

It must not be supposed that the prevalent type of stronghold in the twelfth century was one in which a square solid keep was the really important part of the fortress, and the rest merely subsidiary. Far more usual was another type, on which the name of shell-keep has been bestowed. It consists of a ring of fortifi-cation surrounding an open court, and assuming many different shapes of a circular or polygonal sort. The shell-keep was the form of work usually selected by the Norman architect, when he was improving one of the old palisaded mound-castles. It was formed by substituting a ring of masonry for the earlier structure of earth and stakes round the crown of the hillock. Unlike the square and solid keep of the rarer type, it is a regular evolution from the stage of fortification which had gone before it. When architects grew more competent and masons more numerous, it was an obvious improvement to substitute stone and mortar for earth and beams. Hence, as a general rule, the first mound-castle was followed by a Norman shell-keep. It seems also to be true that in many cases the loose artificially-made soil of the mound was not strong enough to bear a solid structure, and could only support a ring-wall.[1] Within the circle of masonry were erected the buildings which sheltered the owner and his garrison ; they were built with the ring-wall for their back, and faced inwards into the little court ; often they seem to have been mere slight timber structures, for even in Norman days the lord did not always live in his stronghold, but only repaired thither in time of war, spending most of his time in riding from manor to manor, with his large and miscellaneous household and retinue. Only in exposed frontier fortresses such as those of the Welsh Marches, did the master find it necessary to make his keep his permanent abode.

Berkeley and Arundel may be taken as showing good specimens of the shell-keep built upon an original mound. A plan of the former, with its later additions, is annexed on Plate XXI. Abroad the same type is very common ; such was the old burg at Leyden, where the ring-wall circles the crown of an early Frisian mound. The castle of Bôves in Picardy, besieged and taken by Philip Augustus in 1185, shows a similar character ; but the shell-keep on its steep mound was strengthened by a square tower, which acted as a last refuge for the garrison when the miners of the French king broke the ring-wall. There are ruins of structures of the same sort both in Eastern and in Western Germany. Wherever the old mound-fortresses existed, the shell-keep was the first and most natural stage in their evolution into regular mediæval castles.

Both the square solid keep and the shell-keep were normally supplemented by outer defences, either at their first construction or at a later date. It is rare to find examples of them without any additional walls outside—though Bowes Castle in North Yorkshire seems to be such an exception. The original English

---

[1] My friend, Mr. Doyle, of All Souls College, pointed out to me an interesting phenomenon in the little castle of Tretower, near Crickhowell, where a Norman shell-keep had been utilised by a later owner as the outer wall of his fortress, a very narrow tower being erected in the centre of the shell-keep, so as to make a little "inner ward" of the ground between the new building and the old shell.

or continental mound-fortress was of small extent, but round it grew up the dwellings of the owner's retainers, and presently some light defences of ditch and hedge were drawn round them, so that the keep or motte became only the citadel. The outer enclosure was known as the "bailey"; it might be large or small, single or double, all on a level, or staged to suit the shape of a hill. When the defences of the bailey were made stronger, and walls supplanted ditch and hedge, we have arrived at a very common eleventh- and twelfth-century type of fortress— the keep surrounded by a curtain-wall containing a considerable space of ground. The enclosed area may be large, and a whole town may be built within it. On the other hand, it may be quite small, only affording room for the few buildings and storehouses needed by the garrison of the keep. As a general rule the keep lies not in the middle of the space, but at one end of it, or set in the wall. This was often due to the fact that the mound was the end of the spur of a hill or rising ground, cut off from it by the excavation of its ditch. The extension of the fortress was along the top of the spur, not below that front of the mound which looked towards the plain. So we often find a castle with its original keep on the end of the spur, its first extension just beyond the original ditch, and then a second extension, or "outer ward," still farther remote from the early citadel. When a castle was not on a spur, but upon an isolated mound in the plain, it must of course have been more or less a matter of chance on which side the outgrowth began. But as a general rule the keep stands at one end of the enclosed space, not in its midst. The same is true of towns and their citadels —the normal type has the castle at one end of the place, like London, Winchester, or Oxford. It is rare to find it set right in the midst of the inhabited space, though Ferrara and Evreux may serve as examples. Obviously there was danger in the close juxtaposition of houses to the citadel : they gave too much cover to an enemy, and if set on fire might stifle the defenders of the stronghold which they surrounded.

The castle-builder tried as a rule not to place his fortress on an absolutely flat site—but, of course, it was sometimes merely the guardhouse of a great town of the plains, where the whole terrain for miles around was level—as, for example, at Milan, Ferrara, Leyden, or Ghent. There he was forced to build on low ground, with at best an artificial mound to give the castle some slight dominating power. Normally he looked for hills and eminences, or in default of these sought difficult spots protected by water, where a lake or a marsh formed an outer defence, as at Leeds in Kent, Caerphilly, Kenilworth, the Scottish strongholds of Lochleven and Lochindorb, or the French Chantilly. There was one special advantage in water-girt castles: undermining was impossible against them: if the besieger was unwise enough to try to make subterranean approaches, the water from above would percolate in, and drown the excavators.

When it was possible to contrive a wet ditch, therefore, every attempt was made to add this protection, by damming streams and turning them into the ditch, or by filling it from the overflow of a convenient neighbouring river. But the more common type of castle was built on high ground, where a wet ditch was of course an impossibility—since water refuses to run uphill. In such cases the only resource was to cut the ditch both steep and deep—so far as the hardness of the soil permitted.

The growing impregnability of fortresses, as the builder's art developed, became the despair of kings and overlords who had to cope with vassals owning many of them. For to deal with a well-designed castle by escalade was almost impossible : undermining was hopeless if the place were surrounded by a lake or a marsh, or (on the other hand) if it were perched on solid rocks against which the mason might toil in vain. Siege machines for battering were still weak and incompetent —it was only in the thirteenth century that they improved— and all the time the art of defence was improving also.

The only certain method by which many of the stronger castles could be dealt with was famine. In the end it was often better not to waste lives by trying to storm a rebel's stronghold, or time and money by trying to batter or under-mine it, but simply to shut it in and trust to the slow work of starvation. But, unfortunately for kings, feudal armies were always wanting to go home at short notice ; a long siege tried their patience, and not even the plunder to be got at a surrender could keep the besiegers in their tents and trenches when October rain or December frost had set in. A well-victualled castle might hold out for months innumerable—as did Pevensey on the one side and Kenilworth on the other during the long strife of Henry III. with his baronage. Some of the Crusading sieges (*e.g.* that of Acre) went on for several years. Happy, then, was the king who could afford to hire war-hardened mercenaries, who never wanted to go home. He could, when his rebel had " gone to ground," block him in, stop all his exits with solid works, and leave his hired bands to see the matter out to the end.

The castles of England, it may be remarked, fall roughly into two classes—the royal and the baronial—which had in the main quite different objects. The royal castles had one or other of two purposes : either they were intended to act as the guardhouses of large and possibly turbulent cities, or they were placed in strategical positions, which had been chosen with the general defence of the realm in view. The king was direct lord of most of the chief towns of England—though a few were in the hands of great vassals, spiritual or temporal—such as Warwick, Leicester, or Durham. But as a rule the king kept the cities for himself, and to watch each of them, built on some strong point inside or alongside of their walls, a castle which would be held by a comparatively small permanent garrison. He could never—owing to the habitual impecuniosity of mediæval kings—afford to pay a large one. The castle served in time of peace as a residence for a castellan, as a gaol, and as a store-house in which any valuable royal property in the district could be placed in safe custody. In time of war it was a final refuge, if the town wall were broken by foreign enemies or domestic rebels. But essentially its main purpose was to overawe the townsmen. Such were the Tower of London, and the castles of York, Bristol, Norwich, or Winchester.

But in addition the king had, outside the great centres of population, other castles which we can only call strategical. Sometimes they were placed to guard an obvious point of entry into the realm from without, like the castles of Dover, Portchester, or Pevensey, each facing an easily accessible landing-place for transmarine enemies. In other cases they were placed at important points within the realm, to guard critical fords, passes, or defiles, such as Windsor and Walling-ford, covering the two chief passages of the Thames, or Newark and Nottingham, watching the most practicable fords on the central Trent.

On the other hand, the baronial castles, save one class of

them in the extreme North and West, to be spoken of hereafter, had for the most part a purely local significance. The head of a great baronial house sought for his stronghold primarily mere strength of resistance, looking for the place in his estates which would enable him to make the longest defence against any enemy, whether the foes of the realm, or (even more probably) his sovereign lord the king. Impregnability was the point sought rather than strategic convenience. Of course a baron whose estates lay mainly in Essex or Kent could not select such fastnesses as were at the disposition of one who held land in Devon or Derbyshire. But he would do his best, and guard himself by marsh and stream if cliffs were unavailable. Hence the larger sort of baronial castle had usually no strategic importance, but was at the most destined to cover a district of which it was the centre and capital—*e.g.* Berkeley, Castle Hedingham, Warwick, or Tonbridge. Such fortresses were usually isolated units, with no interdependence on each other, because (owing to the way in which baronial estates were scattered around the countryside) few families owned in one district a continuous stretch of land large enough to require more than one stronghold to defend it. There were a very few exceptional groups, such as these owned by the earls of Norfolk in East Anglia. But castles on neighbouring sites were more often those of rivals than of friends, and had no purpose of mutual strategical support.

There were, however, two regions where castle-building was on a different scheme, and where the general rule that a baronial stronghold was essentially self-contained and self-sufficing, with no ulterior purpose beyond local strength, and no regard for neighbours, does not hold. The most prominent case is that of the Welsh March, where the conditions of the land dictated mutual support and strategical interdependence to the hardy and persevering baronage who had laid hands on so much Celtic ground. South Wales, as is generally known, was subdued not by royal invasions, but by the successive advances of adventurers to whom the king had given leave to conquer all that they could in the lands of his Welsh enemies. The community of Marcher barons had many feuds among themselves, but their general interests were linked together by their common purpose of holding down the turbulent Welsh tribes on whom they had imposed their yoke. Starting with a group of castles in Gwent and Glamorgan on the south, and in front of Chester and Montgomery in the north, they pressed forward building a new fortress to hold down each conquered valley. For only by such stringent pressure could the Welsh be controlled. In the North the Norman advance was for two centuries limited—the first rush had been stopped by the great defeat on the Menai Strait in 1098, in which Hugh de Montgomery fell. The permanent line of occupation only reached as far as a line of castles in front of Chester—Flint, Mold, Hawarden, Oswestry, Caurs, and Montgomery—leaving the " Four Cantreds " between the Dee and the Conway un-subdued. As has been truly observed, these fortresses formed a belt of fortifications to protect Cheshire and North Shropshire, rather than a series of bases for the absorption of North Wales.[1]

But in the South things went differently, and the great invaders—de Clares, Newmarches, Braoses, Bohuns, Cliffords, Lacys, Verduns, and the rest—went on conquering and to conquer, pressing down the whole countryside by lines of castles steadily built more and more westward, till the coast of the Irish Sea was reached at Cardigan and Pembroke. Each new fortress was supported by the last-built one behind it. The lord of a newly-subdued valley was obviously unable to hold his own unless he was on good terms with his neighbour behind. So in South Wales we trace line after line of castles representing successive growths of occupation. The Marchers had to work together, as each one of them isolated would have been unable to maintain his position, among the turbulent and obstinate natives on to whose lands he had pushed forward. Hence South Wales is more thickly set with castles than any other region of the British Isles. The greatest of them are placed at the exits of main valleys—such are Chepstow, Aber-gavenny, Cardiff, and Kidwelly, generally in comparatively low ground blocking each a valley. On the other hand, the few castles which the Welsh princes built for defence are eagle's nests on lofty cliffs, places of last refuge rather than strategical positions. Such were Dynevor, Caercynan, and Bere.[2]

The only other region of England where interdependence of castles, on a much less marked scale, may be noted, is the Scottish Border. There was here one radical difference from

---

[1] Morris, *Welsh Wars of Edward I.*, p. 7.
[2] For this generalisation see Morris, *Welsh Wars*, pp. 310-311.

the position in Wales—in the latter, castle-building during the twelfth and thirteenth centuries was purely baronial. On the Northumbrian and Cumbrian border, Carlisle and Newcastle [and Berwick later] were royal fortresses, if Bamborough, Alnwick, Wark, Naworth, and others were baronial. But the Scot was an enemy to the baron no less than to the king : hence the whole group, whoever might be the individual owner, were necessarily worked together. It did not much matter whether a ford or a road was blocked by a fortress belonging to the crown or by one belonging to a baron. All had perforce to join in defence against the common national enemy.

Such was the stage at which fortification had arrived in Western and Central Europe, when a new influence was brought to bear upon it. The Crusades put the men of the twelfth century in touch with the Levant, where they had the opportunity of studying the splendid fortresses which the Eastern emperors had built, and of which so many were now in the hands of the Turks and Saracens. To have to undertake the sieges of great fenced cities like Nicæa, Antioch, or Jerusalem was almost an education in itself to the engineers of the West. Their feeble engines and their primitive methods of attack were utterly unable to cope with such strongholds, and as a rule famine or treachery alone enabled them to win the places which they beleaguered. The essential features of Byzantine military architecture were the erection of double and triple defences round the core of the fortress, and the careful provision of towers set at intervals in the " curtain " of the walls. Both were new ideas to the Crusaders, whose notion of a fortress was nothing more than a keep surrounded by a plain outer curtain not strengthened with towers.

Constantinople, the most perfect of all the Eastern fortresses, struck the Franks as absolutely impregnable. The great city was covered successfully for something over a thousand years by one of the last efforts of old Roman military architecture— the Walls of Theodosius II., whose inner *enceinte* was built in 413 by Anthemius, prætorian prefect of the East, and its outer sheathing by his successor the prefect Constantine in 447.[1] Its triple defence consisted first of a ditch or moat, over sixty

---

[1] See Millingen's *Walls of Constantinople*, pp. 47-48, for the problem as to whether "Cyrus," to whom the outer wall is attributed by some chroniclers, is the same person as the Constantine whose name appears on still surviving inscriptions.

feet wide, and at least twenty-two feet deep,[1] with scarp and counterscarp in good masonry. Whether it was filled with water at all times—or at least during times of war and danger— is not quite certain. In some chronicles there is a distinct mention of its being a wet ditch : and certain conduit openings visible in its counterscarp may have conveyed water from distant hills. On the other hand, no account of actual siege-operations during any of its many leaguers chances to mention difficulties of approach caused by water, and certainly during the last great siege of 1453 the moat is spoken of as dry. But by the end of the Empire everything was in a state of decay, and old means of defence may have got out of order. But whether wet or dry it was a formidable obstacle. Along its inner side, above the scarp, was a low battlemented wall about six and a half feet high. This was capable of defence against anything but siege machines, giving good cover for archers ; but it was only a trifle to what lay behind. Sixty feet from this wall and the margin of the moat lay the first real line of resistance.

This was composed of the outer wall, that built by the prefect Constantine. It was a curtain some twenty-seven feet high, set with numerous towers, distant about one hundred and eighty feet from each other ; there were apparently ninety-six in all : they were alternately square and semicircular. All projected some sixteen feet from the front of the curtain, so as to give flanking fire all along its foot. They varied slightly in height, some being thirty, some as much as thirty-five feet above the level of the curtain. There was a narrow parapet-walk, carried on arches, along the curtain, whose upper course was battlemented,

Behind the wall of Constantine was a covered way, some fifty or sixty feet broad, making a complete break between the outer and inner wall, and allowing of the rapid transference of troops under perfect cover, and out of sight of the enemy, from one part of the *enceinte* to another. It was sunk ten feet below the level of the parapet-walk at the back of the outer curtain.

Finally, above this covered way—called the Περίβολος— rose the higher and more important inner wall, that originally built by Anthemius. It rose thirty feet above the covered way, and had a drop of forty feet behind down to the inner level of

---

[1] Millingen, p. 55.

the city. Like the outer wall it was furnished with a lavish provision of towers, but they were about sixty feet high, doubly as lofty and as broad as those of the wall of Constantine. These great towers were placed so as to lie chequer-wise above the smaller towers of the outer *enceinte*, each exactly commanding the space of curtain that lay between two of the towers of the lower wall. Their number, therefore, was the same—ninety-six—as those of the first line of defence. The curtain wall was about fifteen feet thick, all in solid masonry : its front was battlemented, and its parapet-walk passed behind the projecting towers. The roofs of the towers were solid enough to bear heavy military machines, and were battlemented like the curtain.[1] It is clear that any attacking force approaching the moat could be opened upon by four separate lines of mangonels or balistas working from four distinct levels—that of the outer curtain, that of the towers of the outer wall, that of the inner curtain, and that of the towers of the inner curtain. Moreover, the towers were loopholed, so that archery-fire could be given from their interior, to supplement the larger volume of missiles that could be discharged from the main levels. The task of opening approaches toward the moat, for the purpose of crossing it and tackling the outer wall, was such a discouraging one that, as a matter of fact, no hostile force ever dared to attempt a regular attack on this tremendous front till the days of the invention of gunpowder. The Avars, Persians, and Saracens in the seventh and eighth centuries only blockaded the place and tried to starve it out. The Crusaders of 1204 studied the tremendous triple enceinte, found that it was impregnable, and then turned all their energies against the sea face of the city, where there was only a single wall to oppose them. Previous besiegers had never possessed that complete command of the water approaches which made such an attack possible. In the days of Heraclius, Constantine Pogonatus, and Leo the Isaurian, the Byzantine fleet had always been strong enough to render regular assaults on the sea-wall too hazardous. Even when not in complete command of the straits (as, for example, during the Saracen siege of 673), the Imperial navy had invariably been present in strong force within the Golden Horn, and any attempt to assail the water

---

[1] All these details come from Van Millingen's admirable work, see also its illustrative plan.

front would have caused it to sally out and fall upon the besiegers, while their ships, crowded with land troops, were trying to haul in under the wall. Hence such attempts were never made : the " navy in being " of the besieged rendered them too hazardous. But in 1204 the wretched emperors of the house of Angelus had so neglected the fleet that the Venetians were able to draw under the water-wall and assail it without any fear of interruption. Thus it was that Constantinople, for the first time in history, fell before an attack by open force : before, it had never been captured save by treachery from within.[1]

Constantinople was of course quite exceptional in showing a triple line of defence extending over several miles of front: as a rule, it was only citadels and not cities which displayed such a formidable series of walls. Even the wealthy Byzantine Government could not afford to surround places of large size with more than a single enceinte. For castles and fortresses, however, where the space was moderate, the concentric lines were possible, and often were erected : the citadel of Antioch, for example, had a double wall on the north and west sides, though not on the more precipitous southern and eastern fronts.[2] The large town which lay below it, on the other hand, had but a single wall, though this was made very strong by its splendid diadem of towers.

The fortifications of Antioch may serve as an example of the Byzantine methods of guarding a city of first-rate importance. The place had been retaken from the Saracens by Nicephorus Phocas in 968 : in 976 both walls and city were terribly injured by an earthquake, and the whole enceinte had to be repaired. It then remained in the hands of the Eastern emperors till 1086, when the Seljouk Sultan Suleiman captured it by treachery. Thus we see that the Turks had only been in possession of the place for a trifle more than ten years when the Crusaders came against it. The barbarian conquerors had of course added nothing to the Byzantine walls, and the fortifications erected by Justinian, and remodelled in the tenth century by the engineers of John Zimisces and Basil II., were those with which the Franks had to deal in 1098. When Antioch fell, and became the capital of Bohemund's principality, the old walls needed no repair—the siege operations had done

---

[1] *e.g.* As when Alexius Comnenus took it in 1081.
[2] See the Plan in Rey's *Architecture Militaire des Croisés en Syrie*, Paris, 1871.

no harm to them. The Byzantine enceinte protected the Latin
princes for nearly two hundred years : its remains are still
sufficient to enable us to reconstruct the whole system of
defence. It consisted of a line of curtain, in which towers were
placed at frequent but irregular intervals : in the more exposed
parts of the wall the towers were no more than fifty yards apart ;
in the more inaccessible parts they were some eighty or a
hundred yards from each other. Where the walls lie along the
river Orontes to the north-east, and along precipices on the
southern, south-eastern, and south-western fronts (see Map, vol. i.
facing p. 284), they are not furnished with a ditch, but on the
north-western and northern fronts the channel of the Orontes
had been diverted along their foot, as to form a large moat, or
rather a broad marshy depression. The curtain was solid, and
not pierced with loopholes ; its main protection came from the
projecting towers set in it at such close intervals. These
formidable structures were about twenty yards square ; half of
their bulk stood out beyond the curtain-wall, and commanded a
side view of the ditch, or of the ground at the foot of the walls
where no ditch existed. They were about sixty feet high,
and had three storeys ; each storey was loopholed both to the
front and to the sides, so as to furnish a flanking fire along the
ditch as well as a direct fire towards the open country. Being
set in the curtain for half their bulk, the towers blocked the
road round the walls at frequent intervals. No one could walk
for a quarter of a mile along the enceinte without passing through
six or seven towers, and, as each tower had strong doors where
its second storey opened on to the ramparts, each section of
curtain could be isolated by the closing of these doors. So if
by chance the besieger mastered a part of the curtain, the two
towers on each side prevented him from making his way to
right or left along the walls, and, as there was no way of getting
down from the ramparts to the interior of the town (all stairs
being within the towers), the assailant would have gained
nothing but some sixty or eighty yards of narrow rampart
walk. The Crusaders in 1098 were admitted into one of the
towers (that of the " Two Sisters ") by the treachery of the
renegade Firouz,[1] and by means of the gate on the ground floor

---

[1] The first sixty combatants mounted by a rope ladder on to the curtain adjoining the tower which Firouz commanded. He led them from thence into the tower.
Next some descended to break open the postern, while others pushed right and

of the tower got into the town. If they had merely scaled the curtain they would have gained nothing ; but, emerging from the tower, they were able to break open first a blocked postern-gate and then the great bridge-gate (see Map of Antioch, vol. i. facing p. 284) ; through these two entries the main body of the Franks poured in, and the place was won.

Once established in Syria, the Franks not only repaired the castles and city walls which the Moslems had left behind them, but erected an infinite number of new strongholds, varying in size from small isolated watch-towers to the most formidable fortresses of the first class, capable of holding garrisons of two or three thousand men. To trace the exact stages by which they perfected their military architecture is not easy, as most of the castles were being perpetually strengthened, and present now the appearance which they showed in the thirteenth century, when they finally fell back into Moslem hands and were dismantled or left to decay. The most perfect ruins, such as those of Markab and Krak-des-Chevaliers, do not therefore give us so much information as to the twelfth century as could be wished. To ascertain the earlier developments of Frankish architecture in the Holy Land, places must be studied which were surrendered to Saladin after the battle of Tiberias and never again were in possession of the Crusaders, such as Saona and Blanche-Garde (captured in 1187) and Kerak-in-Moab (surrendered in 1188).

An examination of such castles shows that in the twelfth century the two great principles of Byzantine military archi-tecture—the defence of the curtain by towers and the construc-tion of concentric lines of fortification—were thoroughly well understood and practised by the Frankish builders. The early strongholds differ from the later mainly by their want of finish and greater simplicity of detail. In the thirteenth century castles were built not only with more elaborate and ingenious defences, but also with a certain regard to decoration and ornament. They show carvings, shields of arms, and occasional inscriptions, of which the buildings of the preceding age are destitute. But the general principles of construction are the same throughout the

---

left along the curtain. They were so swift and silent that they were able to penetrate into the towers, whose doors were not closed, and to massacre their sleeping garrisons before the alarm was given. Masters of five hundred or six hundred yards of the enceinte, they could not be withstood.

two centuries during which the Franks held their footing in Syria.

It was probably quite early in the time of the existence of the kingdom of Jerusalem that the crusading architects adopted and improved on the Byzantine models. The shell-keeps or square donjons with a plain towerless curtain-wall, which they had left behind them in the West, were so obviously inferior to the military architecture of the Levant that there was no temptation to reproduce them without an improvement. Thus a great change in the fundamental conception of the castle took place early in the twelfth century : instead of being considered as a keep provided with an outer wall, it becomes an enceinte with or without a keep as final place of refuge. Originally the great donjon was the more and the outer wall the less important part in the scheme of defence. But now the main resistance was to be opposed by the enceinte with towers set in it at intervals, and the donjon was a last resort, to which the garrison only retired in desperate extremity. It might even be merely the greatest of the several towers of the enceinte. When King Amaury about 1165 erected the small but strong fortress of Darum on the borders of Egypt, he merely built a square enceinte with four large towers at its angles, of which one was larger than the others.[1] Though this served as a donjon, it only differed in size from the other three.

Another deviation from the old practice of the West was that the strongest tower was sometimes built not in the most secure and well-defended part of the castle, as a place of final refuge, but at the fore-front of the most exposed side of the fortress, so as to bear the brunt of the attack. In this case the keep, if keep we may call it, would be the first part of the place which would be assaulted by the besieger, and the first, perhaps, to fall into his hands. As an example of this kind of castle we may quote Athlit (Château Pelerin), a castle built on a promontory, where the main defensive structure consisted of two massive towers connected by a short curtain and placed across the neck of the promontory. Behind them, seaward, the rest of the castle was only protected by an ordinary enceinte with a few small

---

[1] William of Tyre, xx. 19, describes it as " castrum modicae quantitatis, vix tantum spatium inter se continens quantum est jactum lapidis, formae quadrae, turres habens quattuor in angulis, quarum una grossior et munitior erat aliis." See Rey's *Architecture Militaire*, etc., p. 125, for its present state.

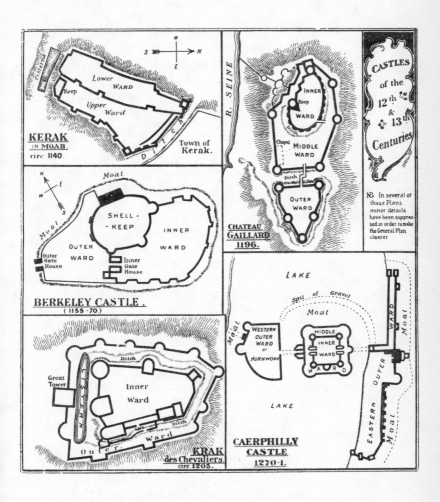

KERAK
IN MOAB.
circ 1140.

Lower WARD

Keep

Upper Ward

Cistern

DITCH

Town of Kerak.

S W N E

BERKELEY CASTLE.
(1155-70)

Moat

SHELL-KEEP

INNER WARD

OUTER WARD

Inner Gate House

Outer Gate House

Moat

N t W S

KRAK
des Chevaliers.
circ 1205.

Great Tower

CISTERN

Ditch

Inner Ward

Outer Ward

Ditch

R. SEINE

CHATEAU GAILLARD
1196.

INNER Keep WARD

Ditch

Chapel

MIDDLE WARD

Ditch

OUTER WARD

CASTLES
of the
12th
&
13th
Centuries

NB In several of these Plans minor details have been suppressed in order to make the General Plan clearer

CAERPHILLY CASTLE
1270-1.

LAKE

Spu of Gravel

Moat

WESTERN OUTER WARD or HORNWORK

MIDDLE INNER WARD

WARD

Moat

EASTERN OUTER WARD

Moat

LAKE

towers. All the strength of the place lay in the two splendid towers at the isthmus. But Athlit was built late (1218), and must not be quoted as an example of twelfth-century architecture.[1]

As a fair example of the strongholds which the Franks erected after they had been seated for a generation in the Holy Land, we may describe Kerak-in-Moab, the eastern bulwark of the kingdom of Jerusalem, built about 1140 by Payn of Nablous, the high-butler of King Fulk. It was only forty years in Christian hands, and seems never to have been much altered from its original shape. It stands on one of the two narrow crests which connect the hill of Kerak with the mountains of Moab. To east and west the slope of the crest is too steep to be accessible : to north and south, where the danger is greater, two enormous ditches have been hewn in the rock, so as to isolate the castle from the rest of the ridge of which it forms part ; they were only to be crossed by narrow bridges removable in time of war. The fortress consisted of a donjon in the south-east angle of the oblong enceinte, and of an upper and a lower ward, separated from each other by a strong wall. The northern front of the castle was the most exposed : it consisted of a curtain flanked by two large towers, which gave a lateral fire into the ditch : the curtain contained at least two stages pierced with loopholes. The only opening in it was by a gate close under the western flanking tower : it was closed by a portcullis, and opened not directly into the court of the castle, but into a long passage between the curtain and a wall built at its back. Two more portcullises were placed at intervals in this passage, and it was only after passing them that the court was reached. (See Plan, vol. ii. facing page 30.)

Kerak-in-Moab proved utterly impregnable to all the attacks of Saladin. Though repeatedly assailed, it was never harmed, nor did the assailants even enter its lower ward. It held out for many months after the battle of Tiberias, and only surrendered when provisions had failed and all hopes of relief were absolutely at an end (1188).

It is safe to say that such a fine example of a fortress with a double line of defence could not have been built anywhere save in the East so early as 1140. Nothing approaching it for completeness of design was reared in England, France, or Germany

[1] All this comes from M. Rey's admirable and oft-quoted work.

till fifty years later, when Richard Coeur de Lion planned his famous Château Gaillard on the bluff above Les Andelys. Richard, we cannot doubt, was utilising his Eastern experience when he erected this splendid and complicated structure, whose arrangements pleased him so well that he boasted that " it might be held even if its walls were made of butter."

Nevertheless, the influence of Eastern military architecture began to be felt in the West not long after the first Crusade, though the Western builders worked on a smaller scale, and were for many years timid copyists of the crusading architects. The old type of the keep standing in a base-court girt by a plain curtain begins about 1130 or 1140 to develop into a more complicated structure. The enceinte wall becomes more important, towers are presently set in it, and the outer line of defence becomes less wholly subordinate to the keep. At the same time the keep itself ceases to depend entirely on its passive strength, and acquires a gate-house, and a larger provision of loopholes.

In a few important castles, instead of building a mere shell-keep or rectangular keep, the architects of the wealthier barons began about 1140–50 to erect a more complicated central pile as the main feature of a new castle. At Alnwick, for example, the powerful Eustace de Vesey set on the ancient mound which he found there existing, not a shell-keep (such as his father would have built), but a circular cluster of towers, enclosing an open court. His outer enceinte was also probably furnished with a few small towers, though these have been so reconstructed by thirteenth- and fourteenth-century holders of the place that it is difficult to be certain on the point.[1] The Tower of London, round which Rufus had drawn a plain curtain-wall,[2] began to be strengthened with towers under Henry II. The Wakefield tower, oldest of those of its inner ward, seems to belong to that time ; the others have been so pulled about by later kings, that it is impossible to attribute any of them with certainty to so early a date.

It must not be supposed that the " adulterine " castles erected in Stephen's reign showed any such improvements. Built hastily by men of precarious fortunes, they were often mere walled enclosures, or at best rough shell-keeps. Hence it comes that they were so easily destroyed by Henry II., and that the majority

---

[1] See Clark's *Military Architecture*, etc., i. 176–185.
[2] See vol. ii. p. 16.

of their sites exhibit very slight traces of masonry. Perhaps
some may have been mere palisaded mounds of the ancient type.
If they had been fitted with massive rectangular keeps of the
first Norman model, or with the more complicated defences
introduced from the East, they would undoubtedly have left
far more solid ruins behind them.

By the end of the twelfth century the military architects of
the West had learned their lesson, and were utilising everywhere
the notions which had originally been borrowed from the
Byzantines. Outer wards and fore-works begin to appear
beyond the original curtain-walls ; towers grow numerous and
strong, and flanking fire is always provided to cover exposed
fronts. It may be worth while to give a sketch of the strongest
fortress of the day, in order to show the enormous advance which
had been made since the first Crusade. Château Gaillard, as we
have already had occasion to mention, was considered the
masterpiece of the time. The reputation of its builder, Coeur de
Lion, as a great military engineer might stand firm on this single
structure. He was no mere copyist of the models which he had
seen in the East, but introduced many original details of his own
invention into the stronghold. It is therefore not exactly a
typical castle of the last years of the twelfth century, but
rather an abnormally superior specimen of its best work.

Château Gaillard was placed in a splendid strategical
position, covering Rouen from all attacks along the line of the
Seine. By the aid of its outworks and the fortified bridge
below, it completely blocked the main avenue of invasion from
France. But it is with the castle itself, not with its dependencies,
that we have to deal. Like so many mediæval strongholds,
it lies on the end of a long spur of steep ground, connected only
by a narrow neck with the hills behind. The slopes below it
are so steep and lofty that it can only be attacked with advantage along the cramped front of the isthmus which joins it to
the main block of the upland. Its fortifications are intended
to oppose four successive lines of defence to an enemy advancing
against the single accessible side. Thus it cannot be called
a " concentric " castle, though each of its wards dominates
and commands that below it. The first of its defences is a
lower ward or outwork at the narrowest point of the isthmus.
This outwork forms an isosceles triangle, with its point facing
toward the enemy. The acute angle at its apex is occupied by

a great circular tower, which is flanked and supported by two other towers placed a little distance down the curtain. The brunt of the attack must therefore fall on these three towers and the short front of curtain between them. If the apex of the triangle was beaten in, the outer ward was lost, and the defenders could retire to the middle ward. This was separated from the outwork by a ditch thirty feet deep, crossed only by a single narrow causeway. Across the ditch lies the middle ward, which exposes to the enemy, when he has gained the outer ward, two massive towers joined by a curtain. Here lay the chapel and many other buildings, whose cellars only now remain. Placed within the northern half of the middle ward was the inner ward, to which King Richard had devoted special attention. Instead of composing it of towers connected by curtains, he constructed the whole wall in segments of circles, so that on a ground plan its outer defences present a scalloped shape. His idea was to give the enceinte all the advantages of towers without their heaviness, for the centre part of each scallop so advances as to command the space between it and the next segment. The general effect is as if he had cut towers into slices, and then placed the slices side by side along the steep edge of the hillside.

The donjon forms part of the western wall of the inner ward : it is not completely round, but has a broad spur projecting into the open court of the inner ward. It splays out towards the bottom—a device adopted both to give greater thickness to its base and to throw outward missiles dropped from its parapet. Moreover, it is furnished with machicolations, intended to command the foot of the wall ; *i.e.* a series of corbels carry round it a narrow gallery with holes pierced in its floor, from which the defenders could shoot downwards, pour liquid combustibles on the enemy, or drop stones on him. This is a very early example of stone machicolation : the majority of builders at the time were only employing wooden galleries (*brattices*), projecting so as to overlook the ground below the wall. It seems that stone machicolation was invented in the Holy Land, where large timber was so scarce that the architects of the Crusaders were forced to replace it by solid masonry.

It is interesting to note the methods by which Château Gaillard was taken by Philip Augustus in 1204. King John neglected it, and allowed it to stand or fall on its own resources without making any vigorous attempt to raise the siege. The French, therefore, were able to beleaguer it at leisure, and employed six months in reducing it by formal siege-operations [1] (September 1203–March 1204). The gallant governor, Roger de Lacy, Constable of Chester, made an obstinate defence, but, getting no help from outside, was bound to succumb in time. King Philip appeared in front of the place in August 1203, and captured the isolated defences in the neighbourhood lying outside the castle. He spent the autumn in erecting works of circumvallation and contravallation round it, and in levelling a platform opposite the apex of the outwork, from which he intended to begin his attack. The French army lay within its lines all the winter, fearing that, if it did not remain before the place in force, King John would appear with a relieving army and raise the blockade.

In February King Philip began the attack by erecting military machines on the isthmus, and battering the great tower at the apex of the outwork and the short curtains on each side of it. He filled the ditch with rubbish, and then set miners to burrow their way beneath the foundations of the masonry. They finally succeeded in undermining part of the defences, which fell in, leaving a breach : [2] through this the outer ward was stormed. The garrison, much reduced by famine, were unable to hold their ground, and retired to the middle ward. This line of defence did not protect them very long : it fell, if Guillaume le Breton is to be believed, by a kind of escalade. In the south-western angle of the ward lay the chapel, whose outer wall formed part of the western front of the enceinte. Where the chapel looked out on the cliff, which lies immediately below it, there were some small windows not very far above the foot of the wall. A little party of French crept along the cliff, and succeeded in clambering into one of these windows, the first to mount pulling up his comrades. They found themselves in a crypt below the chapel : when they had entered they raised their war-cry, and at the same time the main body made a demonstration along the causeway against the gate of the middle ward.

---

[1] Elaborately described in the *Philippeis* of Guillaume le Breton, book vii.

[2] From G. le Breton, vii. 705-10, we should conclude that they got in by throwing down the great angle tower; but Mr. Clark suggests that as that building shows no signs of having been breached and repaired, it must have been the curtain next it which fell in (Clark, i. 384).

The garrison, seeing enemies within the walls, and not realising their small numbers, did not exterminate the few men who had got in below the chapel, but hastily evacuated the middle ward and took refuge in the inner ward, the strongest of all the enceintes of the castle. The small party in the chapel then came out and admitted their friends. Philip now set to work to erect opposite the gate a perrière of unwonted size, which, as Guillaume le Breton says, was called a *Cabulus*.[1] While thus distracting the attention of the garrison, he advanced miners under cover of a large " cat," to sap the foot of the walls. This was successfully done, and then the perrière was set to work on the shaken masonry. Its discharges brought down a considerable mass of stone, and Philip bade his knights attempt to storm the breach. They would not in all probability have succeeded had not the defenders been reduced to great extremities by hunger. There only remained twenty knights and a hundred and twenty men to guard the breach : they failed to hold it, and then (if Matthew Paris may be trusted), instead of retiring into the donjon, tried to cut their way out by the postern-gate and to escape into the open. In this they failed, and were all taken prisoners. (March 6, 1204.)

The real work in this siege, it will be seen, was done by the miners : it was they who broke two of the lines of defence, while the third was taken only by the unlikely chance of an escalade. The siege-engines only contributed an inconsiderable part to the main result : the " Cabulus " might have battered for ever at the scalloped walls of the inner ward if the way had not been prepared for it by the pick of the engineers.

Rounded keeps like that of Château Gaillard were just commencing to supersede the old square Norman shape when Richard built his great castle. The probable reason for their adoption was that such a shape is better adapted to resist the battering-ram, and even the miner's pick, than a rectangular structure, where the corners are the vulnerable point. One of the last square keeps built in England was that of Helmsley, reared about the year 1180. In the next century the circular donjon is very frequent. The best specimen on this side of the Channel is Coningsborough, but on the Continent there were far

---

[1] Guillaume le Breton, vii. 805. Is this strange word short for Catabulus, and equivalent to Catapult (catapulta)? Or is Viollet-le-Duc's derivation from *cable* correct ?

larger and loftier structures.   Not unfrequently these thirteenth-century donjons are not exactly round, but have a projecting spur on one face, looking towards the direction from which attack was most probable.   The great towers of Château Gaillard and of Coucy (wickedly destroyed by the Germans during their retreat in 1918, after weathering seven centuries) both show this feature.

While gaining in solidity by ceasing to be square, the donjon did not profit in all respects.   When the outer defences had fallen and the garrison had taken refuge in their last stronghold, they had an even smaller power of concentrating their fire from the loopholes of a round structure than from those of a rectangular one, and there was a greater difficulty in commanding any given spot at the actual foot of the wall.   The passive strength of the building was still, it would seem, its chief protection, not the rain of missiles which it could direct on the besieger.   But by this time the main line of resistance was far outside the donjon : when the defenders had retired to it they were drawing to the end of their hopes, and, unless relief arrived from friends outside, were unlikely to hold out for much longer.   There were many sieges in which the garrison gave in when the inner ward fell to the enemy, and did not care to protract the game by defending the donjon when all chance of success was over.   It is noticeable that in the great series of sieges 1268–91, which ended the domination of the Christians on the Syrian coast, nearly all the castles surrendered very shortly after their second line of defence was pierced, without any serious attempt being made to hold out in the donjon or (where no donjon existed) in the innermost ward.   Such was the case at Beaufort (1268), Krak-des-Chevaliers (1271), Montfort (1271), and Margat (1285).   Even the tremendous tower which forms the core of the complicated fortification of Château Gaillard fell, as we have already seen, at the same time that the inner ward was stormed by the knights of Philip Augustus. By the thirteenth century the feature of the castle which was originally all-important had sunk to a secondary place in the scheme of defence.   In some of the Syrian castles, as we have already seen,[1] the architect had so far ceased to think of it as a secure place of final refuge, that he placed it in the forefront of the structure to break the first vigour of the besieger's assault.

[1] See vol. ii. p. 30.

It was reserved for the thirteenth century to bring to
perfection the development of castle-building by the invention
of the concentric type of fortress. The places which we have
hitherto been considering, such as Kerak-in-Moab, or Château
Gaillard, are not rigidly and logically concentric, although they
oppose a series of barriers to the assailant. Each enceinte in
them is not wholly surrounded by that lying below it ; the
outer ward does not entirely encompass the inner, nor the inner
the donjon. The latter may be set in one of the exterior walls
of the stronghold, and the inner ward may be placed against the
side of the outer, and not within it. The only idea of the
architect was to fit his buildings upon the ground that lay before
him in such a way that it was reasonably probable that the
assailant would have to deal with the lower lines of defence before
he could get at the core of the castle. It was conceivable that
an enemy who attacked on an unlikely front and in an unexpected
manner might gain possession of the donjon or the inner ward
without having first to deal with the front line of defences.[1] In
such a case the latter would of course prove useless.

To guard against such chances as this, the only possible
resource was to make the castle absolutely concentric, i.e. to
place each ward so completely within the next that the besieger
could not conceivably reach the centre point of the defences
without having worked through every one of the exterior lines.
A system of fortification embodying this principle appears in
the Levant very early in the thirteenth century : there is some
reason to think that it was first put in practice after the terrible
earthquake of May 20, 1202, which threw down great portions
of nearly all the fortresses occupied by the Syrian Franks.[2] At
any rate, the majority of the thirteenth-century castles of the East
show an attempt to reach this ideal which we do not find so
clearly visible in those which belong to the previous age. Most
of the strongholds which show, by their well-developed, pointed

[1] To take a modern example : Wellington in 1812 failed in his main attempt to
storm the breaches in the enceinte of Badajoz, but succeeded in escalading the
castle by a secondary attack. The castle commanded the town wall, which had
therefore to be abandoned, though it had been maintained against all the desperate
onsets of the main storming columns.

[2] Tortosa alone is said to have escaped unharmed. But even Tortosa shows
much thirteenth-century work, and is planned on the concentric style, and many of
the details of its architecture show distinct thirteenth-century features. No doubt the
Templars rebuilt it on the newest lines during the early thirteenth century. The
rectangular keep, however, belongs to the previous age.

architecture, their display of architectural ornament, and their stone machicolation, that they belong to the later half of the crusading period, are distinctly of the concentric type. Krak-des-Chevaliers, Chastel-Blanc (Safita), and the castle of Tortosa are good examples—the last only differing from the other two in that one of its sides rests on the sea. At the first-named fortress the outer ward is so thoroughly separated from the inner that a wet ditch divides them for a great part of their extent. (See Plan, vol. ii. facing p. 30.) At the last named the outer ward, the middle ward, and the donjon each has a ditch of its own, wholly cutting it off from the line of defence immediately beyond it.

It was not till much later in the century that the concentric castle became common in Western Europe. English writers on architecture have often styled the type " Edwardian," because some of the best specimens of it in this island were built by the greatest of the Plantagenets. But the name is inappropriate, as the earlier examples of the system go back to the reign of Henry III. : the Tower of London became a very perfect instance of a concentric castle when that monarch added to it its outer ward, between the years 1240 and 1258. Caerphilly, too, the largest and most imposing example of its class, was completed a year before King Edward came to the throne. To say, therefore, that he brought the design back from the East after his crusading tour in 1270 is obviously absurd. It was used in England, and still more on the Continent, long before that date. The Emperor Frederic II., a great builder of castles in his unruly Italian dominions, sometimes employed it in the latter half of his reign (1230–50). Carcassonne, as remodelled by St. Louis about 1257–65, is practically concentric, the outer enceinte completely surrounding the inner ; only, the fact that the castle forms part of the outer wall of the inner enceinte prevents it from being a perfect example of the type.

Among the castles on our own side of the Channel, Beau-maris, Caerphilly, and the Tower of London are absolutely complete examples of the style. Harlech and Kidwelly are for all intents and purposes concentric, though in each of them for some short fronts of wall the defences of two of the wards are blended, and only two lines of resistance presented to the assailant. It is to be noted that in all these strongholds save the Tower of London there is no longer any donjon. The final refuge of the garrison is not a massive keep standing alone, but a quadrangular enclosure guarded by several towers, which forms the inner ward of the castle. If the Tower of London forms an exception, it is only because Henry III. found the old Norman keep already existing : if he had been building on new ground, he would have made the inner ward the last core of his fortress.

Caerphilly is worth describing as the grandest specimen of its class. It has failed to meet with the fame which its splendid architecture should command, because no great historical memories cluster around it. The Marches of South Wales were completely reduced to order just after it was built, and so it never endured a siege in the Middle Ages,[1] and was only once assailed in the whole of its history—when wrecked by the Parliamentarians in 1648.

The castle was erected by Gilbert de Clare, Earl of Gloucester and lord of Glamorgan, and was finished about 1271. It stands on a mound of gravel, in an artificial lake formed by damming up two watercourses and turning a marsh into a sheet of water. The inner ward consists of a quadrangular enclosure flanked by four large round towers at its corners, and with massive gate-houses rising above the curtain in the midst of its east and west fronts. Completely encircling the inner ward is the middle ward, a narrow space bounded by a curtain-wall much lower than that of the inner ward, and commanded by it at every point. Its corners are low semicircular bastions, into which the towers of the inner ward look down. The middle ward is encompassed by the lake on every side : the only access to it from the shore is given by two causeways in its eastern and western fronts : each of these passages is broken in the middle by a wooden drawbridge, which could be removed at will. A curious spit of gravel (see the Plan, vol. ii. facing p. 30) separated the moat from the main lake on the northern side of the middle ward, but does not seem to have been properly connected at either end with the outer ward.

Beyond the bridges we come to the outer ward, which is composed of two separate works of very unequal size, each destined to play the part of a tête-du-pont. The eastern and

[1] Unless some obscure allusions to a surprise attack in 1315 which burst the outer ward and another to "William de la Zouche and his accomplices who are molesting the castle of Caerphilly" in 1329 (Rymer, *Foedera*, iii. 755) merit the name of siege operations.

smaller defence is a hornwork forming an irregular pentagon
with a curtain fifteen feet high. It is completely surrounded by
a moat of its own, and the only approach to it is through two
strong gatehouses. Its sides run back to the lake, so that it
forms an island, joined to the inner ward at one side and the
open country at the other by well-guarded bridges.

The western outer ward is a much more important and
imposing structure. It partakes, like the hornwork to the east,
of the nature of a tête-du-pont, both of its ends touching the
water of the lake, while its middle portion projects towards the
open country. This central and salient section of the work
consists of a great gatehouse-tower, forming the main approach
to the castle : from each side of it curtains run north and south
till they touch the brink of the lake. The northern curtain,
which is absolutely straight, terminates in two strong square
towers set side by side at the water's edge. The southern
curtain, on the other hand, curves back considerably at its end,
and terminates in a group of three towers where it reaches the
water. The outer ward has a moat of its own, communicating
with the lake at each end. It is cut in two by a dividing wall,
so that, if its northern end fell, the southern could still be maintained, and *vice versâ*.

Thus an enemy attacking Caerphilly either by the eastern
or the western face (the northern and southern are rendered
inaccessible by the lake) would have had to cross two moats and
three lines of wall before he could make an end of the garrison's
power of resistance. It is small wonder that the place was
never assailed—much less taken—in the days before gunpowder
became the ruling power in war.

It is obvious that concentric castles could only be built in
situations where there was room to develop their special form
of strength. On the open ground, on islands, or on plateaux
of considerable breadth they might well be erected. But it was
impossible to place them upon long narrow sites, such as the
crests of hills or the ends of rocky spurs. Where breadth was
not obtainable, it was only feasible to set ward behind ward,
the outermost facing the normal approach, the innermost
receding as far as possible from it. Edward I. showed at
Harlech and Beaumaris that he fully appreciated the merits of
the concentric system, but, when he had to build castles on
sites which were not of sufficient lateral extent, he merely

placed his wards one behind the other, each covering the full breadth of the crest which they crowned. Caernarvon, for example, resembles an hour-glass or a figure-of-eight in shape. The lower ward and the upper are connected only by a broad and lofty gatehouse-tower. Conway, built at the steep end of a promontory, is a parallelogram divided by a cross wall into a lower and larger and an upper and smaller section. It has also, it must be mentioned, a very elaborate system of gate defences projecting from the lower ward towards the town, which it dominates. Where cliff or water sufficiently protect three sides of a castle, the advantages of the concentric system were practically secured by wards placed one behind the other, each commanding that below it, and all facing towards the one point whence attack is to be feared. It is obviously unnecessary to pile wall on wall upon fronts where the enemy cannot possibly appear. Conway and Caernarvon, therefore, resemble Château Gaillard rather than Beaumaris or Harlech, merely because they are set in positions similar to that of the great Norman fortress, where only one front needs serious defence and the rest are protected by the strength of their sites.

CHAPTER III

SIEGECRAFT (1100–1300)

WITH the concentric castle we have reached the final development of the military architecture of the Middle Ages. There was to be no further change of importance, till the introduction of gunpowder in the first half of the fourteenth century introduced an entirely new factor into the art of war, and began to turn in favour of the offensive the advantage which the defensive had hitherto enjoyed. In 1300 we leave the balance still inclined to the defender : the art of building strongholds had improved during the last two centuries far faster than that of destroying them. Siegecraft had made notable advances since the simple days of the first Crusade, but its developments always lagged behind those of military architecture. There was a limit to the mechanical application of the three powers of torsion, tension, and the counterpoise on which the engineer had to rely when constructing his siege-artillery. If he tried to gain increased force by enlarging the size of his machines, they not only grew too costly, but became hopelessly unwieldy and slow in their action. If, on the other hand, he tried to prevail by increasing their number, it was impossible, on account of their short range and great bulk, to concentrate the fire of a large quantity of them on a single piece of wall.

The artillery and siege engines of the twelfth and thirteenth centuries were, with one important exception, the same in general character as those of the previous age, with which we have dealt in the sixth chapter of our Third Book. Many improvements in detail were made, but only one notable introduction of a new principle. This was the invention of machines worked by counterpoises, the chief of which was the Trebuchet. This engine did not depend for its power on either torsion or tension, but on the sudden releasing of heavy weights. It consisted of a long pole, balanced on a pivot supported by two uprights at about one quarter of the distance between its butt end and its point. The longer part was pulled down to the ground, and the missile was placed either in a spoon-shaped cavity in its end or in a sling attached to it : it was held down till the moment of discharge by ropes or wooden catches worked by a winch. Meanwhile, the shorter part of the pole at its butt end was loaded with heavy weights of iron or stone, attached to it in a sort of box or basket or permanently bound to it with cords. The heavy weights would have dragged down the butt of the pole to the ground if the small end had not been already fixed back by its catches. When these were suddenly released, the counterpoise at the other end of the pole was able to act : it dropped suddenly, and tossed the thin end and the missile attached to it into the air. The stone flew off in a great parabolic curve, like that of a bomb from a modern mortar.

By the end of the thirteenth century several kinds of trebuchets were in use, all built on the same principle, but differing slightly in the way in which the weights were worked. Egidio Colonna, who wrote his treatise *De Regimine Principum* for the young Philip the Fair of France somewhere about the year 1280, gives four varieties. The first has a fixed counterpoise, composed of boxes filled with earth, sand, stones, or iron. The second, which he calls *biffa*, has a movable counterpoise, which is shifted closer to or farther from the butt of the pole, according as the engineer wishes to lengthen or shorten the distance to which he intends to discharge his missile. The third has one fixed counterpoise at the butt, and another movable one which can be made to slide up and down the beam : this gave a greater power of exact shooting than either of the first two forms of the machine. It was called the *tripantum*. In the fourth (which is not properly a trebuchet at all) the place of the counterpoise was taken by a number of ropes destined to be pulled down by the main force of men's arms. This device was inferior in accuracy and force to the other three, but had the one advantage of being easily transportable : it was the counterpoises which made the other shapes so heavy and so difficult to move. The light machine could be moved about from place to place, and set to batter a new point of the wall before the enemy could make any provision against it by erecting counter-machines or strengthening the fortification

of the assailed point.[1] The trebuchets generally discharged
stones, but not unfrequently they were used to throw pots or
barrels of combustible material, destined to set fire to the
brattices of roofs of towers, or to start a conflagration in the
town which they were employed to bombard.[2]

Egidio Colonna calls all these shapes of the trebuchet by
the general name of *petrariae* (perrières), but that word is not
unfrequently used in the thirteenth century for other machines
working by the older principles of tension or torsion rather
than by counterpoises. Many chroniclers call every machine
that casts stones a perrière, whether it was of the older mangon
type or the newer trebuchet type. Where we find the names
of mangonel and perrière mentioned together after 1200, the
latter generally means the trebuchet : it was obviously a more
powerful engine than the mangon. Guillaume le Breton, describing the missiles discharged at the siege of Château Gaillard,
writes—

> " Interea grossos petraria mittit ab intus
> Assidue lapides, mangonellusque minores " (*Ph.* iii. 673, 674).

But when *petraria* occurs in writers of the twelfth century,
before the trebuchet and its counterpoise had been invented,
we must evidently look for another meaning to the word. As
petrariae and *mangana* are sometimes found mentioned together,
it is evidently not the same as the latter. Not improbably it
was the machine with beam and pivot, but without counterpoise,
worked with ropes and the force of men's arms, which Egidio
Colonna describes (somewhat illogically) as the fourth kind of
trebuchet in the passage which we have just been quoting from
his work.

As another example of the hopeless way in which the
nomenclature of military engines was confused by the chroniclers, we may mention the passage in Otto of Freising, where he
calls the mangon a kind of balista. The balista, as will be
remembered, was properly the machine working by tension and
throwing darts, while the mangon worked by torsion and cast
stones. But Otto chooses to use *balista* in the widest sense for
" military engine " at large. He says that a stone cast " vi
tormenti e balista quam modo mangam vulgo dicere solent " fell

---

[1] *De Regimine Principum*, iii.
[2] For a trebuchet loaded with a fire-vase, see the Arabic picture in Plate XXIII.

into the midst of the beleaguered town of Tortona, and, splitting into fragments against a wall, killed three knights, who were taking part in a council of war before the cathedral door [1] (1155).

A careful examination of the confused terms of the writers of the twelfth and thirteenth centuries shows that under the great variety of words which they employ only three or four kinds of machines are really concealed.   In the twelfth century the balista or catapult of the original sort, working by tension and throwing shafts rather than balls, is known, but not so frequently employed as engines working by tension and casting heavy stones.   In the thirteenth, on the other hand, the mangon is no longer so prominent, but is largely superseded by the more powerful trebuchet.   At the same time the original balista-catapult of the crossbow type comes to the front again ; it was largely used by the Emperor Frederic II. in his Italian wars. About the end of the century it receives the new name of *springal* (*espringale*), and is found mounted on wheels and used in battle as a sort of light movable artillery.[2]   It was nothing more than a large arbalest whose cord was pulled back by winches, and hence it is sometimes called merely a *balista de turno*.

Before leaving the subject of military engines, we must make some mention of Greek fire, an appliance which the nations of Western Europe never seem to have thoroughly understood, but which was not unfrequently used against them by the Byzantines and the Moslems.   It was invented, we are told, by a Syrian architect named Callinicus of Heliopolis about the time of the great siege of Constantinople by the Saracens in 673.   Callinicus fled to Constantine Pogonatus, and put his device at the disposition of the emperor.   It was a semi-liquid substance, composed of sulphur, pitch, dissolved nitre, and petroleum boiled together and mixed with certain less important and more obscure substances.   Constantine fitted fast-sailing galleys [3] with projecting tubes, from which this mixture was squirted into hostile vessels. When ejected, it caught the woodwork on which it fell and set

---

[1] Otto of Freising, *Gesta Friderici*, ii. § 16, p. 123.

[2] As, for example, in the battle of Mons-en-Pevéle, where Philip the Fair used two in the open field against the Flemings.   See General Köhler's *Kriegsgeschichte*, iii. 189.

[3] They are called by Theophanes δρόμωνες σιφωνοφόροι.

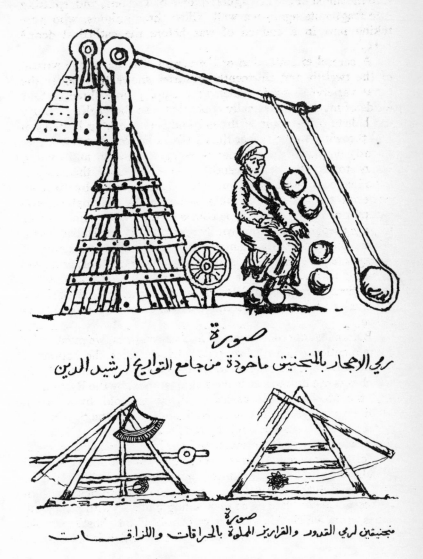

صورة

رمي الاحجار بالمنجنيق ماخوذة من جامع التواريخ لرشيد الدين

صورة

منجنيقين لرمي القدور والقوارير المملوءة بالحراقات واللزاقات

SARACENIC TREBUCHETS (LATE THIRTEENTH CENTURY)

Illustrations from the *Jami-ul-Tawarik* of Raschid-ed-din (published in 1310). The inscription below the smaller trebuchets states that the machines can cast incendiary vessels as well as stones.

it so thoroughly on fire that there was no possibility of ex-
tinguishing the conflagration.   It could only be put out, it is
said, by pouring vinegar, wine, or sand upon it.   The combustible
was successfully used against Saracen fleets by Constantine in
673 and by Leo the Isaurian in 718.

Leo the Wise directs that every war-vessel should have a
brazen tube at its prow, protected by a solid scantling of boards,
from which " prepared fire with thunder and smoke " is to be
shot at the enemy.[1]   But he does not give any account of its
ingredients—the composition was a great State secret, not to be
committed to paper.   He also suggests that jars of the substance
should be cast into the enemy's ships from above, " so that they
may break out into flames," and adds that his officers " may also
use the other device of little tubes discharged by hand from
behind iron shields, which are called ' hand-tubes,' and have
lately been manufactured in our dominions.   For these can cast
the ' prepared fire ' into the faces of the hostile crews." [2]   We
could wish for a better description of these small weapons, which
were presumably some kind of large squirt easily worked by a
single man.   They are probably constructed on the same principle as the devices used by the Byzantine garrison of Dyrrhachium against the Normans in 1108, which Anna Comnena
describes as having been long hollow tubes [3] filled with a
powder composed of resin mixed with sulphur, which shot out
in long jets of flame when a strong continuous blast was blown
down the tube, and scorched the enemies' faces like a lightning
flash.

The Greek fire was of course a much more complicated and
formidable substance than the simple mixture employed by the
defenders of Dyrrhachium.   How it was used may be gathered
from a description of a sea-fight with the Pisans given by Anna
in her eleventh book.   She says that her father, knowing that
the enemy were skilled and courageous warriors, resolved to rely
on the use of the device of fire against them.   He had fixed to

[1] Leo calls it (xix. 51) τὸ ἐσκευασμένον πῦρ μετὰ βροντῆς καὶ καπνοῦ.

[2] Χρήσασθαι δὲ καὶ τῇ ἄλλῃ μεθόδῳ τῶν διὰ χειρὸς βαλλομένων μικρῶν σιφώνων
ὄπισθεν τῶν σκουταρίων σιδηρῶν κρατουμένων, ἅπερ χειροσίφωνα λέγεται.   Ῥίψουσι
γὰρ καὶ αὐτὰ τοῦ ἐσκευασμένου πυρὸς κατὰ τῶν προσώπων τῶν πολεμίων (Leo, xix. 57).

[3] Ἀπὸ τῆς πεύκης . . . συνάγεται δάκρυον εὔκαυστον.   Τοῦτο μετὰ θείου τριβομένου
ἐμβαλλέται ἐς αὐλίσκους καλάμων καὶ ἐμφυσᾶται παρὰ τοῦ παίζοντος λάβρῳ καὶ συνεχεῖ
πνεύματι, καθ' οὕτως ὁμιλεῖ τῷ πρὸς ἄκραν πυρὶ καὶ ἐξάπτεται καὶ ὥσπερ πρηστήρ
ἐμπίπτει ταῖς ἀντιπρόσωπον ὄψεσι (A. C. xii. § 3, p. 189).

the prow of each of his galleys a tube ending in the head of a lion or other beast wrought in brass or iron, " so that the animals might seem to vomit flames." The fleet came up with the Pisans between Rhodes and Patara, and, pursuing with too great zeal, did not attack in a body. The first to reach the enemy was the Byzantine admiral Landulph, who shot off his fire too hastily, missed his mark, and accomplished nothing. But Count Eleëmon, who was the next to close, had better fortune : he rammed the stern of a Pisan vessel, so that his prow stuck in its rudder chains. Then, shooting fire, he set it in flames, after which he pushed off and successfully discharged his tube into three other vessels, all of which were soon in a blaze. The Pisans then fled in disorder, " having no previous knowledge of the device, and wondering that fire, which usually burns upwards, could be directed downwards or to either hand at the will of the engineer who discharges it." [1] That the Greek fire was a liquid, and not merely an inflammable substance attached to ordinary missiles, after the manner used with fire arrows, is quite clear from the fact that Leo proposes to cast it on the enemy in fragile earthen vessels which may break and allow the material to run about, as also from the name πῦρ ἔνυγρον, " liquid fire," which Anna uses for it.[2]

The Moslems are found in possession of Greek fire in the end of the twelfth century. The story of the Damascene engineer at the siege of Acre who burnt all the siege-machines of the Crusaders in 1190 is well known. He flung jars of the fluid on the " beffrois " and other structures which the Franks had reared against the walls, and wherever the vessels broke there arose an inextinguishable conflagration. The author of the *Itinerarium Regis Ricardi* describes the substance as " oleum incendiarium, quod vulgo Ignem Graecum nominant," [3] and says that it could only be put out by sand or vinegar. He adds that it stank abominably, burned with a livid flame, and did not go out even if it fell on stone or iron, but continued to blaze up till it was consumed. Joinville, who saw St. Louis' machines and " cat-castles " destroyed by it at Mansourah, says that it was discharged by the Saracens both from perrières and from great arbalests. " It was like a big tun, and had a tail of the length of a large spear : the noise which it made resembled thunder, and it appeared like a great fiery dragon flying through the air, giving such a light

[1] Anna, xi. § 10.   [2] Anna, xiii. § 3, p. 192.   [3] *Itin.* i. 81.

that we could see in our camp as clearly as in broad day "
When it fell it burst (presumably the fragile vessel containing
it was shattered), and the liquid ran along the ground, burning
in a trail of flame, and setting fire to all that it touched. Its
progress could only be stopped by smothering it with sand.[1]
All this description applies only to the fire cast from the perrières;
that discharged from arbalests cannot, of course, have been
thrown in the same way. Apparently tow or some such substance must have been soaked in the oil and then fixed to the
arbalest bolt. The latter would lodge itself in the wood of the
French machines, and then the flaming substance attached to it
would lick up the boards. Such a device must have been much
inferior in effect (owing to the small quantity of the blazing
material) to the jars hurled from the perrière.[2]

Having dealt with the artillery of the twelfth and thirteenth
centuries, we must turn to the other siege-appliances of the age.
For the most part they are only perfected types of the machines
of the previous age. The movable tower and the penthouse
are still the most notable of the structures employed. The
latter, under the name of *cat* (less frequently *sus* or *vinea*), is the
invariable concomitant of every siege of the time ; it was still,
in its essential form, nothing more than the wooden framework
of the earlier centuries, but as carpenters grew more skilful it
became a stouter and stronger building. Its front parts were
even faced with iron plates to keep off combustibles, and the
timbers of its roof were made more and more solid as the
projectiles of the improved machines grew heavier. A variant
of it was the " cat-castle," such as St. Louis used in Egypt in
1249, where the penthouse was combined with a tower built
above it. The latter was filled with archers or arbalest men, who
tried to keep down the fire of the enemy, while the men below
in the penthouse were filling the ditch.

The movable tower (generally called *beffroi, berefredum,
belfragium*) is more prominent in the twelfth than in the
thirteenth century. It is unnecessary to give lists of the innumerable sieges at which it was employed in West and East,
from Bohemund's siege of Dyrrhachium in 1108 to the great

---

[1] Joinville, ii. 407.
[2] For the appearance of these Saracen trebuchets see the three machines on
Plate XXIII., taken from the *Jami-ul-Tawarik* of Raschid-ed-din, published in
A.D. 1310.

leaguers of Acre in 1189–90 and Château Gaillard in 1204. In the succeeding age it was less used than the mine : apparently the improvement in combustibles had made the towers more liable than ever to the danger of fire ; Coeur de Lion before Acre had even been driven to the costly expedient of coating his beffrois with iron plates. At any rate, the device does not play any great part in the later sieges of the thirteenth century.

The art of mining, on the other hand, which, though always known,[1] had not been very much practised before the twelfth century, was at its prime in the thirteenth. There is hardly a siege in which it does not appear ; only when a castle was water-girt or rock-built was it fruitless. Normally the assailants would advance their " cats " to the foot of the wall and endeavour to pick out stones, if they could not actually undermine the fortifications. The garrison, if they ascertained that the enemy was mining, would try the effect of counter-mines, and, when the line of approach had been discovered, would dig into it, slay the miners or smoke them out, and break down their works. The counter-mine is found as early as the mine, e.g. at the sieges of Dyrrhachium (1108) and Tortona (1155). For an elaborate instance of the employment of the device both by besiegers and besieged, the often-quoted document relating to the siege of Carcassonne (17th September to 11th October 1240) may be cited.[2] William des Ormes, the seneschal of the city, reports to the regent, Queen Blanche, that the rebels under Reginald Trencaval, Viscount of Béziers, after finding that their siege-artillery availed them little, set to work to mine. Carcassonne was then only defended by the ancient Roman or Visigothic works and an outer enceinte of palisading (lices). Its elaborate later works had not been added.

" The rebels," writes the seneschal, " began a mine against the barbican of the gate of Narbonne. And forthwith, we, having heard the noise of their work underground, made a counter-mine, and constructed in the inside of the barbican a great and strong wall of stones laid without mortar, so that we

[1] We have seen it used by the Danes at Paris (i. p. 141), and by William the Conqueror at Exeter (i. p. 134). Bohemund employed it largely in 1108, at his siege of Dyrrhachium. Yet that it was not very frequently tried seems to be shown by the passage in Otto of Freising, where in 1155, at Tortona, Frederic Barbarossa "inusitato satis utens artificio, cuniculos versus turrim Rubeam per subterraneos meatus fieri jubet " (O. F. ii. § 16, p. 124).
[2] From the document in the *Bibliothèque de l'École des Chartes*, ii. 2. p. 372.

thereby retained full half of the barbican, when they set fire to the hole in such wise that the wood having burnt out, a portion of the front of the barbican fell down.

" They then began to mine against another turret of the *lices* ; we counter-mined, and got possession of the hole which they had excavated. They began therefore to run a mine between us and a certain wall and destroyed two embrasures of the *lices*. But we set up there a good and strong palisade between us and them.

" They also started a mine at the angle of the town wall, near the bishop's palace, and by dint of digging from a great way off they arrived at a certain Saracen [1] wall, by the wall of the *lices* ; but at once, when we detected it, we made a good and strong palisade between us and them, higher up the *lices*, and counter-mined. Thereupon they fired their mine and flung down some ten fathoms of our embrasured front. But we made hastily another good palisade with a brattice upon it and loopholes ; so none among them dared to come near us in that quarter.

" They began also a mine against the barbican of the Rodez gate, and kept below ground, wishing to arrive at our walls, making a marvellous great tunnel. But when we perceived it we forthwith made a palisade on one side and the other of it. We counter-mined also, and, having fallen in with them, carried the chamber of their mine."

After this, abandoning mining, the assailants tried to storm the barbican below the castle. The assault failed, and a week later, news arriving that an army of relief was close at hand, the rebels abandoned their lines and retreated.

We have already had occasion to mention the use of the mine in English sieges of the thirteenth century—as at Rochester by King John in 1214, and at Bedford against the adherents of the turbulent Fawkes de Bréauté in 1224. There is in our history, however, no such example of complicated mining and counter-mining as that of the siege of Carcassonne. In the Levant, on the other hand, mines come prominently to the front, during the sieges of the last crusading strongholds by the great Mameluke sultans of Egypt. How thoroughly their power was recognised may be shown by the incidents of the fall of Markab

---

[1] *i.e.* Ancient Roman or Visigothic. All walls in the south of France were often ascribed to the short-lived occupation by the Saracens in the eighth century. In this case it must have been an outwork rather than the main wall of the city.

in 1285.[1] Sultan Kelaun having taken the outer defences, the knights of St. John, to whom the fortress belonged, retired into the inner enceinte. The Egyptians next set to work and mined a section of the curtain ; they brought down part of a tower and made a practicable breach, which they then attempted to storm. The knights repulsed the assailants with great loss and barricaded the breach. Kelaun then set the miners to work again, and in eight days succeeded in driving a gallery right under the great tower. He then summoned the garrison to surrender, offering to allow them to send engineers to survey his mine before making their answer. The knights accepted the proposal, and their envoys inspected the works and reported to the governor that the firing of the mine must certainly be fatal. Thereupon the Hospitallers surrendered on terms, quitting Markab with their horses, baggage, and treasure, and retiring to Acre.

General Considerations on Fortification and Siegecraft, 1100–1300.

We have already had occasion to remark (i. p. 380) that the ascendancy of the defensive over the offensive in the matter of siegecraft is the main reason for the fact that the twelfth and thirteenth centuries show comparatively few engagements in the open field when compared with other ages. The weaker side was always tempted to take shelter behind its walls rather than to offer battle. With modern standing armies such strategy would be faulty, since the combatant who renounces all attempts to take the offensive must almost inevitably fail in the long-run. But in the Middle Ages a feudal host could only be kept together for a few weeks, and a mercenary host was so costly that many princes could not afford to purchase its services. Hence a city or castle might hope to tire out the patience or the resources of its besiegers, long before its own inevitable fall by famine came about. A ruler who was both obstinate and wealthy, and did not disband his men at the approach of winter, might be certain of attaining his end—like Philip Augustus at Château Gaillard. But men of Philip's type and provided with Philip's resources were rare.

It is the number and strength of the fortified places of Europe which explains the futility of so many campaigns of the period.

[1] See the Arabic authors (Ibn-Ferat, etc.) quoted in Rey's *Architecture Militaire des Croisés*, pp. 36, 37.

A land could not be conquered with ease when every district was guarded by three or four castles and walled towns, which would each need several months' siege before they could be reduced. Campaigns tended either to become plundering raids which left the strongholds alone, or to resolve themselves into the prolonged blockade of a single fortified place. A narrow line of castles might maintain its existence for scores of years against a powerful enemy, as did the crusading fortresses of the Levant during the whole course of the thirteenth century. This is the most notable instance of such a resistance during the whole of the age, for the Mameluke sultans were formidable foes, furnished with inexhaustible resources and utilising the best engineering methods of the day. After three generations of incessant strife they ultimately achieved their end when crusading energy ran low, and after a long series of leaguers had broken the Christian line of defence at many points. At last the final departure of the Franks was the result of despair; they resigned the game because they were certain that no more help was to be expected from the West. It will be remembered that even after Acre fell in 1291, there were still isolated strongholds of formidable strength in the hands of the Crusaders; but they evacuated the triple concentric enceintes of Tortosa and the sea-girt castles of Athlit and Sidon because their hearts failed them, and they judged it useless to protract the inevitable end.

Similar chains of castles, when used against more barbarous foes destitute of perseverance and unprovided with the resources of engineering, almost always achieved their purpose, and held firm. We need only mention the line of forts which kept the English Pale in Ireland, and the " burgs " by which the Teutonic knights first subdued and then held down the warlike savages of Prussia.

It is of course possible to overstate the superiority of the defensive in the days before the invention of gunpowder. Towns and castles often fell, not only by treachery or faint-heartedness, but before open force. Weak situations or ill-designed and ill-built walls might prove fatal. A garrison too weak to hold a long front might be crushed by the easy expedient of simultaneous escalades directed against many points at once. A very large and well-provided besieging army might by the mere multitude of its crossbowmen and the incessant use of its military engines wear down the defenders of a post. There is a limit to the power of fortification, and a commander reckless of the loss of life and possessing a measureless superiority of numbers might often win his desire.   Such was the explanation of many of the successes of the Mameluke sultans over the castles of the Levant.   A hundred men, unless placed in a stronghold of exceptional natural strength, cannot resist ten thousand. But if they are crushed, their failure does not in the least vitiate our general statement that the defensive had an enormous advantage over the offensive in the age with which we have had to deal.   Otherwise, we should have to acknowledge that the victory of Zulus over a British battalion at Isandhlwana proved that the Martini-Henry rifle had no advantage over the assegai.

The thesis which we have asserted merely lays down the rule, that with any reasonable proportion of resources between the besiegers and the besieged, it was the latter who during the early Middle Ages had the best chance of success.   Hence come two of the main characteristics of these centuries—the long survival of small States placed among greedy and powerful neighbours, and the extraordinary power of resistance shown by rebellious nobles or cities of very moderate strength in dealing with their suzerains.   These features persist till the invention and improvement of artillery made the fall of strongholds a matter of days instead of months.   In the fourteenth century the change begins, in the fifteenth it is fully developed, in the sixteenth the feudal fastness has become an anachronism.

BOOK VIII

ENGLAND, WALES, AND SCOTLAND, 1296–1333— DEVELOPMENT OF THE LONGBOW

CHAPTER I

EDWARD I. AND HIS WARS IN WALES, 1277–1295— DEVELOPMENT OF THE LONGBOW

DOWN to the time of Edward I. we may roughly say that all the fighting in which English armies had been engaged had fallen into one of two categories. The larger part of the wars had conformed to the ordinary continental type of the day, and had been waged mainly by mailed horsemen, the infantry only appearing as an auxiliary arm of no very great efficiency. Such had been all the English wars with France, and all the civil wars from Lincoln to Evesham. The other class of war had been waged against irregular enemies such as the Welsh and Irish, who lurked in hills or bogs, generally refused battle, and were only formidable when they were executing a surprise or an ambuscade. Campaigns against them had been numerous, but had affected the English art of war no more than Soudanese or Trans-Indus expeditions affect the higher military science of to-day.

The reign of Edward I. forms a landmark in the history of the English army, as showing the first signs of the development of a new system of tactics on this side of the Channel, differing from continental custom by the much greater importance assigned to infantry equipped with missile arms. It is, in short, the period in which the longbow first comes to the front as the national weapon.

The bow had of course always been known in England. In the armies of our Norman and Angevin kings archers were to be found, but they formed neither the most numerous nor the most effective part of the host. On this side of the Channel, just as beyond it, the supremacy of the mailed horseman was still unquestioned. It is indeed noteworthy that the theory which attributes to the Normans the introduction of the long-

bow cannot be substantiated. If we are to trust the Bayeux
Tapestry, the weapon of William's archers was in no way
different from that already known in England, and used by a
few of the English in the fight of Senlac.[1] It was the shortbow
drawn to the breast, not to the ear. The archers who are
occasionally mentioned during the succeeding century—those,
for example, who took part in the Battle of the Standard—do
not appear to have formed any very important part of the
national host. Nothing can be more conclusive as to the
insignificance of the bow than the fact that it is not mentioned
at all in the " Assize of Arms " of 1181. In the reign of Henry
II., therefore, we may fairly conclude that it was not the proper
weapon of any class of English society. A similar deduction is
suggested by Richard Coeur de Lion's predilection for the arbalest : it is impossible that he should have so much admired it,
and taken such pains to secure mercenaries skilled in its use,
if he had been acquainted with the splendid longbow of the
fourteenth century. It is evident that the bow must always have
a great advantage in rapidity of discharge over the arbalest :
the latter must therefore have been considered by Richard to
surpass in range and penetrating power. But nothing is more
certain than that the English longbow at its best was able to
rival the crossbow on both these points. The conclusion is
inevitable that the weapon superseded by the arbalest was
merely the old shortbow, which had been in constant use since
Saxon times.

However this may be, the crossbowman continued to occupy
the place of importance among infantry till the middle of the
thirteenth century. Richard I., as we have said before, valued
the arbalest highly; John maintained great numbers both of
horse and foot arbalesters among those mercenaries who were
such a curse to England. Their evil memory is enshrined in
the clause of Magna Carta which binds the king to banish the
" alienigenas milites, balistarios, et servientes, qui venerunt cum
equis et armis ad nocumentum regni." [2] Fawkes de Bréauté,
the captain of John's mercenary crossbowmen, is one of the
most prominent and the most forbidding of the figures of the
civil war of 1215–17. Even in the reign of Henry III., the

[1] *e.g.* by the diminutive archer who crouches under a mailed thegn's shield, like
Teucer protected by Ajax.

[2] Magna Carta, § 51.

epoch in which the longbow was beginning to come into
prominence, the arbalest was still considered the superior
weapon. At the battle of Taillebourg, a corps of seven hundred
men armed with it were considered the flower of the English
infantry. Though Simon de Montfort must have had both
crossbowmen and archers at Lewes, the former receive most of
the small notice which the chroniclers take of the infantry in
that fight. The archers in the actual battle receive less mention
than the men armed with the archaic and very inefficient sling.

To trace the true origin of the longbow is not easy: there
is, however, good evidence to show that its use was originally
learned from the South Welsh, who seem to have been provided
with it as early as the reign of Henry II. Giraldus Cambrensis
speaks repeatedly[1] of the men of Gwent and Morganwg as
excelling all other districts in archery. For the strength of
their shooting he gives some curious evidence. At the siege
of Abergavenny in 1182 the Welsh arrows penetrated an oak
door four inches thick. They were allowed to remain there as
a curiosity, and Gerald himself saw them six years later, in 1188,
when he passed by the castle, with the iron points just showing
on the inner side of the door. A knight of William de Braose
received an arrow, which went first through the skirts of his
mail-shirt, then through his mail breeches, then through his
thigh, then through the wood of his saddle, and finally penetrated far into his horse's flank. " What more could a bolt
from a balista have done ? " asks Gerald. He describes the
bows of Gwent as " neither made of horn, ash, nor yew, but of
elm : ugly unfinished-looking weapons, but astonishingly stiff,
large, and strong, and equally capable of use for long or short
shooting." It was only among the South Welsh that archery
had become efficient. Their neighbours of Gwynedd and Powys
were essentially spearmen, and showed no vocation for the bow.
Llewellyn's auxiliaries, lent to Simon de Montfort for the
Tresham campaign, were certainly not bowmen. On the other
hand, it was the South Welsh archers of Strongbow and his
fellow-adventurers—as we have seen [2]—who made the Norman
Conquest of Ireland possible.

It is noticeable that on the first occasion when an English
king made really decisive use of archery in a great pitched

---

[1] Pp. 54, 123, 127 of the Rolls series edition of the *Itinerarium Cambriae.*
[2] See vol. i. pp. 409 *et seq.*

battle,[1] we are told that his infantry were mostly composed of Welshmen. But the first mention of the bow as much used by the English is, curiously enough, not from any district near the South Welsh border, but from Sussex, where in 1216 more than a thousand bowmen under one Wilkin are said to have molested the army of the Dauphin Lewis and the rebel barons as they marched through the Weald. But the great landmark in the history of archery is undoubtedly the "Assize of Arms" of 1252. After ordering that the richer yeomanry who own a hundred shillings in land should come to the host with steel cap, gambeson, lance, and sword, that document proceeds to command "that all who own more than forty and less than a hundred shillings in land come bearing a sword and a bow with arrows and a dagger." Similarly, citizens with chattels worth more than nine marks and less than twenty are to be arrayed with bow, arrows, and sword. There is a special clause at the end of the paragraph providing that even poor men with less than forty shillings in land or nine marks in chattels should bring bow and arrows if they have them, instead of the "falces gisarmas et alia arma minuta" which are spoken of as their usual weapons.

In face of the provisions of the Assize of Arms, made twelve years before the battle of Lewes, it is most curious to find that in the campaigns of 1264 and 1265 the crossbow—an essentially foreign weapon, and one not prescribed for the use of any class of subjects of the realm—should still keep the upper hand. It is, as we have already remarked, named far more frequently than the bow by the chroniclers of the barons' war. The only notable mention of archery is—characteristically enough—that which describes the attack made on King Henry's marching columns in the Weald by De Montfort's Welsh auxiliaries.[2] But there is a case, not mentioned by any chronicler, which shows that archers could be raised in good numbers and at short notice in a region very remote from the Welsh frontier. In 1266, even after the great disaster of Evesham, the relics of the baronial party made head against the king in certain quarters. Among the disturbed regions were

---

[1] At Falkirk, according to Walter Hemingburgh, who gives far the best account of the battle : "Numerati sunt pedestres qui aderant, et quasi omnes erant Hibernici et Wallenses" (p. 159). This exaggerates ; see Chapter II. of this Book.

[2] Wykes, 1264, § 5.

Essex and also the Cinque Ports, against which the king sent
out an expedition under Roger de Leyburn. A writ issued in
May orders Leyburn to add to certain other troops assigned to
him five hundred archers to be raised in the Weald.[1] They
were to be called out for short service, and given pay for only
the shortest of terms—under three weeks Apparently the
trouble in Essex which had caused their levy soon died down.
It is suggestive to find that Leyburn's archers are raised exactly
in the same district where Wilkin had made things uncomfort-
able for the French in 1216; yet I have come on no other
indication that the Weald was a special centre for the development of archery.   Possibly all the woodland regions were early
proficient in bowcraft, because of their notorious proficiency in
poaching : we know that Sherwood and Chiltern were famous
for their archers in later days.[2]

The longbow comes to the front only in the wars of Edward
I., and its predominance in later English wars is directly due to
the king's own action.   Edward, after much experience, found
that more advantage might be got from a judicious combination
of cavalry and of infantry armed with missile weapons, than
from the use of horsemen alone.   We have no signs that he had
learned this at the time of Lewes and Evesham, but it appears
clearly enough during his Welsh wars.   In expeditions among
the hills of Gwynedd the horseman was often useless : he could
not storm crags or scramble down ravines   Welsh fighting was
mainly work for infantry, and the king—as his conduct in
the Evesham campaign had shown—was ready to learn in the
school of war.   Having come to know the strength and the
weakness of infantry as well as of mailed knighthood, he was
quite capable of combining his lessons.

The Welsh Wars of Edward I.—1277-1295.

The long and persistent struggle in which Edward I. solved
that problem of the conquest of North Wales which had foiled all

[1] For this interesting reference from Exchequer Accounts, Army and Ordnance,
3 S. 6., I am indebted to Mr. Ernest Jacob of All Souls, who chanced on it and
showed it to me. The force contained three sorts of archers, *Wallenses*, *Waldenses*,
and *alii*.

[2] As late as 1588, in the muster-rolls of the army raised to face the Spanish
Armada, we find that the Chiltern shires—Oxford and Bucks—were the only counties
in which the levy included far more bowmen than arquebusiers : they were the last
regions to give up the longbow.

earlier kings, is perhaps most interesting to the military historian because it contains the two first instances of the scientific combination of cavalry and archery, since Hastings, which we have found in English annals. These were the battle of Orewin Bridge, won by Edmund Mortimer and John Giffard in 1282 over Llewellyn of Gwynedd (who there met his death), and the battle near Conway in 1295, where William Beauchamp, Earl of Warwick, defeated Madoc, Llewellyn's son, the last champion of North Wales. Of these we shall speak in their due place.

Less exciting, but quite as instructive, is the study of the military methods at large by which Edward completed the subjugation of the Principality which had successfully defied so many of his ancestors. The root-matter of the whole story is the fact that a normal short-service feudal host was unsuitable for the conquest of a race of hardy and obstinate mountaineers, who retired into the fastnesses of Snowdonia when driven from their valleys, and there waited for the inevitable break up of the invading army in the autumn. When the enemy had retired before October rains or November frost, the Welsh descended from their eyries and reoccupied their devastated lowlands. The whole conquest had to be begun again *de novo* in the next spring.

Edward's three receipts for dealing with this problem were : (1) the raising of paid non-feudal armies, with a large proportion of infantry, which could keep the field through the winter ; (2) systematic castle-building at the main strategical points ; (3) road-making in a land hitherto provided with nothing better than Celtic trackways, save where the ruins of a few old Roman roads were dimly visible.

To call out the whole feudal levy of England for a Welsh war was to ask for many more horsemen than were required, and to ensure their service for a much shorter time than was necessary. It is obvious that a summons for all the tenants by knight-service or sergeantry to appear in arms at once could only be really needed in two sorts of crisis. It might be justified in face of a foreign invasion—but nothing of that sort had been seen since Louis of France came over in 1214 to claim the crown of King John. Or, again, it might be required in the case of widespread rebellion and civil strife—such as the rising of de Montfort and the " Barons' War " of 1264.

The full amount of horsemen due from the realm of England

would seem to have been in the reign of Edward I. something well over six thousand, though well under seven thousand. The elaborate calculations in Mr. Morris's *Welsh Wars* [1] show that it is impossible to fix the exact number. This total is practically the same as that which has been worked out for the reign of Henry II. [2] For dealing with a Welsh insurrection no king would require six thousand five hundred horse : they could not have lived in the mountains of the West, and, moreover, no commander-in-chief would wish to call out the whole of his reserves at once. The size of the tool employed must be proportioned to the work that is asked of it.

Now Scutage, the system already explained in an earlier chapter, by which the knight's liability to serve for his forty days could be bought off for a sum of money, was quite well remembered all through King Edward's days. Many tenants-in-chief gave money instead of service. But there was an exception to its general employment—feudal public opinion (if we may use the phrase)—considered that earls had a special military obligation; it was beneath their dignity to be perpetual absentees in time of war. Unless an earl was a minor, or a chronic invalid, or very old, he was expected to answer the king's summons in person. " Feudal etiquette," as Mr. Morris observes, " made a strong distinction between earls and others as regards service. An earl, having the number of his *quota* fixed, was expected to bring that number of knights *plus* an adequate complement of troopers, and was expected to serve— and to maintain his status as a great feudatory actually did serve—for over forty days." Hence the proportion of earls in the field in a great campaign is greater than that of the lesser barons, who might compound for their contingent or, if they did not, would serve their forty days and depart, or else claim that (their duty being discharged) they should be paid by the king for any further time that they spent with the army.

The system on which Edward I. worked his long Welsh campaigns was apparently that of making a rough bargain with the tenants-in-chief that they should not be expected to appear with their full *servitium debitum* of knights for the feudal forty days, but that they should bring a smaller—generally a much smaller—*quota*, and undertake to keep the field when the feudal obligation was over, on condition that the king

[1] See *Welsh Wars of Edward I.*, pp. 35-41.   [2] See vol. i. p. 368.

should begin to pay them and their retinue from the forty-first day onward. Only the earls were not expected to take wages—there are a very few exceptional cases in which they did, but the number is negligible.[1] The result of this compromise was that the king got a moderate but sufficient contingent for his Welsh wars, which varied from year to year, according as the military need was greater or less. The relation between the old full *servitium debitum* and the retinue with which the earl or baron actually appeared seems to vary incomprehensibly between different persons; *e.g.* in the Welsh war of 1294 the Earl of Lancaster, lord of two hundred and sixty-three knightly fiefs, appeared with fifty followers : the Earl of Norfolk, with two hundred and seventy-nine fiefs, came with only twenty-eight : the Earl of Warwick, with one hundred and thirty-five fiefs, numbered twenty-one horsemen : Hugh Courtenay, the greatest baron of Devon, had ninety-two, and showed only twelve men,—all these are very low contingents : some of the barons brought a following with a much larger proportion to their full obligation; *e.g.* Robert de Tatteshall owing sixty-nine shields brought twenty, John de Vesey owing thirty-six came with fifteen, Baldwin Wake owing twenty-eight brought no less than sixteen.

As Mr. Morris has pointed out, there were a few exceptional barons of the lesser sort who seem to have laid themselves out for a purely military career : they came early, with a retinue out of all proportion to that shown by greater men, and stayed to the very end of the war, drawing pay sometimes for much more than their proper contingent. They were the first examples of the great " contractors " or *condottieri* of the next century. Such were Walter de Huntercombe, who owing only seven knights' fees, came with twenty followers to Wales in 1295, and with eighteen to Scotland in 1298, and Maurice de Berkeley the younger, who on his father's fee was liable for five shields only, but brought fifteen, and engaged himself to serve with that number in the following of the Earl of Pembroke in 1297.

When a campaign had got into its second month, and the feudal forty days were over, the large majority of the Edwardian cavalry were paid men, only a minority belonging to the earls were unpaid. By this means the king contrived to keep a considerable force on foot even during the winter months, and

[1] See Morris, *Welsh Wars*, p. 57.

to provide permanent garrisons for outlying castles. It would of course have been impossible to find the necessary money for such an army from the proceeds of scutage alone—but the general taxation of the realm, tending steadily to increase, made the feat of maintaining a large force for many months on end possible.

It should be remembered that there was a standing nucleus round which any army could be mobilised—the king's personal retinue *familia regis*, a staff rather than a bodyguard, for it comprised a disproportionate number of knights and even of bannerets, though of course the majority were only sergeants. There would seem to have been in normal times about thirty or forty of the knights, from sixty to ninety of the sergeants. Many were always doing detached duty, serving as castellans of castles, as commanders of small isolated bodies of troops, carrying messages and orders of importance, raising relays of shire-levies, or superintending the transport of material or of money. But there were always some scores of them about the king's person, and when he was present at an action they were of course responsible for his personal safety. To serve in the *familia* was a career of promise : many of the sergeants became knights, some of the knights got promotion to such posts as that of Justiciar of North or South Wales or Seneschal of Gascony. In time of peace those of them who were not actually at court received a regular retaining fee, on condition that they were ready to rejoin when wanted.[1]

What with his *familia*, his paid horsemen, and the feudal *quotas* that were for the moment in his camp, the king could easily count on keeping ten hundred or twelve hundred horse in the field, in addition to those whom the Lords Marchers were maintaining at the same time for the private defence of their own lands. Feudal *quotas*, as they melted away, were replaced in winter by paid squadrons, in which many of the fief-holders and their retainers were content to stay, provided that they got the king's wages. This would be for an ordinary Welsh war : for such great efforts as the campaign of Falkirk it would seem that well over two thousand, perhaps as many as two thousand five hundred, horsemen were in the field.

But cavalry, as has been observed above, was not the arm

[1] For all this see Morris, *Welsh Wars*, pp. 84-87.

most required in the Welsh campaigns; indeed, there were many regions in which it was practically unusable. Hence the need for infantry. A large proportion of this was always composed of South Welsh "friendlies," mainly the foot-archers of the Lords Marchers, who were invaluable on hills and in woods resembling those of their own homeland. A few other similar men appeared, belonging to Welsh chiefs who remained loyal to the king—probably from old family feuds with the house of Llewellyn. The majority, however, of the foot consisted of English shire-levies, almost always drawn from the regions abutting on, or not very far distant from, the Welsh border. Their relative efficiency would seem to have varied in proportion to their distance from that land of perpetual strife. Cheshire or Shropshire troops would be better trained for war than those of the Midlands. The farthest counties ever called upon for a serious contingent were Derbyshire and Nottingham-shire—probably because their woodlands bred the Sherwood archery. For the rest, Gloucester, Hereford, Stafford, and Lancashire were habitual contributors. The more remote Midlands and North were barely touched on a single occasion of special crisis.[1]

The infantry were levied by " Commissioners of Array " who organised their contingents in hundreds and thousands, under *centenars* or constables, and *millenars*. They were on service only for brief periods, it being the duty of the Commissioners of Array to see that drafts came up at short intervals, to replace time-expired groups. Three months seem to have been the limit, and it was hard to keep the men together for so long—the pay-rolls prove that desertion was always rampant. In the war of 1277 the largest figure of infantry simultaneously under arms seems to have been fifteen thousand, of whom the larger half were Welsh " friendlies." In 1282 the largest gather-ing of foot at one time seems to have been eight thousand. But of course heavier figures are found in later years used for the great invasions of Scotland.

Archery was growing in importance, and we occasionally find whole units composed of it—as, for example, certain South Welsh bodies and a corps of Macclesfield men. But the bow was not yet the regular weapon of the English foot-soldier, despite of the ordinance of Henry III.[2] Shire-levies are often

[1] See Morris, *Welsh Wars*, pp. 92-93.   [2] See above, page 60 of vol. ii.

called *sagittarii et lancearii*, and the proportion between the
two is never given—as it is in many documents of the next
century. The fact that the bow had not yet achieved the
reputation that it was to acquire in the next generation is best
shown by a fact already mentioned above—the arbalesters still
received better pay than the archer, in the proportion of threepence to twopence a day. Their numbers were usually
moderate : in 1277 the king had two hundred and fifty with
him, of whom one hundred were Gascons and other foreigners.
In 1282 about two hundred and fifty English crossbowmen
were in the field, and a much larger number of Gascons—at least
six hundred of them,[1] of whom a few were mounted men.
Horse-arbalesters were a very rare phenomenon in any European country, as has already been observed. But in the
campaign of 1289, against the rebel Rhys, there were only
one hundred and five crossbowmen present among a total
force of eleven thousand infantry : in 1292 the largest force
of them mentioned is seventy. In the invasion of Scotland
that culminated at Falkirk there were two hundred and fifty
out of a total infantry force present of twelve thousand five
hundred. At no time, therefore, did the arbalest appear as
a predominant weapon in the English service, and in the next
century it was destined to go altogether out of use, as archery
continued to improve.

The number of troops, horse or foot, employed in Wales
was not the decisive factor in Edward's conquest of the country.
What really settled the matter was that he succeeded in keeping
a great part of them on foot all through the winter months, and
so held his enemies penned up in their hills to starve. In 1277
the invaders, as we read, destroyed all the harvests in Anglesey
and along the Menai Straits, and remained encamped in
Gwynedd—whereupon Llewellyn submitted in October. In
1282–1283 the effort was much greater, for the English army
was out on service for fifteen months continuously. The
decisive battle at Orewin Bridge, which cost Llewellyn his life,
was fought at midwinter—on December 11th ; the last desperate
remnant of the enemy surrendered in June 1283—long before
the harvest was ripe. In 1287 the rebel Rhys-ap-Maredudd
started his second insurrection in November, hoping no doubt for

---

[1] There were thirteen hundred Gascons in all present in 1282, but many were
cavalry, and not all the infantry were arbalesters.

a respite during the season of bad weather, but had been crushed by January 1288, the English having kept up operations through the three worst months of the winter.   The last rising, that of Madoc-ap-Llewellyn, broke out on September 30, 1294 —the king had five thousand foot under arms by October, marched himself from Chester on December 11th, heard of the decisive victory of the Earl of Warwick at Conway on January 22, 1295, and had the insurrection crushed by April.   There was no hope for the Welsh when they had to do with a king and army who were prepared to go on fighting for a whole winter.

To conquer Wales was one thing.   To keep it subdued was another.   This was achieved by Edward's great system of strategically-placed castles.   Following the method by which the Lords Marchers had already tamed the South, he framed his scheme for dominating the habitable parts of the land by impregnable strongholds.   The building started in 1283, immediately after the conquest—Conway was to command the coast road from Chester into Snowdonia, Carnarvon the Menai Strait : the guard here was strengthened at a later date (1295) by building Beaumaris on the other side of the water, to hold down Anglesey, the granary of Wales.   Harlech over-looked the lands around the head of Tremadoc Bay.   Each was a first-rate fortress of the newest "concentric" style, that we have described in the chapter on Fortification.   In addition, the old Welsh fortresses of Bere, Criccieth, and Dolwyddelan were repaired and garrisoned.   Between them they encircled the mountain group of Snowdonia, the former summer refuge of insurgent princes of Gwynedd on all sides.   The chief strong-holds—Conway, Beaumaris, Carnarvon, Criccieth, Harlech— were all by the seaside, and could be revictualled by a fleet, if ever the land-communication with England should be cut. The device succeeded—the castles held out and strangled insur-rection : Carnarvon, it is true, was captured by surprise in 1294, but recaptured almost immediately and rebuilt on a stronger and improved scale in 1295.

But while relying on water-transport for the reinforcement of the new castles in time of extreme need, Edward also turned his mind to road-building.   We find his armies accompanied by "labour battalions"—in August 1277 he had fifteen hundred to eighteen hundred woodmen and ditchers (*fossa-*

tores) employed in making a road from Flint by Rhuddlan to Conway: in September there were still one thousand.[1] Even the chroniclers, generally not much interested in such engineering, were struck by the magnitude of the operation.[2] Only by road-building could communication between the army and its base be kept up—the plan was Roman in conception. Pioneers are mentioned in some of the later campaigns, but never on such a scale as this.

So much for the general features of the Welsh wars. It remains that we should describe the two incidents for which the military historian finds them most interesting, the cases in which a battle was won by the deliberate combination of horse and archery. From the example of these two half-forgotten combats we trace the sequence to Falkirk, Dupplin, Halidon Hill, and all the glorious continental successes of Edward III. and Henry V.

The first battle was that of Orewin Bridge, near Builth, fought on December 11th, 1282—the mid-winter date is well worth noting. Llewellyn had left his stronghold in Snowdon, in order to raise rebellion in Mid and South Wales : unless the area of insurrection were spread, he saw that starvation was threatening his followers. He won considerable success in Brecknock—the countryside rose, and the castle of Builth was beleaguered. Against him there went forth two Marcher lords, John Giffard and Edmund Mortimer, with their own vassals, aided by a Shropshire shire-levy. Llewellyn took up a strong position above the banks of the river Yrfon, a tributary of the Wye, blocking Orewin Bridge. It was a bare steep hillside, only accessible, as it appeared, if the bridge were forced. The Welsh stood in a solid array of spearmen, out of bowshot from the farther bank. A local "friendly," however, showed the Marchers a ford some way up-stream, by which their infantry crossed at dawn unseen, and fell upon the flank of the Welsh position. Llewellyn, by some chance of war, was not on the spot when the fighting began : he was some miles away, at a conference with certain chiefs of doubtful loyalty, according to the native version of the story. At any rate his troops were without a commander when the action started. They clustered together on the hilltop, abandoning the bridge in front, and

---

[1] See Morris, *Welsh Wars*, p. 139.
[2] Wykes in Rolls series, *Annales Monartici*, iv. p. 272.

thus suffering the English cavalry to pass the Yrfon.[1] Giffard and Mortimer brought up their archers against the mass of spearmen, who offered only a passive but an obstinate defence. When a great many of them had fallen, the men-at-arms charged uphill, and broke into the gaps in the mass. The majority were cut to pieces, the rest fled over the hills. Llewellyn, hurrying back at the rumour of battle, was too late to join his men—he chanced to fall in, somewhere on the outskirts of the fight, with an isolated Shropshire man-at-arms, one Stephen de Frankton, who slew him in single combat, not knowing who he was. His death was discovered only when the corpses were being stripped after the battle.

The story reminds one somewhat of Hastings. A mass of infantry, not sufficiently equipped with missile weapons, may hold out for a time against the joint attack of archery and horse, but is doomed to extinction in the end.

The second battle was that won near Conway on January 22, 1295, by William, Earl of Warwick. He was marching from Rhuddlan to raise the blockade of Conway Castle, in which lay King Edward, who had been cut off for a moment from his communication with England by an irruption of the rebels of Madoc-ap-Llewellyn. The Welsh were encamped above the road, on a bare hillside between two woods, into which they intended to retire if pressed too hard. But Warwick, by marching all night, was able to come upon them at dawn, so that they had no time to retire, and turned both their flanks. " Then," says Nicholas Trivet,[2] " seeing themselves surrounded, they fixed the butts of their spears in the earth, with the heads pointing outward, to keep off the rush of the horsemen. But the Earl placed a crossbowman (or, no doubt, an archer)[3] between each two knights, and when by their shooting a great part of the spearmen had been slain, he burst in among them with his horse, and made such a carnage as no Welsh army (it is believed) had ever suffered before." This reads like a repetition of the tactics of Orewin Bridge, only more successful in slaughter

---

[1] " Steterunt Wallenses per turmas in supercilio montis : ascendentibus nostris per sagittarios nostros (qui inter equestres mixti erant) corruerunt multi, eo quod animose steterunt. Tandem nostri ascenderunt equestres et caesis aliquibus reliquos in velocem fugam compulerunt " (Hemingburgh, vol. i. p. 11).

[2] Trivet, *sub anno* 1295, p. 282.

[3] The number of crossbowmen in English armies in this year was so small that Warwick *must* have used archers in addition to his few score arbalesters.

because the enemy's flanks had been turned before the fight began, and he had no line of retreat left open. Among the leaders present on the English side was John Giffard,[1] one of the victors of the earlier fight: it has been suggested, with reason, that he may have been the man who showed Warwick how to deal with the problem before him. He was wounded in the battle, and received a special letter of commendation from Edward, " *quia regi potenter subvenit his diebus.*[2]

In Edward I.'s inglorious French wars in Aquitaine we find little sign of the proper combination of horse and foot. The English armies in those campaigns were largely composed of the king's Gascon vassals, whose military ideas were wholly continental ; but it is curious to find that their English leaders seem to have taught them nothing. Take, for example, the battle at Peyrehorade (near Bayonne) in 1295. The Earl of Lincoln with six hundred men-at-arms and ten thousand foot set out to relieve the town of Belgarde, then threatened by the Count of Artois. Issuing from a wood, his vanguard was suddenly charged by the French, who were waiting for them with fifteen hundred horse ranged in four " battles." The English cavalry came up successively, forcing their way out of the forest-road, and engaged—not very advantageously—with the French. But the footmen " hung back in the wood without advancing, and did no good whatever," [3] though the knights were in grievous need of infantry, " qui projectos armatos hostium spoliarent vel interimerent." The last clause shows the very modest task which Lincoln expected his foot-soldiery to discharge.

It must have been from the experience of his Welsh expeditions and the teaching of such officers as John Giffard that King Edward learned how to combine horse and foot with such effect in his great Scottish victory at Falkirk. The interest of the Scottish war, from the military point of view, lies in the alternate success and failure of the English according to the manner in which they were handled by their leaders. The Scottish tactics were uniform, and were dictated by the fact that the northern realm was hopelessly inferior to England in the number and quality of its men-at-arms. Not only were the Scottish

[1] See Morris, *Welsh Wars*, p. 258.
[2] See Morris, p. 256, and Patent Rolls under the date January 24, 1295.
[3] Hemingburgh, vol. i. p. 74.

nobility and knighthood too few to cope with the English, but
throughout the war a large proportion of them adhered to King
Edward's cause, and were often found fighting beneath his
banner. The Scots therefore were forced to rely almost
entirely on their sturdy yeomen, whose hearts were firmly set
against the Southron. On no occasion did Wallace or Bruce
bring to the field so much as a thousand heavy cavalry, and no
good feat of arms can be set to the credit of their horsemen
save a single charge at Bannockburn, which we shall have to
describe in its proper place.

CHAPTER II

ENGLAND AND SCOTLAND, 1296–1328—FALKIRK AND BANNOCKBURN

DIFFERENT as were the results of King Edward's attempts to conquer Wales and to conquer Scotland, the two enterprises had a superficial resemblance to an unintelligent contemporary observer. Both were fought out in hilly and thinly-peopled countries, where roads were few and provisions hard to find, and against a foe whose reliance lay on his infantry. But there were crucial points of difference. The most obvious, and the one that struck the minds of the men of that day, was the difference in the moods of the two hostile races. The fiery but unstable Welsh loved rapid, headlong attacks in passes or ravines, and seldom or never fought in the open of their own free will. The Scots' array had more of the nature of a regular army—they had a proportion of men-at-arms (though it was usually small) as well as of archery. They relied on the power of steady resistance, and several times accepted a pitched battle. The Welsh, as Giraldus Cambrensis had observed a hundred years before, risked everything on the result of one tempestuous charge,[1]—in five minutes they were either victorious, or routed and in full flight for their hilltops. The Scot came on less wildly to the fray, or even waited to be attacked, but he grew sterner and harder as the day wore on, and was capable of any amount of dogged resistance. Between these two nations of spearmen there lay all the difference between the Celtic and the Teutonic temperament—for the Scottish war was mainly waged by the Lowlanders, not by the Gael from beyond the Grampians, who took small part in the struggle.

Yet it was, on the whole, geography rather than national temperament and tactics which brought about the disastrous

[1] *Itinerarium Cambriae*, p. 209.

end of the attempt of Edward I. to subdue Scotland. Wales lies close into England, stretched along the side of the Midlands, where English resources were great and easily accessible. No part of the Principality is more than seven days' march from one of the three English bases of mobilisation, Chester, Shrewsbury, or Hereford, from which expeditions were wont to set forth. A Midland levy to restrain the Welsh could be got together in a few days, and could be in the heart of the Principality a week later. Another important factor in conquest was that Wales could easily be sailed round on the sea side, and taken in the rear by landed troops while it was being threatened in front by the main army. Edward habitually brought up considerable naval forces, not only from the West English harbours but from the Cinque Ports, and even occasionally from Gascony. The castles which he built along the farther shore—Conway, Beaumaris, Carnarvon, Harlech, etc.—were revictualled and remanned, as countless records show, by ships coming not only from Bristol or Chester, but even from Dublin, which is conveniently placed opposite them on the other side of St. George's Channel.

But geography also worked in another way. The citadel of Welsh resistance—the Snowdon group and its dependent ranges to south and south-east, in which the enemy always took refuge—had, after all, a comparatively small area contrasted with the bulk of remoter Scotland beyond Forth and Clyde, to which a beaten Scottish army could retire. We may add that in the Lords Marchers, already planted deep in Wales, with their serried array of castles and their military organisation, Edward had allies on the spot far more valuable than any that he possessed in Scotland. For though no inconsiderable part of the northern baronage adhered to the invader at one time or another, they did not help with zeal, as did the Marchers, but from purely materialistic aims, and against their conscience, so that they often fell away to the national cause in moments of enthusiasm.

But the main drawback for the invader, after all, was the extreme remoteness of central and northern Scotland from the English base of mobilisation, which was practically York, for Newcastle, Durham, and Carlisle were all small places lying in regions of no great wealth or population. To bring a Midland levy to Carlisle or Newcastle was a far harder thing than to bring it to Hereford or Chester. When York had once been passed, there was a long march through a thinly-peopled and resourceless country before the Scottish Border was reached. And when the Border had been passed, and Lothian and Galloway overrun—as they often were—the enemy had a limitless retreat into the Highlands. English ships were sometimes brought up from Hull or Chester to the Firths of Forth or Clyde, bearing food and munitions. But there was no chance of getting them farther north, especially into the tangle of unknown isles and peninsulas on the western coast. When Robert Bruce, after the rout of Methven (1305), took refuge in the Hebrides, he became inaccessible to King Edward in a way that Llewellyn had never been, even when he had hidden himself in the remotest recesses of Snowdon. Such a fugitive could not be pursued, and could always return at his pleasure, to strike at some point of the English line in Scotland, where the garrison was weak and the countryside ripe for rebellion. The hunting down of Scottish patriots was an interminable and heart-breaking task. For though a costly army might be raised, conducted to the Border, and led up and down for many weeks in a trackless and foodless country, it could not catch enemies who took to the limitless hills and isles of the extreme north and west.

It took some time before the invader began to realise this. In Edward's first invasion of Scotland, which terminated with the rout of Dunbar and Baliol's resignation of the crown, there was no serious fighting. The struggle did not begin in earnest till the rebellion of Wallace—a purely popular rising in the interest of national independence, which was viewed with very scant sympathy by the greater part of the Scottish baronage. For many nobles of the land held manors south as well as north of Tweed, and were almost English in blood and in sympathies. The insurgents found no leader but an obscure outlawed knight of Strathclyde, who was treated with small courtesy by such of the baronage as chose to dally with the cause of independence.

Battle of Stirling Bridge, September 11, 1297.

The first important engagement of the war gave a fine object-lesson as to the way in which a Scottish army ought not to be encountered. Edward had left, as his representative beyond Tweed, John Earl of Warrenne, the hero of the well-known incident of the rusty sword during the *Quo Warranto* inquest. The earl had served at Lewes [1] and Evesham,—though with no particular credit,—and was now nearing his sixtieth year.   He appears to have been a type of the ordinary stupid and arrogant feudal chief, who had learned nothing of the art of war though he had gone out on many campaigns.   The insurgents had been making head beyond the Forth, and had just captured Perth. Warrenne therefore concentrated his army at Stirling, where he drew together some hundreds of men-at-arms [2] and a large body of foot-soldiery raised in the six northern counties and in North Wales.   Wallace and the Scots at once set out to check him at the Forth, camping on the wooded hills which overlook the sinuous course of that river as it passes Stirling.   Their host counted no more than a hundred and eighty mounted knights and squires, but many thousands of sturdy spearmen.   The sole bridge over the stream was that sometimes named from the town, sometimes from the abbey of Cambuskenneth.   It was a long, narrow structure, on which no more than two horsemen could ride abreast.   Towering above it only a few hundred yards away was the Abbey Craig, the steep wooded height which forms the end of the Ochil Hills : on it Wallace lay encamped.   Finding that the Scots treated his summons to lay down their arms with derision, Warrenne determined to cross the bridge and storm their position.   The wiser heads in his camp were filled with dismay at a resolve inspired by a foolish and overweening contempt for the enemy.   Sir Richard Lundy, a Scottish knight of the English party, pointed out to the earl that it would take eleven hours for his whole host to defile over the bridge in face of an active enemy less than a mile away.   He pointed out a ford not far off, at which men could cross thirty abreast, and begged that the army might pass there, or that at least he might be permitted to take a few hundred horsemen and create a diversion on that point.   Warrenne refused to listen to him, and bade his troops begin to defile across the narrow bridge. Wallace was observing every movement of the English from

[1] He was one of those who had deserted Prince Edward and fled away at the end of the first-named battle.   See vol. i. p. 430.

[2] Numbers not accurately ascertainable.   But as Mr. Morris remarks (*Welsh Wars*, p. 283), when the king and many barons were absent in Flanders, and a political crisis was raging at London, Warrenne's numbers can not have been very great.   Only four of Edward's prominent baronets—Percy, Huntercombe, Twenge, and Cressingham—are known to have been at Cambuskenneth.

his lofty post on the Abbey Craig, and his men were lurking in a solid mass behind its woods. He allowed the enemy's van-battle, commanded by Sir Marmaduke Twenge and Hugh Cressingham the Treasurer, to cross the water and to begin to form up on the northern bank. Then, when the main-battle was still on the farther side, he flung his whole army down the hill, against the troops who had crossed. A picked body of spearmen charged for the bridge-head and reached it in the first rush, while the mass of the Scots fell upon Twenge and Cressingham's men. The bridge-head once seized and firmly held, Warrenne could not push forward, nor the van-battle retrace its steps. After a short struggle the whole body that had crossed was either trampled down or flung into the river. Twenge by prodigies of valour cut his way back across the bridge almost alone. But Cressingham and more than a hundred knights, with several thousand English and Welsh foot, were slain or drowned (Sept. 11, 1297).

Warrenne, whose whole conduct contrasts most shamefully with Wallace's splendid action, was so cowed by the encounter, that, instead of preparing to defend the line of the Forth, he threw a garrison into Stirling and retired to Berwick, abandoning the whole of the Lowlands to the enemy.

Wallace followed up the victory of Cambuskenneth Bridge by a fierce inroad into Northumberland and Durham. His ravages drew King Edward in person into Scotland in the next year, with a very heavy force of both feudal and stipendiary squadrons at his back. He brought apparently some two thousand five hundred men-at-arms, mustered under the colours of more than a hundred barons and bannerets. For foot-soldiery he had not summoned the full shire-levies under the sheriffs, but only a picked force. There were some ten thousand Welsh—Marchmen to the number of six thousand, and over three thousand from North Wales,—"for they were always ready to serve for plunder."[1] But the English foot were comparatively few, apparently only two thousand five hundred, mostly from Cheshire and Lancashire.[2] The enormous figures

---

[1] Hemingburgh, i. p. 259.

[2] For interesting calculations as to the strength of this army, see Morris's *Welsh Wars*, pp. 286-291. He makes out for the cavalry one thousand three hundred stipendiary horse, a thousand feudal horse, and the king's *familia* of over a hundred. Some Scots were serving, including Robert Bruce, the future king, the Earl of Angus, a Seton, and a Kirkpatrick.

given by the chroniclers for the array of infantry—fifty or even eighty thousand—are of course absurd ; and the usually reasonable Hemingburgh multiplies the horse nearly threefold.

Battle of Falkirk, July 22, 1298.

When Edward marched from Berwick into Lothian, and began to waste the land and storm the few castles which were defended against him, Wallace did not make any attempt to protect the plain. He had summoned all Scotland to his banner, yet he cannot have had the thirty thousand foot and the thousand men-at-arms [1] with which the more sober of the English chroniclers credit him. But he had withdrawn them into the Torwood, the great forest which lay between Falkirk and Stirling, and there kept quiet. He was resolved to take the defensive in a favourable position, and not to meet the king's overwhelming force of cavalry in the open.

It seemed for a moment possible that no battle might take place, for Edward spent so much time in Lothian that his provisions began to run low, and no more could be procured from the wasted countryside. He could not hear of any hostile army in the field, and was beginning to think of returning to England. But presently there came to him the Earls of March and Angus, two Scottish lords of the English faction, with news that Wallace lay only eighteen miles away at Falkirk, and that, hearing of the approaching retreat of the royal army, he was preparing to fall upon its rear and harass its march. " He shall not come to me, for I will go to him," exclaimed Edward, and straightway set his army—famine-stricken though it was— to march on Falkirk. He slept at Linlithgow on the night of July 21 ; that night he had two ribs broken by a kick from his horse, but, though suffering much pain, he pushed on next morning to seek for Wallace. A Scottish reconnoitring party was sighted early in the day, but promptly retired. Following it up, and moving past the town to the south, by the hillside called Slamannan Muir, the English at last came in sight of the enemy. Wallace had selected a very strong position on a hill- side about two miles south of Falkirk, not very far from the

---

[1] The wilder guesses of others make the Scots a hundred thousand or even three hundred thousand strong. Even the usually sensible Hemingburgh gives the latter figure (i. p. 165). Ten thousand foot and two hundred horse would be a more probable estimate.

edge of the forest which covered all the face of the country to the west. His front was protected by a broad morass—now called Darnrig Moss. His pikemen were arrayed in four great masses—"schiltrons," as the Scots called them ; behind them were the two or three hundreds of mounted men-at-arms which composed his cavalry. On each flank, and also between the schiltrons, were a few thousand archers—mainly from Ettrick and Selkirk. The whole hope of Wallace lay in the solidity of his impenetrable masses of spears ; he was resolved to fight a thoroughly defensive battle, and knew that all depended on the steadiness of his followers. " I have brought you to the ring," he is reported to have said ; " now hop (dance) if ye may." [1]

Edward at once formed up his men on the opposite side of the Moss, in the three " battles " dear to the mediæval general.[2] The vaward or right wing was led by Roger Bigot Earl of Norfolk, the Marshal, and by Humphrey Bohun Earl of Hereford—the pair whose constitutional opposition to the king had led to the *Confirmatio Cartarum* in the preceding year. The main-battle was headed by Edward himself ; the left wing was entrusted to Antony Beck, the warlike bishop of Durham. Each column contained from thirty to thirty-five banners of barons and bannerets. The vaward first started to the charge, but rode into the Moss, and found it wholly impassable. The Earl Marshal, therefore, drew back his men, and started to turn the obstacle by a long march round its flank. The left wing had observed the morass more clearly, and the bishop, without making any attempt to pass it, wheeled off and rode round its flank. Arriving at a point at right angles to the line of the Scots, he halted his battle, and waited for the king, whose division was following him. This delay maddened the rash barons of whom he held command. " Stick to your mass, bishop, and don't teach us the art of war," cried Ralph Basset of Drayton. " Sing your mass here to-day, and we will do the fighting." [3] So saying, he led his horsemen against the flank schiltron of the Scots, and all the other banners streamed after

---

[1] The elaborate story of Falkirk in Blind Harry's *Wallace* is hopelessly garbled and useless. Bruce does all the fighting on the English side !

[2] Some say that there were *four* battles, apparently counting the king's "main-battle" into two brigades, one commanded by Warrenne, the other by Edward himself. See Morris's *Welsh Wars*, p. 314.

[3] " Non est tuum, episcope, docere nos de militia : vade missam celebrare si velis," etc. (Hemingburgh, p. 164).

him, in despite of their commander. A few minutes later the
Earl Marshal's battle completed its detour round the Moss, and
executed an equally headlong charge against the other flank of
the Scottish host.

The result of the onset of the two English cavalry corps was
indecisive. Wallace's archers were ridden down and scattered ;
the squadrons of men-at-arms in his rear rode off the field in
disgraceful flight without striking a blow for Scotland. But the
great schiltrons of pikemen easily flung back the onset of the
horsemen. The front ranks knelt with their spear-butts fixed
in the earth ; the rear ranks levelled their lances over their
comrades' heads ; the thick-set grove of twelve-foot spears was
far too dense for the cavalry to penetrate. Many English riders
fell ; the rest wheeled round and began to re-form for a second
charge. Now came the decisive moment of the day ; if the
onsets had been repeated with a similar fury, the English cavalry
would undoubtedly have failed, and Falkirk would have been
even as Bannockburn.

King Edward and the main-battle had now arrived on the
ground. His quick eye at once grasped the situation ; instantly
he applied the tactics which had been so successful in his Welsh
wars. The knights were ordered to halt for a moment, and
the bowmen, Welsh and English, were brought up. They
were bidden to concentrate their fire on fixed points in the
hostile masses. Loosing their arrows at point-blank range into
the easy target of the great schiltrons, they soon began to make
a fearful slaughter. Nor could there be any retaliation ; the
Scottish archers had been ridden down and driven away, while
the pikemen dared not break their ranks to chase off their
enemies while the English cavalry were waiting to push into the
gaps. Accordingly, the result of a few minutes of the deadly
arrow-shower was that many points of the masses had been
riddled, and the whole had been rendered unsteady. Then
Edward bade his knights charge for the second time, aiming at
the shaken sections of the enemy's front. Bursting in at points
where the killed and wounded were thicker than the unstricken
men, the English men-at-arms broke all the schiltrons in quick
succession.

The rest of the fight was little more than a massacre. One-
third of the Scottish host was left on the field ; the survivors,
among whom Wallace was numbered, only saved themselves by

a prompt flight into the woods.   Those who were at the eastern end of the line, and too far from the friendly shelter of the trees, had to rush down the rear slope of the hill and save themselves by swimming the river Carron.   Many thousands were cut down, and a considerable number more were drowned in the stream.   Of the Scottish chiefs there were slain Sir John Stuart of Bonkill, the leader of the Selkirk archery, Sir John Graham, Macduff, the uncle of the Earl of Fife, and about twenty knights more.   The English loss was small, consisting mainly of the horsemen who perished on the pikes in the first charge :   the only person of note who fell was Brian de Jaye, the Master of the Templars.[1]

The lesson which Falkirk taught to those who could read its true importance was much the same as the lesson of Hastings : that even the best of infantry, if unsupported by cavalry and placed in a position that might be turned on the flanks, could not hope to withstand a judicious combination of archers and horsemen.   Such, without doubt, would have been the moral which King Edward would have drawn from it, had he left us a written record of his military experience.   Such was the way in which it was viewed by Robert Bruce, who saw the fight from the English side, for he served in the left-hand battle under Bishop Beck.   We shall note that at Bannockburn, when it fell to him to face the selfsame problem that Wallace had vainly tried to solve, he took special care that his flanks should be covered and that his cavalry should be turned to good use. But it is clear that less capable men on both sides overlooked the real meaning of the fight.   Many of the English forgot that the archers had prepared the way, and only remembered the victorious charge of the knights at the end of the day.   Many of the Scots, equally misreading the facts, attributed their defeat to the treachery of their runaway horsemen, or to the jealousy which the other leaders felt for Wallace, instead of imputing it to the inherent weakness of pikemen unsupported by any other arm.

There was much fighting of the minor kind between Falkirk and the day of Bannockburn.   For the greater part of the

[1] Mr. Morris notes (*Welsh Wars*, p. 293) that the king paid, after his custom, compensation money for the horses of a hundred and eleven knights and men-at-arms in the stipendiary squadrons, which had been killed.   Many belonged to the *familia*, so the main-battle was well engaged.

sixteen years which intervened between them, hostilities on a
larger or a smaller scale were going on in some part of Scotland.
On the whole, the English had the advantage, owing to the
disunion of the Scots and their inability to find any leader
whom his equals would obey.   On half a dozen occasions
Edward's armies marched up and down the land without
meeting open opposition : the Scots meanwhile retired to the
hills, and only came down when their enemies had turned
homewards.   The fact was that summer campaigns could not
subdue the obstinate race of the Scots.   It had already been
found in Wales that to keep the army in the field during the
winter, and to allow the enemy no rest to recuperate, was the
only way of finishing the game.[1]   After several campaigns in
which he penetrated far, but found that he had achieved nothing
permanent, Edward seems to have resolved that the expensive
policy by which he had tamed Wales must be resumed.   In
1303 he resolved to keep the war on foot all the year round : he
brought up the Courts of the King's Bench and Exchequer
to York, in order to keep them near him, raised both the feudal
levy and a large stipendiary force of cavalry with a moderate
force of infantry—seven thousand at the most—and betook
himself over the Border.

He was to spend no less than fifteen continuous months
in Scotland on this occasion.   His first march took him far
north of the Forth—the farthest point reached was the remote
cathedral city of Elgin, and he took Perth, Aberdeen, and many
other towns.   He wintered at Dunfermline with the nucleus
of his army around him, the rest being garrisoned in towns and
castles.   Next spring he besieged Stirling, the central fortress
of Scotland, and the only place that made a really creditable
defence against him : it surrendered in July.   Even before the
fall of Stirling, John Lord of Badenoch, " the Red Comyn,"
and many barons had given in their submission.   At last,
in August 1304, Edward returned to England, believing the
matter finished.   It seemed indeed to be so, when Wallace,
who had reappeared after his long eclipse since Falkirk to
lead the last remnants of the rebels, was captured and executed.
In 1305 a new Constitution for Scotland, leaving it a separate
parliament, judicature, and administration, was framed and
published.   And then, within six months, a new rebellion

[1] See above, pp. 67–68.

flared up (January 1306) under Robert Bruce, and the whole conquest of Scotland had to begin again ! The problem was insoluble for an aged and moribund king. Edward marched once more northward, but was forced by bodily weakness to halt at Lanercost, near Carlisle. He called his last parliament at the remote Cumbrian capital, and after dismissing it, strove to take the field once more, rode a few miles, and fell fainting from his horse, to die at Burgh-on-Sands, only seven miles from Carlisle and still on the English side of the Border.

So the war went on in the old style, for Edward II. was no man for winter campaigning. Since Falkirk there had been no pitched battles : such fighting as there was mainly consisted in ambuscades and surprises—such, for example, was the rout of Roslin in 1302, when John de Segrave's army was surprised by the Scots in three separate cantonments six miles apart. Segrave's own division was cut to pieces at dawn ; the other divisions under Robert Neville came up only in time to save a few of the fugitives, and then retired from the field. A similar instance on the other side was the rout of Methven, when Aymer de Valence, Earl of Pembroke, scattered Robert Bruce's host by just such another assault at daybreak. A much greater interest attaches to a fight on a far smaller scale, that of Loudon Hill in 1307, if we can trust the details— sufficiently probable in themselves—which Barbour gives of it. In its own way it was a forecast of Bannockburn. Bruce, with his six hundred followers, was lying on Loudon Hill, when De Valence, with a force which the Scottish chroniclers give at three thousand men, came to hunt him down. Bruce had found a position about two bow-shots broad, through which a road ran. On each side of it was a broad moss. He narrowed the front of the position by cutting three lines of ditch from the edges of the morasses on each side, so as to leave open only the road and about fifty yards more on each side of it. On this short front he drew up his men, all on foot and with pikes levelled. De Valence should of course have sent his archers to the front, and, as Bruce could not have advanced, might have mishandled him dreadfully. But, instead, he committed the usual fault of feudal commanders : he sent his cavalry to charge down the road, expecting to ride easily over the pikemen. Two furious onsets were promptly turned back by the line of spears ; then, seeing more than a hundred men-at-arms lying dead in front of the Scottish line, De Valence tamely withdrew, though his infantry and his rear-battle had not struck a blow.

Without any pitched battle, but by a long series of sieges, raids, and adventurous assaults on castles, Bruce had by 1314 cleared the English out of the whole land. Nothing but the strongholds of Stirling, Dunbar, and Berwick remained in the power of Edward II. It was to relieve the first-named place, the most important strategic point in the whole of Scotland, that the imbecile son of Edward Longshanks at last bestirred himself. The governor of Stirling, Sir Philip Mowbray, had promised to yield unless he were relieved before St. John's Day, June 24, 1314. And not even Edward of Carnarvon could view unmoved the loss of the last of his father's conquests.

Battle of Bannockburn, June 24, 1314.

When once Bruce knew that the King of England had sworn to raise the siege of Stirling, and was spending the spring in summoning up contingents not only from England and Wales but from Ireland and Gascony, he had ample time to devote to the choice of a good position for standing on the defensive against the great host which was coming against him. He determined to make no opposition in Lothian, but to let the English army push well into the bowels of the land. Two reasons led him to this conclusion : the enemy would be much harassed by want of food in passing through the devastated lands between Tweed and Forth, and the nearer he fought to Stirling the more certain would he be of intercepting the enemy, who, if the battle was offered to him at a greater distance from the place, might easily slip off to right or left and turn the Scottish host without an engagement.

Bruce mustered his men in the forest of Torwood, the same trysting-place which Wallace had chosen before the battle of Falkirk. But it was not his intention to fight on the banks of the Carron, but much nearer to Stirling. The position which he had selected was no more than two and a half miles south of the beleaguered castle, on the rolling hillsides which overlook the Bannock Burn.

Passing southward out of Stirling, a gentle ascent leads to the village and church of St. Ninians ; half a mile farther on, the crest of the ascent is reached, and a new valley comes in view. Down this depression, which is less than a mile broad, runs the Bannock Burn, now an insignificant brook. In its upper course it flows from west to east, coming out of woods and steep ground, but lower down it makes a sharp turn north-ward, and swerves off through flat, boggy land to join the Forth not far from its mouth. In 1314 the burn was a much more formidable obstacle than now ; its lower course ran through pools[1] and mosses into the mud-flats of the Forth, and at its mouth it became a small tidal estuary into which the sea water came up.[2] In many parts of its length, however, the Bannock could be crossed, though with some difficulty, by both horse and foot ; there were some places where it broadened out into impassable pools, others where it goes between abso-lutely precipitous banks ; but these were exceptional. The only thoroughly good passage was that in front of the present farm of Redhouse, where the main road to Stirling, originally an old Roman way,[3] crossed the burn and valley, running south-east to north-west. The Scots were holding the plateau which this road crosses, before it dips down to enter Stirling. The western half of it was covered by the trees of the " King's Park," a wooded tract which Alexander III. had afforested : the eastern half, in the open fields of the village of St. Ninians, sloped down toward the bogs of the Carse—the flats by the estuary of Forth. It would seem certain that the modern road from Stirling through the Carse (Crookbridge, Airth, Grangemouth) cannot have existed in the fourteenth century, when all this region was water-sodden, and there is no indica-tion of it in any account of the battle. The only practicable highway was the Roman road. The slope of the plateau is well marked, looking southward and northward, but forms a gentle glacis on its eastern front ; at its north-western corner is Coxet Hill, a small humped eminence higher than the rest of the ground. At the Borestane, the central point of the plateau, where Bruce's standard is said (probably with truth) to have been planted, its height is two hundred feet, its western end, among the trees of the Park, reaches two hundred and forty feet.

[1] I was delighted to find these pools, of which no trace now exists, in Arrow-smith's detailed sheet-map of Scotland (1807). Barbour very distinctly mentions them in Book xii. lines 395-7, 404-5, etc.

[2] The Chronicle of Lanercost calls it (p. 226) *fovea magna in quam intrat fluxus maris.*

[3] Coming out from Antonine's Wall to serve the outlying posts (Ardoch, etc.) beyond Forth.

It would seem that the wood extended as far eastward as the road, perhaps even a little farther, as the road is described as an "entry" between thickets, where cavalry would find it hard to operate.[1]

When the English army, advancing from the Border over Lammermuir, passed Edinburgh and Falkirk, King Robert fell back from the Torwood into his chosen position. His intention was to hold the plateau north of the Bannock Burn, and his expectation was that the English would try to force their way to Stirling along the main road. He therefore made special preparations for receiving them on this front, by digging a great quantity of "pottes," or small circular holes three feet deep, at the head of the slope upward from the Bannock, and especially on the east side of the road, where the country was more open and free from wood. They were covered with branches and grass, so as not to be visible to the advancing foe, and were intended as traps for Edward's horsemen. The precaution was excellent, but (as we shall see) did not come into serious use, since the English (contrary to expectation) did not deliver their main attack on this front.[2]

[1] Bruce is made by Barbour to say that the Scots will fight at advantage if the enemy come this way :

"For in the Park amang the treis
The horsemen always cummerit beis" (xii. 296).

[2] The "pottes" have given some trouble to the narrators of the battle. Some of the English chroniclers do not mention them. Others, e.g. Baker of Swinbrook, speak not of a number of small holes, but of one long ditch : "Scoti locum nacti opportunum, subfodiebant ad mensurum trium pedum in profundo, et ad ejusdem mensurae latitudinem fossas protensas in longum a dextro in sinistrum cornu exercitus, operientes illas cum plexis et viminibus." But an even better authority than the very sensible Baker is Robert Baston, the unfortunate prisoner whom Bruce compelled to celebrate the victory in Latin verse. He says that

"Plebs foveas fodit, ut per eas labantur equestres.
Machina plena malis pedibus formatur equinis
Concava, cum palis, ne pergant absque ruinis."

This certainly means a series of holes, not a ditch, and fully bears out Barbour's account of the "pottes." As to their position, Barbour says (xii. 387):

"On either side the way wele brad
It was pottit, as I have tald.
Gef that their faes on horse will hald
Furth in that way, I trow they shall
Not well escape withouten fall."

And in another passage he speaks of the "pottes" as "in ane plane field by the way." I suppose that "the way" means the Roman road, and that the pits lay on each side of it, but more especially to the east, where the ground was open and no woods existed to check horsemen.

But there was a chance that the enemy, disliking the look of the wood behind the main road, or discovering the " pottes," might cross the Bannock downstream, and attack up the gentle slope of the eastern front of the plateau, south of St. Ninians, threading their way along the edge of the damp Carse. But to do so they would have to pass over a morass, and its " sykes " (wet hollows) would put them in confusion, so that they could be attacked at advantage.[1] Wherefore the position on the plateau, from in front of St. Ninians to the edge of the New Park could be utilised for defence against either form of attack : the army concentrated around the Borestane could face either south or east as was needful, and would have no distance to move.

King Robert told off the Scottish host into four " battles " and a small cavalry reserve. Only five hundred picked men-at-arms were kept on horseback, under Sir Robert Keith, the Marshal of Scotland ; the rest of the knights and squires descended to fight on foot among their retainers—obviously to stiffen the general levy, as the Yorkshire knights had done at the Battle of the Standard. Bruce explained that whether for fighting among trees, or for fighting at a marsh-passage, the foot-soldier has an advantage over the horseman. The " vaward " was given in charge to Thomas Randolph, Earl of Moray, the centre to the King's brother, Sir Edward Bruce, the " rearward " to Walter, the young Lord Steward, and Sir James Douglas.[2] The king himself had a fourth brigade to form the reserve, composed of his own retainers from his earldom of Carrick, and of the men of Argyle, Cantyre, and the Western Isles, with some Lowland troops in addition. Normally, as we have often seen in other battles, a " vaward " took the right wing of an army in position, and a " rearward " the left. But the exigencies of manœuvre would seem to

> " But gif that they beneath us ga,
> And our the marras pas, and swa
> We shall be at avantage there . . .
> And the sykes alswa there doun
> Shall put them to confusioune."
>
> Barbour, xi. 286–8 and 300–1.

[2] We are not told what regions furnished the men for each of the three front-line divisions, the only local specification being that the king had the levy of Carrick, with those of Argyle, Cantyre, and the Western Isles (Barbour, xi. 330–4).

have produced at Bannockburn a divergence from custom. Randolph, though he had the "vaward," actually got engaged on the extreme left of the line. The whole force may have amounted to ten thousand men at the most, perhaps to a few thousands less, though the best Scottish historian gives the figure of thirty thousand or a little over.[1]

The marshalling having been arranged, the army retired into camp in the New Park, out of sight of the approaching enemy, behind the wooded eminence now known as "Gillies' Hill," after sending forth some horsemen as outriders to watch for the approach of the enemy. On the afternoon of Sunday, June 23, the vanguard of the English came in sight on the low line of hills which formed the southern horizon. Edward II. had brought with him what seemed a very formidable host to a fourteenth-century chronicler. The feudal levy had been called out, and though the self-seeking Thomas of Lancaster and many of his friends had found excuses for not appearing themselves,[2] they had sent their normal contingents to join those of the more loyal baronage. Adding the usual stipendiary squadrons of paid horse, and the king's *familia*, with some Gascon knights and even a few Germans known to have been present, there were probably near three thousand horse in the field, but possibly a few hundred less.[3] This was a special effort, and it is not unlikely that the numbers of Falkirk were a little exceeded. The Earl of Gloucester alone had raised a squadron of five hundred horsemen. But no absolutely safe computation can be made. For infantry we have certain official figures to serve as a base for calculation. Writs had been issued to the sheriffs of twelve English counties, to the Lords Marchers, and the justices of North and South Wales. The total of foot-soldiers requisitioned was twenty-one thousand

---

[1] Barbour is, like Hemingburgh, a good narrator, but with no accurate sense of figures or their meaning. His thirty thousand (xi. 428) Scots are probably as wild an estimate as his hundred thousand English.

[2] Lancaster made the very poor excuse that the king, according to the Ordinances of 1311, ought to have consulted Parliament before levying his host.

[3] The author of the *Vita Edwardi* gives only two thousand knights, but has obvious reasons for stating the numbers of the army as low as possible. A contemporary Scottish writer, Bernard abbot of Arbroath, gives three thousand one hundred, probably very close to the real figure. See Mackenzie's *Bannockburn*, pp. 23, 24.

five hundred and forty.[1] No man was summoned from any region south of Warwickshire and Staffordshire, and the Midland contingents were light, save those of Lincolnshire and of Shropshire, a district always relied upon for good service, because of the old experience of its men in Welsh wars. Cheshire and Lancashire, shires in which Edward I. had been wont to place much confidence, appear very poorly represented by five hundred men each. And Cumberland and Westmoreland show no figures at all—perhaps their levies were told off for frontier guard on the West March. In addition, writs were sent off to Ireland, at an earlier date than the issue of the English and Welsh summonses, asking twenty-five chiefs or kinglets to supply four thousand men ; they were brought over by Richard de Burgh, Earl of Ulster.[2] With a few Gascon crossbowmen and other foreign driblets, as also small contingents brought by certain desperate adherents among the Scots, there might have been twenty-six thousand or twenty-eight thousand infantry in all, if every shire had done its duty.

But even in the best days of Edward I. the English infantry levies had been hard to assemble in full force, and even harder to keep together when once gathered. There had been occasions when not more than 50 per cent. of the designated contingents had appeared at the front.[3] In 1314 there was widespread discontent in the realm, and Edward of Carnarvon was not a popular king, so that it is quite possible that no more than fifteen thousand or eighteen thousand foot were really collected. On the other hand, the occasion was a pressing one, and the national honour was at stake for the relief of Stirling,[4] so that

[1] Rymer's *Foedera*, May 27, 1314. The figures are perhaps worth giving. They run as follows :

	Men.		Men.
Yorkshire	4000	Leicestershire and Warwickshire .	500
Northumberland . . .	2500	Justices of South Wales, *i.e.*	
Bishopric of Durham . .	1500	counties of Cardigan and Car-	
Lancashire	500	marthen	1000
Lincolnshire. . . .	3000	Certain Marcher Lords . .	2040
Notts and Derby . . .	2000	Justices of North Wales, *i.e.*	
Salop and Stafford . .	2000	counties of Anglesea, Carnar-	
Cheshire	500	von, and Merioneth . .	2000

[2] Rymer's *Foedera*, iii. 432, 1314.

[3] See in Morris's *Welsh Wars*, p. 301, the very bad case of the army raised in 1300, where of sixteen thousand men ordered up only seven thousand six hundred and nineteen ever reached the front. But this was an exceptionally bad record.

[4] In the writ of May 27, the language used is very strong.

there is some danger that the numbers present may be under-estimated.   As to whether the Irish contingent had joined, we have no good authority discoverable.   Shipping had been provided for them, and Barbour says that there was in the English host " a great meinie from Ireland," [1] but there is no mention of them in the fight.   Their presence might raise King Edward's infantry to twenty thousand men, but it cannot be regarded as certain.

The horse was told off into ten " battles," probably (like the French at Courtrai) in three lines of three battles each, with the tenth forming an advanced guard.[2]   We have no proper details of the marshalling, knowing only that the Earls of Gloucester and Hereford led the " vaward," and that the king with the Earl of Pembroke headed the rear-battle.   But details as to the array are of little importance, because (as all accounts agree) the host was so cramped and crushed together on the battlefield that to the enemy it appeared all one vast " schiltron," speckled from front to rear with the flags of barons and bannerets.   Only the " vaward " was distinguishable, the rest was one large weltering mass.[3]

The English advance guard arrived on the field on the after-noon of the 23rd June, and proceeded at once to reconnoitre the position.   Two bodies of cavalry pushed forward on two points, one crossing the burn at the Roman road, the other making a detour through the Carse to endeavour to communicate with the castle, by riding round the marshy ground on the left of the Scottish line.   The first body came on until it found Bruce in force at the head of the slope.   Its advance was only noticeable for the chivalric incident of Sir Henry Bohun's death.   Bohun was in the van of the party which came up the road, and caught sight of King Robert, with his crown conspicuous on his helm, riding up and down some distance in front of his pikemen. Setting spurs to his horse, the daring knight charged at the Bruce, hoping to end the war with his single lance.   Robert, though he was not horsed on his barded destrier, but only on a little hackney, and though he had no lance in his hand,

[1] xi. 100.

[2] Barbour speaks of ten "battles" in one place (xi. 155), and of nine in another (xii. 537).   The tenth battle may have been the "vaward."   The poet in the first is dealing with arrangements before the battle, and in the second with the actual engagement.

[3] Barbour, xii. 429–35.

but only the axe at his saddlebow, did not shrink from the single combat. Warily awaiting his adversary's charge, he turned Bohun's lance aside with his axe, and as the knight passed him, brained him with a tremendous blow on the back of his helmet. The rest of the English party drew back, losing a few other casualties.

The other attempt of the English to feel the eastern flank of the Scottish position led to more serious fighting. Three hundred men-at-arms, under Sir Robert Clifford and Henry de Beaumont, made such a wide sweep through the Carse that they were close below St. Ninians Kirk before the Earl of Moray sighted them.[1] Burning to repair this neglect, Randolph rushed down the hill with five hundred pikemen and threw himself across their path. Clifford bade his knights ride over the Scots, and delivered a furious charge which utterly failed to break the compact mass of spears. For many minutes the English horsemen rode round and round the Scots, trying to burst in, and angrily casting maces and lances into their ranks, in the hope of making a gap. Some scores perished among the pikes, including William Deyncourt, a well-known knight. The rest, finding their efforts all in vain, and seeing succour under James of Douglas coming down the hill to Randolph, at last rode off foiled ; a few of them who had pushed too far north to be able to retreat by the way they had come, are said to have fled beyond Randolph's flank, and to have taken refuge in Stirling Castle, which now stood unblockaded.

The result of the two reconnaissances of Sunday afternoon was to convince King Edward's military advisers that the attack along the Roman road, on the " entry " in the wooded park, where the Scots had been found in force, was unadvisable, but that there was good open fighting ground on the gentle slopes east of St. Ninians, over which Clifford's detachment had ridden before it became engaged with the Earl of Moray. There is no evidence that they were deterred from trying the southward approach by having discovered the " pottes," which (as we know) were " on *each side* of the way full broad," but not actually on it : apparently Bohun's party had kept to the

---

[1] Tradition would have it that the fight took place at Randolfsfield, in the actual suburbs of modern Stirling. This is possible, but the spot seems very far north. See the map annexed.

road, and not spread out on a wide front before they were checked.

But to reach the hard slopes it was necessary to cross the Bannock and its bogs much lower down its course than the place where the Roman road ran. Apparently the points of passage selected were beyond Bannockburn village,. where the stream has taken a sharp turn northward and reached low ground. Where the Roman road crosses the burn it is flowing at one hundred and thirty-seven feet above sea-level ; half a mile lower down, by the village, the height of the water is only ninety-three feet above that level. Another half-mile north, only forty-one. From a little way beyond the village the Scottish bank ceases to command the east bank, the stream having meandered away from the neighbourhood of the Borestane–St. Ninians plateau, whose slope it had been hugging in its upper course. From the spots now marked by Crookbridge and Redhall it was a mile from the water's edge to the fifty-foot contour at the eastern foot of the plateau. The enemy, in order to dispute the passage, would have to come down from his position, and fight on ground which he had not chosen.

The weak point of the plan for crossing between Bannock-burn village and the modern Crookbridge was that the ground was wet in the extreme. In modern maps we see it surrounded on both sides by running water—the Bannock on the east side, the " mill-lade " which serves the Kerse Mills on the west. Arrowsmith's map of 1807, exaggerating perhaps, represents the whole space between these two watercourses as a watery expanse a mile and a half long and over half a mile broad. In 1314 there was no " mill-lade " of course, and the water now carried off by it lay in soggy pools among comparatively dry patches. There was no proper road or causeway by which the crossing could be made—apparently no path of any kind in the Carse, from Bannockburn village northward. When the army picked its way in the late afternoon towards the chosen points of passage, I cannot believe that its train followed. Documents show that Edward had brought to Scotland a vast quantity of transport, necessary (no doubt) in a land where food was hard to get, but cumbersome to a degree. One chronicler records that on the march it would take up over twenty leagues of road.[1] We are told that on the night of the

[1] *Vita Edwardi Secundi*, p. 147.

23rd–24th the English encamped on the flats of the Carse. This must, I think, be taken to mean the ground on each side of the Bannock, since it is quite clear that ox-wains and four-horse carts could not have got over the burn, though foot and horse might.   " The English," says Barbour, " harboured them that night down in the Carse, and made their preparation and got ready their apparel for the battle of the next morning ; and because the Carse was full of pools, they broke down houses and thatch,[1] and bore them to make bridges where they might pass.   And some say that the garrison in Stirling Castle, after nightfall, when they got to learn of the difficulties, came out in strength, bringing with them doors and window-timber, so that before daylight they had bridged the pools, and every man had got across, and the horsemen had occupied the hard ground, and were ready to give battle." [2]   This can only mean that the pioneers were at work all night, and that the rear only got over shortly before dawn.   Indeed, one can hardly believe that a mediæval army, twenty thousand strong, moving in the dark over unknown, swampy ground, can ever have got into proper array even by morning.   The cavalry, we are told, kept on their armour, and the horses were not unbitted.   Horse and foot alike must have had a sleepless night[3] of standing about in the swamp ; and the night was short, for on St. John's Day the sun is up by 4 a.m.   Hence it was a tired and dispirited army that lay before St. Ninians that morning, with the mud-flats of Forth behind them, and their main line of retreat towards one flank only, in case they should be beaten.   The stories of carousing in the English camp, given by Baker and Baston, are most improbable.   But very probably tired soldiers may have taken a draught of wine or beer as they stood or lay in rank.

Bruce had not expected that his enemy would take this course—he had supposed that they would attack along the high road, as his planting of the " pottes " had shown.   But, having his men concentrated and ready, he could easily change his dispositions, for a fight looking eastward and not southward. Having discovered the English getting into order on the first dry land along the edge of the Carse, but apparently neither ready for advance nor yet completely drawn up in their proper

---

[1] No doubt from Bannockburn village and from outlying farms.
[2] Barbour, xii. 391–407.   [3] *Scalachronica*, pp. 54–55.

divisions, he resolved to take the bold step of charging them while they were still in disarray.   This involved an infantry advance in a line of columns downhill, for the best part of a mile at least—a hazardous experiment, for it is hard for un-disciplined troops to preserve their order when on the move. Pikemen can hold out against cavalry well enough when stationary—as Falkirk and Courtrai had shown in recent years—but for pikemen to advance against a force of both arms and of superior numbers was a different matter.   Perhaps Bruce was as much psychologist as tactician on this day, for we are told that he had been joined during the dark hours by a Scottish knight deserting from the English camp, one Alexander Seton, who told him that the enemy had lost heart and were in a panic at the idea of being attacked before they were ready ; they were tired out, and if charged at dawn would break.[1]

At any rate, the English can only have been getting into order when three Scottish " schiltrons " emerged one after the other from the woods of the New Park, and bore down upon their enemy, apparently in an échelon of columns, the right leading.   The king and the reserve were not at first visible, nor the five hundred horse of the Marshal, Keith.   The reason why the right—Edward Bruce's corps—formed the front échelon was probably that it was nearest to the enemy, the high ground to the south-east corner of the plateau, where it had originally been posted, being immediately above the flats where the hostile left was lying.   The second échelon, if we may trust Barbour, was Moray's corps, which had originally lain about St. Ninians ; the third that of Douglas and Walter Stuart, which had originally been in support of Moray.

The English did not refuse the battle for a moment, though they were all in disorder.   The one body that was ready was Gloucester's " vaward " of cavalry, which charged at once up-hill against the corps of Edward Bruce.   Meanwhile the rest of the army appeared to the Scots a weltering mass.   It had been the original intent of the English staff to send out a front line of archers, but this plan would only seem to have been developed on the right—the part of the line most remote from Edward Bruce.

---

[1] *Scalachronica*, p. 55.   Gray, telling this tale, gives the rather improbable addition that Bruce had been thinking of retiring into the Lennox and allowing Stirling to be relieved, and was stirred to prompt action mainly by Seton's news.

At the south end of the battle-front the combat began with a sheer clash of horse against foot, both being on the move. " The two hosts so came together, and the great steeds of the knights dashed into the Scottish pikes as into a thick wood ; there arose a great and horrible crash from rending lances and dying horses, and they stood locked together for a space," says the Lanercost chronicler. But if Gloucester's horsemen, with the impetus of their first charge, had failed to break into the Scottish schiltron, much less were they able to do so when they had been brought to a standstill, and could only cut and thrust away at the pikes. The young de Clare himself fell very early in the fight : his horse was speared, and he himself slain ere he could get to his feet. It is said that he was not well supported by his meinie : " Twenty men might have saved him, but out of the five hundred men-at-arms whom he had brought at his own cost, few but himself were slain." [1] The mass drew back a little to re-form, and then repeated feebler charges.

Meanwhile matters had been moving in the centre and the north end of the battle-front. On the right, at least, as we are told, some of the English archery got out in front of the nine corps of horse, and met Scottish archers in inferior numbers, whom they drove in, and then began to let fly into the Scottish schiltron behind — presumably Douglas's column.[2] " The English shot so fast that, if only their shooting had lasted, it would have been hard for the Scots." [3] But King Robert, " who well knew that archers were dangerous and their shot hard and right grievous," had provided for this chance by bringing up the five hundred horse of Keith to his left flank. They charged in diagonally upon the bowmen, and scattered them with great loss—they left the field in rout, or at best fell back on the mass of foot behind the fighting line. Therefore, as we are told, the Scottish archers came out again and opened a not ineffective fire against the English cavalry.[4] Keith was able to draw back and act as a flank guard ; he had no further occasion to move, as the enemy made no second attempt to establish a flank fire of archery.

While this episode was in progress, the three Scottish " schiltrons " were all frontally engaged with the English

[1] *Vita Edwardi Secundi*, p. 149.   [2] Barbour xiii. 55–71.
[3] *Ibid.* xiii. 77.   [4] Chronicle of Lanercost, p. 225.

horse—Edward Bruce apparently with the rallied remains of
Gloucester's " vaward," Moray and Douglas with the remainder
of the front line cavalry, " nine broad battles with many
banners," but all in disorder. " Whether it was through the
narrowness of the front that they were fighting upon, or whether
from demoralisation, I know not ; but it seemed that they
were all in one mass, except the vaward, who were arrayed by
themselves," [1] says Barbour.   One English chronicler remarks
that the rear ranks could never get up to the fighting-line,
because they were blocked by their own front ranks, no intervals
having been left.   " They could not help them, and nothing
remained but to think of retreat, so a trustworthy eye-witness
told me." [2]   Another says that he knew of one body of two
hundred men-at-arms which never drew sword or struck a
blow,[3] and left the field without casualties.   For the front line
fought desperately, died by scores on the pikes, and were too
courageous to fall back and own themselves beaten.   Individuals
may have got a chance of pushing forward to replace the
fallen, but the majority stood helpless.

Still more helpless were the disordered mass of infantry
behind the cavalry battles.   Setting aside the troops who had
been cut up by Keith's charge, there must have been ten or
fifteen thousand archers and spearmen waiting on the contour
just above the bog doing nothing.   Some of them, according
to one chronicler,[4] tried to help by letting fly arrows at a
high trajectory over the heads of their own horsemen in
front.   The result was not encouraging.   " They hit some
few Scots in the breast, but struck many more English in
the back."

The whole of both hosts were now locked in one great mêlée,
for King Robert had brought up his infantry reserve, the fourth
Scottish battle, to strengthen his front line.   We are told that
he came in " on a side "—almost certainly his left—and that
this flank attack thrust back the enemy perceptibly.[5]   The
advantage was definitely on the side of the Scots : the English
cavalry was " fought out," and only kept from recoiling by the
masses behind ; Gloucester and the majority of the other barons
who led it had fallen, and in front of the Scottish line was a

[1] Barbour, xii. 430–35.   [2] Chronicle of Lanercost, p. 225.
[3] *Vita Edwardi Secundi*, p. 151.   [4] Baker of Swinbrook, p. 10.
[5] Barbour, xiii. p. 132.

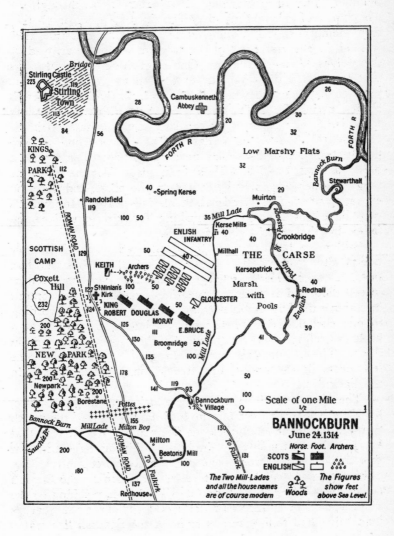

Stirling Castle 223
119
Stirling Town
113
Bridge
84
56
KINGS PARK 112
Randolsfield 119
SCOTTISH CAMP
Coxett Hill 232
127
KEITH
St Ninian's Kirk
124
KING ROBERT DOUGLAS MORAY
125
130
NEW PARK
200
Newpark 155
Borestane
200
200
178
141
119
Fottes
Milton Bog
Bannock Burn
MillLade
200
Sauchie
180
137
Redhouse
ROMAN ROAD
To Falkirk
Milton
Beatons Mill 100

28
Cambuskenneth Abbey
20
FORTH R
32
Low Marshy Flats
32
26
30
FORTH R
Bannock Burn
Stewarthall
40 Spring Kerse
29
Muirton
100 50
35 Mill Lade
Kerse Mills 40
ENLISH INFANTRY
50
40
Archers
100
50
50
GLOUCESTER
50
E.BRUCE
III
Broomridge
100
50
Millhall
THE CARSE
Kersepatrick
Marsh with Pools
40
40 Redhall
39
41
Crookbridge
English Pouls
50
100
50
100
Bannockburn Village
130
131
To Falkirk

Scale of one Mile
0   ½   1

BANNOCKBURN
June 24. 1314

Horse. Foot. Archers.
SCOTS
ENGLISH

The Two Mill-Lades and all the house names are of course modern

Woods

The Figures show feet above Sea Level.

great bank of slain and wounded horses and men, which no one
could now pierce.   Meanwhile, the English rearward had stood
for hours vainly trying to get to the front, and losing heart when
the impossibility of doing so was fully realised.   It only needed
some impulse from outside to turn the whole host backward ;
apparently this was supplied by Bruce's thrust ; soon after,
the cry " On them, on them! they fail!"[1] was heard along the
whole line, and the English front broke to pieces.

If we are to believe Barbour, some moral assistance was
given toward causing the panic by Scottish camp-followers, of
whom there were several thousands.   These " yeomen, swains,
and poveraille " had been watching the fight from behind the
screen of trees on the slope of Gillies' Hill.   Seeing that their
enemy seemed faltering, they were seized with the happy
inspiration of making a demonstration against the English
flank.   Snatching up such irregular weapons as the camp
afforded, and raising coloured cloths on spears to simulate
banners, they came down the wooded slope of the hill, blowing
horns and shouting " Slay, slay ! "[2]

Imagining that a new Scottish reserve was about to operate
against their flank, the English, as Barbour tells the tale, lost
heart, and began to melt away to the rear, long before the
emptiness of the demonstration could be perceived.   It is
probable that the thrust of Bruce's reserve really sufficed to
settle the matter.   Edward himself hastily left the field with
five hundred knights, and when he was gone his followers
thought it no shame to flee away also.   The Scottish line pushed
down the slope after the fugitives, taking many prisoners, and
thrusting their enemies by heaps into the bogs and the burn,
where many hundreds were drowned or smothered.[3]   Those
who got off made at once for the English border, and considered themselves fortunate if they reached Berwick or Carlisle
without being intercepted and butchered by the peasantry.
Edward himself had a curious line of flight   Seeing the ground
behind him clearer to the north than to the south, he rode to
his right, making for Stirling Castle, which he intended to enter.
The gates, however, were barred, and the governor, Mowbray,

[1] Barbour, xiii. p. 205.   [2] *Ibid.* xiii. p. 229.
[3] Chronicle of Lanercost : " Quum ante transissent unam foveam magnam, in
quam intrat fluxus maris, nomine Bannockburne, et cum confusi vellent redire, multi
nobiles ceciderunt . . . et nunquam se explicare de fovea potuerunt " (p. 225).

besought him not to come in, because the Castle would have to surrender at once, and he would be taken prisoner. This was wise advice, and Edward, guided by a Scottish partisan, rode off below the Castle westward, and escaped by a long detour between the King's Park and the Campsie Fells.

Never in all history was there such a frightful slaughter of the English baronage as took place at Bannockburn : even the red field of Towton was far less fatal. There fell one earl, Gilbert of Gloucester, forty-two barons and bannerets, and many scores of knights.[1] Humphrey Earl of Hereford, twenty-two barons and bannerets, and sixty-eight knights, were taken prisoners either on the field or in the pursuit.[2] Of men-at-arms and foot-soldiery the numbers slain were enormous, but no safe guess can be made at the exact figures : the Scots gave thirty thousand as their estimate, but this exceeds the total of the English army. The victors are said to have lost only two knights, but very many of their pikemen—which is not at all improbable.

So ended the most lamentable defeat which an English army ever suffered. Its lessons were obvious. With the experience of Falkirk and Loudon Hill before him, Edward II. and his military advisers showed themselves absolutely incapable as tacticians. They moved their army by a confusing and fatiguing night-march among bogs, just to the farther side of a difficult military obstacle, the Bannock and its pools. Assailed at dawn before they had got into proper array, they could only try to win by cavalry charges, since the mass of their infantry was to the rear, and not yet deployed. They had expected that Bruce would wait to be attacked, as Wallace had at Falkirk : and were entirely taken by surprise when, instead of allowing them leisure to form up, he came plunging down the slope into the thick of their army. To be attacked yourself when you are in the midst of arranging for an advance, is a sufficiently discomposing experience for any general. But to be attacked and beaten when, by your own fault, you have no power to utilise superior numbers and superior armament, is the mark of a bad general—and (we may add) of a bad staff. It was their obvious duty to fight so as to be able to use their

[1] Barbour says two hundred, and seven hundred esquires.
[2] Hereford was betrayed at Bothwell Castle by its governor, a Scot who turned patriotic on the news of the battle.

archery and their horse together — as at Orewin Bridge,
Conway, or Falkirk. Probably owing to the initial blunder
of supposing that their enemy would observe a strict immobile
defensive, they were forced to fight in such a way that the
archery were practically useless, and the cavalry wasted itself
in the endeavour — already known to be a dangerous one — of
trying to break unassisted into solid masses of pikes.

For the conduct of the fight on Bruce's part no praise can
be too great. It was the culminating point of that whole
method of war which he left as a legacy to his subjects. The
lines in which his " testament " was committed to memory by
after-generations are well worth quoting—

> " On fut suld be all Scottis weire,
> By hyll and mosse themselff to reare.
> Lat woods for wallis be bow and speire,
> That innymeis do them na deire.
> In strait placis gar keip all store,
> And byrnen ye planeland thaim before.
> Thane sall thai pass away in haist
> When that thai find na thing but waist.
> With wyles and waykings of the nyght
> And mekill noyis maid on hytht,
> Thaim sall ye turnen with gret affrai,
> As thai ware chassit with swerd away.
> This is the consall and intent
> Of gud King Robert's testiment."

The fourteen lines contain all the principles on which the
Scots, when well advised, acted for the next two hundred and
fifty years. They were to maintain the defensive, only to fight in
strong positions among hills and morasses, to trust to retirement
into the woods rather than to the fortifying of castles, to ravage
the open country before the advancing enemy, and to confine
their offensive action to night surprises and ambushes.

The fifteen years which followed Bannockburn differed from
most of the periods of war between England and Scotland, in
that for the greater part of the time the southern realm was on
the defensive. It is not till the battle of Dupplin Muir in 1332
that the balance turned again in favour of the English. The
period is of no very great interest from the military point of
view, being mainly covered by a series of skilful raids of the
Scots into the northern counties, which reached sometimes well-
nigh to the gates of York. They came not to conquer, but
merely to ravage, and were as a rule more set on carrying their

plunder safely home than on meeting the enemy in battle.   So great was Bruce's caution in risking a general engagement that, even in 1321, he allowed an English army to march as far as Edinburgh unfought with, and turned it back only by a careful cutting off of its commissariat.   There were, however, two considerable collisions between English and Scottish hosts during the time, in both of which the latter had the advantage.   At Mytton in 1320 the Yorkshire levy, under the leading of its archbishop, was easily scattered by the Earl of Moray and James of Douglas.   This was a rout rather than a battle, the Yorkshiremen having retired as the Scots drew near, without any serious attempt at a fight.   At Byland in 1322 Bruce himself won his last victory, beating up the English quarters by a sudden attack at dawn, both in front and in flank.   There was no regular fighting, as the English were surprised, and those of them who rallied only strove to defend a narrow pass long enough to let their master King Edward escape, which he did with great difficulty, leaving his kinsman, John of Bretagne, Earl of Richmond, in the hands of the Scots.[1]

NOTE ON BANNOCKBURN

In company with many other historians, I have had to own myself convinced by the arguments of Mr. W. M. Mackenzie, who in his edition of Barbour's *Bruce* in 1909 proved, I think, that the traditional battlefield of Bannockburn, south of the Borestane, is not the true fighting ground.   I had walked twice over the field before writing the narrative in my first edition of this book, with no doubt that I could accept the old site.   But I was wrong—like all my predecessors.   In 1921 I went over the neighbourhood again, and found that I must fall in with Mr. Mackenzie's conclusions.   The crucial difficulty of the old version is that King Edward could not possibly have ridden past Stirling Castle if the fight had been south of the Borestane.   The agreement of Barbour, the *Scalachronica*, the *Vita Edwardi Secundi*, and the Bridlington Chronicle, that this was his line of retreat overrides its omission by Baker of Swinbrook and many writers of short narratives.

[1] Cf. Barbour with Baker of Swinbrook, p. 14.

CHAPTER III

CONTINUATION OF THE SCOTTISH WAR: FIRST COMBINATION
OF ARCHERY AND DISMOUNTED CAVALRY — DUPPLIN
AND HALIDON HILL

WITH the disasters of Mytton and Byland the second
period of the Scottish war comes to an end. King
Robert died on June 7, 1329, and with his death the ascendancy
of the Scottish arms passed away. Taught by their misfortunes,
the English were about to try a new tactical combination.[1]
They had failed in many disastrous attempts to cut off Scottish
raiders, and had suffered many checks when they still attempted
to take the offensive. The well-intentioned device of raising
mounted infantry, "hobilars" in the Border counties, in order
to keep up in pace with the Scottish raiders had no great success.
The first campaigns of the young Edward III. had been perfectly
fruitless. When at the head of a vast levy of all the strength of
England he tried to hunt down Douglas and his plundering
bands in 1327, he had been obliged to return to Newcastle
wearied out and utterly foiled.[2] The "Shameful Peace" of
Northampton had followed (May 4, 1328). Four years of
uncertain truce intervened, and then the English and Scots
met again with changed fortune.

In 1332 an invasion of Scotland was prepared. The disinherited nobles of the English party, who had adhered too long
to the cause of the Plantagenets, backed by the many English
barons and knights who had been granted, and had since lost,
Scottish estates, were determined to attempt the recovery of

---

[1] The first conscious attempt on the English side to use *dismounted* men-at-arms
combined with archers may be Andrew Harcla's petty victory over the Lancastrian
rebels at Boroughbridge in 1322, when we are told that he dismounted all his cavalry
'in the Scottish fashion' to assist his archers to hold a bridge and a ford. But this
was a very small affair. See Professor Tout in *English Historical Review* for 1906.

[2] Froissart's account of this chase on the Northumbrian moors may be incorrect
in detail, but well deserves reading as a picture of Scottish tactics.

their fiefs.   The peace of Northampton had provided that they
should receive back their holdings on doing homage for them
to the Scottish king, but Bruce had distributed most of the land
in question to his own partisans, and the regents who ruled after
his death made no attempt to carry out the terms of the treaty.

The leaders of the " Disinherited " were the young Edward
Baliol, son of the unfortunate King John, Gilbert Umphraville
Earl of Angus, David Earl of Athole, Henry de Beaumont, who
had married the heiress of Buchan, and Walter Comyn.   The
rank and file of their little host was almost entirely composed
of Englishmen, with a few Scots and still fewer foreign mercenaries, among whom the Netherlander Walter Manny (destined
to be one of the prominent figures of the Anglo-French wars) is
the only name of note.   Their number was no more than five
hundred knights and men-at-arms, with between one thousand
and two thousand archers.[1]   King Edward had refused to
afford them help, holding himself bound by the Treaty of
Northampton.   He had even prohibited them from crossing
the Tweed, and given his Wardens of the Marches order to
use force to prevent any such attempt.   The Disinherited therefore collected at Ravenspur near the Humber mouth, hired
ships, and passed into Scotland by sea.

They landed near Kinghorn in Fife, drove off the Scots
who tried to hinder their disembarkation, and then moved on
Dunfermline.   From thence they marched on Perth, but soon
found a large army under the regent, Donald Earl of Mar,
lying across their path on the other side of the river Earn.   All
Central Scotland had been roused, and the least estimate given
(too high, no doubt, as usual) of Scots on Dupplin Muir is
two thousand men-at-arms and twenty thousand foot.[2]   It
might have been expected that the Scots would cross the
river at once to attack the small body of invaders ; but the
Earl of Mar was cautious : either he feared treachery in his own
host, or he grossly over-estimated the number of Baliol's men.
He contented himself with placing the flower of his army at the

[1] The Bridlington Chronicle, p. 106, says five hundred men-at-arms and one
thousand foot.   Knighton, i. p. 462, gives three hundred men-at-arms and three
thousand foot—not such a likely proportion, for the archers were never ten times the
number of the cavalry in English armies of this time.   The Lanercost Chronicle
gives fifteen hundred, but says that some gave two thousand eight hundred.

[2] Forty thousand is the figure of Knighton, vol. i. p. 462, and the Bridlington
Chronicle, p. 106.   Ten thousand in all would be a more likely figure.

bridge which crosses the Earn, intending perhaps to force the passage next morning.[1]

Battle of Dupplin, August 9, 1332.

The Disinherited were quite conscious that their attempt was a mere forlorn hope, and that their only chance of success lay in extreme audacity. When the dusk had fallen, they set forth to make a night attack on the regent's camp, crossing the river by a ford pointed out to them by some of the Scottish exiles.[2] They fell on to the rear of the Scottish bivouac and made a dreadful slaughter of the foot-soldiery who lay on its outskirts. But when day dawned they found the regent and all his men-at-arms marching against them in good order : being at the other side of the camp, near the bridge, they had escaped the surprise, and had gained time to arm and array themselves.[3] The Scots advanced in solid columns, two in number according to the Chronicle of Lanercost,[4] while the Bridlington Chronicle's clearer narrative gives the more probable statement that there was one large central column flanked by two smaller ones.[5] All were on foot, according to the ancient custom of the Scots.

Seeing the enemy approaching in such force, the invaders drew back from the Scottish camp and ranged themselves on the slope above it.[6] The knights and men-at-arms dismounted and stood in a single mass in the centre ; the archers were drawn out in a thin line on either flank, scattered among the heather of the hillside, and presenting no formed body at which an enemy could strike. Forty men-at-arms, all continental mercenaries, were alone told off to remain on horse-

[1] "Omnes equites et armati pontem pariter obsidebant, aestimantes advenas vada ignorare (Brid. Chron. 106).

[2] "Instructi per quosdam patriam et vada fluminis cognoscentes" (Brid. Chron. 105). Scottish tradition said that Andrew Murray of Tullibardine guided them.

[3] I must here make my acknowledgments to Mr. J. E. Morris, whose article on the battle of Dupplin in the *English Historical Review*, 1897, pt. iii., first set me studying the details of the fight. He undoubtedly is the discoverer of the true meaning of it.

[4] "Fuerunt duae magnae acies, in quibus erant vexilla duodecim" (Chron. Laner. p. 268).

[5] "Dispositis itaque turmis et sagittariis suis, ut *collaterales* cuneos hostium invaderent, ipsi armati [the barons and their men-at-arms] *magnum exercitum* [the Scottish main body] expugnabant" (Brid. Chron. 106).

[6] "Festinaverunt ascendere montem, ubi Scoti hospitati sunt, in sinistra parte" (Knighton, p. 463).

back and form a reserve,[1] destined to deliver a last desperate charge, or, in the event of victory, to strike in as pursuers. It seems clear that the archers were arrayed not in the same straight line as the men-at-arms, but with their flanks thrown forward so that the whole army resembled a half-moon.

The English can hardly have been in array for more than a moment when the Scottish columns, with twelve banners of earls and great barons waving over them, rolled up the hillside. Utterly neglecting the archers on the wings, the regent made for the central clump of men-at-arms, and dashed into it with lances levelled. The first onset was so heavy that the " Disinherited " were borne back some paces. It was with the greatest difficulty that they held together and preserved themselves from being trampled down. But the impetus of the Scots being deadened by the first shock, and the slope being against them, they were for a moment checked, and the two hosts stood pressed together, with their spears locked, and hardly room to swing a sword.[2] Ralph Lord Stafford, seeing that the fight had now become a matter of pushing rather than of hacking and hewing, called to his men to turn sideways and thrust with their shoulders instead of opposing their breasts to the enemy. Using this device, and struggling desperately, the invaders succeeded in holding their line unbroken for some time,[3] and brought the Scots to a stand.

Meanwhile, the archers on the wings had closed in upon the enemy, and were pouring a blinding shower of arrows upon the smaller flanking columns which protected the sides of their main body. At first the Scots seem to have paid no heed to them, but to have set all their attention on pushing forward in the centre. But the shafts fell like hail, and so deadly were they that the advancing masses involuntarily swerved inwards and refused to face the incessant shower.[4] They thus fell in

[1] " Praeliari coeperunt, exceptis xl armatis qui venerant de Alemannia in auxilium Anglorum, qui se a latere continebant *ascensis equis suis*" (Knighton, p. 463).

[2] " Facto congressu Scotorum impetum primo non ferentes aliquantulum retrocedere compelluntur : sed de superius animati resistunt " (Knighton, p. 106).

[3] " Clamabat Baro de Stafford, 'Vos, Anglici, vertatis contra lanceas vestros humeros et non pectus,' et ipsi hoc facientes Scottos protinus repulerunt " (Chron. Lanercost, 268).

[4] " Hostium vero minores turmae per sagittarios plurimum lacerati adhaerere magno exercitui compelluntur et in breve conglobati alius ab alio premebatur " (Chron. Brid. p. 106).

upon the centre column and became blended with it. The enormous lateral pressure produced by their junction with the "main-battle," which was already so hotly engaged with Baliol's men-at-arms, had the most disastrous results. The whole mass was hustled together and wedged in hopeless confusion, which only became worse when the archers again closed in on the flanks and continued to pour their arrows into the heaving mass. "In a short space they were thrust so close that they were crushed to death one by another, so that more fell by suffocation than by the sword."[1] They were soon piled into a great heap, which grew higher as the inward pressure continued, and " a marvel never seen or heard of before in any battle of the past was observed, for the heap of dead stood as high from the ground as the full length of a spear."[2]

Unable to break through to the front, and horribly galled on the flanks, the Scottish host at last broke up, and all who could escape from the press made their way to the rear. Henry de Beaumont and some of the " Disinherited " then sprang on their horses and chased the fugitives for several miles. The Scots were not merely beaten, but well-nigh exterminated. Only fourteen knights are said to have escaped.[3] Among the slain were the regent, Donald Earl of Mar, the Earls of Menteith and Moray, Robert Bruce Earl of Carrick, the young king's bastard cousin, Alexander Fraser the High Chamberlain, eighteen bannerets, fifty-eight knights, eight hundred squires, twelve hundred men-at-arms, and an innumerable multitude of foot-soldiery.[4] Not one single living man was found in the frightful heap in the centre of the host. Among the " Disinherited " there fell thirty-three knights and men-at-arms, of whom the chief were John Gordon and Reginald de la Beche : not a single archer is said to have been slain ; the Scots had never come to handstrokes with them.[5]

The battle of Dupplin formed the turning-point in the history of the Scottish wars. For the future the English always

---

[1] " Ita a suis suffocati et magis quam gladiorum ictibus verberati, acervum valde mirabile composuerunt : sicque condensati ac si fuissent funibus colligati miserabiliter expirabant " (ibid. 106).

[2] Chron. Lanercost, p. 268.

[3] Knighton, p. 107.

[4] Chron. Brid. p. 107. Knighton gives (p. 463) twelve bannerets and more than a hundred knights.

[5] Knighton, p. 463.

adopted the order of battle which Baliol and Beaumont had discovered, dismounting their heavily-armed men and forming the centre from them, while the archers were thrown forward on the flanks. This was the array which King Edward III. used at Halidon Hill in 1333 : it is to be noted that Edward Baliol, Gilbert Umphraville, Beaumont, and David of Athole, the victors of Dupplin, were all serving under him in that engagement ; it must have been from them that he learned the most effective way of dealing with the Scottish masses.

Battle of Halidon Hill, July 19, 1333.

The main facts of Halidon Hill are very clear, though we are not so well furnished with its details as might be wished. Edward was besieging Berwick when a great Scottish host appeared to deliver it. Leaving a considerable portion of his troops in the trenches, to keep up the blockade, the king marched with the rest to beat off the army of succour. He took up a position such as Bruce would have loved, on a hillside with a marshy bottom below it and a wood on its brow. Edward made all his knights and men-at-arms dismount, and formed them in line with the archers. The host was divided into three " battles," each furnished with small wings. The right division was headed by the Earl Marshal, Thomas Earl of Norfolk, the king's half-uncle ; he had with him Edward's young brother, John of Eltham, and Henry de Beaumont. The wings of their corps were composed of troops under the Earl of Athole on the right and the Earl of Angus on the left. In the centre was the king himself, on the left wing Edward Baliol ; each of their divisions was furnished, like the right-hand " battle," with small wings. All the knights fought on foot.[1]

The Scots were forced to attack, as Berwick could not be relieved unless the English were beaten in the open field ; after the event of Bannockburn they were prepared to take the offensive. Dupplin Muir had not warned them. They arrayed themselves in the great masses which formed their habitual order of battle, and came lumbering down the opposite

---

[1] This is expressly stated by Baker of Swinbrook : " Hic didicit a Scotis Anglorum generositas dextrarios reservare venationi hostium, et contra morem suorum patrum pedes pugnare " (p. 51). He had evidently not appreciated the importance of Dupplin in the military history of England. Herein all historians have followed him, wherefore Mr. Morris deserves the more credit for calling attention to that much-neglected field.

hillside in four columns.[1] The marsh at the bottom forced
them to slacken their pace, but, pushing through it, they began
to climb Halidon Hill. They could not, however, win far up
its side, for such a terrible storm of arrows began to beat upon
them the moment that they commenced to mount the slope,
that all the front ranks went down together. The masses
strove to push forward, but each party as it emerged from the
weltering crowd and tried to climb higher up the slope was
promptly shot down, and it seems that very few of the Scots
struggled up so far as the line of English men-at-arms on the
brow. When at last the mass wavered and began to tail off
to the rear, King Edward bade his knights mount, charged the
fugitives, and pursued them fiercely for five miles. There
fell of the Scots Archibald Douglas, the regent of the realm,
Hugh Earl of Ross, Kenneth Earl of Sutherland, Alexander
Bruce Earl of Carrick, three other earls,[2] and such a multitude
of barons and bannerets, that Bannockburn was well repaid.
As the English ballad-maker sang—

> "Scottes out of Berwick and out of Aberdeen,
>   At the Burn of Bannock ye were far too keen,
>   King Edward has avenged it now, and fully too, I ween."

Halidon Hill is the second, as Dupplin is the first, of a long
series of successful battles fought against the Scots, and won by
the skilful combination of archery and dismounted men-at-arms.
Neville's Cross, Homildon, Flodden, Pinkie, are all variations
upon the same theme. At the first-named fight the archers so
riddled the Scots right wing that it broke up when attacked by
the English men-at-arms, and left the centre bare to flank
attack. At Homildon they so teased the Scottish masses by a
careful long-range fire, that they came storming down from a
strong position (like Harold's axemen at Hastings), and were
thrown into disorder and discomfited by perpetual concentric
volleys before ever they could reach the English line of battle
on the opposite hill. Flodden and Pinkie fall outside the limits
of our period; in their main features they belong to the same

---

[1] Hemingburgh gives for their army the very moderate and probable figures of
twelve hundred men-at-arms and thirteen thousand five hundred pikemen. At the
same time he says that the available force of Edward was smaller. Many of the
English authorities give absurd figures for the Scottish losses, running up to sixty
thousand !

[2] Apparently Lennox, Strathearn, and Athole, the last-named being the Scottish
claimant who disputed that title with David of Strathbogie.

class as Dupplin, Halidon, Homildon, and Neville's Cross. The moral of all is the same : invaluable against cavalry, the Scottish pikemen were helpless when opposed by a judicious combination of lance and bow.   It was in vain that enlightened men in the northern realm, like King James I., tried to encourage archery : for want of old tradition and hereditary aptitude, Scotland never bred a race of archers such as flourished south of Tweed. When she got the better of England in war, it was always through a careful adherence to " good King Robert's Testament," by the avoidance of general engagements, the harrying of the land before the advancing foe, and the confining of offensive action to ambushes and night surprises,—" the wyles and wakenyngs of the night," which that wise and cautious soldier had prescribed.

BOOK IX

THE LONGBOW IN FRANCE AND SPAIN

1337-1396

CHAPTER I

COMMENCEMENT OF THE HUNDRED YEARS' WAR—
THE ARMIES OF EDWARD III

WE have seen that the result of the thirty years of almost uninterrupted war between England and Scotland, which began at Dunbar and lasted down to Halidon Hill, had profoundly modified the habitual tactics of English armies. Taught by the events of Falkirk and Bannockburn, they had abandoned the old idea that battles were won solely by the charge of armed horsemen. Success, it had been found, depended far more upon the judicious use of archery. But archers alone would not be sufficient to decide the day ; they could be driven off (as at Bannockburn) by a charge of horse, unless they were properly supported. For an offensive battle the support might consist of mounted men (as at Falkirk). For a defensive battle dismounted men would be more useful, for all history has shown that cavalry cannot easily defend a position : once tied to a fixed spot, they lose the impetus which is their strength. If an army is forced to take the defensive, by reason of weakness, it had better dismount the greater part of its horsemen.

Edward III., as we shall see, was a very competent tactician, but a very unskilful strategist. It fell to him and to the professional soldiers bred in the experience of the long Scottish war to apply its lessons to a new struggle, fought on a larger scale and under very different conditions. The use that was made of them was excellent, and led to such successful results that it stereotyped the tactics of English armies for the next century and a half.

England was now about to engage in war with a power which excelled her in military strength much in the same proportion in which she herself excelled Scotland. Just as England surpassed the realm beyond Tweed in the size of her hosts, and especially in the number of heavy cavalry that she could put

into the field, so did France surpass England in those points.
To hope to meet the French, lance for lance, in the open field
was just as impossible for Edward III. as it had been impossible
for Wallace or Bruce to set knight against knight at Falkirk or
Bannockburn.   Hopelessly outmatched in the numbers of his
mounted men, Edward had to bethink him of some way in which
the superiority of the French in that respect might be neutralised.
His resolve was to adapt to continental war the tactics recently
developed in the Scottish campaigns—to fight defensive battles
in good positions, and keep off the horsemen by a steady and
unbreakable line of infantry.   But he had an advantage which
Bruce had never possessed—that of being able to command the
services of a very numerous and efficient archery, far surpassing
any continental troops armed with missile weapons that then
existed.   The strength and adaptability of this arm was now
known to every English commander, but it was wholly un-
suspected beyond seas, for its development had taken place
since the last continental campaigns of the Plantagenets in
the thirteenth century.

Edward's great experiment, therefore, first worked out at
Crecy, was to apply the tactics of Dupplin and Halidon Hill—
which had told so well against masses of spearmen on foot—
against masses of cavalry.   In France those absurd perversions
of the art of war which covered themselves under the name
of Chivalry were more omnipotent than in any other country of
Europe.   The strength of the armies of Philip and John of
Valois was composed of a fiery and undisciplined *noblesse*,
which imagined itself to be the most efficient military force in
the world, but was in reality little removed from an armed mob.
A system which reproduced on the battlefield the distinctions
of feudal society was considered by the French aristocracy to
represent the ideal form of warlike organisation.   The French
knight believed that, since he was infinitely superior to any
peasant in the social scale, he must consequently excel him to
the same extent in military value.   He was therefore prone not
only to despise all descriptions of infantry, but to regard their
appearance on the field against him as a species of insult to his
class-pride.

A few years before, the self-confidence of the French
nobility had been shaken for a moment by the result of the
battle of Courtrai (1302).   A few words on that famous fight

are necessary. Its details bore an extraordinary likeness to those of Bannockburn, a fact which struck both Baker of Swinbrook and Sir John Gray of the *Scalachronica*, the two most intelligent observers in the next generation. Philip of France had imprisoned Guy Count of Flanders, and declared his earldom annexed to the royal domain for treason. He had garrisoned several Flemish towns and nominated French officials to administer the county. But he had misjudged the loyalty of the Flemings to their captive lord. In May 1302 a general insurrection swept over northern Flanders, and in a few days little was left in French hands save the towns of Ghent and Cassel and the citadel of Courtrai. Philip entrusted the task of crushing the rebellion to his kinsman and brother-in-law, Robert Count of Artois, a haughty and bellicose prince of no great capacity. He was put in charge of the feudal levy of all Northern France, and of bodies of Genoese mercenary crossbowmen, and of Basque and Gascon javelin-men ("bidets"), besides other foot-soldiers of less repute. Many lords of the Low Countries, from Hainault, Brabant, and Luxemburg lent him aid. His army was large, though it cannot have attained the seven thousand five hundred horse and forty thousand foot of the contemporary chroniclers. No doubt was entertained that it was amply sufficient to trample down the insurrection, all the more because a considerable part of the Flemish *noblesse* was lukewarm in the cause of independence, and some (the so-called "Leliards") had actually taken the French side. This was exactly what happened in Scotland at the time of Falkirk : the insurrectionary army was hopelessly destitute of its proper complement of cavalry. The force which was led by Guy of Namur, a younger son of the imprisoned count, and his cousin William of Juliers was essentially an infantry levy of burghers and peasants, with only enough knights present to serve for staff purposes to the commanders. To French observers their resistance seemed presumptuous, to Flemish observers it was a desperate exhibition of reckless patriotism.

When Robert of Artois crossed the frontier (July 2) the Flemish army abandoned the siege of Cassel, before which it was lying, and drew back to a chosen position in front of Courtrai, whose castle was considered in a very evil plight— the garrison being on the edge of capitulation. The battle which followed was one of those where an army of relief sets itself to thrust away an army which is covering a siege. It is therefore exactly parallel to Bannockburn. And, as in the Scottish fight, the strength of the insurrectionary army was that it had got into a position well protected by marsh and streams. The Groeninghebeke (like the Bannock) was a very modest watercourse, running to join the Lys river a mile below Courtrai among bogs and pools. Behind it the Flemings had taken post, across the Menin-Courtrai high road, with the Lys and a Franciscan nunnery covering their left flank, and swampy meadows and a ditch running into the city moat their right. They are said to have dug *trous-de-loup* in front of their line, just as Bruce prepared his " pottes " at Bannockburn. The position was good in itself, but a death-trap if the army should be beaten, for behind it lay the citadel of Courtrai, still in French hands, and only two bridges leading into the town across the broad moat (Hoegen Viver) which encircles it. In case of a disaster the Flemings had no retreat save by a pair of narrow defiles. This was visible to every one, and their commanders had made them understand that if they gave way they were doomed to annihilation.

The Flemish army took up its position behind the Groeninghebeke in one solid phalanx—apparently with a front of about one thousand yards, which, since the Chroniclers insist on the depth of the formation, implies a mass of ten thousand men at least. In addition there was a small reserve behind the centre, under a knight named John van Renesse, while a contingent of twelve hundred men from Ypres were left to block the exits from the castle, lest the garrison should make a sally to take the army in the rear during the action. The Flemings had a certain number of arbalesters, who were thrown forward close to the edge of the stream, but the vast majority of the host was composed of infantry well armed with steel hat and gambeson, and bearing pikes, or the celebrated " goedendag," a queer, heavy weapon composed of a long club-like shaft with a spike protruding from its upper end. Its shape may be seen in the illustration from the curious " Courtrai Chest " in New College, Oxford,[1] of which three episodes may be seen in the plate facing

[1] This unique relic I was lucky enough to identify in New College, some fifteen years ago, and to have the chance of showing to Professor Pirenne, who agreed in the identification. It contains a series of carvings illustrating the chief incidents of the campaign.

page 118. It could be used equally for striking club-fashion, or for thrusting like a spear.

Robert of Artois, on arriving within touch of the Flemish army, halted for some time to investigate the situation. It is said that some of his advisers urged him to leave the enemy alone, and march on Ghent by another road, a move which would compel the Flemings to quit their position and follow him. But full of the feudal contempt for infantry, he resolved to make a frontal attack : " a hundred horse are worth a thousand foot " is the saying attributed to him,[1] and he held the Groeninghebeke no sufficient obstacle to prevent a cavalry charge.

He first sent out his light troops, mainly Genoese cross-bowmen, who advanced to the west bank of the stream and opened upon the Flemish arbalesters on the other side of the water. After a prolonged exchange of missiles the Flemings gave way and retired, thus uncovering the front of their own phalanx, which was near enough behind to be exposed to the enemy's bolts. These told so much that the two counts ordered their men to draw back some scores of yards, so as to get out of range. This manœuvre, a difficult one to try with untrained troops, was successfully accomplished—a good testimony to the steadiness of the Flemings.

Seeing the enemy retiring, Robert of Artois thought it time to charge with his cavalry, ten heavy squadrons of men-at-arms in three lines. He sent orders to the light infantry to clear off at once, and launched his vaward at the enemy. As happened afterwards at Creçy, the advancing knights got mixed with the retiring crossbowmen, rode some of them down, and arrived at the brook in great disarray. They plunged into it, however, but found it deeper and muddier than they expected, and on reaching the far bank got stuck in the marshy meadow and trapped in many cases in the *trous-de-loup*. Those who struggled through were massing themselves to continue the charge, when they were surprised to see the whole hostile phalanx bearing down upon them with levelled weapons. The Flemish captains had resolved to take the offensive when the knights were in disorder and had lost their impetus—had Bruce heard of this manœuvre when he took

---

[1] But only by the Flemish Chronicle-poet Van Velthem, who is perhaps not the best authority for words spoken at a French council of war.

exactly the same step at Bannockburn ?   The two lines met—
the one advancing in order with a level front, the other consisting of a number of groups of horsemen, with gaps between
and in no array at all.   To their intense anger and surprise
the whole French vaward was rolled back toward the
Groeninghebeke.   Robert of Artois at once led forward his
main-battle to aid his failing front-line squadrons ; they
crossed the stream and marsh with the same hindrances as
their predecessors, and only got up, in great disorder, just in
time to prevent their comrades from being exterminated.
Lurching forward in groups and slowly against the Flemings,
they cut and hewed at the pikes, and strove desperately to
break in.   Only at one point in the centre of the line did the
enemy give back for a time, and here the game was ended by
Van Renesse bringing up the reserve of pikes to stop the gap.
Finally, just as at Bannockburn, the horsemen were fought
out—their chargers stabbed by hundreds in the bowels, the
riders knocked on the head before they could rise.   Robert of
Artois himself was brained as he tried to get to his knees, crying
his name and asking for quarter.   " We don't understand
French," said his slayer—the order had gone round that no
enemy wearing the spurs of knighthood should be spared.
At last the struggling mass of horsemen was thrust back
into the Groeninghebeke, in which many hundreds of them
perished.   The third French line and the infantry went off the
field without attempting to renew the attack.   A fruitless
sortie by the garrison of Courtrai Castle had already been
repelled by the men of Ypres, who had been left to block
their exit.

When the Flemings stripped the slain and fished the
drowned out of the Groeninghebeke, they identified sixty-three
counts, barons, and bannerets, including, along with Robert
of Artois himself, the Counts of Eu, Tancarville, Dammartin,
Aumâle, and Grandpré, Godfrey of Aerschot uncle of the
Duke of Brabant, Jean " Sans-Merci " heir of the Count
of Hainault, Thierry son of the Duke of Lorraine, Raoul
de Nesle Constable of France, and the two Marshals, Jean de
Trie and Guy de Nesle.   Seven hundred pairs of knightly
spurs of gold were stripped off the heels of the fallen, and
hung up as a thank-offering for victory in the high church
of Courtrai.

It is obvious that Robert of Artois lost his life and his army by persisting in attacking a steady enemy placed in a narrow position, with well-covered flanks and the frontal defence of a belt of stream and marsh. But it is also obvious that the scale of the disaster was caused by the counter-attack of the Flemings, on an enemy who had just crossed in disorder a dangerous obstacle and had not yet gathered himself together for a new advance. If the French vaward had been given time and space to mass itself for a new charge, and the Flemings had remained motionless, the results might have been different. But the knights were given neither the time nor the space, since the Flemings came down on them before they had re-covered themselves, and left them no open ground on which to rearrange their ranks or to get up impetus for a second advance. Nor could the French fall back in order to re-form, since the marsh and stream were immediately behind them. Had William and Guy kept their original position, and not attacked, the result of the battle might have been more like that of Cortenuova [1] than that of Bannockburn. Hence Courtrai is a very important fight, showing that infantry with covered flanks might not only hold out against horse, but thrust them back, provided that there was no co-operation between the cavalry and the missile-bearing infantry of the hostile army. The extent of the disaster resulted (as at Bannockburn) from the marsh obstacles in the rear of the defeated party.

The result of the battle shocked and puzzled contemporary observers of the knightly caste, not only in France, but (as Chronicles show) all over western Europe. To explain it a whole crop of legends sprang up within the next few years. They have been carefully collected by Professor Pirenne in an ingenious pamphlet.[2] Some of the French writers alleged treachery—cowardice of the reserve and of the Genoese infantry. Others accused the Flemings of unknightly conduct—the most absurd story is that of Guiart, who inserts an idiotic episode in the fight. The Flemings cry out to the French to give them more space for a fair fight, and when the simple knights retire many yards to oblige them, charge them suddenly in the rear while their backs are turned. Another version declares

[1] See vol. i. pages 494-6.
[2] *La Version Flamande et la Version Française de la bataille de Courtrai.* Brussels, 1898.

that there was no fight at all; the knights charged into a deep morass, and were engulfed up to their middles—then the Flemings came down and murdered them as they sat helpless on their sunken steeds. A third relates that there was in front of the Flemish line not the *trous-de-loup* but a vast ditch dug out and covered in with hurdles and grass, into which the French vaward plunged unwittingly, and were annihilated. A fourth alleges the misinterpretation of signals made from the garrison of the castle, which led to the adoption of an absurd line of advance. The whole settled down finally into a version which threw all the blame on the improvidence of Robert of Artois, insisted much on the importance of the *trous-de-loup*, but made the fall of the knights into the Groeninghebeke the main episode of the battle, while really it was only the disastrous corollary of their failure on the other side of the water. The moral that on certain ground, and under certain conditions, and with certain tactics, infantry might defeat cavalry was shirked and ignored.[1]

The French *noblesse* comforted themselves with the reflection that it was the morass and not the Flemish infantry which won the battle: they were confirmed in their views by the event of the two bloody fights of Mons-en-Pevèle (1304) and Cassel (1328). The fate which had on those days befallen the gallant burghers of Flanders was believed to be only typical of that which still awaited any foot-soldier who dared to match himself against the chivalry of the most warlike aristocracy in Christendom. Pride goes before a fall, and the French nobles were now to meet infantry with new tactics, of a quality such as they had never supposed to exist.

Against these presumptuous cavaliers, the king's mercenaries, and the disorderly militia of the French communes, the English archer was now to be matched, in the long struggle that lasted with a few truces from 1337 to 1396. The men whom Edward III. led over-seas were not hasty and miscellaneous shire-levies such as had fought at Bannockburn. In the beginning of the war the English armies were entirely

---

[1] It may be noted that in the above narrative I have said nothing about the vast turning movement of the French army round the end of the Groeninghebeke morasses of which General Köhler makes much. He gets it all from some lines in Guiart, a very poor authority, and not an eye-witness. I agree with Dr. Delbrück in ignoring this supposed movement, of which the best authorities show no traces.

raised by Commissions of Array, under which designated commissioners selected from each county a definite number, usually a very moderate one, of picked men-at-arms, archers, and other infantry.

The time had not yet come, though it was near at hand, when the whole of the foot of an English army, with the exception of Gascon, Welsh, or Irish auxiliaries, was to be armed with the bow. Since Bannockburn many experiments in the combination of arms had been tried. Edward II. had once (1322), apparently in a stupid misreading of the meaning of his great Scottish disaster, levied a host in which nothing but spearmen were asked for, the bow being contemned. More capable men had tried another experiment, the development of mounted infantry (hobilars), who would be able to cope with Scottish raids by keeping up with the cavalry, and to dismount when the enemy had been caught up and brought to action. The hobilar was a spearman ; but before long the same idea was applied to archers. It was useless to try to run down the evasive Scot with a dismounted force, but infantry on any sort of nags might come up with him, and if spearmen, why not also bowmen ? After Dupplin Muir and Halidon, the efficiency of the longbow had been revindicated, and a few years later we find the mounted archer appearing. In 1337 the small army with which the earls of Salisbury and Gloucester invaded Lothian had nearly two thousand of them, a much greater number than that of the foot archers. But this innovation was obviously considered specially suited for Scottish campaigns only, and the first armies which Edward III. took to the French War had few or none of these mounted bowmen. Even as late as the siege of Calais in 1347 only one quarter of the king's archers had horses : they received sixpence a day instead of the normal threepence of their pedestrian comrades.[1]

It is rather surprising to find that the obvious moral of Dupplin and Halidon took such a long time to work out that some of Edward's early armies of the Hundred Years' War

---

[1] Yet, a few months before, Lancashire had sent to the campaign of Neville's Cross nine hundred and sixty horsed as against two hundred and forty foot archers, and Yorkshire over three thousand. Clearly counties accustomed to deal with the Scot had an abnormal proportion of mounted men. See Morris's *Bannockburn*, p. 102.

had only half their infantry strength composed of bowmen.[1] But the proportion steadily mounted up as the war went on ; and by its end, English contingents normally consisted of men-at-arms and archers only.

Of the men raised by Commissions of Array, a considerable number, no doubt, would be willing men who volunteered to serve.   Provision was made for allowing those who were unfit, or reluctant, to provide themselves with substitutes, on the principle of scutage, by paying a reasonable sum of money in compensation.[2] The commissioners themselves were responsible for seeing that the deputy should not be a waif or a wastrel, but a competent and proper representative of the man who stayed at home.   Yet Sir John Falstaff's methods, it is clear, were not unknown in the fourteenth century, for we frequently get complaints as to the kind of recruit that was provided.   In the army that fought at Halidon Hill there were criminals and poachers, who required pardons.   But the achievements of

[1] The muster-rolls of the arrays of Feb. 1339, given in Rymer, II. vol. ii. p. 1070, may be worth giving in full.   The archers, it will be noted, form exactly half the foot.   The "armati" are "hobilars," as it would appear.

	Men-at-arms.	Armati.	Archers.		Men-at-arms.	Armati.	Archers.
Yorkshire .	200	500	500	Cambridgeshire .	18	70	70
Gloucestershire .	63	250	250	Huntingdonshire	18	70	70
Worcestershire .	30	120	120	Buckinghamshire	20	80	80
Staffordshire .	55	220	220	Bedfordshire .	20	90	90
Shropshire .	55	220	220	Lancashire .	50	300	300
Herefordshire .	30	120	120	Norfolk .	40	160	160
Oxfordshire .	20	80	80	Suffolk .	25	100	100
Berkshire .	15	60	60	Northumberland	70	250	250
Wiltshire .	35	140	140	Westmoreland .	25	150	150
Devonshire .	35	160	160	Cumberland .	50	200	200
Cornwall .	25	100	100	Lincolnshire .	80	350	350
Hampshire .	30	120	120	Nottinghamshire	35	150	150
Somersetshire .	35	160	160	Derbyshire .	35	150	150
Dorsetshire .	25	100	100	Leicestershire .	25	120	120
Sussex .	50	200	200	Warwickshire .	30	120	120
Surrey .	20	80	80	Northamptonshire	35	160	160
Kent .	35	140	140	Rutland .	10	40	40
Essex .	35	160	160				
Hertfordshire .	18	70	70		1407	5600	5600
Middlesex .	10	40	40				

[2] e.g. in the year of the levying of the Creçy army the arrayers of arms are allowed to make agreement "ad tractandum et concordandum cum omnibus hominibus ad arma et hobellariis qui fines, pro progressu suo, facere voluerint, habita consideratione ad bona et catalla sua : ita quod loco eorum de denariis illis provenienti-bus alios homines conducere valeamus," etc. (Rymer, 1346, p. 78).

the English hosts are the best testimonials to the character of the men who served in them.

As the long struggle with France wore on year after year, we find the king dropping more and more the custom of raising national forces by Commissions of Array, and falling back upon the system which his grandfather had adopted when collecting the cavalry for his Welsh, French, and Scottish wars—that of making contracts with his barons and knights to raise men for long service. Edward I. had applied this to the mounted arm alone, as we have seen in a previous chapter, supplementing the not too willing feudal levies by large squadrons of horse serving " at the king's wages." [1] Edward III.—infantry having become much more important than in his grandfather's day—applied the same principle to foot-soldiery. The contractors agree to supply him not only with horse, but with infantry, and after a time these infantry are all found to be archers. The idea prevalent in the late thirteenth century that the earls, at least, ought to discharge their feudal obligation,[2] and serve unpaid, vanishes; and they, no less than other men, contract to take the king's wages from first to last. After a time the system of " Indentures " is applied, not only to contingents raised for a campaign, or for a longer period, but to other purposes. For example, a banneret or knight may contract to maintain a certain fort or garrison at his own risk, in return for certain payments and allowances to be made him by the sovereign. The contract was wholly outside and unconnected with feudal obligations; it was a pure matter of bargaining. The contractor might not even be a vassal of the king's: Sir Walter Manny, Wolfhard of Ghistelles, and other well-known captains were aliens born. A simple knight with only a few acres of his own might contract for hundreds of men, if he was a popular and capable leader whose name would attract numerous volunteers.

The use of the " Indenture " system saved the king the friction and show of compulsion caused by enforcing the conscription carried out by Commissioners of Array. The men brought in by the contractors were all freely enlisted and willing soldiers, serving under the leader of their own choice. They would also be, on the average, more efficient than the pressed men from the shires. The long continuance of the wars had

---

[1] See above, pp. 64–65.   [2] See above, p. 63.

created a large class of adventurers who had seen one or two campaigns on compulsion, but had then stuck to the trade of war from choice. These professional soldiers were as ready to make their bargain with the holder of an indenture as the latter was to make his bargain with the king. Thus came into being the mercenary armies of the second stage of the war, composed of hardy unscrupulous veterans, terrible to the enemy's host, but still more terrible, from their habit of scientific plunder, to the peaceable inhabitants of any district through which they chanced to pass. The best of soldiers while the war lasted, they were a most dangerous and unruly race in time of truce or peace, for they had no wish to return to their homes and fall back into civil life.

As a normal example of the forms used in the system of indenture, the agreement signed by the king and Thomas Holland Earl of Kent, on September 30, 1360, may be noted.[1] The earl contracts to serve the king, " at the accustomed wages of war," for a quarter of a year : the sum due is to be paid him beforehand, in order that he may have sufficient ready money for the equipment of his contingent. He is to provide sixty men-at-arms, of whom ten are to be knights and one a banneret, and a hundred and twenty archers, all of whom are to be provided with horses. The high proportion of " spears " to " bows " deserves notice, and also the fact that all the archers are to be mounted ; it was by this provision of horses for even the infantry that the English armies were enabled to move so fast in the later French campaigns.

In the case of indentures providing for the custody of fortresses on French soil, we may note some curious provisions for the protection of the contractor. When Sir John Chandos undertakes to garrison a castle, it is stipulated that if the king or any of his sons pays him a visit, the castellan shall have an extra allowance for entertaining them : again, if any English forces pass by and consume the stores of the garrison, the king undertakes to pay an additional sum to make up the value of the food which Chandos supplies to them. But the ordinary expenses of war must be defrayed by the governor from the regular allowance guaranteed in his indenture.

In the first period of the Hundred Years' War, Edward III. experimented freely with a system of treaties of subsidy with

[1] Rymer, *Foedera*, etc. iii. p. 510.

foreign princes. At one time and another he took many lords of the Netherlands and Germany into his service, each undertaking to supply a fixed contingent at stated rates of pay. But the experiment was found costly and unsatisfactory. No such obedience could be got from sovereign princes, serving as subsidised allies, as could be obtained from English national troops, or from regular hired mercenary bands. Each duke or count had his own political axe to grind, and cared little for the King of England's main line of policy. They came late, departed early, intrigued against each other, gave scamped service, and were always clamouring for more money. Edward found himself bankrupt, and had achieved none of his ends. Hence after the ignominious failure of his campaigns of 1339 and 1340 he gave up for ever the idea of winning the war with subsidised foreign armies, and relied for the future on his own subjects, and his bands of veteran mercenaries, serving on " indentures," under professional officers of high capacity, most of them English, but some foreigners.

CHAPTER II

THE LONGBOW IN FRANCE—CRÉCY

FROM the very first moment of the Hundred Years' War we find the English archery exercising a preponderant influence in battle. The first clash of arms came when the Earl of Derby landed in Flanders on St. Martin's Eve, 1337. The English had to force their way on shore, which they did under cover of a rain of arrows which completely drove off the Flemish crossbowmen who had lined the quays of Cadzand haven.[1] Then, when the expedition had landed, there was a sharp fight on shore : the earl posted his archers on his flank, a little in advance of his men-at-arms.[2] The Bastard of Flanders, who commanded the enemy, charged the English when they were formed, but was completely routed, mainly owing to the irresistible flank fire of arrows, and taken prisoner with most of his chief followers.[3]

When King Edward himself came over to Flanders in 1339, and called in to his aid the German princes that he had subsidised—the Margrave of Brandenburg, the Dukes of Brabant, Gueldres, and Juliers, and the rest—he had under his hand the largest army that any English king ever set in battle-array on continental soil. Of men-at-arms there were said to be twelve thousand,[4] and the Flemish and Brabançon infantry swelled the host to enormous proportions. With such forces at

[1] Froissart, K. de Lettenhove's edition, vol. ii. p. 436: "Traioient arbalestier a leur pooir, mais Englais n'en faisoient compte, car archier sont trop plus isniel au traire que ne sont arbalestier."

[2] MSS. de l'Arsenal, 148, p. 187: "Luy et ses gens descendirent à terre et les archiers à l'un des lés ung peu devant eulx, et commenchérent a traire moult druement."

[3] Froissart, K. de L. ii. p. 436: "Au vrai dire li archier ensonnoient trop grandement les assallants et deffendants Flamens, . . . et finablement li Flament ne peurent porter ne soustenire le faix," etc.

[4] Baker of Swinbrook, p. 64. No doubt a figure much too high.

his command, we might have expected that Edward would have brought the enemy to action at all costs, even though Philip of France had arrayed against him an even greater multitude. He was planning, however, to fight a defensive engagement, and to employ the very tactics that had served him so well at Halidon Hill. The army was formed up in front of La Flamengerie in three lines. The front line was composed entirely of English, and was divided into a centre with two smaller wing divisions, or *échelles*, as the king himself calls them in his account of the campaign. In each division the whole of the men-at-arms were dismounted and formed in line, with the archers ranged on each flank of them. The Margrave of Brandenburg and the German princes composed the second line, the Duke of Brabant's contingent the third. In these lines it would seem that, according to the custom of the Continent, the knights were on their steeds, for it is recorded that the Margrave and the Duke of Brabant, riding forward to view the king's order of battle, were much surprised to see the array that he had adopted, though they concluded, after inspection, that it was admirably arranged.[1]

If King Philip had advanced from Buironfosse and attacked the confederate army, there would have resulted a battle on the same lines as that which took place seven years later at Creçy, but on a much larger scale. But the English tactics were not yet to be put to the test: the French king ranged his host in order at a prudent distance; he entrenched himself, covered his front with *abattis*,[2] and refused to move forward. He, no less than Edward, wished to be attacked. Thus it came to pass that no general engagement took place, and that the enemies retired each toward his own base when they had exhausted the provisions of the countryside.

The seven years that followed were singularly deficient in

---

[1] The French original of the "Ordonnance des Anglois à la Flamengerie" clearly enough states that the archers were on each side of the knights : "Le roy fist touts ses gents descendre à pié, et mis ses gents en arraie, les archiers à l'encoste des gentes d'armes." The English chroniclers who translated the document, *e.g.* Hemingburgh rendering *à l'encoste* by *juxta*, make the arrangement obscure and vague.

[2] So says King Edward in his rather angry letter to his son in England : "He made trenches all about him and felled big trees in order to prevent us from reaching him. We waited all day on foot in battle-array and at dusk it seemed to our allies that we had waited long enough."

events of any decisive tactical interest. The long bickering of the French and English alike in Flanders, Brittany, and Aquitaine led to no single engagement of first-class importance. The war was carried on by a series of forays, sieges, and chivalrous but unscientific exploits of arms, which led to no strategic result. The one really striking event of the time, the battle of Sluys, was a fight on sea, not on land. Such encounters as did take place ashore were for the most part surprises, ambuscades, or night attacks—like the Earl of Derby's brilliant surprise of the Gascons at Auberoche[1] (October 11, 1345), or Sir Walter Manny's victory at Quimperlé[2] (June 1342). The combat of Morlaix (September 29, 1342) was something more like a regular battle. William Bohun Earl of Northampton and Robert of Artois took up a defensive position between woods, and dug pitfalls along their front, placing their dismounted men-at-arms behind the obstacles. Charles of Blois' cavalry fell into the trap and were much mishandled. But no chronicler mentions the use of archery by the English.[3]

All the more startling and important, therefore, was the event of the battle of Crécy, when the new English tactics were first put to the proof on a large scale. It was not till it had been fought that the importance of this new development of the art of war was realised on the Continent.

King Edward, as we have already had occasion to observe, was not a great strategist, and the details of the campaign which led up to the battle of Crécy are as discreditable to his generalship as those of the actual engagement are favourable. Disgusted at the repeated failure of his attempts to invade France with the aid of an army of German or Breton auxiliaries, he had sailed from Portsmouth on July 5, 1346, at the head of a host composed entirely of his own subjects.

---

[1] Adam Murimuth gives all the credit of the fight of Auberoche to the archers (p. 190 of the Rolls Series edition).

[2] Sir Walter surprised the fleet of Louis of Spain in his absence, routed the troops left to guard it, and then encountered the enemy as he hastily returned homeward, and beat him by suddenly dashing out of woods against his flanks.

[3] See De la Borderie's *Histoire de Bretagne*, ii. 467, utilising Murimuth and Knighton. Baker of Swinbrook comments on the fact that the enemy got to close grips with the English, a thing that happened neither at Halidon nor Crécy. Possibly the archery were not properly employed.

This force consisted, as far as the mounted arm went, entirely of troops raised under the system known to Edward I., in which barons and bannerets collected squadrons of volunteers, and offered these " retinues " to the king, to serve him at the usual wages of war.   The horsemen were obtained by bringing pressure on all landowners of a certain income either to serve in person, under such a lord as they might choose, or to pay a monetary contribution like the old scutage. Parliament had assented in 1345 to a scheme by which every man owning land or rents to the value of £5 should find an archer, those rated at £10 a hobilar (or spearman furnished with a horse), those rated between £10 and £20 two hobilars, and those with holdings of the value of £25 a man-at-arms, and so in proportion upward " according to the quantity of their lands." [1]   The sheriffs and commissioners of array had to make lists of the landowners and their obligations, and to see that the number due from their county was sent to the place of muster (Portsmouth in 1346).   Landowners unable to serve in person could provide substitutes—sons or brothers for choice—for their personal duty, and could enlist any other persons liable to serve to make up the full number of horsemen due from them.   Any one who neither came himself, nor sent a substitute, was liable to pay a heavy fine.[2]   But most of the assessed persons seem to have hastened to offer their services to the baron or banneret of their preference, from the knight responsible for two or three lances to the small £5 freeholder who had to produce a single archer.   The rolls of 1346 and 1347 are full of dozens and scores of writs to the sheriffs not to molest assessed men who had either gone to the war themselves or sent a competent substitute.[3]   The

---

[1] This arrangement may be found stated in full in the writ to the Sheriff of Devon, of February 26, 1346.

[2] Cf. writ of March 31, 1346, to all Supervisors of Array, permitting them to receive fines from all men-at-arms, hobilars, and archers who wish to make fines nstead of crossing to France, and with the money to hire others (Wrottesley's *Crecy and Calais*, p. 79).

[3] *e.g.* take such notices (all from the long rolls in Wrottesley's *Crecy and Calais*) as the fol lowing :

Writ to the Sheriff of Lincoln to supersede assessment on William de Croxby for an archer, the said William having sent his son Roger, well furnished with horse and arms, to Portsmouth.   Ditto, to John de Hundon, also assessed at one archer, who has sent Robert his son.   [June 28.]

Writ to the Sheriff of Warwick to suspend all demands on Sir William Careswell

" retinues " as they were originally drawn up in June 1346 have unfortunately not been preserved, but only the names of many, but not all, of the knights who served in them, so that it is impossible to arrive at the accurate figure for the horse-contingents of the expedition.   But we have the complete list of the king's army before Calais in the next year, which shows the proportions of the various arms in each of the contingents of the earls, barons, and bannerets, and can see from these (analysed on a later page) that on an average each knight was accompanied by about three or four troopers (esquires, men-at-arms, constables) and a somewhat larger number of archers.   In a well-organised retinue the large majority of the archers were mounted.   There was the widest variety in exact proportions between knights, men-at-arms, and archers—*e.g.* Richard Lord Talbot had fourteen knights, sixty esquires, eighty-two archers ; but John de Vere Earl of Oxford has twenty-three knights, forty-four esquires, and sixty-three archers.   If, as seems probable, the total cavalry force on the Creçy expedition was about two thousand four hundred men, we may take it that there were about five hundred knights, one thousand nine hundred men-at-arms, and some two thousand five hundred archers in the " retinues."

But in addition to the troops raised in this fashion, there were the infantry levies of the shires and towns, men not belonging to the contingents of the earls, barons, and bannerets. We chance to possess for this part of the army the full writs of summons made to the sheriffs and commissioners of array of the counties, and to the mayors or other corporate officers of the cities and boroughs.   All the shires south of Trent were told to provide archers, in very moderate contingents—

for men-at-arms, as the said William is serving in the retinue of Sir Bartholomew de Burghersh.   [Nov. 4.]

Writ to the Sheriff of Staffordshire to supersede any demands on Edmond Lys for a hobilar, as the said Edmond sent Thomas de Stonleye, a hobilar, who served in the retinue of Sir William Careswell, till he was killed at Melun. [Dec. 16.]

Writ to the Commissioners of Array in Warwick and Salop, that whereas William le Boteller of Wem has been assessed at ten men-at-arms, of which the king has remitted six, as it now appears that the said William has devised away the greater part of his lands, and has no more than 200 marks of rent, the king remits three men-at-arms more, but William shall find one man-at-arms for the retinue of the Earl of Huntingdon.   [June 7.]

they run to three thousand seven hundred and eighty in all.[1]
The urban levies originally summoned came to about seventeen
hundred more, of which London had to provide a hundred
men-at-arms, but all the rest were *armati*,[2] which would
seem to be equivalent to hobilars and not to archers. But in
March many coast towns were told to hold back their men
for home defence, as French counter-raids were possible.
And for many other towns reductions were made, perhaps on
the same ground, cutting down the number of men ordered
to Portsmouth to two-thirds or one-half of the original contingent required. When allowance is made for these wholesale
countermands, it would seem that the total of these urban *armati*
who actually sailed must have been under one thousand. For
the reduction in numbers had fallen on many of the towns with
the largest contingents; such as Norwich, Bristol, and Lynn.[3]

In addition to the English infantry, which amounted, if we
add the retinue-men to the shire-archers and the urban *armati*,
to perhaps seven thousand five hundred in all, very large Welsh
contingents had been ordered out : the Principality of Wales
was assessed at three thousand five hundred and fifty men, half

[1] The shire figures are worth giving. They are :

Kent	280	Wiltshire	200	Suffolk	100	Worcester	80
Sussex	200	Essex	200	Dorset	100	Leicester	80
Norfolk	200	Somerset	160	Surrey	100	Hampshire	60
Northants	200	Oxford	160	Bucks	100	Bedfordshire	60
Lincoln	200	Warwick	160	Herts	100	Hunts	60
Gloucester	200	Hereford	160	Cambridge	100	Middlesex	60
Shropshire	200	Berkshire	120	Stafford	100	Rutland	40

Total three thousand seven hundred and eighty. From the county of Chester
there were a hundred more, reckoned among the Prince of Wales' Welsh.

[2] I cannot understand why the towns should not have been asked for archers,
but there is only one trace of such a demand, a writ of March 5, ordering the Mayor
and Sheriffs of London to postpone the mobilisation of three hundred and twenty-five
archers from Sunday in mid-Lent till fifteen days after Easter (*Creçy and Calais*,
p. 70). But on February 10 London had been asked to send no *archers* but five
hundred *armati*. Yet that the summons to the towns to send *armati* meant a request
for hobilars is shown by a writ of May 25, 1347, stating that seven named persons
had been "*chosen to serve as hobilars*" by the vill of St. Albans, and with two others
from Watford, had sailed with the king, and were still serving abroad. Now St.
Albans is rated at eight *armati* and Watford at three in the "reduced lists" of
March. Allowing for casualties in the year's campaign it is clear that these persons
represent the requisitioned men of March 1346.

[3] Of the cities London was originally assessed at a hundred men-at-arms and
five hundred *armati*; Norwich at one hundred and twenty *armati*; Bristol at sixty;
Lynn, fifty; Lincoln and Coventry, forty each; Oxford, Winchester, St. Edmundsbury, Hereford, Shrewsbury, Salisbury, and Exeter, thirty each; Northampton,

spearmen and half archers—though archers had in earlier generations been rare in North Wales. With them went, as part of the following of the Prince of Wales, a hundred bowmen from Cheshire. The Welsh Marcher Lords were assessed at another three thousand three hundred and fifty men, half spearmen, half archers, and not all archers as we might have expected from earlier precedents. It may be doubted whether such a large number as six thousand nine hundred Welsh was ever collected; for in the next year, at the siege of Calais, we find the English infantry contingents nearly five times the total of the Welsh, instead of only a bare thousand stronger, and this was in spite of the fact that the Welsh, no less than the English, contingents had been recruited by drafts since the previous year. It would be a fair guess to put them at four thousand five hundred in the Creçy army rather than at six thousand nine hundred.

Including perhaps a thousand hobilars, a handful of cross-bowmen and other small units, such as the king's personal retinue and guard, we may suppose that the whole army which set sail from Portsmouth may have numbered two thousand four hundred horse and twelve thousand foot.[1] This was a

twenty-five; Cambridge, Canterbury, Chichester, Colchester, Gloucester, Worcester, Reading, and Bodmin, twenty each; the others vary from fifteen down to the modest two of places like Luton, Hungerford, Frome, and Yeovil.

The completely countermanded contingents were those of Bristol, Lynn, Chichester, Canterbury, Maidstone, Ipswich, Exeter, and several smaller towns.

The partly countermanded contingents were those of Norwich (reduced from one hundred and twenty to sixty men), Lincoln (forty to twenty), Northampton (twenty-five to twelve), St. Edmundsbury (thirty to fifteen), Wells and Ely (fifteen to eight), Stamford (twelve to six), and very many more smaller places (*Creçy and Calais*, pp. 70–71).

Is it possible that the king recognised that *armati* were less useful than archers, and so left many at home? And is the above-recorded diminution of contingents the result of such an idea, rather than of the scare of French invasion? And may we possibly consider the three hundred and twenty-five unexpected London *archers* named in the last note as being possibly a composition for the five hundred London *armati* originally asked for?

At the siege of Calais in the next year only five hundred hobilars were present, a considerable diminution from the number which must have taken the field in June 1346, when the urban *armati* were added to the hobilars of the assessments. This looks as if the arm had been judged inferior, and archers substituted.

[1] Including among the foot both hobilars, who were but mounted spearmen, and the mounted archers. For neither fought on horseback, though they had nags to carry them to the field. It is not quite safe to take hobilars and *armati* as interchangeable terms. For sometimes *armati* seems to be used as a general word to cover all infantry not archers.

very formidable force, since in the " retinues " at least there were already a large number of professional soldiers of all ranks and arms, trained in the wars of Scotland, Flanders, and Brittany.

At the moment of sailing, the general impression on board the fleet had been that the expedition was destined for Guienne, where the Earl of Derby had been calling for succour. But, much to the surprise of the army, the king, when well out of sight of land, sent orders round the squadron to steer for Cape La Hogue, as he was about to invade Normandy. Strategical reasons might conceivably have dictated such an invasion. Edward might have purposed to land as near as possible to Paris, and to make a dash at the capital, with the object of doing something to justify his claim to the French crown. On the other hand, he might have aimed at a conquest of Normandy or some part of it—the projecting peninsula of the Cotentin, perhaps—in order to secure a firm basis of operations for future attacks on France. Or, again, he might have aimed merely at causing such a diversion in the north as should compel the French to abandon their pressure upon the Earl of Derby in Aquitaine.[1] But Edward's conduct of the campaign shows no proof that any of these rational schemes was definitely formulated in his mind, and the expedition finally assumed the character of a chivalrous adventure, or of a great raid of defiance pushed deep into France to provoke its king.

Edward landed at La Hogue on July 22, and marched at a leisurely pace [2] through Normandy for twenty-eight days, wasting the countryside, spoiling open towns, and accumulating much plunder, but making no attempt to secure any hold on the land by seizing and garrisoning its fortresses. The only important place which fell into his hands was Caen, a rich but unwalled town, which was captured on the 26th of July, after

[1] This is the version given by Froissart (4th redaction in Kervyn de Lettenhove's edition): he makes the Norman exile, Godfrey of Harcourt, persuade the king to attack Normandy merely because of its wealth and defencelessness. Edward perseveres in his plan of sailing to Gascony, till Harcourt points out that a foray into Northern France will probably cause the French to raise the siege of Aiguillon and evacuate Guienne. It is impossible to verify the story.

[2] e.g. on July 26 he marched only three miles, on July 24 only five : he halted five days after taking Caen, July 26–31, and three more at Lisieux. For the itinerary and its dates, carefully worked out, see the excellent notes in Maunde Thompson's edition of Baker of Swinbrook, pp. 255, 256.

a severe engagement, in which the militia of Normandy was scattered, and the Counts of Eu and Tancarville, the Constable and Chamberlain of France, were taken prisoners, with more than a hundred knights of their following. Pushing eastward, the king made a movement on Rouen, but he found all the bridges of the Lower Seine broken, and could not harm the city. Philip of France, on receiving news of the English invasion, had called out the whole ban and arrière-ban of his realm. He had sent for aid to the army of his son John, who was facing the Earl of Derby in Guienne, and had ordered a large body of Genoese crossbowmen, who lay on board his fleet at Harfleur, to come to his assistance. Breaking all the bridges of the Seine, he hoped to confine the ravages of Edward to Western Normandy until he should be able to muster a force large enough to justify him in advancing against the English.

Finding the Lower Seine impassable, and knowing that a great army was gathering at Paris, King Edward had now to make up his mind what course to pursue. As it would appear, his policy was settled for him by a strange piece of indiscipline on the part of his fleet. Permission had been given for many vessels to return to England with sick, wounded, and the spoils of Normandy. When these sailed, the rest followed them without leave, thus deserting their master. Meanwhile, King Philip's host was growing larger day by day, and ere long he would be able to take the offensive with a vast superiority of numbers. Nor was there now any chance of catching Paris inadequately garrisoned, as there might have been if Edward had hurried on after his landing without stopping to plunder Normandy.

The English king therefore was forced to plunge into a very dangerous adventure. It was hopeless to think of conquering all Northern France, and it was necessary to get into touch with a friendly base of operations. The choice was between Brittany and Flanders, and the last was chosen, probably because Edward had just received information that his allies the Flemings had crossed the frontier and laid siege to Bethune. To join them it was necessary to cross the Seine and the Somme, both formidable obstacles, and to march past Paris, where the enemy was known to be in force. Edward took the risk, and pushed across the Isle de France, wasting the country, and burning several open towns. He found all the Seine bridges broken, as he tried each on his way up-stream, till he was getting quite close to Paris, where he was told that King Philip had now the best part of a hundred thousand men under arms, camped on the plain of St. Denis. The figure is no doubt fantastic, but the force was a heavy one.

King Philip had grown so strong that he sent a message of defiance to the English, and bade them meet him in the open field if they dared, offering to fight on whichever bank of the Seine they might prefer. Such a proposal must have been a sore temptation to the chivalrous spirit of Edward, but the risk was too great to allow him to accept it. Putting it aside, he hastily repaired the broken bridge of Poissy (near St. Germain-en-Laye) and crossed to the northern bank of the Seine. A great body of the communal militia of Amiens and other northern French towns came up while he was completing his bridge, but they were beaten off with loss, and the English were able to start on their march northward, before King Philip and his main army could reach them (Aug. 13–14). The time for leisurely movement was now past, and in four days Edward pushed on nearly sixty miles, with the French not far behind him. He was now nearing the greatest obstacle that lay in his path—the broad river Somme and the long line of peat-bogs which border its banks. Edward sent on his two marshals, the Earl of Warwick and Godfrey of Harcourt, to find a suitable place for his crossing. A disagreeable surprise awaited him : the marshals made four separate attempts to force a passage—at Pont-à-Remy, Fontaine-sur-Somme, Loucq, and Picquigny. They were foiled at every point : the bridges were broken, and the fords held by the levies of Picardy in such strength that it was impossible to cross. Nor was this all : King Philip and his host had marched parallel with the English, and their van had reached Amiens. Thus Edward found himself shut into a triangle, whose three sides were closed by the Somme, the sea, and the French army. The position was most hazardous : it seemed that Edward must turn and fight, in a position from which there was no retreat.

But, just as he was beginning to despair, he learned that there was one more chance to be tried. The lowest ford on the Somme was that of Blanchetaque below Abbeville, where the river grows tidal. Twice a day the ford was passable for a few hours, but it was guarded by two thousand Picard men-at-arms under Godemar de Fay and a large body of crossbowmen. Under the guidance of a peasant, who was tempted by the bait of a hundred gold nobles, Edward marched down to the passage. His knights entered the water and made for the farther bank, while the archers kept up a long-distance flight of arrows over their heads. The Picards made a stout defence, but were beaten off after a hard struggle, and the English poured over the ford in such haste that King Philip only came up in time to capture a little of their baggage. The tide then rose, the French could not follow, and Edward was saved (Aug. 24).

Battle of Creçy, August 26, 1346.

He had now secured a clear retreat on Flanders, and made two short marches, which took him to Creçy-en-Ponthieu, where he halted. No longer solicitous about being surrounded, he had resolved to face about, and strike a blow at the French if they should pursue him too rashly. At Creçy he had found a position which pleased his eye, and he announced to his host that " being now in Ponthieu, his own inheritance,[1] he should await his enemies there, and take such fortune as God might send him."

Ponthieu is a country of rolling downs, which slope down to the course of two small streams, the Maye and Authie. The downs are for the most part low and gentle elevations of not more than a hundred and fifty or two hundred feet in height. The district is, except at one point, rather bare of trees, though each village is set in the midst of its own elms and orchards. But one great wood, the forest of Creçy, stretches across the district and forms its most prominent natural feature. The forest of Creçy lies due north of Abbeville, and has a length of some ten miles and a breadth of four or five. It forms an impassable military obstacle, and the two great roads which run northward from Abbeville to Hesdin and Montreuil turn aside to avoid it. A single narrow path, however, cuts through the heart of the wood, and this line Edward had taken, conscious

---

[1] The county of Ponthieu had been the dowry of Eleanor of Castile, the wife of Edward I., whose mother Joanna had been Countess of Aumâle and Ponthieu in her own right. But Edward III.'s own mother Isabella had also a charge of two thousand crowns a year upon it in her marriage settlement, so that the king's statement was doubly true.

that his adversary would hardly dare to pursue him along it. Having reached the northern side of the wood, the English lay on the banks of the Maye, above the little town of Creçy, " subter forestam de Creçy," as the chronicler puts it. The French king could pursue only by two roads ; and one of these, that through the wood, was practically barred to him by the impossibility of deploying from the single narrow path in the face of the enemy. It was probable that he would, as indeed he ultimately did, take the Abbeville-Hesdin road, which turns the eastern end of the forest, and comes near to the English position when it reaches the village of Fontaine-sur-Maye.

Edward had therefore to face south-eastward to await the approach of his enemy, and just outside Creçy town there lies a position eminently suited for a defensive battle. The rolling hills between the Maye and the Authie are here cut by a lateral depression or cross-valley, running from south-west to north-east. It is the best defined break in the line of downs which forms the watershed between the two little rivers : for this reason the engineers of to-day have utilised it when they built the Abbeville - Dompierre railway. At no other point could the rolling slopes be crossed at such an easy gradient. The little valley is about one and a quarter mile long : on each side of it a gentle ascent rises to the main level of the downs. When this ascent is climbed, to right or left, the pedestrian finds himself on an undulating plateau. On that to the right (or east) lies the village of Estrées ; on that to the left (or west) lies the village of Wadicourt. Each of these little places is set in the midst of its belt of trees, and barely shows a few roofs and chimneys through the greenery. South of Estrées lies the ground where the French army formed up for battle ; Wadicourt is the northern end of the English position. Creçy, which gave its name to the fight, lies low, pinched in between the southern descent of the Wadicourt downs and the little river Maye, a quarter of a mile behind the English line. A bowshot beyond the town, and on the very edge of the water, commences the forest of Creçy, a fine well-grown wood, covering the whole southern horizon.

The Creçy-Wadicourt position is bounded to the south, not by the Maye,—an insignificant thread of water, fordable any-where,—but by the thick, impenetrable forest ; for there is no sufficient space for an enemy to thrust himself along the river-bank between the downs and the wood so as to turn the southern flank of the English line. At the northern end, at Wadicourt, the protection is not so strong : the village and its straggling orchards are sufficient to prevent any attempt to attack from the immediate flank ; but there is nothing to hinder an enemy approaching from the south-east from making a wide sweep along the summit of the plateau in the direction of Ligescourt. It is possible that in 1346 the country north of Wadicourt was more wooded than it is now, but there is only the vaguest evidence to prove it.[1] As things actually went, the French arrived and attacked in such disorder that they made no attempt either properly to reconnoitre or to turn the position.

Edward's army had seen some fighting since it landed at La Hogue, and had suffered, as all armies must, from the wear and tear of two months' active campaigning.[2] But it cannot have been very greatly diminished in numbers, and we shall prob-ably not be far out if we estimate it at two thousand men-at-arms, five thousand English bowmen, and three thousand five hundred Welsh, half of these last archers, who would be serving with the English, the other half spearmen,[3] plus some five hundred or six hundred hobilars.

The host was divided into the usual three " battles." Two formed the front line, the third a reserve. On the right wing lay the Prince of Wales, with eight hundred men-at-arms, two thousand archers, English and Welsh, and perhaps one thousand spearmen from his own Principality,[4] probably three thousand

[1] The Valenciennes Chronicle, which seems to have no good topographical knowledge, says that Edward was encamped on the edge of the wood which lies between Creçy and La Broie. This is probably a mistake for the wood which lies between Creçy and Abbeville. No other chronicler mentions a great wood to the north.

[2] Michael of Northburgh says in his contemporary letter, written from Calais just after the fight, that from Caen to Creçy the army lived by foraging, "à grand domage de nos gens." Many sick, including the Earl of Huntingdon, had gone home on the fleet.

[3] The figures of Froissart's second edition are two thousand men-at-arms, four thousand two hundred archers, and a thousand Welsh. That the last number is wrong we may pretty certainly conclude, from the fact that in the muster-rolls in Rymer we learn that the king summoned out six thousand Welsh. They may well have been reduced by now, but certainly not to one thousand.

[4] The contingent of the Principality, as opposed to that of the Marches, had been summoned three thousand five hundred and fifty strong, but we may doubt if more than two thousand, half archers, half spearmen, were now in line.

eight hundred all told. The men-at-arms, all on foot, were
formed in a solid line—perhaps six or eight deep—in the
centre of the " battle." The archers stood in two equal
divisions to the right and left of the men-at-arms : Baker of
Swinbrook, the best authority for the battle on the English side,
remarks that " they had their post given them not in front of
the men-at-arms, but on each flank of them, as wings, so that
they should not get in their way, nor have to face the central
charge of the French, but might shoot them down from the
side."[1] He adds that while waiting for the French the archers
dug many small holes, a foot square and a foot deep,—like the
Scottish "pottes" at Bannockburn, — to cause the French
cavalry to stumble if they chanced to charge in upon them—
which, as he adds, the French did not do. Those of the Welsh
infantry who bore spears were placed behind the archers, not
in the front line.

The prince's division occupied the hillside from the point
where it sinks down to the banks of the Maye as far as half-way
to Wadicourt. North of them, but somewhat drawn back, so as
to form an échelon rather than a parallel line with him, lay the
Earls of Arundel and Northampton with the second " battle."
This was somewhat smaller than the first, consisting of five
hundred men-at-arms and twelve hundred archers : we do not
hear that any Welshmen were attached to it. But very probably the South Welsh archers may have been here, a thousand
strong. It was drawn up in the same array as the prince's
division, with the dismounted men-at-arms in the centre and
the archers on the wings. From the left rear of the first battle
it reached as far as the enclosures of the village of Wadicourt.[2]

The king himself with the reserve lay on the plateau above
the slope, in front of the wood of La Grange : he seems to have
stationed himself in the rear of his son's battle, nearer to Creçy

---

[1] Baker of Swinbrook, pp. 83, 84 : "Effodiebant foramina . . . . ut si, *quod
abfuit*, equites Gallorum nimis fuissent insecuti, equi ad foramina titubassent."

[2] What are we to make of Froissart's puzzling statement that the English archers
were drawn up "in the fashion of a *herse* with the men-at-arms *au fond de la
bataille*"? On the whole I am inclined to agree with Mr. H. B. George's theory,
stated in his *British Battles*, that the English line was compared to a harrow, the
archers making the projecting points, and the knights lying a little to their rear.
Certainly, the point where Prince Edward's archers touched Warwick's must have
presented an angle to the approaching French. My plan of the battle (Plate XXVI.)
will make the array clear. The line would have three projections, and two retiring
spaces where the men-at-arms stood, hence the comparison to a harrow (*herse*).

than to Wadicourt. His corps consisted of seven hundred men-at-arms, two thousand archers, and those of the Welsh spear-men who were not with the prince, perhaps a thousand strong. Presumably the hobilars, five or six hundred strong, joined the men-at-arms with their spears, and were distributed in all three divisions. Edward himself took post on the windmill at the southern edge of the plateau, the spot from which the whole battlefield can be best embraced with a single glance.[1]

Behind the English line, on each side of the road to Liges-court, the whole baggage of the army had been parked in a square enclosure, with the horses tethered inside. A very slender guard was told off for its protection.[2]

The better part of the baronage of England had followed Edward over-seas : we read that in the right-hand battle the prince had under him Thomas Beauchamp Earl of Warwick, John de Vere Earl of Oxford, and the Lords Stafford, Cobham, Latimer, Willoughby, Scales, Lovel, Mohun, Clifford, Burg-hersh, Bourchier. In the second corps lay Richard Fitzalan Earl of Arundel, William Bohun Earl of Northampton, and the Lords Say, Fitzwalter, Audley, Dudley, and Basset. In the king's reserve were the Bishop of Durham, Robert de Ufford Earl of Suffolk, William Montacute Earl of Salisbury, and the rest of the barons present.

On the same morning that King Edward drew up his host on the hillside of Creçy, his adversary had started from Abbe-ville to continue the pursuit. He had no knowledge whether the English intended to fight or to continue their retreat ; indeed he had lost touch of them since they crossed the Somme at Blanchetaque. Hence it came to pass that he started forth on the Abbeville-Montreuil road, to go round the western side of the forest of Creçy. It was only after the head of the army had reached Braye, some eight miles north of Abbeville, that the news arrived that the English had crossed the forest and thrown themselves on to a more easterly and inland road. Philip on receiving this intelligence sent off in haste four knights, who were charged to gallop round the eastern end of the forest

---

[1] Walking carefully over the field, I found no spot commanding such a good general view as that where lie the foundations of the ruined mill, now no more than a ring mound and a few stones. Local tradition still calls it the Moulin d'Edouard.

[2] It is certain that the two or three foreign chroniclers who speak of the waggon park as a part of the English line (e.g. Villani) are wholly wrong. None of the good authorities place it anywhere save in the rear.

and search for the enemy.   Meanwhile, the army was wheeled
to the right, and set to march by a cross-path on to the Abbeville-Hesdin road.   The French had no conception that King
Edward was waiting for them only a few miles away ;   they
marched in great disorder, and straggled over the whole face of
the country.   The rear, indeed, had not yet left Abbeville when
the van was at Braye.

The four knights who had been sent out to seek for the
English had no sooner reached the village of Fontaine than they
suddenly came in sight of the whole English army, not retreating
(as they had expected) along the Hesdin road, but drawn up
in its three battles on the hillside by Wadicourt.   Hastily
returning to King Philip, they informed him of what they had
discovered.   Their spokesman, Alard de Baseilles, a knight of
Luxemburg, who followed the King of Bohemia, besought him
at once to halt his host and defer the battle till the morrow.
For the head of the vanguard was now but a mile or two from
the English position, and would soon come in sight of it, though
the host was in disorder, neither arrayed for battle nor at all
expecting it.   The French king fully saw the danger of running
blindfold upon the English position, with his host strung out
for miles upon the roads behind.   He sent orders for the van
to halt, and for the troops in the rear to advance no farther,
but make ready to encamp.   For the afternoon was now far
advanced, and vespers were at hand.

Philip, however, had failed to take into account the rashness
and insubordination of a feudal host.   " The king's orders were
soon passed round among his lords, but none of them would
turn back, for each wished to be first in the field.   The van
would not retire because they had got so far to the front, but
they halted.   But those behind them kept riding forward, and
would not stop, saying that they would get as far to the front as
their fellows, and that from mere pride and jealousy.   And when
the vaward saw the others pushing on, they would not be left
behind, and without order or array they pressed forward, till they
came in sight of the English.   Great shame was it to see such
disobedience, and better would it have been for all if they had
taken the counsel of that good knight who advised the king to
stay his march.   For when the van came suddenly in face of
the enemy, they stopped, and then drew back a space in such
disarray that they pressed in upon those in their rear, so that all

behind thought that the battle was begun, and the vaward already routed.   And the foot-soldiery of the cities and com- munes, who covered the roads behind as far as Abbeville, and were more than twenty thousand strong, drew their swords, and began to cry, ' Death to those English traitors !   Not one of them shall every get back to England.' " [1]

In consequence of the utter confusion in which the French arrived in the presence of their enemy, it resulted that they never succeeded in forming any orderly and definite line of attack.   The host had been told off, before leaving Abbeville, into a number of battles—nine or ten according to some authorities, five according to others.   But these divisions were not repro- duced on the field, for each contingent scrambled to the front as best it might, and took post where it found a gap.   The only vestige of order which remained was that the picked infantry who had marched with the " vaward " battle—the Genoese crossbowmen disembarked from the fleet—had got forward to their proper place, and had time to deploy south of the village of Estrées on the slope that faced the English position. Behind them was nothing but a seething mass of feudal contin- gents jostling each other and seeking to thrust themselves forward as best they might, while the communal militia in the rear was still crowding up to join the horse.

What the exact strength of the French army was it will never be possible to ascertain.   That it was at least thrice that of the English is clear ;   the lowest estimate for its cavalry given by any chronicler of repute is twelve thousand men-at- arms.[2]   Froissart and other non-contemporary writers raise this figure to twenty thousand.   The crossbowmen are called six thousand strong—though the fifteen thousand given by some writers is of course a ridiculous overstatement of their force. The communal militia was certainly present in force, and the total muster of the foot was swollen by a number of mercenaries other than the Genoese, the " bidets " of whom Jean le Bel, Froissart, and the rest make mention, as well as by those of the retainers of the feudal chiefs who did not serve on horseback. We can hardly state the whole host at less than thirty thousand strong ;   it included not only the whole levy of Northern France,

[1] Froissart's narrative is too vivid to omit, though we have more contemporary chroniclers to help us.

[2] Villani's figure, and that of Northburgh in the letter from Calais.

but some portion of the army which had been serving in the south. The names of many chiefs who had been operating against the Earl of Derby in Guienne, two months before, are to be found among the list of the slain or the captives of Creçy. Nor was it French forces only which had taken the field ; there had come to Philip's aid John King of Bohemia, and his son Charles, afterwards emperor, who already styled himself King of the Romans. They had brought not only a contingent of Bohemian and German knights, but a large body of men-at-arms from their ancestral duchy of Luxemburg. Other subjects of the Holy Roman Empire were present in great numbers under the Duke of Lorraine and the Counts of Namur and Hainault, of Salm, Montbéliard, Blamont, and Saarbrücken. James, the exiled King of Majorca, had also come to fight for his host, King Philip. Of the vassals of the French crown there were present the Counts of Flanders, Blois, Alençon, Aumâle, Auxerre, Sancerre, Harcourt, St. Pol, Roussy, Dampierre, Beaujeu, Forez, the Dauphin of Auvergne, and many scores of barons of more or less note—all the nobility, in fact, of Northern and Central France.

When King Philip struggled to the front, he found his army so close to the English line that it was impossible to draw it back with safety. The whole face of the earth between Estrées and Fontaine was covered by the weltering mass, but the more advanced troops were forming up in some semblance of array on the hillside south of Estrées. Despairing of his power to get the chaos into order, or carried away by his anger and vexation at seeing the English army sitting quietly on the slope by Wadicourt, Philip gave orders for the vaward to move on. The long line of crossbowmen under the two Genoese condottieri, Odone Doria and Carlo Grimaldi, prepared to open the fight, and a deep mass of men-at-arms under the Counts of Alençon and Flanders formed up in their rear. The rest of the host was still in utter disarray, presenting no semblance of any division between foot and horse, main-battle or rearward.

The hour of vespers was now past, and the French were moving towards the edge of the Estrées plateau, when a sudden thunderstorm swept up from the sea and burst just over the field. The combatants on both sides were drenched to the skin, and the darkness caused the advancing columns to halt. But in a few minutes the clouds rolled by, and the evening sun burst forth with great brilliance, shining brightly in the eyes of the French army.[1]

At once the crossbowmen began to descend the valley which lies between Estrées and Wadicourt. Twice they halted, uttered a shout of defiance, and saw to the alignment of their advance. Then they moved on for the third time, cheered once more, and began to let fly their bolts at the enemy. It was at long range, and English accounts say that they slew hardly a man, their missiles falling short a few yards in front of the mark. Far otherwise was it with the answering volley. The English archers took one pace forward, drew their arrows to the head, and shot so fast and close that it looked as if a snowstorm were beating upon the line of Genoese. Their shafts nailed the helmet to the head, pierced brigandine and breast, and laid low well-nigh the whole front line of the assailants in the first moment of the conflict. The crossbowmen only stood their ground for a few minutes ; their losses were so fearful that some flung away their weapons, others cut their bowstrings, and all reeled backwards up the slope which they had just descended.[2]

The Count of Alençon and his horsemen failed to perceive the plight in which the Genoese had been placed ; they imagined that treason or cowardice was driving them back. Instead of opening intervals in their line to let the routed infantry pass to the rear, they came pricking hastily down the slope, crying, " Away with these faint-hearted rabble ! they do but block our advance," and crashed into the panic-stricken mob which was recoiling towards them. Then, finding themselves caught in the press and unable to get on, they drew their swords and began to slash right and left among the miserable Genoese, to force their way to the front. This mad attempt to ride down their own infantry was fatal to the front line of the French chivalry. In spite of themselves they were brought to a stand at the foot

[1] Only one chronicler, and he not one of the best, the second continuer of William de Nangis, mentions the often-repeated allegation that the shooting of the Genoese was spoiled by the wetting of the crossbow cords in the storm.

[2] We need not lay much stress on the statements of Villani and the *Grandes Chroniques de France* that the English had two or three small cannon in their front line, which scared the Genoese and the horses of the men-at-arms. The English had a few cannon in 1346, and (as will be seen in Chapter II. of Book X.) King Edward ordered some small pieces, *ribauldequins*, to be shipped to France, but we have no proof that they went. Moreover, no English chronicler mentions guns at Crecy.

of the slope, where the whole mass of horse and foot rocked helplessly to and fro under a constant hail of arrows from the English archery. " For the bowmen let fly among them at large, and did not lose a single shaft, for every arrow told on horse or man, piercing head, or arm, or leg among the riders and sending the horses mad. For some stood stock-still, and others rushed sideways, and most of all began backing in spite of their masters, and some were rearing or tossing their heads at the arrows, and others when they felt the bit threw themselves down. So the knights in the first French battle fell, slain or sore stricken, almost without seeing the men who slew them."

Only a few of the men-at-arms of the Counts of Alençon and Flanders succeeded in piercing through the press and drawing near the English line. It is doubtful whether a single rider reached it, and got to handstrokes with the enemy. The battle, however, was but commencing ; the main body of the French host made no attempt to allow the vaward to draw off and clear the way, but pushed down the slope to rescue them. In the second charge fell King John of Bohemia, who, though blind, or nearly so, had refused to hold back. He bade the knights at his bridle-rein " lead him so far forward that he should have one fair blow at the English." He had his desire : his followers succeeded in piercing through the press and reaching the line of the Prince of Wales' men-at-arms, by " coasting along the archers," so that they were able to ride in upon the English spears. But their charge was but an isolated effort, and the whole party fell dead around the king, save two squires who cut their way home to tell of his fate. Charles of Luxemburg, who had been separated from his father early in the battle, left the field unharmed, and survived to wear the Imperial crown for thirty years.

The battle of Crecy was but a long series of reckless and ill-ordered charges, such as that which John of Bohemia led. After the first onset there was no attempt to set the main-battle and rearward in array, or to arrange for a simultaneous onset all along the English line. As each body of French knights worked its way to the front, it launched itself at the English, and soon fell back discomfited into the seething mass behind. By far the greater part of the loss was due to the arrows of the English archery, who succeeded in maintaining their position all through the fight, and kept up a deadly flank discharge on each

wave of assailants that surged forward.   The main assault of
the French seems in every case to have been directed against the
English men-at-arms : as they advanced, the arrows beat upon
the outer riders and slew or dismounted them, but the central
section of each squadron, protected by their fellows' bodies from
the flanking fire, sometimes reached the front of the prince's or
Arundel's dismounted knights and pressed hard upon them.
The main stress seems to have fallen on the southern " battle,"
probably because the enemy emerging from the Fontaine-
Abbeville road made haste to strike at the nearest foe.   On one
occasion [1] at least an attack was pushed home with such
dangerous vigour that those about the prince sent a hasty
request for succour to the king.   Edward, commanding the
whole battlefield from his post at the windmill, was better able
to judge of the general aspect of the fight, and refused to move
his reserve, though he consented to send down thirty knights
under the Bishop of Durham [2] to strengthen his son's division.

The prince's battle, though hard pressed at this time, did
not yield a foot, and the stress which lay upon them was
apparently drawn off when the Earls of Arundel and Northampton pushed forward their corps, which had hitherto lain
somewhat farther up the hillside, and aligned it with the first
battle on a level front.   As the dusk advanced, the assaults of
the French grew more and more haphazard and partial ; but
the barons of the rear divisions still persisted in pushing to the
front and trying their fortune.   A few seem to have ridden in
among the archers, and Froissart records the fate of a Hainault
knight who pierced their line at one point, rode unharmed
along their rear, and galloped back through a gap towards the
French, before he was shot down and disabled. [3]   But the late-
comers, as well as those who opened the battle, seem to have
spent themselves in trying to ride down the men-at-arms rather
than in the more rational attempt to dispose of the bowmen.

From first to last the English counted that fifteen [4] or
sixteen [5] separate and successive attacks were delivered against

---

[1] This is the time when the prince, according to Baker, was actually beaten to his
knees, and to which the celebrated saying in Froissart about " the boy must win his
spurs " belongs.

[2] Baker of Swinbrook, p. 84, and the Valenciennes Chronicle, p. 232.

[3] Froissart in K. de Lettenhove's edition, v. p. 61.

[4] Baker of Swinbrook, p. 84.

[5] Northburgh's letter from Calais in Avesbury.

them, all with equal ill success. The fighting lasted long after dusk—indeed it was not till midnight, according to one trust-worthy authority, that the last broken bands of the French ceased to dash themselves against the impenetrable line. But since the sun set the more faint-hearted of the enemy had gradually begun to withdraw themselves from the field, and as the night wore on the host melted away, and Philip of France at last found himself with no more than seventy lances beside him as he rode up and down the slope below Estrées and tried to organise one more hopeless assault on the hostile position. Then John Count of Hainault laid his hand on the king's bridle and led him to the rear, to take shelter for the night in the castle of La Broye, six miles behind the battlefield. Philip had had a horse killed beneath him by one arrow, and had received a slight wound in the neck from another.

The English, well content to have beaten off their enemies, and not fully conscious of the fearful damage they had wrought, lay down in their ranks to snatch a few hours of repose before the dawn. The morning of the 27th was misty, and it was impossible to see what had become of the French army, though the piles of corpses in the valley at the foot of the English slope and on the hillside below Estrées showed clearly enough that the enemy had suffered tremendous losses. Accordingly the king bade the Earls of Suffolk and Northampton take five hundred men-at-arms and two thousand bowmen, and push forward on to the French position and beyond it. This reconnaissance led to a sharp skirmish: the earls found still lingering about the field many of the bodies of communal militia, who had come up too late to take part in yesterday's battle, as well as a force of men-at-arms under the Archbishop of Rouen and the Grand Prior of the Hospitallers who had only just arrived from Normandy. Both these corps were scattered with much slaughter: it is said that as many as two thousand of them fell.[1]

When the last of the French had been driven away, King Edward allowed his army to break their ranks and strip the slain. The heralds went round to identify the nobler dead, and found that one thousand five hundred and forty-two lords and knights had fallen:[2] the number of those not of gentle blood who

---

[1] Baker of Swinbrook, p. 85.
[2] Northburgh's letter in Avesbury, p. 369 of Rolls Series edition.

had perished was never clearly ascertained ; chroniclers' wild guesses vary from ten thousand upward. But it is clear that the main loss fell on the men-at-arms, and that the infantry, save the Genoese, were little engaged, so that their casualties may have been moderate. On the other hand, the English had lost no more than two knights, one squire, some forty men-at-arms and archers,[1] and a few dozen Welsh, who, as one eye-witness[2] says, " fatue se exposuerunt " by running out from the line between two charges to slay or plunder the disabled knights who were lying about at the foot of the English slope.

The most notable among the slain in the defeated army were the King of Bohemia, the Duke of Lorraine, the Counts of Flanders, Alençon, Auxerre, Harcourt, Sancerre, Blois, Grandpré, Salm, Blamont, and Forez. Among the few prisoners were the Bishop of Noyon and the Archdeacon of Paris, who had unwisely thrust themselves among the fighting men. The Counts of Aumâle, Montbéliard, and Rosenberg were borne wounded from the field : the last-named died of his wounds two months later.

The fight of Creçy was a revelation to the Western world. The English but a few years before had no special fame in war :[3] their victories over the Welsh and Scots were hardly known on the Continent ; their French wars under Henry III. and Edward I. had brought them no glory. It was contrary to all expectation and likelihood that with odds of three to one against them they should easily discomfit the most formidable chivalry of Europe. But the moral of their victory was not fully grasped at first. It was obvious that they had won partly by their splendid archery, partly by the steadiness of their dismounted men-at-arms. The real secret was that King Edward had known how to combine the two forms of military efficiency. But that it was the combination which had been

---

[1] Oddly enough, a writ to his executors gives us the name of this squire, Robert Brent, of Audley's retinue (*Creçy and Calais*, p. 125). The knights are unidentifiable, though we have a list of forty who died during the expedition and the siege of Calais—mainly at the latter (*Creçy and Calais*, pp. 280–281).

[2] Wynkeley's letter, Avesbury, p. 216.

[3] See Jean le Bel, *Chroniques*, i. p. 154. "Encore sachez que quant ce noble roy Edoward premiérement reconquist Angleterre en sa joeunesse, on ne tenait rien des Anglais, communeurent : et ne parloit-on point de leur proesse ne de leur hardiesse : ne ils ne sçavoient armer de plates, ne de bachines à barbière . . . Or ont-ils appris les armes au temps de ce noble roy Edoward, qui souvent les a mis en œuvre, que le sont les plus nobles et les plus fresques combatants qu'on sache."

his stroke of genius, was not altogether understood by his enemies. They dreaded the English arrow for the future ; they copied the English practice of sending the horses to the rear. But they did not show, by any improvement in their tactics, that they had grasped the meaning of the English victory.

CHAPTER III

FROM CREÇY TO POICTIERS, 1346–1356

IN modern war a general who had just inflicted a crushing defeat on the main hostile army would be expected to turn his victory to some strategic account—more especially, perhaps, when he had won his victory by a new tactical device, as startling and demoralising to the enemy as was the twentieth-century introduction of poison-gas or tanks on the battlefield King Philip's army had gone to pieces—nothing lay between Edward and Paris, Rouen, or any other goal that he might have selected.

But here came in an essential difference between fourteenth-century and twentieth-century war. There still existed that overwhelming superiority of the defensive over the offensive in the matter of siegecraft of which we have spoken in an earlier chapter. All that Edward had won at Creçy was the power to devastate as much of the open land of Northern France as he pleased, or else the right to lay siege to any first-class city that he might select—which assuredly would be a long business. With a wearied army, provisions only gettable by marauding, and no near base of operations, he opted—and reasonably from a fourteenth-century point of view—in favour of placing himself in touch with the friendly Flemings, and laying siege to Calais. The town was close to allied soil—Dunkirk, still a part of the county of Flanders, was only twenty miles away. And Calais was not only the nearest French port to England, but also the headquarters of a privateering system which made the Straits of Dover, and many a sea-mile on each side of it, unsafe for English merchant shipping.

Edward resolved to make the capture of this highly important seaport the reward of his recent victory. He marched thither undisturbed, came in front of it on September 4, and opened up his communication with the Flemings. He then threw a line of circumvallation round Calais, settled down in it with the best contingents of his army, and was soon in touch with a fleet from the Cinque Ports, which took over to Dover many sick and wounded, some valuable French prisoners, a quantity of miscellaneous plunder, and a great number of knights and barons and esquires who got leave for a long furlough. Others of all ranks followed *recreationis causa* — the departure of many being nothing less than desertion, as we learn from writs sent to sheriffs to hunt up the truants.

The places of the missing men were no more than filled up by drafts received from England. Long before Creçy orders had been sent over-seas to raise reinforcements, and some of them dropped in at intervals during the autumn months. But there were distractions—particularly the long-expected Scottish invasion of Northumbria, against which Edward had guarded by calling out no contingents from the counties beyond Trent for his French expedition. It had hung fire all through the summer, but took shape on a grand scale in October, when King David Bruce crossed the Border with a large army, and after capturing the Castle of Liddell made a fierce raid right across Northumberland and as far as the heart of the Palatinate of Durham. At Neville's Cross—quite close to the cathedral city—he was brought to action by the Northern barons in a fight of which we know lamentably little in the way of detail (October 17). It would seem, however, that the Scottish king was completely surprised by the rapid mobilisation of the enemy, and was attacked long before he expected to have to fight. An interesting light is thrown upon this fact by the muster-rolls of the English force called out to resist the invasion, which contain an enormous proportion of horsed archers as compared with foot archers.[1] The " hobilars " of the Northern counties were also of course mounted men, though they turned their nags loose when it came to battle. The English army was nominally under William de la Zouch, Archbishop of York, but really managed by the Lords Percy, Neville, and Mowbray, and by Gilbert Umphraville, the exiled Scottish Earl of Angus, son of the Earl who had fought so well at Dupplin and Halidon.

---

[1] Lancashire sent nine hundred and sixty horsed to two hundred and forty un-horsed archers.

It was only when a Scottish raiding party under Douglas, " the knight of Liddesdale," fell into, and was cut up by, the English van, a few miles from his camp, that King David realised that he was let in for a battle.   He took up a position on a hillside, among hedges and cuttings, which proved a snare, as they prevented the three corps of the Scottish army from keeping in close touch with each other.[1]   The array was the normal one—three great " schiltrons " of pikemen, among whom the knights mingled themselves, with some archers thrown out on front and flank.[2]   The " van," *i.e.* right wing, was led by the Earl of Moray, the centre by David himself, the left or rear-ward by Robert Stuart (afterwards king as Robert II.) and by Patrick Earl of March.   The English halted for some hours before the position, obviously to reconnoitre its possibilities of attack—though some insincere *pourparlers* sent in by the clergy took up time.   They appear finally to have assailed it in *échelon* formation, the left leading, while the right was " refused " and never got into serious action with the Scottish " rear-ward."   The English left, under Henry Percy and Ralph Neville, outflanked the Earl of Moray's " schiltron " with swarms of archers, who drove off the Scottish light troops, and then continued to empty their shafts into the mass of pikemen in deadly fashion, till it broke up—part left the field, part fell back on the king's corps.   It is said that Sir John Graham asked for a hundred horse, offering to do with them what Keith had done at Bannockburn—to disperse the archers by a flank charge,—but he could not obtain them from the king, and failed in a vain endeavour to carry out his idea with his own small retinue.   The English left then closed in upon the flank of the Scottish main-battle, while the centre, under the Arch-bishop's nominal leading, attacked it in front.   The matter was not entirely settled by archery, as the masses of spearmen were seriously engaged for some time at close quarters.   But the king's corps finally gave way, and was terribly cut up ; when they were seen to be losing ground, the left Scottish division under Stuart and March hastily left the field—the

---

[1] At least so say the *Scotichronicon*, xiv. 2, and Wyntoun, viii. 40.

[2] According to the Lanercost Chronicle, David had a large force—two thousand men-at-arms, twenty thousand "hobilars," *i.e.* spearmen who dismounted to fight, and ten thousand archers and miscellaneous infantry.   The figures are probably thrice too large.

English right under Lord Mowbray had apparently contented itself with " containing " them, probably deterred from close attack by the character of the ground.   The Lanercost Chronicle waxes sarcastic at the prudence of these two magnates, who, like St. Peter on the night of the Betrayal, " followed afar off " and abandoned their master.[1]   The slaughter among the beaten party was considerable—among the slain were the Earls of Moray and Strathearn, and three great officers of the Crown, David de la Hay the Constable, Robert Keith the Marshal, and Thomas Charteris the Chancellor.   But the prisoners were still more numerous.   They included the king—badly wounded by an arrow in the face—the Earls of Fife, Menteith, Wigtown, and Sutherland, Douglas of Liddesdale, and many scores of notable bannerets and knights.

This was a battle of somewhat different type from Dupplin or Halidon, since the English took the offensive, and the Scots acted on a purely defensive policy.   It might be compared to Falkirk, save for the important difference that the combination which ruined the Scots was that of spearman and archer, not that of horseman and archer.   But obviously it was essentially one of the class of battles in which the English won by dint of archery—it was the flank fire of the bowmen which rendered the frontal attack of the knights and hobilars on foot certain of success.   But details are much lacking—it is a pity that Baker of Swinbrook—so illuminating on Halidon and Dupplin —devotes only a short notice to this fight : he makes it clear, however, that there was much hand-to-hand fighting in the centre.

But to return to King Edward before Calais.   Much cheered by the news of Neville's Cross, which showed that the Scottish danger was at an end, he resolved to persist in the winter siege of the coveted seaport.   It was essentially a water-fortress, girt with wet ditches which made mining impossible, and by marshes where the soil was too soft to bear military engines suitable for battering work.   The garrison under John de Vienne, a knight of Burgundy, was obstinate and resolute, and the siege became a blockade by sea and land.   Such enterprises took up an enormous tale of weeks, and were costly to besiegers in the bad months of the year.   Though Edward hutted his men for the winter, we know that there

[1] Lanercost Chronicle, p. 380.

were many casualties from disease.[1] When it became clear that spring would come before the garrison was starved out, the king realised that he might look for a desperate attempt to relieve the place by all the forces that France could muster by land and sea. He prepared to resist any such enterprise by casting up works of contravallation, covering the approaches by road, and sent across to London for such store of cannon as he owned to place in them. But most especially did he press for the raising of reinforcements, and having got a liberal grant from Parliament, he was able to collect by May and June such an army as no Plantagenet had ever raised before. For some few weeks at Midsummer it would seem to have risen to as much as thirty-two thousand men—an almost incredible force for England to keep under arms even for a short emergency. To get this force together the Earl of Lancaster and a large retinue had been brought round from Guienne, several bannerets from the Scottish Border, and the Earl of Kildare from Ireland, while two German counts — Holstein and Freiberg—and certain other foreign auxiliaries had been hired. But the total number of foreigners was very small—not much over one thousand all told. The roll of the army, fortunately preserved in the accounts of Sir Walter de Wetewang, Treasurer of the Household, works out as follows :

The Prince of Wales	1	Centenars of foot		52
Earls [2]	10	Vintenars of foot		794
Bishop of Durham	1	Hobilars [spearmen with horses]		528
Two German counts	2	Archers, of whom 4025 mounted		20,076
Barons and bannerets	78	King's household yeomen, etc.		140
Knights	1066	German panzenars [mailed foot]		339
Esquires, sergeants, and banner-bearers of horse	4182	Crossbowmen		111
		Standard-bearers of foot		6
Total of horse	5340	Armourers		6
		Artificers (including 12 gunners)		339
		Welsh foot		4572
		Total of foot, etc.		26,963

General total, 32,303.[3]

[1] The tables in Wrottesley's *Crecy and Calais*, pp. 280-1, show that fifty-three tenants-in-chief died during the expedition of 1346-47, and of these very few fell at Crecy, and not many by the enemy's hand. Among the victims of disease were the Earl of Surrey and the Lords Lovel and Fauconberg.

[2] The earls were Lancaster, Northampton, Warwick, Arundel, Suffolk, Huntingdon, Oxford, Pembroke, Kildare, and Hugh Despencer, doubtfully classed by Wetewang as Earl of Gloucester apparently, though he was never confirmed in the title.

[3] The moderate number of foreign auxiliaries to be deducted from this total is only 1012, viz. :—

That this enormous and unparalleled force was kept together only for a few midsummer weeks, is sufficiently shown by the total of expenses disbursed by Wetewang, which is so comparatively modest as to show that during the greater part of the siege there must have been a much smaller army in the trenches. The rates of pay are interesting—the Prince of Wales received £1 per day, the Earls and the Bishop of Durham six shillings and eightpence each, the barons and bannerets four shillings each, the knights two shillings, the four thousand one hundred and eighty-two squires and men-at-arms a shilling. The foot archers had threepence, the horsed archers double that sum, the hobilars sixpence also: the Welsh pikemen only twopence.

In the late summer King Philip, as had been expected, made an effort to raise the siege of Calais. He had called out the whole levy of France for Whitsuntide, but the contingents were slow in mobilising and in reaching Amiens, the chosen point of concentration. Evidently the memory of Creçy lay heavily upon the mind of the whole country. However, on July 18, the Earl of Lancaster, who had been sent out to watch the roads from the south, reported that the enemy was on the move in full force. Philip advanced as far as Sangatte, near Wissant, and from thence sent a message to his adversary, offering to fight him in the open on August 2. The reports

2 German Counts [Holstein and Freiberg], with	86 knights.
	400 esquires.
	339 panzenars [mailed infantry].
Auger de Monthaut, Lord of Mussidan, with	9 esquires.
	5 hobilars.
	5 foot archers.
Peter d'Espagne, with	20 esquires.
Hugh Calkyn of Flanders, with .	4 esquires.
Henry of Flanders, with	4 knights.
	25 esquires.
	16 panzenars.
John de Lovendal of Brabant, with	4 knights.
	12 esquires.
	16 panzenars.
William of Granson (a Burgundian), with	7 esquires.
	8 panzenars.
4 knights of Hainault, with	21 esquires.
	2 crossbowmen.
	5 panzenars.
1 knight of Lorraine, with	2 esquires.
	2 panzenars.

General total, barons and knights, 107; esquires, 497; panzenars, 386; hobilars, 5; other infantry, 7.

as to the English lines of circumvallation round Calais were so depressing that Philip's advisers assured him that it would be madness to attack them. Edward naturally refused to give up his tactical advantage; if chivalry was in question, he could say with truth that he had defied Philip to come out from behind his *abattis* at Buironfosse in 1339, and had failed to move him. Why should he be more obliging in 1347?

Thereupon King Philip gave up the game, set fire to his cantonments between Boulogne and Wissant, marched off, and demobilised his army at Amiens. The garrison of Calais, on getting the news, surrendered on August 4. On the far-reaching effects of the gain of this magnificent *tête-de-pont* in France on English invasion-strategy we shall speak in its proper place. Here we are concerned rather with tactics.

King Philip had obviously found no solution to the problem of dealing with English armies and their new system of battle. It is therefore most interesting to see what experiments were made by his vassals and generals during the next few years, in their endeavour to arrive at some device for neutralising the effect of English archery.

The first on record is a purely defensive venture. In the Breton War, Charles of Blois, the claimant to the duchy who was supported by the French, had in 1347 to deal with Sir Thomas Dagworth, the bold professional soldier, who had relieved the Earl of Northampton in command of the English auxiliary forces which upheld the cause of John of Montfort. Charles was all through the summer engaged in the siege of the strong fortress of La Roche Derien, held by a garrison under Richard of Totesham. He expected to be attacked by a relieving army, and, as Dagworth tells us in an interesting letter preserved in the Chronicle of Avesbury, "made great fortification of ditches about him, and outside his fortifications had scraped all the face of the country for half a league round him, and levelled all the hedges and ditches, *by means of which my archers might have had advantage over him and his folk*, so that we were forced to fight in bare fields."[1] Evidently

---

[1] Letter of Dagworth in Avesbury (Hearne's edition), pp. 159–160. "Lequel Monsieur Charles hors de sa forteresse avoit fait planir et enracer à demi-league du païs tout manères de fosses et de haies, par quei mes archiers ne puissent trover leur avantages sur lui, mais convient à fyn force de combattre en plains champs" (Robert of Avesbury, p. 159).

Charles thought that he could compel the English to take the offensive by entrenching himself in contravallations, and that their archers would find no cover, while his own men were palisaded and protected from arrow-shot. Dagworth, recognising that archers are of little use against entrenchments, took the desperate step of attacking the entrenched camp before day-break, launching his men against it in a column. He sacrificed entirely the advantage of archery, since the whole fight was in the dark, but won a most hazardous victory. The enemy had not expected such a move, his lines were pierced, and when attacked in the rear by the garrison of La Roche Derien he was broken and routed. Duke Charles was taken prisoner, severely wounded, with many of his barons, and the flower of the party of Blois was destroyed.[1] Archery, then, did not win the battle—but fear of archery had caused the enemy to shut himself up in entrenchments, thereby surrendering all the advantage of his superiority in cavalry (June 27, 1347). The victory was a *tour de force*, won by inferior numbers purely through surprise.

The English continued, whenever they found it possible, to accept a defensive battle, and not to take the offensive as at La Roche Derien. The next two combats of some importance seemed to justify this policy, wherever it could be tried. In the obscure fight of Lunalonge (1349) we only know that they dismounted every man, while the French kept to their horses and tried a charge in the Creçy style, with no success.[2] But being much inferior in numbers, the victors retreated by night, after having inflicted a severe check on their adversaries. In 1351 there were two other engagements, of much greater interest, since the French were now trying another policy. The first was the combat of Saintes or Taillebourg (April 8), which Froissart describes as merely " a good joust," but which held real tactical importance, since the French Marshal, Guy de Nesle, first among his countrymen, dismounted the main body of his knights after the English fashion, but kept two considerable bodies of them horsed, and set them to turn the

---

[1] Blois had two roads to cover, and had fortified lines blocking each of them. One-third of his army, according to Breton sources, was absent in the other lines, and owing to the attack being made in the dark, did not get up in time to join him before the decision had been won. See Laborderie's *Histoire de Bretagne*, iii. p. 503.

[2] See the *Chronique Normande du xiv. Siècle*, ed. Molinier, and Professor Tout's comments on it in *English Historical Review* for 1905.

hostile flanks.   The plan failed, though *why* we are not told by
the *Chronique Normande*, which only states that the slowness
of de Nesle's manœuvring allowed the English garrison of
Taillebourg to come up and turn the tide of battle.   Tactical
explanation is deficient.[1]   But de Nesle was taken prisoner
with many others, and had to be ransomed by his master, the
French king, who was a great believer in his military talents

The other fight of 1351, the combat of Ardres, ended less
fortunately for the English, probably because they had with
them far too small a proportion of archers to enable their
proper line of battle to be formed.   Sir John Beauchamp had
pushed out of Calais with three hundred men-at-arms and
three hundred mounted archers.[2]   He swept the countryside
as far as Boulogne and St. Omer, and collected many hundred
head of cattle and much miscellaneous plunder.   There was
a considerable French garrison in St. Omer, headed by Edward
of Beaujeu, Marshal of France, which turned out to pursue
the raiders.   The Lord of Beaujeu himself, with a hundred
horse, outstripped the rest of his force, and soon came in sight
of the English.[3]   The remainder of his followers, both horse
and foot, were straggling along the road for miles to the rear.
Seeing the enemy at hand, Beauchamp resolved to stand and
fight, in order to cover the escape of his convoy.   He sent the
cattle and carts forward, under charge of twenty men-at-arms
and eighty archers, and stopped behind himself with the rest.
He got off the road and ranged his men behind the ditch of a
large field, sending all the horses to the rear.   Edward of
Beaujeu wanted to hurry matters, since, unless he drove in the
English quickly, the convoy would get away clear.   He dismounted his men, and, though much inferior in numbers,
attacked Beauchamp frontally along the line of the ditch.   As
was to be expected under the circumstances, he was killed, and
his small corps almost annihilated.   But before the fight was
quite over other parties of the French came hurrying in ;

[1] Therefore we can say nothing towards drawing a tactical moral.   Mr. Bentley's
Saintes and Mauron monograph [Guildford, 1918], for which I was much obliged to
the donor, is (naturally) more interested in Sir Walter Bentley than in tactics.

[2] These are the figures given by Baker of Swinbrook.   Froissart gives Beauchamp four hundred men-at-arms and three hundred archers, but is much less good
authority than the two contemporary chroniclers.

[3] Baker seems to imply that Beaujeu got ahead of Beauchamp's retiring force, as
he calls the first attack an *imboscatio* or ambush, *i.e.* an attempt to block the way.

Guichard of Beaujeu led a second charge to avenge his brother
—he was wounded, but his men succeeded in crossing the
ditch and getting to close quarters with the English.   Shortly
after another body of French men-at-arms, under the Count
of Château-Porcien, came riding up on the flank, coasted round
the archers of one English wing and cut them up.   Finally
the infantry of the garrison of St. Omer, " five hundred *brigans*
armed with spear and shield," arrived on the scene, and, turning
the whole mêlée, came in upon the rear of the disordered English,
who were already giving way.   Beauchamp was made a prisoner,
and the survivors of his men-at-arms were captured to a man.

The English captain's error is easily seen : he had too few
archers with him,—only two hundred and twenty after the
plunder had been sent off,—and these had used up their arrows
before the third French division came on the field.   He had
taken a position which had some cover in front, but none on
the flanks, and could easily be turned by superior numbers.
Lastly, he might have retired after checking the first French
onslaught and slaying the Lord of Beaujeu, but stayed to fight
again, " animose sed non sapienter," out of mere chivalrous
enterprise.

All these fights were much less important than the engagement at Mauron in Brittany on August 14, 1352, which rose
to the dignity of a battle from the number of combatants
engaged.   The English were under Sir Walter Bentley, his
predecessor Dagworth having been betrayed and killed in an
ambush by a Breton renegade a few months before.   Bentley
selected a position in the Creçy style, along a hedge and ditch
on the upper slopes of a bare hill [1]—the men-at-arms dismounted
in the centre, the archers forming two wings.   His opponent
was the same Guy de Nesle who had been defeated at Saintes
in the previous year, and the tactics adopted were identical—
evidently the Marshal considered that his failure in 1351 had
been caused by mismanagement, not by an error of theory.
He dismounted his main body of knights, but sent one hundred
and forty picked riders under the Sieur de Hangest to make a
sweep around the archery of the English right wing, and to
fall in upon their flank.   Whether the dismounted horsemen
advanced in one column or in two does not appear, but as the

---

[1] In his report, given in full by Avesbury, Bentley makes a point of the fight
being *en plein champ*, without wood cover.

French left wing is spoken of as composed of men on foot, it is probable that they were distinct from the main-battle.

The results of the experiment were inconclusive from the tactical, and disastrous from the practical point of view. De Hangest was fortunate—probably he had the easiest slope of the hill before him—at any rate he succeeded in closing with the archers, and riding many of them down: the rest fled too soon for their credit. But he did not, for some reason unexplained, fall on the flank of the English main-battle. Whether he was prevented from doing so by the ground, or by his followers being led away by indiscipline into a reckless pursuit, does not appear. But it is certain that meanwhile the rest of the French army suffered a complete disaster; the foot on the right were so shot down by the archers of the English left wing that they never succeeded in closing. The main-battle in the centre was woefully delayed and disordered by furze and gorse bushes which covered the front of Bentley's line, but got to hand-strokes nevertheless—no doubt because the success of de Hangest's attack had saved it from any arrow-volleys from the left flank. But being in bad array and exhausted by a long climb in heavy armour, the French centre delivered a weak assault; it thrust back the English men-at-arms some way, but failed to break the line. A counter-attack by Bentley's men followed, and set the Marshal's main-battle rolling down-hill again—the intact English archery of the left wing joining in the repulse. The time had now arrived when armour had become so heavy that it was very dangerous to broken troops, who could not retreat at any pace. The Marshal himself was slain, refusing to fly, and with him the best of his knights: scores of others were taken prisoners as they lurched slowly down the slopes. It is said that one hundred and forty knights and esquires fell, and eightscore were captured, and that the Franco-Breton loss in horsemen was altogether five hundred and forty. The fate of the party of Charles of Blois was settled for many a year, and the Montfort faction dominated Brittany till the end of the war.[1]

---

[1] See Mr. Bentley's *Saintes and Mauron* for lists of the very heavy losses of the Franco-Breton army. Many details are to be got in Laborderie's history of Brittany (vol. iii. pp. 531-2). Baker of Swinbrook (p. 120) tells us that Bentley was so disgusted with the conduct of the archers of his right wing that he had thirty of them executed for cowardice.

The victory of Ardres had given the French no more certain a receipt for how to deal with an English line of battle than had the defeats of La Roche Derien, Lunalonge, Saintes, and Mauron.   In the next general action, one on a very different scale from all the engagements just narrated, we find them still groping for the solution of the problem.

CHAPTER IV

POICTIERS, SEPTEMBER 19, 1356

SUCH secondary combats as Ardres or Saintes or Mauron had settled nothing. The next military lesson of real interest is only found when we reach 1356, and investigate the details of the celebrated battle of Poictiers. In the autumn of 1355 the Black Prince had sallied forth from Bordeaux and pushed a destructive but rather objectless raid as far as Toulouse and Narbonne. The French had not dared to meet him in the open field, and he had returned to Bordeaux loaded with spoil. In the summer of 1356 he resolved to conduct a similar foray into the heart of Central France—the districts along the upper and middle course of the Loire. Like his father, the younger Edward does not shine in the sphere of strategy. Though he seems to have had some vague idea of ultimately pushing northward to join the force under his brother John of Gaunt, which was operating on the borders of Normandy, his route and his whole conduct of the campaign show that his primary object was merely to harry as much of France as he could, to defy King John, and to bring back to Bordeaux as large a store of plunder as his men could convey.[1] His army, indeed, was too weak to do much more than execute a destructive raid, mustering only between three thousand and four thousand men-at-arms, two thousand five hundred or three thousand archers, and a thousand light troops of other kinds, " sergeants," " brigans," and Gascon " bidowers." Apparently the bowmen were all mounted, that they might be able to keep up with the knights if hard marching became necessary. This

---

[1] The prince's own dispatch (given in *Memorials of London*, 285–6) only says that he moved north to have news of his father's "passage" into Normandy. Apparently, then, Edward III. had originally intended to sail himself, and handed over the business to John of Gaunt too late to allow his elder son to get the news.

fact accounts for the small proportion in which they appear in the host; ordinarily the archers outnumbered the men-at-arms three or fourfold in an English expedition. But on this occasion a very large part of the prince's army was composed of the *noblesse* of Guienne, who brought with them hardly any followers of value save their contingent of mailed horsemen.

The prince started from Bergerac on August 4; he swept through Limousin and Berry as far as Châteauroux and Vierzon; then, turning somewhat westward, he wasted the valley of the Loire, confining himself to its southern bank because all the bridges had been broken by the French. He made no attempt to seize on garrison towns,—indeed the castle of Romorantin in Berry was the only fortified place which he assailed,—but pushed steadily on, not tiring his men by long marches, but covering only three or four leagues a day, and gathering in a vast quantity of plunder.

Meanwhile, John of France had begun to collect his army at Chartres, to repel the invasion with which the Duke of Lancaster had threatened Normandy. But when the duke's expedition had failed, he was able to turn his attention to the far more dangerous attack from the south. Accordingly he marched against Prince Edward, who was now feeling his way westward along the southern bank of the Loire. When the English had reached Tours, and were battering away at its suburbs, they learned that King John, with an army of some forty thousand men, had crossed the Loire at Blois, thirty miles east of them, and was hastening to throw himself between them and their base in Aquitaine. The great road southward from Tours to Bordeaux ran through Poictiers, and John was marching on that town, where he would be in a good position for intercepting the invaders' retreat. On hearing that his enemy had moved southward, Prince Edward hastily abandoned his demonstration against Tours, and made off in the very direction which the king had expected him to take. Baker of Swinbrook says that he was looking for the enemy. But the prince's actual manœuvres show rather a desire to get his plunder and his small army [1] back in safety to Bordeaux.

The intelligence department of both hosts seems to have been conducted with even more than the usual slackness of the Middle Ages, for they finally collided in the most casual way,

[1] See Baker, p. 141.

almost, as it were, by haphazard. Though they were converging on the same place, they remained entirely ignorant of each other's exact position, with the result that on September 17 the prince, marching from Châtelherault on Poictiers, suddenly came on the rear of the French army, which had been marching across his front all the morning as it moved from La Haye on Poictiers. The English vanguard pounced on the straggling corps at the tail of the French host, routed them, and took prisoners the Counts of Auxerre and Joigny. If John had been a little slower in moving, or Edward a little quicker, the result would have been that the English would have struck into the very midst of the French host. As it was, they not only avoided this danger, but found that, most providentially, the enemy had overshot his mark, and left the way to Bordeaux open to them.

Accordingly the prince, now certain of his rival's position, avoided Poictiers, pushed southward by a cross-road, and halted for the night at the little village of Maupertuis, seven miles south-east of the ancient city.

To halt even for a few hours was to risk a battle, but the English were now fatigued with several days of forced marching, and no doubt their beasts of burden were tired out. The huge mass of booty, heaped on waggons or piled on the backs of sumpter-horses, must have brought down their speed to a mere three miles an hour, and rendered rapid motion wholly impossible. Edward had now to choose whether he would sacrifice his plunder and execute a hasty retreat on Bordeaux, or whether he would risk a fight rather than abandon his baggage. The first alternative would have been safe, but wholly ignominious to one who, with all his military virtues, was, after all, a typical knight of the fourteenth century. He resolved to take his chance, and to stand his ground on the next morning, ready to receive the French if they should move against him, but ready also to move off and avoid a conflict, if the enemy should hang back long enough to allow him to start off his train on the Bordeaux road.[1]

So far our chronicles are fairly unanimous ; but as to the circumstances which led up to the actual opening of the battle there are two divergent accounts, between which we have to choose. They turn on the topography of the field, concerning which it is necessary to say a few words.

The prince's position lay close to the village of Maupertuis,

[1] See his own letter, printed in *Memorials of London*, p. 288.

a place which has now entirely disappeared, and is represented only by the isolated farm of La Cardinerie. The whole face of the country was much covered with trees and thickets, and behind lay the dense wood of Nouaillé. The ground was fairly level all around ; there is only some twenty or thirty feet of difference between the highest and the lowest level of the rolling plateau. But to the south the field was bounded by the river Miausson, a stream with a deep muddy bottom, running along a marshy valley some hundred feet below the level of the plateau. It was crossed to the left rear of the English position by a ford named the Gué de l'Homme, over which lay the line of retreat on Bordeaux. If the prince could have been certain of getting his enormous train over the Miausson without being attacked, he might have gone on his way with a light heart. But it was obvious that, while baggage and army were defiling across the ford, there would be great danger of a disaster if the French made a brisk assault on the rear of the long line of march. For King John and his army were too close to the English to be easily eluded : their watchfires were in sight of Maupertuis, and both sides were watering their horses at the same river.

It seemed inevitable that a collision would take place when the morning of the 18th dawned, and the prince made hasty efforts to strengthen his position. He seems to have lain facing north-west, with his right placed in the thickets which ran out from the north end of the wood of Nouaillé, and his left somewhat beyond La Cardinerie (Maupertuis). Behind his right centre was a low hill, if a rise of twenty feet deserves that name, which has still preserved the name of " La Masse aux Anglais." His horses were parked so as to be hidden from the French by this rolling ground. The whole position was so masked by hedges and thickets that it was difficult to reconnoitre it, or even to ascertain its limits. On one or both flanks waggons had been hastily drawn together, to cover gaps in the line of scrub and bush. This is said to have been specially the case on the flank farthest from the river.[1] The front of the position was formed by a thick thorn hedge with a ditch in front of it,

---

[1] I conclude that when the French scouts on September 19 reported that they had reconnoitred the English line, and found *the left* so barricaded, that they meant their own left, and did not put themselves in the prince's position and think of *his* left.

pierced only on one point by a country road wide enough for four horses abreast : this was probably the path that led down to the Gué de l'Homme, the prince's line of retreat.

To hold this position Edward had divided his army into the usual three " battles " of the mediæval host. The vaward was led by the Earls of Warwick [1] and Oxford,[2] but consisted to a very large extent of the prince's Gascon vassals under the seigneurs of Pommiers, Albret, L'Esparre, Montferrand, and Mussidan, and the Captal de Buch. The main-battle, under the prince himself, included the English barons Audley, Cobham, De la Warre, Despenser, Burghersh, and the pick of the professional soldiers who followed the English banner—Sir John Chandos, Sir William Felton, and Sir Nigel Loring. The rearward was given to the Earls of Salisbury [3] and Suffolk,[4] who had with them the Lords Willoughby, Multon, and Basset, Sir Maurice Berkeley, and some of the prince's mercenaries from the Netherlands, under Daniel Pasele and Denis of Morbeke. Each battle contained somewhat over a thousand men-at-arms, about the same number of English archers, and a few hundreds of Gascon light troops

In the original drawing up of the host Warwick must have held the northern and Salisbury the southern end of the position. But, as we shall see, the array of the host was wholly changed before the battle, and it was the rearward which ultimately opened the fight, the vaward taking post south of it, and not in its proper place.

The prince's position, however, was not destined to be assailed on the 18th. That the fighting did not occur till the next day was due to the well-intentioned but hopeless intervention of the Cardinal of Perigord.[5] This good prelate had been hovering about the two armies for some days, in the hope of prevailing on the princes to spare the effusion of Christian blood by concluding a treaty of peace. He now begged John to allow him to visit the English camp and offer his services as intermediary : the invaders, indeed, were in a position sufficiently

---

[1] Thomas Beauchamp, then a man of forty-three, a veteran of Creçy.

[2] John de Vere, aged forty-three, like Warwick, and also, like him, a Creçy man.

[3] William Montacute, aged twenty-eight, had served as a youth at Creçy, and been knighted by the Prince of Wales.

[4] Robert de Ufford, then aged fifty-eight, had served in Flanders, and at Creçy.

[5] Bearing the name, destined to be famous four hundred and fifty years later, of Talleyrand de Perigord.

hazardous to justify Edward in thinking twice before refusing reasonable terms.   The French king very unwisely granted the cardinal's request : he should undoubtedly have spent the morning in endeavouring to march round the English flank, either on the left or the right bank of the Miausson : such a movement would have forced the enemy either to abandon his baggage and decamp at once, or to risk being surrounded.

The negotiations, as was to be expected, came to nought. According to Froissart's account, the prince offered to dismiss his prisoners without ransom, to give up any castles or towns he had taken during the expedition, and make a seven years' truce. The French demanded that he and a hundred chosen knights should give themselves up as hostages, and on this point the discussion was broken off.   Chandos Herald gives the more probable statement that Edward replied that he was not authorised to make any treaty or truce without his father's knowledge and permission.   It is at any rate certain that English and French commissioners met between the two armies, discussed terms, and parted without any satisfactory result.

The cardinal's futile diversion had wasted the greater part of the 18th of September : while the negotiations were going on, Edward might probably have absconded, for the French army had not properly reconnoitred his position nor taken any measures to watch the exits from it.   But knightly honour demanded that no movement should take place during time of truce, and the prince deferred all action till the 19th.

Of his plan for the next morning we have two distinct accounts.   Chandos Herald, a very fair authority with a good military eye, tells us that he had determined to draw off from his position and march quietly for Bordeaux.   " The prince," he says, " put his men in order, and willingly would he have avoided an action, if he could have managed it.   But he saw well what he had to do : . . . accordingly he summoned the Earl of Warwick, gave him charge of the van, and said to him, ' You shall first go over the passage and take our baggage in charge : I will ride after you with all my knights, that if you meet with any mischance we may reinforce you : and the Earl of Salisbury shall follow behind and lead our rear-battle.   Let us each be upon our guard, and, in case the French fall upon us, let every man dismount as quickly as he can, to fight on foot.' "   So they settled the matter over-night, and in the morning " the prince left his quarters and set out to ride away, for on this day he did not think to fight, but thought rather that he could avoid an action." Warwick had already passed the Miausson with the convoy, and the prince himself had marched off, when the French hastily moved forward and assailed Salisbury and the rear-battle, who were still holding the position of the previous day, to cover their comrades' retreat. To save Salisbury, the prince had to wheel back and take up his old line of defence. But ere he had returned, the covering force had beaten off the first French assault, " long before the van-battle could be turned and pass back to them, for it was already beyond the river."

This account of the circumstances which brought about the battle is eminently probable and rational, but unfortunately it does not coincide with any other narrative, English or French. Froissart, the majority of the chroniclers who wrote from English sources, and also the French historians, speak of Edward as having made no movement to the rear, but as having deliberately waited for the assault of the enemy in his old position. Only one of the English writers, Baker of Swinbrook,[1] speaks of the prince as having been occupied in drawing off the field at the moment when Salisbury was attacked, and his account differs in its details from that of Chandos. " The prince," he says, " saw that away on his flank there was a hill girt round with hedges and ditches, with its top occupied partly by scrubby pasture-ground, partly by ploughed fields and vineyards ; he thought it probable that a body of French might be hidden in these fields.[2] Between us and the hill was a considerable valley with steep banks, and a marsh with a stream flowing through it. The prince's battle and the convoy of baggage passed the stream at a narrow ford, and, having crossed the valley, made its way through the hedges and ditches and occupied the hill, where he was hidden from view by the thicket, and yet himself commanded a view of the enemy. The French, seeing the prince's banner clearly in sight at first, then gradually moving off, and finally concealed from their sight by the intervening ridge, thought that he was retreating." Accordingly

---

[1] But Baker, it is to be remembered, is much better authority than Froissart, or even than the Chandos Herald. The other chronicles are short and poor.

[2] I imagine myself that it was the hill partly covered by the Bois de St. Pierre on the south side of the Miausson. (See Plate XXVI.)

they fell hastily upon the English position, and became engaged with Salisbury and the rear-battle.

So far this account might pass for a variant of the tale told by Chandos. What the latter considers to have been the commencement of a general retreat, Baker may have chosen to represent as a lateral movement destined to occupy the hill beyond the Miausson, and so to prevent the main position from being turned by any French corps detached to the south of that stream. But the difficulties of Baker's version only commence when the prince has reached the outlying hill, for he never gives any account of Edward's return from that position, and presently speaks of him as joining in the resistance to the later attacks of the French. Either, therefore, he has forgotten to describe Edward's recrossing of the Miausson, or he conceives of the flanking hill as on the north side of that stream, and not out of touch with the rest of the English army. Sir Edward Maunde Thompson in his learned exposition of Baker's story leans to the latter view, and holds that the stream and " marsh " which the prince crossed on his way to the hill were the little runlet which flows, or rather once flowed, from a long-vanished pool [1] near La Cardinerie, down to the Miausson. I must confess that I cannot recognise in the " ampla profundaque vallis et mariscus torrente quodam irriguus " of which Baker speaks, the fifteen or twenty feet dip in the hillside with a mere trickle of water running down it, which lies south-west of Maupertuis. Allowing for all possible exaggeration in the description, I fail to see that Baker can be speaking of any stream except the Miausson. When his narrative is read along with that of Chandos, the identification of his *torrens* with the Herald's *rivière* seems absolutely necessary. The only alternative, therefore, which remains to us, is to believe that Baker, in his hurry to get on to the picturesque details of the fighting, forgets to say that the prince, when he saw Salisbury beset by the French, reversed his lateral movement and came back to join his rear-battle on the original position. I shall adopt this hypothesis in my account of the engagement.

The French king had drawn up his army early on the 19th for a general assault on the English line, but was still very imperfectly informed as to the strength and exact position of

---

[1] The " Abreuvoir aux Anglais " of Colonel Babinet, the local antiquary, who has done much to fix the sites of the battle.

his enemy. The countryside was so masked with woods and hedges that he had not been able to learn much from the knights whom he had sent out to reconnoitre the hostile front.[1] They could only report that the English were " strongly posted along a road with a hedge and a ditch beside it, with the hedge lined with archers, and the men-at-arms drawn up behind among the vines and thorn bushes, all on foot ; the hedge had but one gap in it, where four knights might ride abreast ; save at this point there was no way of getting at the English except by breaking through the archers, who were never easy to dislodge."[2]

In preparing his assault on the English position, King John adopted the method of fighting which had been tried by Guy de Nesle at Saintes and Mauron with such moderate success.[3] At the suggestion of William Douglas (as Baker tells the tale), he resolved to make the greater part of his men-at-arms dismount and assail the English on foot. Only a body of picked horsemen, a kind of forlorn hope, was to precede the main army and endeavour to break through the archers by a sudden charge, so as to prepare the way for their comrades.

The reasons which led John to adopt this order of battle were much disputed at the time, and have caused much discussion in after-ages. The approach to the English position was difficult for horsemen, and the ground all about it was sown thick with bushes and trees, which might have thrown a great body of cavalry into disorder. The deadly accuracy of the arrows of the English archers, who had made such havoc among the horses at Creçy that the French knights had never been able to push their charge home, was a second reason. If on the bare downs of Creçy the horsemen had been completely checked, they would fare far worse on the plateau of Maupertuis, with its scrubby thickets, hedgerows, and vineyards.[4] Apparently the king, like the Marshal de Nesle at Mauron, made an unskilful argument by analogy—the English of late had always been

---

[1] They were sent out before the Cardinal's intervention ; John does not seem to have made any second reconnaissance on the 19th.

[2] This account in Froissart agrees very well with Baker's statement that "at the upper end of the hedge, where it was farthest from the slope down toward the marsh, was a gap or opening, made by carters, and our third (or rear) battle was drawn up a stone's throw in rear of this gap, under the Earl of Salisbury."

[3] There were several of the vanquished of Mauron on the field, notably the Marshal d'Audrehem.

[4] This is John le Bel's view : "Tous se combattoient a pyè, pour doubtance des archers, qui tuoient leurs chevaulx, comme à la bataille de Creçy" (vol. ii. 197).

successful by dismounting, why should he not turn their own tactics against them? He forgot, unfortunately, that the English victories had all been won by acting on the defensive, and that tactics which might be admirable for a small army defending a position against superior numbers might be absurd for a large army striving to evict a lesser one from its chosen ground.   Baker of Swinbrook may perhaps be right in attributing this unhappy suggestion to William Douglas, who—as he says—told John that " since the present king came to the throne the English have generally fought on foot, imitating the Scots ever since their disaster at Bannockburn.   Wherefore he advised that the French should copy the Scots manner, and attack the enemy on foot rather than on horseback."   But whether a Scot, or one of the survivors of Mauron, conceived the idea, it was a hopeless misapplication of the facts that lay before them.   The French men-at-arms of 1356 were now far too heavily armed to make it easy for them to march a mile on foot, scramble through bush and brier, and assault a well-guarded position : like their comrades in the battle of 1352, they were to find that the knightly armour was grown too cumbrous to allow of operations which would have been quite feasible eighty years before, when chain mail had not yet been superseded by plate.   All through the day they were fighting against fatigue and over-exhaustion as much as against the enemy.   Very different was the case of the English, who, as at Halidon and Creçy, had only to hold their ground and keep their line, and did not move to the assault till the last phase of the battle. Finally, we should remember that King John forgot, in his misapplied endeavour to learn the secret of victory from his enemy, that the essential part of the English tactics was not the mere dismounting of the men-at-arms, but the proper combination of them with the archery : Creçy and Halidon were won by the bowmen even more than by the knighthood.   The latter would in each case have been surrounded and overwhelmed but for their auxiliaries on the wings.   At Poictiers John had a considerable body of troops armed with missile weapons,—two thousand arbalest men besides many other light troops,—but he did not attempt to combine them with his men-at-arms after the English fashion.   He sent the crossbowmen, indeed, forward with his first battle, but did not dispose them so as to endeavour to check the English archery; in this respect he seems to have acted even more unreasonably than his father at Creçy; Philip had at any rate given the Genoese some opportunity of trying their mettle in 1346. John so mixed them up with his men-at-arms that they never had a fair chance of using their weapons.

His disposition of his forces must be shortly stated. The first battle, which was smaller than the other three, was given to the two Marshals D'Audrehem and Clermont. Under them were arrayed the three hundred picked horsemen whom we have already mentioned ; their orders were to ride in rapidly upon the English, and at all costs close with them and cut up the archers. Next behind the forlorn hope came the main body of the first battle, which included a considerable body of German auxiliaries under the Counts of Saarbrücken, Nidau, and Nassau. These, like the marshals' three hundred, kept to their horses : with them marched the two thousand crossbow-men of whom we have spoken above, and two thousand " sergeants à pied," armed with darts and javelins.

The second battle was led by the king's eldest son, Charles Duke of Normandy, and the Duke of Bourbon : it is said to have mustered four thousand men-at-arms. The third was under the king's brother, Philip Duke of Orleans, and is reckoned at three thousand men-at-arms. The fourth and far the largest battle marched under the command of John himself, who had at his side his youngest son, Philip, a mere boy of fourteen. In his company were the Counts of Eu, Longueville, Sancerre, and Dammartin, and twenty-three banners in all of great counts and lords. The division is called at least six thousand strong.

The French, no doubt, mustered much less than the sixteen thousand cavalry and some four thousand or five thousand foot-soldiery, these latter all trained mercenaries, at which they are calculated by the Chroniclers. Froissart is undoubtedly stating the numbers of the French too high when he reckons them at forty thousand or fifty thousand strong. A good corrective to his exaggerated figures is to be found in the letter written from the field by Bartholomew Lord Burghersh, who estimated the beaten army at no more than eight thousand horsemen and three thousand footmen.[1] But Burghersh may

---

[1] Baker of Swinbrook also speaks of "eight thousand men-at-arms, to take no account of sergeants, under eighty-seven banners." He makes no mention of foot-soldiery, but we know from Chandos Herald and Burghersh that they were present to the number of some thousands.

have slightly underrated the enemy. Froissart's figures are hopelessly impossible.

It was apparently the half-descried withdrawal of the English van and main body which led King John to order the advance. At once the marshals and their battles pricked forward at full speed, leaving the three great bodies of dismounted men-at-arms to follow as best they could. They reached the English line long before their fellows were on the field, for their only care was to close in haste before the enemy should have withdrawn. Clermont is said to have wished to hold back and allow the main body to come up, but D'Audrehem taunted him with sloth and over-caution, and, after a sharp exchange of words, both dashed forward towards the hedge. Clermont made for the gap in it, towards the north end of the English position ; D'Audrehem attacked lower down.

The result of this hasty and inconsiderate charge was as disastrous as might have been expected. The English archers lined the hedge and shot down the horses of the greater part of the three hundred knights of the forlorn hope; the survivors and the German men-at-arms who followed them were only able to close slowly and in small parties. A fierce combat raged all along the hedge, but Salisbury held his own without difficulty, and he was presently relieved by the hasty return of Warwick and the Prince of Wales, who had left the convoy to take care of itself when they saw the French approaching, and had hurried back to fall into line with the rearward. The rout of the battle of the marshals and the Germans was completed by a device of the Earl of Oxford, who hastily led out part of the archers of the vaward into the marshy low ground by the Miausson, at right angles to the English line, and bade them shoot up the valley at the flank of the French.[1] Harassed beyond endurance by this side attack, the hostile van broke up and retired in disorder. The Marshal Clermont had been killed, his colleague D'Audrehem and the German Counts of Saarbrücken and Nassau had all been taken prisoners—cast down, no doubt, by their slain or wounded horses, and left at the mercy of the English.

The defeat of the French van had been completed, before the three great bodies of dismounted men-at-arms which formed

---

[1] This they could do with safety, because the ground where they stood was too marshy to allow the French cavalry to make a dash at them.

the bulk of their host could reach the field. The first of them, the Dauphin's battle, just arrived in time to be somewhat incommoded by the fugitives sweeping past its flank. It is said that some cowardly spirits took advantage of the disorder to call for their horses and make off in company with the wreck of the marshals' division. But the main bulk of the Dauphin's men came steadily to the front, and attacked the whole length of the hedge. So vehement was their onslaught that the Prince of Wales had to put into line against them not only Salisbury's and Warwick's troops,[1] but all his own battle, save four hundred picked men-at-arms whom he retained as a last reserve. The struggle was long and hard; but the line of the hedge was sternly held, the French could never pierce it, and at last the Dauphin's knights, after suffering a dreadful slaughter, gave back, and repassed the little valley across which they had advanced to assault the hedge.[2] They were not pursued save by a few hot-headed young knights like Sir Maurice Berkeley,[3] for the prince knew that half the French army had not yet come into action, and refused to allow his men to break their line.

Meanwhile, a wholly unlooked-for piece of good fortune had befallen the English : at the sight of the rout of the Dauphin's battle, the division under the Duke of Orleans, which ought to have delivered the next assault on the English line, was completely demoralised. Without having struck a blow or suffered any loss, the duke's whole corps followed the defeated battle in hasty flight, and made off north-eastward in the direction of La Chaboterie. Only a few scores of knights and squires, who scorned to copy their leader's example, stayed behind and joined the king's still intact reserve.

[1] To meet this attack, says Baker, the battles of Salisbury and Warwick had to get together and re-form in close line, "nostra prima secundaque custodia pariter se glomerarunt." The place taken by the prince's own battle is not given; but at the end of the attack everyone had been engaged, "demptis solis cccc qui vexillo principali subservierunt reservati," etc.

[2] Baker and Chandos Herald agree that the fighting with the Dauphin's division raged all along the hedge. They differ, however, in that Baker says that Warwick was back in position before the marshals' battle was entirely beaten, and that his archers took part in routing it; while Chandos says that Warwick arrived much later, after the marshals had been wholly discomfited, and only just in time to prevent the Dauphin from forcing the hedge (line 1220).

[3] Both Froissart and Baker tell with some differences of detail the story of Berkeley's foolish pursuit of the French, and of his capture.

King John himself was in a very different frame of mind from his cowardly brother.   Furious at the disgraceful repulse of the leading divisions, he urged on his own corps, and pushed to the front to resume the combat.   Nor was he without reasonable hope of success.   In numbers he was still almost or quite equal to the English, whose ranks had been fearfully thinned by the two desperate mêlées in which they had been engaged. His troops were fresh, while the prince's were utterly exhausted. The English line presented a by no means cheering spectacle as described by Baker.   " Some were carrying the wounded to the rear and laying them under the shelter of trees and thickets, others were replacing their broken swords and lances from the spoils of the slain ;   the archers were trying to replenish their stock of arrows, even pulling them out of the bodies of the dead and wounded.   There was in the whole host no one who was not either hurt or utterly worn out with the battle, save only the reserve of four hundred men whom Edward still kept about his standard."   As the king's battle rolled up the hill, a knight of well-tried courage remarked to the prince that all was over and defeat inevitable.   But the English leader's spirit was still high ; he threw an angry rebuke at the doubter,[1] and gave his orders for the new combat with an undaunted bearing.

Seeing the French sending their last reserve into action, and conscious that there was nothing more to be feared if it could be beaten off, Edward had now resolved to take the offensive. Putting his four hundred fresh men into the front of the battle, and hastily forming all the exhausted host into a single mass, he bade his standard-bearer, Walter of Wodeland, bear his ensign straight against that of King John, and charged down the gentle slope.[2]   One last precaution he had taken : before the moment of the shock, he had directed the Captal de Buch, the best trusted of his Gascon vassals, to take sixty men-at-arms and a hundred archers—all that he could spare—and to fall on the flank or rear of the French battle, after fetching a compass unseen behind the slight rising ground, the Masse aux Anglais, where his baggage had been stacked on the preceding night, and through the thickets which bounded the field of battle on the north.

---

[1] " Mentiris pessime vecors, si me vivum posse vinci blasphemeris " (Baker, 150).
[2] Froissart says that he bade his knights mount for the final charge, but Chandos and Baker do not mention it, and they would have done so if it had happened.

Meanwhile, the two main bodies had met on equal fronts at the foot of the slope below the English hedge, with a clash which, as one chronicler tells us, could be heard as far as the walls of Poictiers, seven miles away. Both sides were desperate, and for many minutes the two hosts stood locked together, neither winning nor losing ground. The English archers, having exhausted their last few arrows, threw themselves into the mêlée, and fought hand to hand among the men-at-arms. Fierce as had been the fighting during the two preceding encounters, it was as nothing compared to this final shock. The victory was still hanging in the balance, when the Captal de Buch and his small detachment suddenly appeared in the left rear of the French. He had gone round the Masse aux Anglais, taken a turn to the north-west, which brought him on to the ground from which King John had originally started, and then followed the enemy's track on to the scene of the combat.[1]

Ignorant of the small numbers of the force which had charged them from behind, the French wavered, and the more fainthearted began to melt away to the right rear, in the direction of Poictiers, where the way of retreat was still open. King John himself, however, utterly refused to fly, and held his ground, surrounded by his personal retinue and the most loyal of his vassals. It took the English some time to crush the resistance of this faithful band, but at last the mass was broken up, and the king, with his young son Philip, who had stuck to his side to the last, were made prisoners. All those who had stayed by them were either captured or slain : the routed main body of the French rear-battle reached Poictiers, though many were taken by the way ; the English made no great slaughter of the fugitives, being far more intent on taking prisoners with good ransoms than on shedding blood.

Thus ended a battle far more hazardous and far better fought than that of Creçy. From first to last it had filled some seven hours : " the first attack had commenced at prime, and the last of the English had not returned from the pursuit till vespers." Considering the long struggle, the French loss in killed was not

---

[1] "Graditur iter obliquum, sub declivo recedens a monte quem cum principe nuper dimisit, et occulte girans campum venit ad locum submissum primae stacionis coronati. Exinde conscendit altiora campi per viam Gallicis ultimo tritam, et subito prorumpens ab occulto, per veneranda signa Georgica significavit se nobis amicum" (Baker of Swinbrook, p. 151).

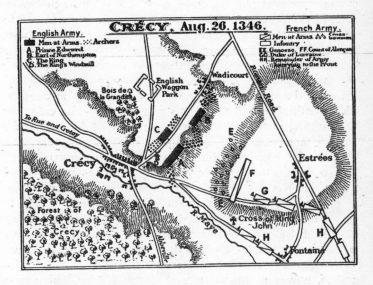

CRÉCY, Aug. 26. 1346.

English Army.
■ Men at Arms ∴ Archers
A. Prince Edward.
B. Earl of Northampton.
C. The King.
D. The King's Windmill.

French Army.
☐ Men at Arms ∴ Cross bowmen
Infantry
EE. Genoese. FF. Count of Alençon
GG. Duke of Lorraine
HH. Remainder of Army hurrying to the Front

Bois de la Grandière
English Waggon Park
Wadicourt
To Rue and Crotoy
Crécy
Forest of Crécy
R. Maye
Estrées
Cross of King John
Fontaine

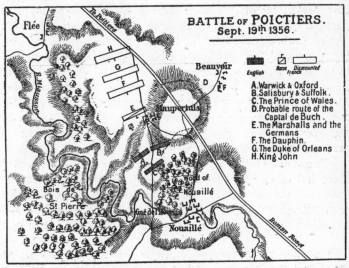

BATTLE of POICTIERS.
Sept. 19th 1356.

■ English ☐ Horse French ☐ Dismounted

A. Warwick & Oxford.
B. Salisbury & Suffolk.
C. The Prince of Wales.
D. Probable route of the Captal de Buch.
E. The Marshalls and the Germans
F. The Dauphin.
G. The Duke of Orleans
H. King John

Flée
To Poitiers
R. Miausson
Beauvoir
Maupertuis
Bois St Pierre
Gué de l'Homme
Nouaillé
Wood of Nouaillé
Roman Road

so large as might have been expected, though several of the greatest lords of France had fallen. On the other hand, the number of prisoners of the highest rank was almost unparalleled. The slain are said to have been two thousand five hundred, of whom just two thousand were knights and men-at-arms.[1] The chief of them were the Marshal Clermont, who had led the first division ; Gautier de Brienne Duke of Athens,[2] the Constable of France ; Peter Duke of Bourbon ; Guichard lord of Beaujeu, younger brother of the Edward of Beaujeu who had fallen at Ardres in 1351[3] ; Robert of Durazzo, a cousin of the King of Naples ; Geoffrey de Charny, who bore the oriflamme that day ; Renaud Bishop of Chalons ; and the Viscounts of Brosses and Rochechouart. Far more striking is the list of the prisoners : they included King John himself and his son Philip ; James Count of La Marche, John[4] Count of Eu, Charles Count of Longueville, John Count of Tancarville, Bernard Count of Ventadour, John Count of Auxerre, Henry Count of Vaudemont, John Count of Sancerre, Charles Count of Dammartin, John Count of Vendôme, John Count of Nassau, John Count of Saarbrücken, John Count of Joigny, Robert Count of Roussy, William Archbishop of Sens, Arnold d'Audrehem, the marshal whose inconsiderate advance had opened the battle, ten more great lords bearing banners, and two thousand five hundred others, of whom nineteen hundred and thirty-three were men-at-arms and knights.[5] The English loss must have been considerable : unfortunately, no trustworthy chronicler has stated it : only Lord Burghersh's letter gives figures—the impossibly small total of four men-at-arms and sixty others.

The political results of Poictiers were, owing to the king's captivity, very considerable, but the immediate strategical results were *nil*, as the prince retired to Bordeaux with his plunder and his more important prisoners, dismissing the rest under a pledge

[1] The Black Prince in his letter to the Bishop of Worcester gives two thousand four hundred and six men-at-arms, besides the princes and barons whose names he cites. The letter of Burghersh speaks of two thousand men-at-arms and five hundred others.

[2] Only titular duke, as his father, Gautier I., had been deprived of the duchy and his life by the Catalans at the battle of the Cephissus in 1310.

[3] See p. 156.

[4] It is curious to notice the preponderance of the name John among the prisoners; nine out of sixteen bore it.

[5] The figures of the Prince of Wales and Lord Burghersh, agreeing closely together, and both sent from the actual field, can no doubt be trusted.

to surrender themselves again, or to bring in their ransom on a fixed day. He made no attempt to hold Poitou or any of the neighbouring districts. Evidently his intention was to attain his political ends by bringing pressure to bear on his prisoner, and not by the series of lengthy sieges which would have been required to secure the results of his victory.

Experience proved that this was the right policy: the attempts of the English during the next four years to complete the conquest of France came to nothing. Though King Edward marched to and fro through the heart of the land, ravaging Champagne, Burgundy, and Isle de France, and encamping at the very gates of Paris, he could make no permanent lodgment. Cowed by the results of Creçy and Poictiers, the French refused to meet him in the open field, and shut themselves up in their towns and castles. To take one by one these innumerable strongholds would have been an interminable process; it did not suit his temper, nor were his resources adequate for such an enterprise. But he obtained some considerable part of what he had desired by playing on King John's dislike of captivity, and on the desire of the French estates to put an end to the anarchy which had resulted from his absence. Hence came the Treaty of Bretigny (8th of May 1360), ratified at Calais on October 24, which gave up to the English Poitou, Angoumois, Limousin, Rouergue, and many districts more, so as almost to reconstitute the old duchy of Aquitaine as it had been held by Henry II. two hundred years before. Nor was this all: the English got back Ponthieu at the Somme mouth, and retained the all-important harbour of Calais, the open gate of Northern France.

Thus ended the first act of the Hundred Years' War; yet fighting was by no means at an end in France. There were two quarrels still on foot which were fated to cost much blood. The long war of succession in Brittany between Charles of Blois and the younger John de Montfort was not yet settled, and Charles the Bad, the intriguing king of Navarre, was still trying to fish in troubled waters, and get some private profit from the misfortunes of his cousin John of Valois. The disbanded mercenaries, French and English, who had been fighting in the main war gladly hired themselves to serve in the minor struggles. It was not till the battles of Cocherel (May 16, 1364) and Auray (September 29, 1364) had taken place that France could really be said to be at peace. Both these combats were practically fought out entirely by the free companies ; at Cocherel two-thirds of the French army and five-sixths of the Navarrese army were veteran mercenaries.   At Auray half the army of Charles of Blois was composed of French free companies, and four-fifths of that of John de Montfort of English auxiliaries of the same kind.   Neither fight is of any permanent importance in the art of war ; they are only interesting as showing the way in which the lessons of Creçy and Poictiers had impressed themselves on the minds of the professional soldiers of the day.   Both sides in each of the fights descended and fought on foot ; the only exception to this rule being that Du Guesclin at Cocherel kept a small reserve of thirty horsemen, who were ordered to wait till both sides were locked in close combat, and then dash in at the person of the hostile leader, the famous John de Grailly Captal de Buch, who had struck the decisive blow at Poictiers.   It is noteworthy that the Captal at Cocherel and Sir John Chandos at Auray both adopted the tactics they had learned under the two Edwards, and took a defensive position on a slope, on which they waited to be attacked by the superior forces of the enemy. The Captal was prevented from carrying out his plan by the rashness of one of his wing-commanders, the condottiere John Joel, who was lured down into the plain by a feigned flight of the wily Du Guesclin.   At Auray Chandos was more lucky, and received on his chosen ground the attack of the French and Bretons, who crossed the river and ascended the slope to assail him.[1] Both the Captal and Chandos, though commanding mercenaries who had long fought under the English flag, were very short of archers.   It was only in a national levy that these could be found in proper proportion to the other arm.   At Cocherel there were only three hundred archers to twelve hundred men-at-arms, a number insufficient to have any influence on the event of the battle.   At Auray Chandos had about a thousand archers to eighteen hundred men-at-arms, a larger but still an insufficient proportion.   It was not they who decided the fate of the day ; the four battles of dismounted horsemen,

---

[1] Chandos insisted on taking the defensive, and said to his employer Duke John, who wished to advance :

> " Laissez nous assailir, et François commencier,
> Et tenons nos courois sans nous adesfonquier,
> Car voit-on bien souvent, je te dis sans cuidier,
> Qu'est meschief à celui qui assaut le premier."
>
> Cuvelier, lines 5875-79.

whom Charles of Blois led, all came to hand-strokes with the English in spite of the arrow-flight. That they succeeded in doing so was due to the greatly increased heaviness of the knightly panoply, which had been growing thicker and more complicated year by year for the very purpose of keeping out the arrow. Only a strong shot disabled a man in the new plate armour ; a large proportion of the shafts glanced off the surface obliquely. In serried ranks, and carrying shields before them, the French succeeded in closing without suffering any over-whelming loss. When the mêlée commenced, the archers cast down their bows and joined in the hand-to-hand combat with axe and sword, as they had done at Poictiers. They are said to have done good and efficient service, fighting side by side with the knights, just as their grandsons did at Agincourt fifty years after. Tactically the victory at Auray was decided by the fact that Chandos used his reserve—two hundred lances under Sir Hugh Calverley—to strengthen weak points in his line one after another, never allowing it to become so entangled that it could not be withdrawn for service in another part of the field. The far larger reserve-battle which Du Guesclin had set aside for a similar purpose got mixed with the fighting line, and ceased to be a tactical unit, so that the first break in the French array proved fatal, there being no organised body of fresh men who could be thrust into the gap. It is perhaps worth noting that Calverley made his two hundred men-at-arms strip off their cuissarts (thigh-pieces) to allow them to move about more easily—a proof that the full knightly armour had now grown heavy enough to make all motion difficult, when the wearer had been wearied by long fighting. Without this expedient his reserve would not have been movable enough for use at each point of the line, as it was successively in danger of being broken through.[1]

[1] For a full account of Auray, with much discussion of the relative value of sources, see La Borderie's *Histoire de Bretagne*, ii. pp. 586–95.

CHAPTER V

NAVARETTE AND ALJUBAROTTA

THE details of the tactics of Cocherel and Auray serve to show that the day of the horsemen was now considered to be at an end. After Creçy and Poictiers cavalry ceased to be the preponderant arm in Western Europe for some century and a half. For the future French and Netherlanders, as well as English and Scots, dismount as a general rule for battle. But the new tactics had still to be learned by the nations of the Iberian peninsula ; the lessons which taught the Spaniards and Portuguese the importance of the dismounted man-at-arms were both given by English teachers. In the first, the battle of Navarette (1367), the Black Prince himself showed the Spaniards the same tactics which his father had used against the French at Creçy. In the second, the battle of Aljubarotta (1385), the Portuguese king João (John I.) was directed by English officers of experience, and assisted by a considerable English contingent, so that we may fairly look upon his victory as another of the great series which commenced at Dupplin and Halidon Hill.

It was Navarette which first brought Spain into contact with Western military science. The Castilians, unlike their neighbours of Aragon, had since the first foundation of their State had very little to do with the general politics of Europe. Their history touches that of Portugal, Aragon, and Navarre, but had hitherto been seldom connected to any important extent with that of France. Indeed Castile was not conterminous with any part of the royal domain of France, and only touched at one single point the English duchy in Aquitaine. On the other hand, she was in constant contact with the Andalusian Moors, and the most important part of her history is concerned with their gradual conquest. One hundred and twenty years before, St. Ferdinand had finally penned up the Mohammedans in the kingdom of Granada.[1] But there they still survived, and Moorish campaigns were still frequent. Hence it was natural enough that Castile had shared little in the later developments of the art of war in the fourteenth century, and that the military customs and organisation of her people bore strong marks of their long contact with the Moslem.

When, in February 1367, the Black Prince crossed the Pyrenees to restore Pedro the Cruel to the throne from which he had been driven by his bastard brother Henry of Trasta-mara, the strength of the Castilian army was considered to reside wholly in its cavalry. And among these mounted men the light horse bore a more important part than they had ever occupied in any other European kingdom save Poland and Hungary. The "Genetes,"[2] or "Genetours" as the English called them, took their name from the jennets or light coursers which they rode. They were equipped in a semi-Moorish fashion, with a round steel cap, a large shield, a quilted gambeson, and two long javelins, which they launched at the enemy with good aim, even when galloping at full speed. Their tactics were not to close, but to hover round their opponents, continually harassing them, till they should give ground or break their formation, when a chance would occur of pushing a charge home. What such fighting was like is best shown by the interesting picture of the battle of Higueruela, now in the Escurial, which represents a famous victory of John II. in the year 1431 over Mohammed, King of Granada. The whole front of space between the armies is filled with a whirling mass of the light horse of the two sides, engaged in single combats with the javelin, which is sometimes hurled and sometimes used to thrust. The Spanish *ginetes* wear a certain amount of armour, heavier than that of their Moslem opponents, many of whom have only a shield to protect them. Behind this mêlée we see on the one side the Spanish heavy cavalry in two lines, one led by the Constable of Castile, the other by the king, with two solid masses of infantry in their rear. The Moors on the other side of the field show, behind their screen of skirmishing light horse, two lines,—the first

---

[1] Cordova fell in 1236; Seville in 1248.
[2] The word was used down to the present century for the cavalryman in the Spanish army; a Spanish "morning state" shows the heads *Infantes, ginetes,* and *artilleros* as late as the Peninsular War.

mainly composed of six solid squadrons of mounted lancers, the second entirely of infantry in eight columns. The picture is, of course, late, and was terribly "restored" in 1882, but the old outlines survive, and show admirably the skirmishing tactics, both of the Moors and of the Christian *ginetes*. [Plate XXVII.]

Such troops would have been formidable foes to infantry not armed with missile weapons, or to dismounted men-at-arms ; but against the combination of archers and knights they were ineffective. At Navarette, as we shall see, they were shot down helplessly by the archers, long before they could get near enough to use their javelins. The Spanish heavy cavalry, supplied by the baronage and the great military Orders of Santiago and Calatrava, were in 1367 much in the condition in which English and French feudal horsemen had been fifty years before. They were late in adopting the heavier armour which had been coming into vogue farther north, and their horses were not for the most part " barded," but unprotected by armour. They knew nothing of the new device of fighting on foot, but still charged in mass like their ancestors. They do not seem to have been very highly esteemed by their opponents in this campaign, and are accused of being too prone to fall into the skirmishing tactics of their compatriots the " genetours " when their first charge failed.[1]

The Spanish infantry appeared in considerable numbers on the field, the chartered towns contributing spearmen and crossbowmen, while considerable numbers of slingers were also used. But they played a very poor part in the campaign of 1367, and were of no practical use at Navarette.

The army with which Prince Edward crossed the Pyrenees, though English in name and led by many English leaders, was far less national than that which had fought at Creçy or even at Poictiers. The large majority of the troops were supplied either by the Gascon vassals of the duchy of Aquitaine, or by the huge bands of mercenaries, the celebrated " great companies " whom the prince had raised for this campaign. There were, no doubt, many thousand Englishmen in the ranks of the " free companions," but they were swallowed up in the general mass of cosmopolitan adventurers. Beyond the prince's personal retinue, and those of the English peers and knights who accompanied him, the only contingent from this side of

[1] So Froissart, xi. 182.

the Channel was composed of the four hundred men-at-arms and six hundred bowmen whom John of Gaunt had brought over.

The army which fought at Navarette was larger than most of those which served under the English banner in the Middle Ages. It mustered more than ten thousand men-at-arms, and at least as many infantry, of whom something over half were English archers, all mounted, so that, as Chandos Herald observes, the prince's train comprised no less than thirty-two thousand horses. The van marched under the Duke of Lancaster, the main-battle under the prince himself, the rear under James the exiled King of Majorca, who, driven out of his realm by the Aragonese, hoped ultimately to re-establish himself there by the prince's aid. Edward would have been able, had he chosen, to put an even larger force in the field, for the free companies had flocked in to his call in such numbers that he was obliged to dismiss many of them because of the enormous financial strain on the resources of his duchy. He could not afford to take into his pay all who presented themselves. It was the need of finishing the matter quickly, before his money should run out, which induced him to start so early as February, when the Pyrenean defiles are barely passable. As it was, both his van division and his main-battle suffered terribly from cold and piercing winds, while threading on successive days the lofty pass of Roncesvalles.

The beginning of the campaign was much complicated by the double-dealing of Charles of Navarre, in whose hands the passes lay. He first was bribed by Henry of Trastamara to shut them against the English; then, rather than fight the prince, he made a convention with him, received English gold, and fed the army of invasion while it passed through his realm. Lastly, to avoid committing himself too much against the Castilians, he got himself taken prisoner by Oliver de Mauni, a French knight in the service of the King of Aragon, who seized his person and put him in custody. Under cover of this compulsion, he pretended to be unable to aid either party. But three hundred of his men-at-arms, under his chief confidant, Martin Henriquez de Lacarra, joined the prince's banner.

Charles the Bad having thus sold the passes to the English, the King of Castile had the choice either of defending the line of the Ebro, a fierce and broad river in early spring, or of advancing beyond that river and endeavouring to block the exits

(I) A TYPICAL NORMAN KEEP: CASTLE HEDINGHAM

(II) A TYPICAL "CONCENTRIC" CASTLE: CAERPHILLY

THE BATTLE OF COURTRAI (JULY 11, 1302)

THREE EPISODES FROM THE COURTRAI CHEST AT NEW COLLEGE, OXFORD

(1) The Death of Godfrey of Brabant.   (2) The Flemings in Phalanx receive the Cavalry charge.
(3) The Men of Ypres repel the sortie from the Castle.

N.B.—Note the "Goedendags" of the Flemings.

CASTILIAN "GENETOURS" SKIRMISHING WITH MOORS

From the large picture of the Battle of "La Higueruela (1431)": a victory of King John II.
of Castile over the King of Granada, in the Escurial.

N.B.—This picture was "restored" in 1882 by a modern hand; but its main outlines remain intact.
Observe the early example of a hand-gun in the lower plate.

I

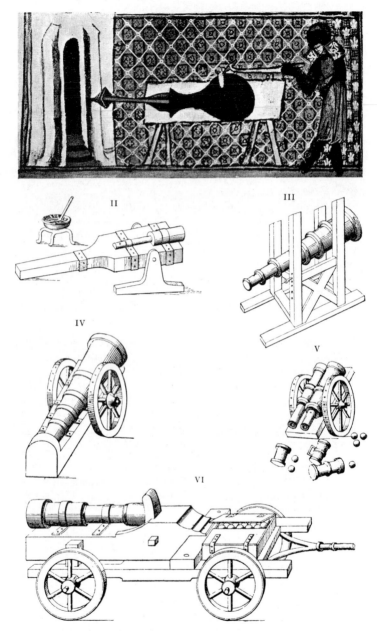

FOURTEENTH AND FIFTEENTH CENTURY CANNON

(I) The earliest known representation of a cannon, 1327, from the Millemete MS. in Christ Church, Oxford.
(II) Small early bombard clamped down to a "gun-stock." (III) A large bombard for siege work.
(IV) Fifteenth-century bombard on wheels. (V) Twin-gun on wheels: one of the objects in front is
a "chamber." (VI) Gun mounted on a carriage, German late fifteenth century.

from Navarre—the defiles which lead out of the plains of Vittoria and Pampeluna, through the mountains of Alava. He chose the latter alternative, broke up his camp at San Domingo de la Calzada, crossed the Ebro, and posted himself at Añastro, so as to block the difficult road which leads from Vittoria to Miranda, the main line of communication between Navarre and Burgos, the capital of Castile. From his new position he sent forward his brother Don Tello with six thousand horse to reconnoitre the English camps round Vittoria. Don Tello carried out his orders with considerable enterprise and cleverness : he beat up the camp of the Duke of Lancaster and the English vaward, did considerable damage before the invaders could get into array, and galloped off before they could harm him. On his homeward way he surrounded and cut to pieces an English scouting party under Sir Thomas and Sir William Felton on the hill of Ariñez. This skirmish had some interest as throwing light on the value of the tactics of the two armies. The two Feltons had little more than a hundred lances with them ; [1] encompassed by the Spaniards, they let their horses loose, and ranged themselves in a solid clump on the hill. They stood firm under the shower of javelins which the genetours of Don Tello cast at them, beat off several charges of the Spanish heavy horsemen, and were only taken or slain when some hundreds of French knights in the Spanish service dismounted, attacked them hand to hand, and over-whelmed them by force of numbers.

For about a week the English and Castilian armies lay opposite each other (March 20–26), the former in the plain of Vittoria, the latter on the hills to the south, each waiting for the other to advance, and both suffering from bad weather and want of food. Don Henry, warned by his French auxiliaries that it would be easier to starve the prince than to beat him, refused to come down into the plain ; Edward, on his part, thought the pass too difficult to force, and matters seemed at a deadlock.

The only exit from this situation was to endeavour to turn the Bastard's position by a sweeping flank march. This the prince at last resolved to undertake : secretly breaking up from Vittoria by night, he left the main road, took a by-path, and then turned southward and crossed the Sierra de Cantabria

[1] Ayala says (p. 446) two hundred men-at-arms and two hundred archers.

at the pass of La Guardia. He reached the Ebro near Viana after a forced march of two days, and shortly afterwards crossed the great river at the bridge of Logroño—a place which, unlike the other towns of Northern Castile, had adhered to Don Pedro. At Logroño the prince was upon the high road from Pampeluna to Burgos, and had completely turned Don Henry's position, blocking the Burgos-Miranda-Vittoria route. The Castilians, who seem to have entirely lost touch of the English army between the 26th and the 30th of March, were forced to break up hastily from their camp on the heights of Bañares and Añastro, and to recross the Ebro in order to throw themselves between Edward and their capital. Passing by the bridge of San Vincente near Haro, the Bastard marched for Najera, the nearest point on the Logroño-Burgos road that he could reach. Here he halted on April 1, his front covered by the Najarilla, a considerable stream which falls into the Ebro from the south. On the same night the prince lay at Navarette, six miles to the eastward of him.

The change in the scene of operations was all in the prince's favour : he had got down into the fertile valley of the Ebro, and between him and the Castilians there was now nothing but the Najarilla and " a fine plain where there was no bush or tree for a good league around." [1] Don Henry was practically under an obligation to fight in the open, unless he should choose to sacrifice Castile and retire into the interior. This course had been urged on him by the French some weeks before, but he had replied that if he retired without fighting, half Spain would go over to Don Pedro : indeed, desertions from his ranks had already begun.[2] He had now only to choose whether he would fight east or west of the Najarilla, and, as he placed his main confidence in his cavalry, he resolved to advance into the broad plain beyond the river, instead of staying on his own bank and waiting for the prince to attack him. Horsemen, as he perhaps reflected, are not suited to defend a position.

Battle of Navarette, April 3, 1367

To the great joy of the prince, his scouts brought him news, at the dawn of April 3, that the Castilians had crossed the

---

[1] Chandos Herald, lines 3450, 3451.
[2] Ayala, p. 454: "Antes que las batallas se ayuntasen algunos genetes e la pendon de Sant Esteban del Puerto pasaronse á la parte del rey Don Pedro,"

Najarilla and were advancing upon him in battle-array. The tactics which the Bastard had adopted for the drawing out of his host were precisely the reverse of those which the French had tried at Poictiers. King John in 1356 had sent a forlorn hope of cavalry in front of his army, and dismounted the rest of his men-at-arms. King Henry in 1367 sent out in front a picked body of dismounted knights, and kept the rest of his army on their horses.

This vanguard was mainly composed of the Bastard's French auxiliaries under the great Breton condottiere Bertrand du Guesclin and the Marshal d'Audrehem, who after his experiences at Poictiers was, we doubt not, glad enough not to have to fight on horseback. To the French, who were, counting knights and squires together, some fifteen hundred combatants, the king added a picked body of several hundred Castilian men-at-arms under his brother Don Sancho and the Grand Master of Santiago. Included among them were the Knights of the Scarf, an order of chivalry founded in 1332, which corresponded somewhat to Edward III.'s better-known order of the Garter. Pedro Lopez de Ayala, the chronicler of the fight on the Castilian side, bore that day the pennon of the Knights of the Scarf. The whole body of dismounted men was probably about two thousand strong (Ayala says only one thousand): to them the king had joined some crossbowmen, who no doubt were drawn up on the flanks of the men-at-arms.

Don Henry's second line was formed of the bulk of his horsemen. It was composed of three bodies, not drawn on a level front, but with the side divisions somewhat advanced, so as to cover the flanks of the vaward " battle " of dismounted knights. On the left wing was the king's brother Don Tello and the Grand Prior of the Hospitallers, with one thousand men-at-arms and a great body of " genetours," probably two thousand strong;[1] in the centre was the king with fifteen hundred chosen knights; on the right Gomez Carillo de Quintana, High Chamberlain of Castile, Alfonso Count of Denia, a nephew of the King of Aragon, and the Grand Master of Cala-

[1] Chandos Herald, lines 3015–20, says that Henry had six thousand men-at-arms and four thousand genetours. Ayala, stating the Castilian numbers at the lowest, no doubt, says four thousand five hundred men-at-arms, and gives no figures for the genetours. Chandos Herald says that the Spanish foot were fifty thousand strong, with six thousand crossbowmen. Ayala states that they were very numerous, but gives no definite number.

trava, with one thousand men-at-arms, and a like number of genetours to the left wing. Some crossbowmen seem to have been attached to the cavalry of the second line, but the great bulk of the Spanish infantry, at least twenty thousand strong, were formed behind the king's battle as a third or reserve line. Little confidence was evidently placed in them, and they did no more than had been expected of them [1] when they fled from the field.

The Black Prince's host was, like the Spanish, formed in three lines, but each of them consisted of men-at-arms and archers in about equal proportions : it is not explicitly stated that in each case the bowmen were drawn up on the flanks of the knights, but we can have no doubt that this was the case. The vaward, led by the Duke of Lancaster, is said to have consisted of about three thousand lances (*i.e.* three thousand men-at-arms and three thousand archers). It contained the personal following of the duke, those of the two marshals of the host, Sir Stephen Cossington and Guichard D'Angle, with those of Hugh Lord Hastings, and of Thomas Ufford, William Beauchamp, and John Neville—the sons respectively of the Earls of Suffolk and Warwick and the Lord Neville. But the core of the division was composed of the twelve hundred veteran lances of the free companies who served under Sir John Chandos' banner, the pick of the mercenary troops of Western Europe.

The prince's own main-battle, like that of Don Henry, was drawn up in a centre and two wings : Edward himself, with Pedro of Spain, governed the centre ; the right wing division was led by the Captal de Buch, the Count of Albret, and Martin Henriquez the Navarrese. The left wing division marched under Sir Thomas Percy,[2] the Breton Oliver de Clisson, and Sir

---

[1] In this account I follow Ayala. Chandos Herald gives the same divisions, but very different numbers. He says that Bertrand's battle on foot was four thousand men-at-arms, that Don Tello had twelve thousand genetours (no men-at-arms apparently), and Gomez Carillo four thousand one hundred men-at-arms (but no genetours apparently). The king, according to him, had fifteen thousand "hommes armés" in his division, besides a vast multitude of arbalesters, sergeants, and other footmen. This makes twenty-three thousand men-at-arms, but a few pages before Chandos had made Henry say that he had but six thousand men-at-arms and four thousand genetours. Obviously these are much more like the real figures. One can but follow Ayala, who served in the Castilian host, and must have known all about it.

[2] Afterwards Earl of Worcester. He was in 1367 a young man of twenty-five. Beheaded after Shrewsbury fight by Henry IV.

Walter Hewett.[1]   Each of the three corps must have contained about two thousand lances.   [See Plate XXVIII.]

Finally, the rearward, under the King of Majorca, consisted of Gascons under the Count of Armagnac, and a great body of free companions led by Sir Hugh Calverley and Perducas d'Albret.   They are said to have been about three thousand lances strong, like the vaward-battle.   The whole amount of the English host should have been about twelve thousand lances, but they had suffered much during the last two months from cold, rain, forced marches, and insufficient feeding, so that their opponent Ayala is probably near the truth when he states that the prince's army contained ten thousand men-at-arms.   Among the corresponding number of infantry who accompanied the men-at-arms there must have been included many Gascon " bidowers " and foreign crossbowmen and javelinmen of all sorts, for there were certainly not ten thousand native English archers on the field.

The prince drew up his host close to Navarette, and then marched forward, not by the high road to Najera, but over the open plain, screening his advance by a rolling hill to the right of the road.   It was only on descending this rising ground that he came in sight of the Castilians.   He then halted, bade his men send their horses to the rear, and marched down to meet the enemy.   Their fronts seem to have exactly corresponded, as we do not hear of any outflanking.   In numbers (as we have already seen) the prince had a large superiority in men-at-arms— probably about ten thousand to five thousand five hundred ; on the other hand, the Spaniards had their four thousand light horse and perhaps twenty thousand foot to oppose to the prince's ten thousand archers.

The course of the battle was very simple : the two vawards first met ; the English archers of Lancaster's division seem to have driven off the crossbowmen, but the two bodies of dismounted knights met and remained locked together fighting desperately.   At the first clash the English are said to have been borne back a spear's length,[2] and Chandos was cast to the ground and nearly slain.[3]   But neither side gained any further advantage, and the fate of the battle was decided elsewhere.

The next bodies which came into collision were the Spanish

---

[1] Chandos puts Sir Thomas Felton here, though he had fallen at Ariñez.
[2] Ayala, p. 457.   [3] Chandos Herald.

knights and genetours of Don Tello and Gomez Carillo, and the flank divisions of the English main-battle, under the Captal de Buch on the right and Percy and Clisson on the left. In these two combats the Castilians were disgracefully beaten ; they never closed with their opponents or came to handstrokes ; apparently they tried their usual skirmishing tactics, intending to hover around the English and cast javelins at them. But the English archery shot down horse and man while the Castilians were still far away, and, instead of closing, the whole horde, genetours and men-at-arms together, turned their bridles and fled off the field. Several prisoners of importance fell into the hands of the English from these divisions, including Gomez Carillo and the Count of Denia ; probably their horses had been shot and they were cast to the earth and unable to get away.

After driving off the Spanish horse, both the Captal de Buch and Percy wheeled their divisions inward, to attack the flanks of the Castilian vaward, which was still hotly engaged with Lancaster's battle. At the same moment Prince Edward came up in the centre to reinforce his brother. To succour his advanced guard, now wholly encompassed with foes, Don Henry hurried up in person with his fifteen hundred chosen knights and the great mass of his infantry. The Bastard, as all the chroniclers agree in stating, showed the greatest courage. He charged three times at the head of his personal following, endeavouring to cut his way to join the vaward-battle ; but he could not break the lines of the English dismounted knights, and was thrice forced to recoil. Meanwhile the English arrows were making fearful slaughter among the great masses of his infantry, who were already beginning to fall into disorder.

At last the King of Majorca and the English rear-battle came upon the scene, striking in on the left of the combat. The Castilians could stand no longer, " for arrows flew thicker than rain in winter-time ; they pierced through horse and man, and the Spaniards soon saw that they could no longer endure. They turned their steeds and commenced to flee away. Then when Henry the Bastard saw them fly he was sore enraged, and three times he tried to turn them back, crying, ' Sirs, for God's sake give me aid, for you have made me king and sworn me your oath to help me loyally.' But his word availed nothing, for the attack grew stronger every moment, and the Spaniards

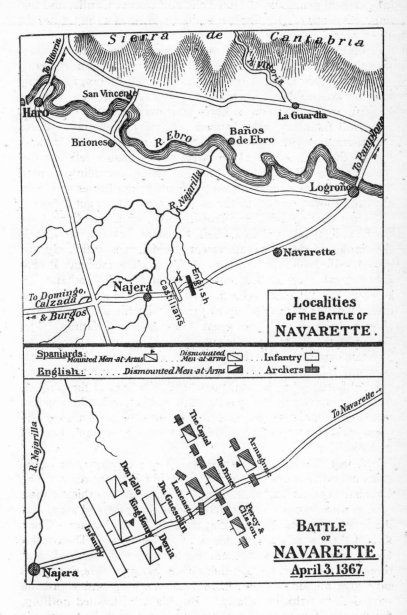

Sierra de Cantabria

To Vitoria

To Vitoria

San Vincente

Haro

La Guardia

Briones

R. Ebro

Baños de Ebro

To Pampylona

Logroño

R. Najarilla

Navarette

To Domingo, Calzada

& Burgos

Najera

Castilians

English

Localities
OF THE BATTLE OF
NAVARETTE.

Spaniards: ..... Mounted Men-at-Arms   Dismounted Men-at-arms   Infantry

English: ..... Dismounted Men-at-Arms   Archers

R. Najarilla

To Navarette

The Capel

Armagnac

Don Tello

The Prince

Lancaster

King Henry

Du Guesclin

Percy & Clisson

Infantry

Denia

Najera

BATTLE
OF
NAVARETTE
April 3, 1367.

turned backward, and every man loosed his rein.   Sore grieved and wroth was the Bastard, but it behoved them to fly, or they would all have been slain or taken.   Therefore he fled down the valley, though the French in his vaward were still standing their ground." [1]

Du Guesclin and his band of dismounted knights, long surrounded by the English, and growing fewer every moment, did not yield till the whole of the Spanish army had been driven off the field.   It is impossible to praise their determined courage too highly.   But, seeing themselves abandoned, they were at last forced to surrender.   More than four hundred of them had fallen, including the Bégue de Villiers, one of the captains of the French mercenaries, and of the Spaniards Garcilasso de la Vega, Sancho de Rojas, Juan Rodrigo Sarmiento, and Juan de Mendoza.   Bertrand du Guesclin gave up his sword to Sir Thomas Cheney ; Audrehem and Don Sancho, the king's brother, were also taken.

The rest of the Castilian chivalry had suffered comparatively little : as the total number of corpses of men-at-arms, counted by the heralds after the fight, was only five hundred and sixty, the divisions headed by Don Henry, Don Tello, and Gomez Carillo must only have lost a hundred and sixty all told.   The unfortunate foot-soldiery, who could not flee so fast, suffered more.   Their masses blocked the bridge of Najera, towards which they all fled, and the English cut down great numbers of them.   A freshet from the mountains had swelled the Najarilla during the morning, so that it was not fordable, and many who strove to escape by swimming were drowned.   Altogether the Spaniards are said to have lost over seven thousand men.   In the pursuit several important prisoners were taken : the Grand Master of Calatrava was caught hiding in a cellar at Najera ; the Master of Santiago and the Grand Prior of the Hospitallers were trapped in a blind entry between high walls into which they had incautiously ridden, and forced to surrender.

The total loss in the prince's host was absurdly small : four knights had fallen—two Gascons, a German, and Sir John Ferrers, son of the English baron of that name ; in addition, forty men-at-arms and twenty archers had perished.   Almost the whole loss must have fallen on the vaward, who had fought so desperately with Du Guesclin's men.

[1] Chandos Herald, line 3385 *et seq.*

Thus ended in disaster the last attempt of continental cavalry to pit itself against the combination of archers and dismounted men-at-arms, which Edward III. and his son had perfected. Nothing could have been more miserable than the show made by the Castilian light-horse and crossbowmen when they came under the deadly rain of English arrows, or that of the Bastard's chivalry when they strove to ride down the English men-at-arms.

The battle, however, was won, but not the campaign. As long as Henry of Trastamara lived, Pedro the Cruel's throne was insecure It was in vain that the tyrant strove to massacre all the Castilian prisoners, and actually, in spite of Prince Edward's opposition, beheaded Gomez Carillo, the Commander of Santiago, and two other knights.[1] No amount of cruelty could secure him the throne that the English had given him back. Less than two years after Edward had retired in disappointment to Gascony, Spain was up in arms again, and Don Pedro had fallen into his brother's hands, and been murdered by his brother's own dagger (1369).

Battle of Aljubarotta, August 14, 1385.

To end the chapter in the history of the art of war which began with Creçy, it only remains that we should make some mention of the battle of Aljubarotta, the last fight in Western Europe in which mounted men were to take a prominent part during the fourteenth century. In 1385 John King of Castile, the son of Henry of Trastamara, was making a great effort to put down his namesake John, the Master of Avis, who claimed the throne of Portugal. In right of his wife, the only daughter of Ferdinand, the last of the male line of the Portuguese house, the Castilian had a better hereditary claim than the Master of Avis, who was but the late king's bastard brother. But the national spirit of the Portuguese revolted against a union with Spain, and the large majority of the people, both gentle and simple, adhered to the Master, who took the crown under the name of João I. To crush him, the King of Castile called out the full levy of his realm, strengthened by a large corps of mercenary men-at-arms, led by certain lords of France, such as Regnault de Solier, Jean de Rye, and Geoffrey de Partenay. So large a proportion of these auxiliaries were drawn from the

[1] Ayala, p. 458.

county of Bearn that Froissart sometimes calls the whole body of them " the barons of France and Bearn." John of Avis, on the other hand, was assisted by a much smaller band of English adventurers who had come in three great ships from Bordeaux under two squires, veterans of the French war, named John Northberry and Hugh Hartsell. They numbered in all about five hundred men.[1]

The Portuguese army was far less numerous than that of the invaders, but, on the advice of his English allies, John of Avis resolved to offer battle. He marched out from Lisbon to Thomar, and looked for a good position. The chosen spot was hard by the abbey of Aljubarotta, where the hills of the Sierra da Estrella sink into the plain. On one of the spurs lie the monastic buildings, thickly surrounded by orchards and plantations. Half-way down the slope the Portuguese took their post; they felled trees so as to cover both their flanks, but left a fairly broad open space opposite their centre.[2] Behind the two flanking abattis were placed the English archers and such native crossbowmen as could be got together, forming two projecting wings. The men-at-arms, all on foot, were formed in one solid battle in the middle, opposite the gap in the barricades. This order of battle was obviously a direct copy of that of the Black Prince at Poictiers : the army was masked by the trees, and the natural gap in the hedge, which figured in the former battle as the sole point of entry into the English position, was deliberately reproduced in 1385 by the extemporised barricades with the open space in their centre. A few yards in front of the line there was a shallow ravine with a thread of water running through it,[3] which reproduced the dip in the ground which lay in front of the farm of Maupertuis. Some way to the side were two other ravines, which guarded the flanks of the army.[4]

The King of Castile had marched from Ciudad Rodrigo by Celorico and Leiria to Santarem : his army consisted of at

---

[1] Lorenzo Fogaça in Froissart (K. de L.), vol. xi. p. 305, says only two hundred.

[2] "Adont firent-ils au costè devers les champs abatre les arbres et couchier à travers, à celle fin que de plain l'on ne peust chevauchier, et laissiérent ung chemin ouvert qui n'estoit pas d'entrée trop large" (Froissart (K. de L.), vol. ii. p. 164).

[3] "Ung fossé, et non pas grant que ung cheval ne peust bien saillir oultre" (Lorenzo Fogaça in Froissart (K. de L.), vol. xi. p. 314).

[4] Ayala, p. 231 : "Los dos alas de los nuestros tienen delante dos valles, que non pueden paser pera acometar à nuestros enemigos."

least two thousand lances of his French auxiliaries, many thousands of Spanish cavalry, light and heavy, like those who fought at Navarette, and a large contingent of crossbowmen on foot. Thus he much outnumbered the Portuguese, whose whole force was estimated at two thousand five hundred knights and men-at-arms [1] and twelve thousand infantry.

On a hot and bright Saturday noon—it was the Vigil of the Assumption (August 14)—in the heart of the summer, King John of Castile received news of the determination of the Portuguese to offer him battle. He was three leagues from Aljubarotta, and doubted whether he should fight that day, or advance to a convenient distance from the enemy and put off the battle till the morrow. Regnault de Solier, whom he had made marshal of his host, hotly urged the propriety of an instant attack, and was supported by nearly all the French knights and many of the younger Spaniards, who had never been present at a stricken field. On the other hand, certain of the Spanish barons spoke in favour of deferring the attack : it would be late in the day, they said, before the host could be properly drawn up in front of the hostile position, and battles begun in the evening seldom lead to a decisive result. Jean de Rye, an aged knight of Burgundy,[2] lent his support to their arguments, but the French talked down the advocates of delay, and the king gave orders to advance. He issued his command to draw up the host in two lines : the vaward was to be composed of the auxiliaries, who were to dismount (like Du Guesclin's knights at Navarette) and to endeavour to force the Portuguese centre. Behind them were to come the mass of the Spanish horsemen, arrayed in a centre and two wings.[3] The crossbowmen and other infantry followed in the rear, guarding the baggage ; it would have been more prudent to allot them to the front division.

Marching through the afternoon, the Castilian army reached Aljubarotta about vespers. When the enemy's line was made out, the French of the vaward pushed forward with unwise haste and proceeded to attack before taking the precaution of ascertaining that their own main body was sufficiently far forward to

[1] Froissart, xi. p. 308. Ayala says two thousand two hundred men-at-arms and ten thousand foot (p. 227).
[2] This we get from Ayala's Chronicle, p. 232, not from Froissart.
[3] The wings are only named by Ayala ; Froissart speaks as if they had been all in one mass. It is he also who mentions that the crossbowmen were in the rear (p. 231).

co-operate in the advance.   As a matter of fact, the king was several miles to the rear, and none of his corps were near enough to act in unison with the French.   Nevertheless the marshal and his countrymen rode briskly forward till they drew near to the enemy, and then turned their horses loose and dismounted to fight on foot.[1]

They advanced just in the way that the Portuguese king had hoped ; neglecting the archers and javelinmen on the wings, they pushed on in one solid mass for the gap in the line of abattis, behind which they saw the men-at-arms arrayed. Crossing the little ravine, they flung themselves upon the hostile centre.   Here they were received with a steady line of glaives and lances, while from both flanks a fierce discharge of arrows, crossbow bolts, and javelins was poured in upon them.   No support came up from the main body : the French were out-numbered, and surrounded on three sides.   Hence it is not sur-prising that after half an hour of desperate hand-to-hand fighting they gave way : nearly half of the division were slain, and a thousand were captured ; only a few hundreds escaped to bear the evil tidings to the King of Castile.

The whole encounter was over before King John had arrayed his line and proceeded to advance towards the hill of Alju-barotta.   He himself was soon apprised of what had happened ; his army, seeing no great back-rush of fugitives, but only isolated French knights making their way to the rear, failed to realise that the vaward-battle had been annihilated.

It was long past vespers and close to sunset when the great masses of horsemen drew near to the Portuguese position.   All along the line the Castilians were protesting against the folly of fighting at such a late hour ; but when their king ordered a general advance, they did not shrink from the assault.   The centre dashed partly against the barricades, partly through the gap in them ; the wings, which by the conformation of the ground had no good view of the enemy, got confused among ravines, orchards, and enclosures, and failed to outflank and turn the Portuguese.[2]   In no part of the field did the Spaniards gain any

---

[1] The account of Lorenzo Fogaça makes the French dismount, as does Ayala ; but Froissart's first version says, no doubt wrongly, that they kept their horses (p. 174).

[2] From Lorenzo Fogaça's version in Froissart, p. 315.   One of Henry's wings under Gonzalo de Guzman got right round to the rear of the enemy, but could not reach them (Ayala, p. 233).

advantage :[1] in the centre, the only point where they were able to close, they suffered very severely from the flanking fire of arrows, bolts, and javelins. So many horses were shot down that " in forty places the ravine was passable over their heaped-up carcases." It was calculated that about five hundred Castilian knights crossed this obstacle, and that the ground beyond it was such a death-trap that not one who had passed came back alive. As the dusk closed, the whole Spanish army reeled to the rear and fled in disorder ; the king and the greater part of the fugitives reached Santarem, but the rest fled devious over the countryside and reached Estremadura by cross-roads.

The loss at Aljubarotta was very heavy : the whole vaward division perished *en masse*, for before the second combat João of Portugal ordered all his prisoners to be cut down (like Henry v. at Agincourt), fearing lest such a numerous body might attack him from the rear, or might at least distract too many of his men from the combat. " So perished four hundred thousand francs of ransom-money." The marshal Regnault de Solier, the barons of Longnac, Esprès, Berneque, les Bordes, and Moriane, were the chief among the two thousand French slain. The Spaniards also suffered severely, though not in such a great proportion to their numbers : sixty barons and bannerets and twelve hundred squires and men-at-arms are said to have fallen, among whom were the Grand Masters of Santiago and Calatrava and the Count of Mayorga. Ayala names also Don Pedro son of the Infante of Aragon, Juan lord of Aguilar, the king's cousin (son of his father's brother, Don Tello), Diego Gomez, Adelantado Mayor of Castile, Juan de Tovar the High Admiral, Diego Gomez Sarmiento and Pero Gonsalvez Carillo the two marshals of Castile, Pedro de Mendoza the High Chamberlain, and many other barons of note.[2] The victors, as usual in these defensive battles, lost but a few scores : the only man of note among them who died was Martin Vaz de Mello, who was pierced right through his body by a dart cast by a Spanish genetour.

Though not discreditable to the courage of the French and Spanish knights, Aljubarotta gives us a very poor idea of their skill in war. All the blunders of Poictiers and Navarette were repeated : the vaward and main body did not co-operate ; the

---

[1] Ayala : "Los dos alas de la batalha del rey non pudieron pelear que cada una de las fallo un valle que non pudo passar" (p. 233).

[2] Ayala, pp. 235, 236.

enemy's position was not properly reconnoitred.   Both corps fell blindfold into the trap which the King of Portugal had laid for them, attacking in a headlong manner the fatal gap which he had left open to allure them between the two wings of infantry armed with missiles.   Instead of charging furiously down this entry, John of Castile should have employed his superior numbers in outflanking and surrounding the whole Portuguese position, and should only have closed when he had thoroughly made out the disposition of the enemy.   Blind assaults are almost inevitably bound to lead to defeat—most of all blind assaults of cavalry on a front securely hedged in with abbatis, from behind which infantry can strike at their assailants without being themselves exposed to the danger of being ridden down.

Such was the result of the last attempt made in Western Europe to defeat the English tactics by unsupported charges of horsemen.   We shall see, when we investigate the course of the second act of the Hundred Years' War, that John of Castile was hopelessly behind the times in his conception of the military art.   Many years before Aljubarotta was fought, leaders of greater wisdom had discovered more effective means of meeting the system by which Edward III. and the Black Prince had won their great victories.

CHAPTER VI

FRANCE AND ENGLAND—FAILURE OF THE POLICY OF EDWARD III., 1369–1396

ALREADY before the Peace of Calais had been signed, it had become evident that the strategical policy of Edward III.—if policy it can be called—had been tried and found wanting. Devastating raids, however sweeping and prolonged, could not conquer France : and the enemy had given up, after Poictiers, any idea of delivering great offensive battles against the invading English armies. Auray might be quoted as an exception ; but this was really no battle of French against a national English force, but a local Breton affair, in which a certain number of English mercenaries (with an unduly low proportion of archers) served as the auxiliaries of one claimant to the Breton duchy against the other—who for his part was supported in a similar way by a large body of French mercenaries. Actually, as well as theoretically, Auray was not a typical conflict between England and France.

Confounded at the blows which had been delivered against their old military system—Crécy, Saintes, Mauron, Poictiers, the *noblesse* of France foreswore the open field, and fell back on that fundamental superiority of the defensive over the offensive in the art of fortification of which we have already had to speak in so many places.[1] No tactical device had yet been found which would enable them to beat the English combination of lance and bow, when the enemy had got himself into a good position and waited to be attacked. Therefore battles for the future had to be eschewed altogether, unless the circumstances were exceptionally favourable. But there remained the possibility of foiling the enemy, by utilising the power of the defensive behind walls. Artillery was still so undeveloped and weak that the resisting power of a city wall

[1] See above, ii. pp. 52–53.

or a strong castle was hardly beginning to grow less. If a great English raid swept through France it could do much damage to the open country, but it could only win a town by a siege of desperate length.   Every one remembered how long Calais had held out in 1346–47 ;   unless the invader were prepared to sit down for months, he could win nothing ; and if he were successful in the end he only gained one city, whose plunder would certainly not repay the expense of keeping an army on foot in hostile territory during the siege.   That a first-rate fortress could not be rushed, even with the help of a few cannon, was sufficiently shown by the six weeks' siege of Rheims in 1360, which Edward III. himself had been forced to give up in disgust.

The Peace of Bretigny was extorted from the French, not by reason of strategical successes, but rather through the desire of the captive King John to get back to his realm, and by the profound desire for peace at almost any price which was felt by a majority of his subjects.   And so King Edward won, not by the sword but by the pen, the immense districts for which he surrendered his unreal claim to the royal crown of France. He made, as we can now see, a fundamental mistake in adding to the limits of the old nucleus of the duchy of Guienne, where nobles and cities alike were old and faithful subjects of the Plantagenets, broad regions like Poitou, Angoumois, Saintonge, Quercy, Marche, and Rouergue which had long been united to the French royal domain, and had a well-justified hatred to the English name, caused by the ravages which they had been enduring for the last twenty years.   Some places, like La Rochelle, held out for months after the signature of the Peace of Calais, in the name of a king who had bartered them away : they had to be besieged and taken by force.   Many nobles retired into French territory and refused their homage.

When the war broke out again in 1369 it was seen at once that the defence of the great principality, won at the treaty of 1360, would be rendered almost impossible by the active or passive disloyalty of Edward's vassals of all ranks.   The large majority of the inhabitants of the annexed districts, both gentle and simple, gave their assistance to the French whenever it was safe to do so,—sometimes unwisely and when it was not safe, as was shown by the fate of the unhappy people of Limoges in the last campaign of the Black Prince (1370).

The younger Edward was by this time an invalid, broken down by the fevers that he had earned in his Spanish campaign ; but even if he had been his old self, it would have been impossible for him to preserve the unwieldy and disloyal heritage with which his father had enfeoffed him.

The policy by which the French ultimately won back all, and more than all, that they had lost at the Peace of Calais, was the same that they had adopted with a heavy heart in the last few years of the old war—a steadfast refusal to give battle in the open, even with defensive tactics and the advantage of numbers ; and a Spartan resolve to sacrifice the countryside. The citizens shut themselves up in their towns, the nobles in their castles, when an English army came by. When it passed on, the local forces emerged to hang upon the rear of the invaders, to cut off their foraging parties, and to make descents on their train when nothing was thereby risked. Even the most formidable English raids accomplished nothing permanent. The most notable of them all, that of John of Gaunt in 1373, was in its way an astonishing feat of arms. The Duke of Lancaster led his army all across France from Calais to Bordeaux, past Arras, Troyes, and Nevers, and through the mountains of Auvergne, till he reached friendly soil in Guienne. But he did not take a single town of importance, nor win the smallest combat, for the French adhered to the policy of the great Constable, Bertrand du Guesclin, and absolutely refused to fight. The army burned a broad tract of devastation across Central France, but accomplished no more. When the autumn went by it found the greatest difficulty in feeding itself, became the prey of cold and hunger, and finally arrived at Bordeaux low in numbers, almost destitute of horses, and riddled with dysentery and fever.

Meanwhile the Constable du Guesclin practised his unpretentious but effective scheme of war. Though he would never fight a battle against an English royal army, he was continually cutting short the limits of the English territory in France. His tactics were to attack the small outlying garrisons, and to stir up the discontented regions of the newly-annexed provinces. He assaulted isolated castles or towns where the garrison was weak or discontented. If he was left alone, he captured them : if an army of succour marched against him he abandoned his siege, marched off, and made a dash at some distant stronghold, where he was least expected. He fought by night surprises, ambuscades, escalades, and stratagems of all sorts, utilising local treachery [or patriotism] whenever it was possible. But he refused to attack an English force, even one smaller than his own, if once it had taken up a good defensive position and got its archers arrayed. He had not been personally responsible for the policy of Navarette or Auray, though he was present at both.

This system wore away the strength of the English, whose tactics were above all suitable for defensive battles in the open. Archers, as is obvious, are better suited for use *en masse* in the field than for employment in small parties in garrisons. In siege-work even the best marksmen could not be very effective against an enemy who hid himself behind palisades and trenches, and advanced under cover of *pavises* (large mantlet-shields) whenever he approached a castle or a town wall.

It does not seem that the disasters of the English in the second stage of the Hundred Years' War were caused by any great decline in their military efficiency, though no doubt some of the forces which fought in France were short of their proper proportion of archers, and had ranks filled up with foreign mercenaries in a larger measure than was safe. The garrisons of the Gascon border were enfeebled rather than strengthened by any attempt to utilise local help—since the spirit of the nominal subjects of King Edward was generally more or less disloyal. Mercenaries, too, are notoriously treacherous to a losing cause. But it is to be noted that when a purely English army crossed the sea, as in 1373, 1378, and 1380, it always failed to win successes on the old scale.

From time to time public opinion grew so angry in England that ministers were accused of mismanaging the war of deliberate malice, either from motives of corruption or profiteering (which may occasionally have been imputed not without some justification), or else from mere treason (which was absurd). When one of these fits of national excitement had been raging, there was repeatedly an expedition on a large scale sent to France, to renew the old triumphs of Creçy and Poictiers. The result was always a disappointment ; but neither treason nor bad tactics were at the root of the failure. The end was impossible : a small state like England could not find either the men or the money needed to cope with such a vast task as the retention or reconquest of the all-too-large and disloyal duchy of Aquitaine.

Nor must it be forgotten that one of the basic conditions which had made the earlier English successes in France possible gradually disappeared in the later years of the war. The complete domination of the seas had come to an end : from Sluys onward the King of England had been able to land wherever he pleased beyond the Channel. But as a direct result of the Black Prince's unhappy championship of the cause of Peter the Cruel, the new dynasty in Castile had been forced into permanent alliance with France, and when its fleet joined that of Charles v. the balance at sea was changed. It was in the main a Spanish squadron which in 1372 beat the Earl of Pembroke off La Rochelle, and from that day onward the Bay of Biscay was no longer safe. It was impossible to rely on regular and swift communication with Bordeaux and Bayonne. The Channel was insecure, and Boulogne privateers in 1377 captured English merchant vessels only a few bow-shots outside Calais harbour. In the same year the Admiral of France, John de Vienne, and his Castilian colleague, Ferran Sanchez de Tovar, sacked Rye and Hastings, and ended their cruise with a daring raid into the mouth of the Thames, where they burned Gravesend. Such incursions were intermittent, but foreboded worse things in the future. Not only were the last loyal regions of Aquitaine threatened with conquest, in the absence of the reinforcements which could not always reach them, but there was serious danger to England itself.

In 1386 it looked as if the command of the sea had been so completely lost that an invasion of the southern counties was imminent—a thing that had not been dreamed of since 1340. In that year the new French king, Charles vi., gathered a great armament at Sluys, and called out all the vassals of France for a naval venture. His army and fleet were so large that the ministers of Richard ii. were in a state of panic from September to November. A fleet was watching the Dover Straits from Sandwich as the first line of defence : but the confidence felt in it was so moderate that all the shire levies from south of Thames were mobilised on the coast, and those of the Midlands round London. The towns of southern England received royal letters bidding them to repair or rebuild their walls— among others Oxford, where the still existent fragments of fortification date from that year.   Fortunately the invasion-scare passed away, partly in consequence of the incapacity of the young Charles VI.—but more from the quarrels of his factious uncles.   The French fleet never left Sluys, and the armament broke up in November.   But this was an un-covenanted mercy—the landing of the French in Kent had been a perfectly possible contingency, whatever the consequences might have been when once they had landed.   Probably a disaster would have resulted for the invaders, for the English bow and lance were still as formidable as before in a defensive position : and the enemy was led by a rash boy and a wrangling pack of princes of the blood, whose quarrels foreboded defeat.

The invasion-scare of 1386 was the last military crisis of the fourteenth century.   When the great Constable du Guesclin and his capable master Charles V. had died within a few months of each other in 1380, the real stress of the war had ended.   The great alarm of 1386 had resulted from a passing freak of megalomania in the brain of Charles VI. rather than from any well-thought-out scheme.   His father would never have dreamed of any such an enterprise, but would undoubtedly have used the resources allocated for it to gain some practical end in Aquitaine.   In 1388 there followed a truce, more lasting than several others which had preceded it, and finally there came after a long interval the definitive peace of 1396, which put an end to the Second Act of the Hundred Years' War, and was followed by the opening of friendly relations between England and France.   When the English king married the young daughter of Charles VI., it seemed that the struggle for the French crown, which had opened in 1338, was at last over, and each kingdom might turn to more profitable activities.

As has been already observed, the most surprising feature of the intermittent periods of war which lie between 1369 and 1396 is that no single pitched battle was fought in them.   Combats there were of the minor sort, and sieges small and great—that of St. Malo in 1378 was undoubtedly an operation on a large scale.   But no new military discovery was made, save indeed Du Guesclin's ingenious if somewhat uninteresting proof that a successful war may be waged without accepting battles in the open.   And this was in a way a confession of despair, arising from the fact that English armies in position had been found invincible : it is difficult to discover in history many instances of generals who, like Fabius, won a reputation by avoiding battles and specialising in minor operations !

As to tactics, we shall see in a later book that the day of the longbow was by no means over. When granted once more the conditions necessary for its proper employment, it was to win in the fifteenth century some of its most surprising victories. And it had already set its mark on the military history of Europe, by deposing cavalry from its ancient supremacy In battles quite outside the English sphere— Sempach, Roosebeke, Verneuil, Arbedo—we shall see the men-at-arms dismounting for battle, mainly in consequence of the lessons of Crecy and Poictiers.

BOOK X

GUNPOWDER AND CANNON

1250-1450

CHAPTER I

THE INVENTION OF GUNPOWDER AND CANNON

IN the chapter of the Seventh Book which dealt with the military machines of the thirteenth century, we had occasion to speak of the early discovery of incendiary compositions, and of the various ways in which they were utilised. By the end of that century a new explosive composition, the parent of the modern gunpowder, had been invented; and early in the fourteenth century it had been discovered that this stuff could be turned to its best use by being employed to propel missiles from tubes, as it had a propulsive power and not merely an incendiary or explosive one. Hence came artillery in its new shape.

The use of fire-projecting machines of all sorts is a long one, and goes back to classical times [1]: as early as the siege of Delium in the Peloponnesian War, the Bœotians had invented something like the German *flammenwerfer* of 1915, a device for spouting flames against stockades or gates by means of bellows [2] and a tube. And, as we have already seen, the notion of fire-projection had reached a considerable development in Byzantine days, and " Greek fire " had been the terror of the Mohammedan and the Italian enemies of the Eastern Empire.[3] But such inventions were purely incendiary, and have nothing to do with modern gunpowder or cannon. Explosive as opposed to incendiary compounds come a good deal later in the history of the Art of War: and for some time after their discovery they were not used for any propulsive purpose, but merely as superior forms of incendiary device, which not only set fire to things with which they came into

---

[1] There is a useful synopsis of such matter in Colonel Hime's *Origin of Artillery*, chaps. i.–iv.

[2] See Thucydides, book ii. ch. lxxvii.

[3] See Book VII. above, pp. 46–49.

contact, but shattered them with a loud noise. To put the matter into modern language, they partook of the nature of rockets, crackers, or petards, thrown by one sort of method or another. The idea of the battering cannon-ball, projected from a tube for the purpose of destroying solid stone walls, is a fourteenth-century notion, and can be traced no earlier.

But in the thirteenth century we find distinct mention of explosive compounds. Their possibility seems to start with the discovery of the powers of saltpetre, a chemical which was never used in the earlier incendiary mixtures, whose essential components were sulphur, naphtha, pitch, or petroleum. The " wet fire " of the Byzantines, shot through tubes or squirts, as described in the third chapter of this volume, had undoubtedly an oleaginous basis. But the mixture which was to be the parent of gunpowder was essentially a dry and granulated stuff. It is mentioned beyond dispute by Roger Bacon (in a letter written in 1249), by Albertus Magnus (*obiit* 1280), and in the collection of incendiary receipts (*Liber Ignium*) which passes under the name of Marcus Græcus. This work goes back in some of its paragraphs to classical antiquity, but its final redaction belongs to the second half of the thirteenth century. As Albertus Magnus quotes it, it must have been current in its latest form before the German philosopher's last works were produced in the 1270's. In all three of these authors, the crucial passages mention saltpetre, and speak of its mixture with charcoal and sulphur, so that the problem of the invention has been solved—though nothing practical has yet come of it.

All attempts to prove that the credit of discovering gunpowder should be assigned to the Chinese, the Arabs, or even the Hindus, come from misconceptions made by modern writers as to the meaning of certain words describing military devices, which they found in the chronicles of those nations. It is very easy for a translator who has no special knowledge of military history to take a vague account of a trebuchet slinging incendiary compositions contained in earthen pots (such as those which the Mamelukes used against St. Louis in 1249) for a description of a cannon shooting shells. And the first pioneers of Western research into Oriental history were almost all of them imbued with a vast reverence for the antiquity and ingenuity of the nations whose annals they were exploring.

We owe to the learned Jesuit missionaries of the seventeenth and eighteenth centuries the oft-repeated statement that the Chinese invented gunpowder centuries before it was known in the West. Struck by the limitless horizon of early Chinese history, and impressed with an immense respect for Chinese mechanical skill, they were quite prepared to detect modern gunpowder in fire-devices of the earliest ages. And it was long before the mistake was corrected—for unfortunately there have been few Western historians acquainted with the tongues of the Far East, and of them hardly one endowed with any technical knowledge of military history. Practically all were at the mercy of a bold and inaccurate translator.

There would seem to be no doubt that the Chinese possessed incendiary compounds, as did the Byzantines, long before the tenth century of our era. But that they had explosive compounds is nowhere proven. There are definite accounts in the story of a siege of 1232, that of the city of Kai-Fung-Fu, of the use of incendiary stuff, which seem to show that it was something of the nature of Greek fire. The besieged Chinese, when the Mongols had pushed up approaches to the foot of their walls, covered by mantlets, swung out by means of chains, great iron pots filled with a mixture called " heaven-shaking thunder." When fire was applied to them, and they were dropped into the Mongol lodgment, the pots broke, and flames darted out from them on all sides, with a roaring noise which could be heard for many miles. The flames licked up a superficial surface of about a third of an acre, and completely consumed the mantlets of the enemy and the men crouching in them. There is nothing in this, except the noise, which suggests anything more than large vessels filled with incendiary compounds, such as we have already heard of in the West. And, no doubt, the simultaneous concussion of many such bursting fire-pots would have created a loud din—though not one to be heard a hundred *li* away (thirty miles !) as the Chinese chronicle declares.[1]

But the best commentary on this story is, I think, the account of the Wars of the Mongols and the Chinese, given by an absolute contemporary of the above-named siege, Giovanni de Plan Carpin, who was in the Far East in 1246, on an embassy to the Great Khan. He says that both sides in their long wars

[1] See the chapter on the Chinese claim in Colonel Hime's *Origin of Artillery*.

used military machines and arrows, and also Greek fire and mines.[1] They were acquainted with the balista and the military sling (mangonel ?).   Occasions had been known where cities had been set in flames by projecting melted fat or tallow into them.   But while Greek fire is mentioned several times, there is nothing about explosives.   The strangest tale in Carpin's account of the warfare of the Mongols is that one of their expeditions against India (where he says that Prester John was reigning !) was foiled by a device of the Indians, who stampeded into the hostile line of battle a herd of horses each bearing a dummy figure of a man.   These figures were stuffed with Greek fire, and burst into flames at the moment of their impact into the Mongol ranks, so that men and horses were scorched and the air blackened with smoke.   The Mongols were thrown into complete confusion, and broke when the Indians delivered their real attack.[2]   If Carpin, who devotes many paragraphs to these wars, and has a long chapter dealing with the best tactics for beating the Mongols, says nothing about any military inventions unknown to the Western world, it is strong evidence that none such existed.

Much the same confusion between incendiary compounds and gunpowder, between fire-projecting machines and cannon, seems to have been made by those who attribute to the Arabs the invention of modern artillery.   We have shown in the sections which treat of the Crusades and Siegecraft, that the Saracens were well acquainted with Greek fire and other such combustibles ; but no contemporary Western author tells of their using anything like gunpowder.   As Colonel Hime has shown,[3] the legend of early Arab firearms seems to start from Michael Casiri, Librarian of the Escurial, 1760-70, who translated many Eastern manuscripts.   He unfortunately rendered Arabic words for incendiary compounds simply as " gunpowder " ; and could turn " a great machine throwing hot naptha-balls against a tower," into " a machine which, when fire was applied, exploded naphtha and balls with much noise against a tower."   The latter rendering distinctly suggests

---

[1] Beazley's edition of Carpin, p. 65, "Qualiter Munitiones obsident." Cf. also p. 82.

[2] *Ibid*. "De Pugna ipsorum [Tartarorum] contra Indiam Minorem," p. 83.

[3] See his chapter on the "Arabs and their Claims," in *Origin of Artillery*, pp. 63-73.

modern artillery—the correct one only gives the normal slinging of fire-balls from a mangonel or trebuchet, a familiar thirteenth-century device. Arab chemical receipts ascribed to Nedj-ed-din Hassan Alrammah (*obiit* 1295) and Yussuf-ibn-Ismail (1311), both contemporaries of Roger Bacon and of Albertus Magnus, speak indeed of saltpetre and its powers of ignition, but do not apply it to explosive military ends.

The claims of the early Hindus to the invention are even more clearly the results of mistranslation by eighteenth and nineteenth century Western explorers into Sanskrit literature, who persisted in rendering fire arrows and incendiary projectiles into rockets and shells. There can be no doubt that cannon came into India from the West, certainly not earlier than the late fourteenth century, and quite possibly as late as the fifteenth.[1]

But that a mixture of saltpetre, sulphur, and charcoal had surprising explosive effects was certainly known to a few Western researchers by the third quarter of the twelfth century. Roger Bacon in his *Epistolæ de Secretis Operibus*, dedicated in 1249 to William of Auvergne, Bishop of Paris, is laying down the thesis that science can produce marvels as great, or greater, than those commonly ascribed to magic. Among his marvels is that saltpetre and sulphur mixed with another substance (charcoal) will produce a loud explosion and a bright flash (*tonitruum et coruscationem*) when touched with fire. And he intimates that the invention will be useful to the State, because it is so terrifying that whole armies may be harmed or scattered in panic by it. In another passage he says that he can produce in the air flashes bright as lightning and sounds loud as thunder —which seems best explainable as referring to the use of his new compound in rocket shape. And he devotes an elaborate if cryptic chapter to a receipt for making pure saltpetre—impure it had a comparatively weak effect.[2]

The compilation *Liber Ignium* which passes under the name of Marcus Græcus contains thirty-five receipts, some of them purely non-military, and others relating to Greek fire and other well-known incendiary mixtures. But a minority of the receipts (five) concern compounds into which saltpetre enters. No. 13 is certainly a rocket: " Take one pound of

---

[1] Colonel Hime, *Modern Artillery*, pp. 74–84.
[2] See Colonel Hime's chapter in *Roger Bacon Essays*, Oxford, 1914.

sulphur, two of charcoal, and six of saltpetre, pound them together in a marble mortar, and place the powder in a long narrow case (*tunica*, presumably a linen case) to make flying fire. There must be a little hole in the bottom of the case, which can be touched with fire: and "you can make a double explosion by placing one case inside another." This receipt can also be used for a cracker or bomb (*tonitrum faciens*), which should be big in the middle and small at the ends, and should be tied round many times, the more the better, to make the longer series of "bangs."

No. 32 is a similar rocket—the mixture of one part of sulphur, three of charcoal, and nine of saltpetre can be placed in a paper sheath, and when lighted will soar up into the air. No. 12 gives a use of saltpetre in a liquid compound—mixed with sulphur and dissolved in linseed oil it can be placed in a cane or wooden tube, and will shoot out in a long jet of flame in the direction in which the tube is pointed, so as to set on fire any object at which it is directed. But this, of course, is a mere incendiary compound, and has nothing to do with gunpowder, any more than has No. 31, which shows how this same liquid can be shot up into the air rocketwise.

Roger Bacon had made his first cryptic advertisement of gunpowder in 1249—twenty-five years later the invention was getting to be well known. In the surviving fragment of his *Opus Tertium* (1265–68), he tells Pope Clement IV. that an explosive mixture of saltpetre, sulphur, and charcoal was being used *in mundi partibus diversis* [1]—possibly the last edition of Marcus Græcus, which contained the rocket and cracker receipts, was now circulating. At any rate, there was no longer any reason to speak of the new stuff in terms of mystery. But gunpowder, as we have already said, was known for over sixty years before its propulsive power was discovered, and utilised to throw missiles. Rockets, crackers, and petards can all be used in war, but they are inventions of much less importance than cannon.

Unfortunately, there is still a gap in our knowledge here. The great step had been made by 1325 — but when, where, and by whom we cannot say. "The world knows little of its greatest men"; and the inventor who saw that gunpowder could best be utilised for the throwing of balls from tubes

[1] See again Colonel Hime, p. 120.

remains unidentified.   Certainly he was *not* Berthold Schwartz, the monk from the Breisgau, who has been sometimes credited with the discovery.   Schwartz may have existed as a specialist in artillery—but he comes thirty or forty years too late to claim the credit of being the first gunner.   His existence depends on a disputed French document of 1354.[1]   But the gun had appeared as early as 1325, and if there is anything in the document it only establishes Schwartz as a brass-founder.[2]

There is (or was before the Bolshevik régime began) an anonymous Arabic manuscript on the Art of War in the Asiatic Museum at St. Petersburg, which gave such primitive and unpractical directions for the use of gunpowder as a pro-pulsive power that one would be inclined to place it at the very beginning of the fourteenth century: and this is permissible, since the last historical date which it gives is that of a battle fought in 1304.   An instrument called a *madfaa* is described as a hollow cylindrical log of wood, short (like a mortar), and rather broader at the mouth than at the bottom.   Its bore was to be filled about half-way up with a mixture in the proportion of sulphur three parts, charcoal four parts, and saltpetre twenty parts, tamped down with a wad.   " If it were more than half filled it would burst."   A ball rather larger than the bore of the muzzle was placed on it, like an egg in an egg-cup, so that there must have been a void space between the wad and the missile.   On being fired through a touch-hole the powder drove the ball forward—but as the latter was only resting on the muzzle, and not rammed down, it cannot have gone far, or have had much battering power.   A second machine is described as suitable for shooting either bolts or very small balls.   It is a long tube five inches broad, in which is placed a sort of iron cartridge case—called *madfaa*, like the above-described weapon ; in this iron case the ball or arrow

[1] A note in the *Registre Lothier*, p. 72, in the Bibliothèque Nationale at Paris, in which King John of France orders an embargo on copper, till it shall be found whether there is enough of that metal in France to make brass guns after the manner recently discovered in Germany by the Monk Berthold.   This note was discovered in 1838 by M. Lacabane, and utilised in his treatise *De la Poudre au Canon et son introduction en France*.   Köhler holds that it is a fifteenth-century insertion.

[2] See Köhler's long note on Schwartz, in his *Kriegswesen*, iii. 1. pp. 242-246. I fancy that he proves the alleged contemporary notice to be an insertion of at least one hundred and fifty years later than 1354.

is placed, the charge of powder being at the bottom of the tube below the *madfaa*. The latter is tied to the tube by a strong silken cord passed through the touch-hole. We are assured that, when the charge is exploded, the cord will prevent the *madfaa* from leaving the mouth of the tube, so that it can be used again and again, but the ball or arrow will be projected with great force ! This seems incredible, for either the powder which could not break a silk cord would be too weak to have much propulsive power, or else the *madfaa* would break the cord and go with the arrow into space.[1] The whole device reads like the description by some sciolist of the " chamber " gun which is described in the next chapter.

The earliest Western gun, however, of which we have an actual picture is almost as weird a machine. This is the vase-shaped bombard of the Millemete MS., the most interesting item in the library of Christ Church, Oxford. It is absolutely datable with accuracy, since the drawing in which it occurs is the headpiece of a dedicatory address *de Officiis Regum* given by Walter de Millemete to King Edward III. on his accession (1327). The picture, which has no connection with the written text above, represents a knight firing by means of a lighted linstock a strange cannon shaped like a vase or bottle. The missile is a heavy feathered bolt, which is seen leaving the mouth of the piece, on its way to break in a castle door. The touch-hole is very unwisely placed in the swelling side of the metal gun, nearly half-way towards its muzzle. The knight is in armour precisely suitable to the date, wearing the *aillettes* which were to go out of fashion a few years later.[2] The extraordinary shape of his gun explains at once why the earliest pieces got the name of *pots de fer* from the French, and of *vasi* from the Italians. Such engines were certainly more like pots than anything else (see Plate XXIX.).

Having ocular proof that guns were known in England in 1327, there is no reason to doubt statements of chroniclers that they were used at a siege of Metz in 1324 :[3] and a Florentine document of 1326 speaking of balls and cannons (*pilas seu pallectas ferreas et canones de metallo*) is an indisputable piece

---

[1] See Köhler's *Kriegswesen*, iii. p. 221.

[2] See chapter below on thirteenth and fourteenth century armour.

[3] The Metz Chronicle calls them *Serpentines*. This is not a contemporary name ; but the fact of their use need not be doubted.

of evidence.   But it is a little dangerous to go forward another ten years with Colonel Hime, and to be positive that certain *bussen met kruyt* dispatched from Ghent to England in 1314 were " guns with powder." [1]   The gunpowder we may pass —though *kruyt* could be used for other stuff: and *busses* were destined to be a definite name for firearms in the Low Countries—as witness *donderbuss* and our derivative " blunder-buss."   But the word had been used in the thirteenth century for devices which preceded modern artillery, and it is prob-able that they still had that meaning in 1314.

But from 1325 onward there is no disputing the existence of cannon all over Western Europe, which gradually developed from their original impractical shape into something like modern weapons.   There is no reason to doubt that the gun which Walter de Millemete drew in 1327 was one of the train of artillery which went forward in that same year to take part in the first campaign of Edward III.   For we can fully accept the statement of Barbour [2]—though he wrote a generation later—that it was in this campaign that the Scots first beheld two military novelties, armorial crests on helmets [3] (*tymmers* = the French *timbres*), and " crakys of war," which were certainly cannon, as all later uses of the word show.   But this was not to remain " wonder for to see " to the Northern host for very long—by 1339 the Scots themselves were using guns at a siege of Stirling.

Meanwhile, we begin to find notices of cannon from all quarters—a German army used them in 1331 at the siege of Cividale in Friuli, where they are called *vasi e scioppi*.   In the same year the citizens of Alicante warned their master the King of Aragon that the Moors were coming against them provided with " iron balls to be cast against us by fire," which by this time must certainly mean that the infidels also had guns.   Eleven years later, when King Alfonso of Castile was

---

[1] See P. A. Lenz's researches into Ghent Archives in his *Notice sur l'invention de la Poudre à Canon*, and Colonel Hime's comment thereon in his book (p. 120), so often quoted in the last pages.   For the result of inquiries into the statement in the Ghent Memorial Book under 1313, that " in this year ' busses ' were devised by a monk in Germany," which is a late addition, not a contemporary entry, see note at end of this chapter.

[2] Absurdly taken to mean wooden helms by many modern writers, as if *tymmer* meant ' timber ' !

[3] xix. p. 394.

beleaguering Algeciras, " thunder machines" (*ingenios de truenos*) were used against him by the besieged, which threw iron balls as big as apples, some of which flew right over the Christian camp. A similar word *tronum* for a " thundering " weapon is used as a synonym for *canonem* in the State accounts of Lucca for the year 1341.[1] It was only to be expected, therefore, that firearms should appear in the Hundred Years' War from its first beginnings.

NOTE ON THE ALLEGED INVENTION OF CANNON IN GERMANY IN 1313

In several books on early artillery, use is made of a statement to be found in certain MSS. of the *Memorial-Boek der Stad Gent*, to the effect that in the year 1313 guns were first devised by a monk in Germany. Being in Ghent this summer (August 1923), I thought it worth while to look up this matter, and got kindly help in my search from Dr. Bergmanns, the librarian of the University Library, in which several copies of the " Memorial Boek " lie. There is another in the city archives, which I also inspected. The result was that the whole story is found to be worthless. The entry only occurs in some late copies of the book, and in the earlier ones it is inserted in the margin in a hand of the early sixteenth century, or even somewhat later. The marginal notes only get into the text in the very latest manuscripts. And in the earliest MS. which contains the marginal note, that labelled " S.G."—the entry occurs not under the year 1313, but under the year 1393! Those in which it is put under the earlier year are later texts. It looks to me as if some copyist had carelessly miswritten MCCCXCIII as MCCCXIII—thereby getting the date eighty years too early! But as guns were certainly known by 1325, this entry by an ignorant scribe of 1500 or thereabouts, is quite valueless.

[1] All these instances are collected by General Köhler in his *Kriegswesen*, iii. pp. 225-6.

CHAPTER II

CANNON IN THE WARS OF THE FOURTEENTH AND FIFTEENTH CENTURIES

THE use of cannon, as we have seen, was already more than ten years old when the Hundred Years' War began, and primitive guns were already as well known in England and France as in Flanders, Germany, Italy, and Spain. But they were not yet making much head as a decisive element in war. Indeed, they were still in a purely experimental stage, and many ineffective forms of artillery were destined to be tried before a definitive shape was arrived at. The best testimony to their unimportance in the middle decades of the fourteenth century is that they very seldom attract the attention of the chroniclers, and that the testimony to their existence is generally drawn only from accounts and inventories. The archetypal gun, as the drawing in the Millemete manuscript shows, had been bottle-shaped, and was intended to shoot bolts rather than balls. And the name *pot de fer*, used both in France and in England, implies a short, broad, wide-mouthed machine. In the very first year of the great struggle between Edward III. and the House of Valois, we find that the French fleet which raided Southampton in June 1338 was furnished by the royal treasurers with the modest provision of one *pot de fer*, three pounds of gunpowder, and forty-eight large bolts with iron "feathers" in two boxes.[1] Clearly this 'pot' can only have been intended for use on special occasions—*e.g.* for the breaking in of a castle gate—since forty-eight bolts would be used up in a few hours. There is no mention of its actual employment in any of the chronicles. In the following year *poudre et canons* were used against the English fortress

[1] From the list of material shipped at Rouen, in a document printed in the *Bibliothèque de l'École des Chartes*, vol. of 1844, p. 36.

of Puy Guillem in Perigord,[1] and also at the siege of Cambrai by Edward III.[2] In the latter case we find them mentioned, by way of exception, in a chronicle. These French guns were apparently still very small, as the bill for their purchase states that they were bought by weight, and gives the price of the iron by the pound, in a total which works out at no more than twenty-five pounds per gun.[3]

In the same year, 1339, we have the first mention of a tentative form of fire-weapon which had some vogue in the second half of the century, but died out soon after it had come to an end. This was a primitive attempt at a *mitrailleuse*, called a *ribauld* or *ribauldequin*, consisting of several small tubes clamped together and with their touch-holes so arranged that one sweep of the linstock would discharge them simultaneously. The *ribauldequins* were mounted on a beam, and furnished with wheels, and with a mantlet to shelter the gunner, so that they made a sort of cart, and they are sometimes called " carts of war." From the small size of the tubes, and the concentrated fire which the *ribaulds* were evidently intended to produce, we must presume that they were mainly defensive weapons, intended to block a passage or gate, or to command a breach, which an enemy might attempt to assault in column. For the fire of such weapons, deadly against human bodies, would have little or no effect against stone walls, or even solid timber work. And obviously they could be used only for one discharge against an assaulting enemy, since it would take a monstrous time to reload a number of juxtaposed tubes, each requiring to be filled with powder, tamped, and then provided with the bolt or small leaden ball which formed its missile. The first mention of them is in the city accounts of Bruges, whose burghers provided themselves with the new invention— *niewen enginen die men heet ribaulde*, and paid a smith twenty-two sous for iron bands to clamp them down to their carts.[4] In 1340 there is an interesting notice relating to the siege of Tournay, which shows that a work containing *ribaulds* had

---

[1] Ducange discovered this note in French Treasury accounts, for the sum spent on gunpowder, and put it under the head "bombard" in his famous glossary.

[2] French accounts show that the cannons, "five of iron and five of metal," were sent for the defence of Cambrai. See Lacabane, quoted before, p. 51.

[3] See the bill quoted in the article by Favé in the set of monographs collected under the name of Napoleon III. as *Études pour l'Artillerie*.

[4] See note in Kervyn de Lettenhove's edition of Froissart, iii. p. 492.

been placed to command the gate of the city—just the sort of purpose for which we should expect them to be employed.[1]

It would seem that Edward III. specialised on *ribaulds* on a large scale when he was preparing for his great invasion of France. In February 1345 he ordered the keeper of the Tower Wardrobe to prepare "guns and pellets" for the projected expedition—the use of the word "pellet" suggests that either the guns were very small, or that nothing more than *ribaulds* were in question. For later in the same year the king directed Robert de Mildenhall, the keeper, to prepare no less than a hundred *ribaulds*, and to collect the timber, wheels, axles, bolts, and other minor materials necessary for the mounting of them.[2] During the six months following the keeper received from the exchequer the modest sum of £124, 18s. 4d. for the manufacture of the *ribaulds* and bolts ordered by the king—if (putting aside the cost of bolts) the engines themselves could be made for something not much over £1 a piece, it is clear that they must have been extremely small. Powder must have been provided at the same time, but it is not till after the expedition had sailed, and Creçy had been fought, that we find Thomas de Roldeston, Clerk of the Privy Wardrobe, ordered to make as much more powder as possible. His first account shows that he had to pay eighteenpence a pound for saltpetre, and eightpence for sulphur, so that the compound was very expensive for a fourteenth-century scale of prices. Thomas, in November 1346, got together seven hundred pounds of saltpetre, and three hundred and ten of sulphur. Next year he procured larger amounts, two thousand and twenty-one pounds of saltpetre and four hundred and sixty-six of sulphur, no doubt to replace powder expended at the siege of Calais.[3]

What became of all these *ribaulds*, and for what precise purpose did Edward III. propose to employ them? He was intending to conduct a campaign of the first class, as all his multifarious preparations sufficiently prove. Were these little engines intended for use on occasion to sweep narrow fronts in siege work, or to block gates and entries? Or was there some notion that if two armies came to a deadlock in front of

---

[1] Froissart, K.D.L., iii. 496.
[2] See Professor Tout's "Fourteenth-Century Firearms" in *English Historical Review* for 1911, p. 670, and text on p. 688.
[3] The date is November 25, 1346. See *Archæologia*, xxxii. p. 381.

each other, as at La Flamengerie in 1339,[1] one might annoy the other by gun-fire, till it took the offensive in order to stop the nuisance ? Guns in later ages were used for this purpose, notably at Formigny in 1450 ; but in 1346 the cannon, and still more the *ribauld*, were of short range, and would have no more effect in teasing the enemy into close action than good archery. But the odd thing about this large provision of *ribaulds* in the months preceding the invasion of Normandy, is that we have no documentary evidence of their being actually taken abroad, and no mention from the chronicles of their being used abroad. Whereas there is good proof that they were employed in the siege of Calais, after Creçy had been fought, along with guns of the more ordinary size.[2] They were requisitioned from England in September, along with much other military material, and used to garnish the king's works round Calais. In particular they were placed in the lines of contravallation, which faced outward, to resist the approach of any relieving army, and which so impressed Philip of Valois that he refused to close.

Such evidence as there is concerning fire-weapons in the Creçy campaign would seem to apply to a very small number of ordinary cannon, not to *ribaulds*. In any case it is scanty, comes entirely from the French side, and is obviously tendencious, being designed to explain the defeat of Philip VI. by showing that his enemies used new-fangled devices. No English account of the battle has any mention of guns, and it is notable that Froissart in an earlier draft of the tale of Creçy does incidentally speak of them, but in the later version, written under English influence, omits the reference. Does this mean that he had learnt from his acquaintances on this side of the Channel that there were no cannon at Creçy ? Or did he deliberately strike out the notice of them, because he thought that English readers would prefer to have the victory made to turn entirely on bow and lance ? Either theory is possible.

The actual authority for the use of guns at Creçy is perhaps worth giving. Two Italian chroniclers, writing a vast way

[1] See above, vol. ii. p. 125.

[2] See the number of entries from the Privy Wardrobe Accounts on pp. 689-90 of Professor Tout's article in *English Historical Review* of 1911. The only sign of their being taken is an order to ship them issued in March, before the storms which caused the prorogation of the expedition. In the following September, when the king has sat down before Calais, requisitions come fast and thick.

from the scene, and obviously relying on self-exculpatory narratives from Genoese mercenaries, speak of them. Villani, a perfectly contemporary author, but one who makes gross mistakes in his tale, says that the arbalesters, when attacking the entrenched laager of waggons in which the English had sheltered themselves (!), were opposed not only by archery but by bombards, which shot little iron balls, made a noise like thunder, and slew man and horse.[1] The author of the *Istorie Pistolesi* is a much more fantastic inventor. He states, to begin the campaign, that King Edward landed in Flanders ! And in the crisis of Creçy he makes the Prince of Wales and his chivalry get to horse, and charge the French line, with the aid of certain wild Welsh (*Gallesi como uomini salvatichi*) and of many bombards![2] Of course, if anything is certain about Creçy, it is that the Prince made no cavalry onset, and equally that the English line was not entrenched. Both the Italian narratives are untrustworthy. There remains the very definite statement in the *Grandes Croniques de France*, a pretty good authority, that at the beginning of the fight the English "getterent trois canons": no further stress is laid on them.[3] Also the statement in the Amiens redaction of Froissart that when the Genoese advanced with shouts "the English kept quite still and loosed off some cannon which they had in their line, to scare the Genoese." [4] Like the *Croniques*, this narrative makes no further mention of the guns.

It is rather difficult to make up one's mind on this often-discussed question. Clearly, from our knowledge of King Edward's preparations, he *might* have had guns at Creçy, and *ribauldequins* also. But we have no documentary evidence that he had them at any moment in the campaign, and not one English chronicler mentions them. On the other hand, two distant but contemporary Italian chroniclers introduce them into obviously erroneous accounts of the battle. If there were not the entries in Froissart and the *Grandes Croniques*, we should have no hesitation in disregarding Villani and his

---

[1] Villani in Muratori, xiii. p. 946. [2] Muratori, xi. 516.

[3] *Croniques*, Book v. p. 460.

[4] Froissart, ed. Luce, iii. 416. "Et li Engles tout koy, descliquièrent aucuns kanons qu'ils avaient en le bataille, pour esbahier les Genevois." Cf. Kervyn de Lettenhove, i. part ii. pp. 46–51, for the decidedly English tone of the second redaction. But he points out that Froissart had *not* become the mere flatterer of England, and had corrected many errors, *e.g.* the presence of Queen Philippa at Neville's Cross.

Pistoian contemporary altogether. But may not Froissart's elimination of the guns in his later redaction mean that he had come to disbelieve in their existence ? There remains only the four words in the *Grandes Croniques* to which no serious objection can be taken. Can we on their authority concede the use of cannon at Creçy ?

In any case there can be doubt that they had no perceptible influence on the fate of the day, or both the *Grandes Croniques* and Froissart would have had much more to say about them. I am myself rather inclined to doubt them, and to ascribe their mention in the writers of the beaten party to the same tendency which made Victor Hugo explain the event of the battle of Waterloo by his imaginary ravine in front of the British line, into which Kellermann's cuirassiers plunged and were smothered—a dry repetition of the disaster of Courtrai. If there were any fire-weapons on King Edward's side, I take it that they must have been small ordinary cannon, and not *ribauldequins*, for the *Grandes Croniques*, our best authority, makes them precisely three in number, while *ribauldequins* would have been numerous, if there had been any at all. They were also quite well-known inventions at the time, and there is no reason why one chronicler should talk of cannons and another of bombards, if the real artillery had been of the *mitrailleuse* type.

When King Edward settled down before Calais, he sent to England not only for powder and guns and *ribaulds*, but also for more ancient forms of artillery, three *magna ingenia* which were probably trebuchets. It is curious to find that the skilled staff to work the bombards and *ribaulds* figures at no higher number than twelve men in the Calais pay-rolls, quoted above on page 152. Obviously they must have been set to train and direct a good many other men, drawn from the ranks of the infantry. The bombards are recorded to have been employed at the sea-end of the king's works, to command the exit of the port of Calais, a fact which would seem to show that at least the biggest of them—Edward had two described as *grossi*— must have had a range of some hundreds of yards.

Mentions of artillery become so numerous in all countries after 1346 that there is no need to pile up long lists of them. Apparently guns began to grow in size, and the practice of casting them from brass or copper rather than iron was continued and proved successful. We have seen that in 1354 King

John is said to have put an embargo on all the copper in France
till it should be discovered whether there was enough of the
metal in the country to cast guns after the new German method.[1]
And in the previous year, 1353, Edward III. had just had four
new guns of copper cast for him by William of Aldgate, brazier.[2]
These must have been small, as the making of them (as opposed
to the metal) only cost thirteen shillings and fourpence apiece,
and so must a gun of *latten* bought from Peter the Joiner
have been, as it cost only £1.[3] But the king had *magni gunnes
de cupro* a few years later, as well as many more *parvi gunnes*
of that metal.[4] The iron weapons, however, were much more
numerous, no doubt because of the far smaller cost of their
metal. By the later years of the reign they were numbered by
dozens, and to be found in every important castle, and not merely
in the Tower of London and at Calais, as in earlier decades.

Small guns in this age continued to be very popular, and
inventions were made which must have increased their efficiency
by facilitating their rapidity of loading. Of these the chief
was the device of movable breech-pieces, allowing of the
charge being put into the tubes without the need of ramming
it down their broad muzzles. These movable charge-cases
were called " chambers," and were loaded with the powder
before being placed in the lower end of the barrel. Another
loaded chamber could be slipped into the piece when the
first had been discharged. Why this useful invention died out
after a time, and was only applied to *ribaulds* and small guns,
seldom to large pieces, is a problem. Two hypotheses suggest
themselves—insufficient means of clamping down the chamber,
when it had been put in position, may have led to "blowing
out at the breech " when the linstock was applied—to the
detriment of the gunner.[5] Or perhaps foulness and lingering
sparks in the barrel may have frequently ignited the new
chamber when it was being placed in position. In the case
of big guns, we need have no doubt that the experiment was
made :[6] if it was not continued, the cause must certainly

[1] See above, p. 211. But the document is doubtful.
[2] See accounts of William de Rothwell, printed by Professor Tout in his
"Fourteenth-Century Artillery" in *English Historical Review*, 1911, p. 691.
[3] *Ibid.* 691.   [4] *Ibid.* 692.
[5] The account comes from the Chronicle of Galeazzo Gataro in Muratori, xvii. p. 559.
[6] A Bologna inventory of 1397 has an entry of wedges for fixing down the
" chamber " into the gun. This looks like a very primitive and dangerous plan.

have been disasters resulting from the want of sufficiently strong methods of fastening down the " chamber " after it had been inserted.

There is a record of three most monstrous *ribaulds* constructed in 1387 by the orders of Antonio della Scala, Lord of Verona. Each contained no less than one hundred and forty-four tubes, in three stories one above another. Each story was divided into four compartments, and each compartment had twelve tubes in it, which could be fired simultaneously. There was one gunner to each story, who fired the groups of twelve tubes in succession, so that twelve salvos of twelve balls each could be delivered. It is said that four dray-horses heavily equipped with armoured barding could draw the car. . Of the time that it must have taken to re-charge the tubes after they had been fired we are told nothing. These super-*ribaulds* must have been at least twenty feet high, and must surely have been a most cumbrous and unpractical device.[1]

Such vast engines of war must have been unique, but we hear of small *ribauldequins* in great numbers during the wars of the later fourteenth century, and even into the earlier years of the fifteenth. The rebellious Flemings of Ghent are said to have put two hundred in line in 1382, when they defeated their Count in front of Bruges, and at Roosebeke they used a great number, though to little effect.[2] But the largest figure on record—it appears incredible—is that ascribed by Juvenal des Ursins to the Burgundian army of 1411, which, he declares, had no less than two thousand pieces of this small artillery with it. One can only suppose that he heard of two thousand *chars*, and made them into two thousand *chars de guerre*.[3] By this time they were beginning to be superseded by infantry armed with one tube each—the original handgun men, who were the ancestors of the arquebusier and the musketeer.

While *ribaulds* and *ribauldequins* had wheels from the first, the gun proper was for some time mounted on carriages unfurnished with that convenience. The Millemete gun in 1327 stands on a sort of four-legged table or trestle, to which

---

[1] For their fate at the battle of Castagnaro, see the account of that action in Book XII. page 298 below.

[2] Froissart, book ii. ch. 154, and Juvenal des Ursins, p. 341.

[3] *Ibid.* p. 462.

it is not apparently clamped down in any way. One is forced to ask whether it had no recoil, and if it had, how it was prevented from jumping backward off its stand. The idea of the trunnion, by which part of the metal of the gun itself is extended sideways to fit into sockets contrived in its carriage, seems not to have been conceived till the sixteenth century.[1] For two hundred years the piece lay tilted up on its beam—called " trunk," " tiller," and later " gunstock "—or on its sledge or stand, and the only way of depressing it was either to shove wedges between the hinder end of the piece and its " gunstock," or else to lift up the cannon bodily on to a frame. (See Figs. 3 and 4 in Plate XXIX.) If, on the other hand, it was necessary to elevate the muzzle, this could be done either by putting the whole machine-gun and stock on a slight up-slope, or by digging down below the trail of the stock and sinking it in the ground. In most pictures of artillery we see the gun fixed to its stand by bands clamped round it and nailed to the wood below. Such a device, one can only suppose, must have shaken the stand to pieces by degrees, since the force of recoil must have given a fierce jerk to the bands every time that the gun was fired. Even when wheels were applied to cannon, as began to be the practice in the fifteenth century, the recoil must still have been a disturbing element, since the gun was not fixed directly to the wheels by means of trunnions, but lay on its stock, as if on a cart. But all the great siege-pictures of the fourteenth and early fifteenth centuries show us the artillery of the beleaguering party not wheeled, but resting on stocks or beams or supports. (See Plate XXIX.) The moving of them must have been a slow and cumbrous business, the moment that guns grew large.

And by the end of the fourteenth century some of them had reached a considerable bulk. Ralph de Halton, Keeper of the Privy Wardrobe to Richard II., bought between 1382 and 1388 no less than seventy-three guns from William Woodward, gun-founder ; forty-seven of them averaged three hundred and eighty pounds apiece, five others three hundred and eighteen pounds, and one vast and exceptional engine at least six hundred and sixty-five pounds. This was a " freak " or experimental gun-mitrailleuse ; it is described as having one bore (*foramen*)

---

[1] It appears, of course, in the works of Tartaglia (*ob.* 1559) and other scientific Renaissance artillerists.

for great stones, and ten smaller ones suitable for " pellets "
or bolts. It is presumable that the ten small bores were arranged
in a circle round the one large one.[1] Probably this monster
cracked or burst very soon—with fourteenth-century founding,
eleven holes in one mass of iron must have involved local
weaknesses and flaws, and the experiment was never repeated.
Double guns, however, are mentioned thrice in the accounts of
1388, and must have resembled the piece shown in Plate XXIX.,
though this is from a French fifteenth-century manuscript of
Froissart, written after wheels had come in.

The larger guns of the late fourteenth century were not
only cast, as their smaller predecessors had been, but also
sometimes made in another fashion. No doubt because casting
led, in the case of big pieces of work, to air-holes and flaws,
the idea was started of making guns of wrought-iron. The
system was to take a wooden core of the desired dimensions,
and then to weld round it iron rods or bars, which were juxtaposed when red-hot, and beaten into a solid tube by the gun-
smith's hammer. As a precaution against insufficient welding,
and weakness in the joining places, iron rings or hoops were
clamped round the outside of the completed gun in varying
numbers, ranging up from two to six or more, according to the
length of the piece. The wooden core being then removed
by boring it out or otherwise, the gun was ready for use. This
system was much employed in the fifteenth century, and may
be seen in early guns preserved in many museums. But it was
quite as unsatisfactory as casting when very large pieces were
in question, and led to many explosions and accidents. The
best remembered of them is that which in 1460 slew King
James II. of Scotland, as he was besieging Roxburgh Castle.
He was personally inspecting the fire of a big hooped bombard,
bought in Flanders, and named " the Lion," when it went to
pieces, and one of its quoins struck him in the chest, killing him
instantly. Other fragments wounded the Earl of Angus and
several gunners. As the art of metallurgy improved, and
castings became more safe and certain, the welded and hooped
gun went completely out of fashion. By the end of the fifteenth
century it had been superseded by the beautiful and artistic

[1] All this interesting material comes from Professor Tout's " Fourteenth-
Century Artillery " in *Eng. Historical Review* for 1911, p. 687, and the excerpts
on pp. 696–99.

long bronze guns of renaissance workmanship which contrast
so strongly with the fat heavy bombards of 1400 or 1450.

But whether guns from 1370–80 onward were cast or welded,
they increased in size very rapidly, and began to be capable of
throwing much larger missiles. The small early pieces had
shot bolts or leaden and iron " pellets," as the fathers of gunnery
called them. Much larger projectiles were now possible, and
since it would be very costly to make them of metal—lead and
copper cannon-balls would be far too expensive, and even
iron ones not too cheap—the stone ball so familiar to those
who wander round castle ruins and museums came into vogue.
Some of them were of enormous size and weight soon after
the fourteenth century had come to an end. At the battle of
Tongern (1408), John of Burgundy is said to have had with
him five enormous bombards, of which the largest cast a stone
of four hundred pounds weight, two others stones of three
hundred pounds, a fourth and fifth—one of which bore the odd
name of Seneca—stones of two hundred pounds. He had also
one copper gun firing balls of one hundred pounds.[1] Since the
metal of this last piece is specially named, we may conclude
that the other five were of iron, which must have been far less
expensive. Stone balls begin to appear in the English Wardrobe accounts between 1382 and 1388, when the Keeper is
found buying from William Woodward, " founder," four great
copper cannon " made and ordered for shooting round stones,"
and weighing between them six hundred pounds. About the
same time he engaged a workman " operans super rotundacionem
lapidum pro canonibus," who received the very handsome wage
of sixpence a day—as much as the pay of a horse-archer. From
this time onward gun-stones occur regularly—in the days of
Edward III. we hear of naught but lead or iron. The wages of
the cannon-ball cutter had risen as high as a shilling a day
by 1399—the pay of a man-at-arms—so that he must have
been considered about the most important of all skilled artisans.[2]

While cannon, and *ribaulds* too, had been used in sieges
from the very first time of their invention, they had been more
useful for shooting at men, or at woodwork, than at stone walls,
so long as they were still small, and discharged but moderate-

[1] Christine de Pisan, *Livre des Faits d'Armes*, ii. ch. 21.
[2] All these figures from the Halton accounts at the end of Professor Tout's
" Fourteenth-Century Artillery " in *E.H.R.* for 1911.

sized missiles. It is only as battering in doors, bringing down brattices, ruining palisades and drawbridges, or smashing in the roofs of towers, or of houses inside the besieged town,[1] that we find them effective. But in the last decades of the fourteenth century we are told that they had become able to play with success on the main stone defences of a castle or city. The first case on record seems to be the battering of the castle of Audrucq, near St. Omer, in 1377, where we are told that the French besiegers shot bolts weighing two hundred pounds apiece, *qui pertuisoient les murs*,[2] and reduced the place. But such achievements were still rare—against the one case of the capture of Harfleur by regular bombardment in the campaigns of Henry V., we have to set his interminable sieges, like those of Rouen and Meaux, where artillery proved unable to finish off its task in any reasonable time. We may almost say that the triumph of artillery only commences in the middle years of the fifteenth century. In the East we see the capture of Constantinople by the Turks in 1453, when the most famous and complicated system of defences in the civilised world was ruined by gun-fire, though all the other known methods of siegecraft, especially mining, were also employed. In the West at the same time the perfected siege-artillery of the brothers Bureau, the great gunners of Charles VII., was reducing the English strongholds in France with a celerity which seemed incredible to those who remembered the leaguers of previous generations. At the siege of Harcourt in 1449, " the first shot thrown pierced completely through the rampart of the outer ward, which is a fine work and equal in strength to the keep." [3] In the re-conquest of Normandy in 1449–50, the French conducted sixty successful siege-operations in a year and four days. The power of the battering-train had become so indisputable that many places surrendered the moment that the big guns had been successfully placed in battery. This was also seen in Gascony—the city of Bayonne, the second most important place in the old Plantagenet holding, held out against Dunois so long as he

---

[1] When the Black Prince took Romorantin in 1356 it was by cannon-fire indeed, but by cannon throwing fire-balls, which set light to the woodwork, roofs, etc., of the outer ward (*basse cour*), and smoked out the defenders (Froissart, K.D.L., vol. v. p. 395).

[2] *Ibid.* viii. p. 411.   [3] Alain Chartier, p. 162.

had only got small guns in position, but asked for terms when the great siege-train came up and was got into action (1451).[1] The same complete mastery of modern cannon over old fortifications was seen in England during the Wars of the Roses, where one of the reasons for the paucity of sieges was certainly the general conviction that the old walls had become useless— though moral and psychological causes were co-operating—as we shall see in a later chapter. Where a castle did hold out, as did Bamborough in the Northumbrian campaign in 1464, it was promptly battered to flinders by King Edward's great siege-train.

Speaking generally, the heavy gun in the fourteenth and earlier fifteenth centuries was seldom used save for siege work, the *ribauld* was the real field-piece. When the larger bombards were seen in line of battle, it was generally in cases where one side had resolved to take up the defensive, had chosen its ground, and even entrenched it on occasion. Such were the conditions at Castillon (1453), Northampton (1460), and Morat (1476), where the French in the first fight, the Lancastrians in the second, and the Burgundians in the third, had built themselves solid lines of defence, in which the guns could play their part and would not need to be moved. For till wheels were applied to the bigger guns they could not manœuvre, and even when the wheels had become usual, it was difficult to move a bombard with rapidity—as Charles the Rash discovered at Granson. But, of course, if the enemy could be lured or forced to attack a regular entrenched position, even the heaviest guns might play their part. If the assailant retained his power to outflank a position, or to make the defensive party come down to meet him on ground that he had not selected, the great gun could not follow in time to be of use. We have an example of this at the battle of Gavre (1453), where the rebellious Flemings had placed themselves in a good position with their guns ranged all along their entrenched front. The Burgundians approached it, did not like the look of it, and after a simulated attack retired, as if giving up the game. The Flemings pursued *en laissant leur engins derrière eulx*, and were surprised to find themselves let in for a general action a mile in front of their chosen ground and their stockaded guns. In dealing in a later chapter with the Wars of the Roses, we shall explain the

[1] Alain Chartier, p. 215.

curious fact that in most of the great battles both parties had guns, and neither got any particular profit out of them. At Granson and Morat the combatant who had heavy artillery was decisively beaten by the adversary who had none.

A few words about the smaller firearms are necessary. The earliest hand-guns, as Professor Tout has pointed out,[1] can be undoubtedly traced back to a development from the small tubes of the lightest artillery—the *ribauldequins*. These minute guns were originally mounted in rows on cars—as we have already seen—and used mitrailleuse-fashion. But within a decade or so it began to be seen that a single tube might be utilised separately, by being fixed on a staff and carried in the hands of a soldier. The ancestor of the musket and rifle was a toy cannon strapped to a pike handle. The earliest definite mention of this device in England is a bill of William de Sleaford, Keeper of the Privy Wardrobe, dating from 1373–5, in which he proves that he has paid thirteen shillings for fitting eight guns with handles (helves) after the fashion of pikes, and also for " helving " ten axes.[2] In 1386 the name " hand-gun " appears—Ralph Hatton sends three of them to the chamberlain of Berwick.[3] Probably he meant the same thing when he ordered " baculos curtos et grossos ligatos cum ferro pro iv cannonibus parvis." [4] Short stout sticks look less like gunstocks for real cannon than staves for portative tubes.

But Italy seems to have been ten years ahead of England in the making of hand-guns. In 1364 the town of Perugia ordered five hundred little bombards of only a palm's length to be made, and it is noted that they were portable and to be fired from the hand.[5] A nine-inch " bombard " of a portative sort is nothing but a hand-gun : it must certainly have been strapped to a staff, not set on a stand. In the same year Modena had " four little *scioppi* for the hand "—which reminds us that *sclopetum* was to become the authorised Latin word for a pistol in later years : these were no doubt much like the Perugian " little bombards." In 1381 Augsburg had thirty " hand-cannon," and in 1386 Froissart records that the French used against the Liégeois *bombardes portatives*.[6] These inconvenient

[1] " Fourteenth Century Artillery" in *English Historical Review*, 1911, p. 684.
[2] *Ibid*. 693.   [3] *Ibid*. 684.   [4] *Ibid*. 697.
[5] Grazzini's Chronicle in *Archivio Storico Italiano*, xvi. p. 197.
[6] Froissart, K.D.L., x. 125.

weapons, if we may trust manuscript drawings of the early fifteenth century, had very long staves, and were held under the soldier's arm, with the butt of the staff resting on the ground, so that the recoil would go into the earth : they can only have been fired at a high trajectory. They do not become short, and are not lifted to the shoulder, till the beginning of the fifteenth century. After 1420, however, the hand-gun though still no more than a tube with a touch-hole, fired by a match, begins to be much shorter and to be aimed from the shoulder.[1] The Hussites were the first to use it on a large scale.

The weapon never had any popularity in England, being slow to load, and hard, in its original shape, to aim. It could not compete with the longbow, and the experimental pieces mentioned above were probably employed only for wall-shooting in fortresses. But on the Continent it was to gain gradual popularity as its shape improved, and to develop into the hackbut, caliver, and musket. The first organised bands of hand-gun men in England were foreign mercenaries—Germans or Flemings—hired in the crisis of the Wars of the Roses. They are recorded to have been seen at the second battle of St. Albans, where they had no effect—wind and rain blew out their matches and wetted their powder.[2] Edward IV. was lent a few by his brother-in-law, Charles of Burgundy, for his expedition of 1471, and Henry of Richmond is also reported to have hired some for his dash at the crown in 1485. But every leader who could get enough English bowmen preferred them to the foreign mercenaries, with their slow and inaccurate fire. It was not till the reign of Henry VIII. that any English soldier would say a word for small firearms—though in the last years of Elizabeth the longbow, much regretted by old captains such as Sir John Smyth, was relegated to the butts or the lumber-room.

[1] There is a good example of a short hand-gun in the great fresco in the Palazzo Publico at Siena, showing the defeat of the Florentines by the Duke of Calabria at Poggibonzi, and another in the fine Burgundian MS. in Sir John Soane's Museum.

[2] Gregory's Chronicle, pp. 212–3.

BOOK XI

THE SWISS

CHAPTER I

ORIGINS OF THE SWISS INFANTRY—MORGARTEN (1315), LAUPEN (1339), SEMPACH (1386)

IN the fourteenth century, as we have already seen, infantry, after a thousand years of depression, at last regained its due share of military importance. Between the catastrophe of Adrianople, of which we told in the first chapter of the First Book, and the group of battles—Courtrai (1302), Bannockburn (1314), Morgarten (1315), Creçy (1346)—which mark the turning-point in tactical history, there had been many fights in which infantry took its share in a victory. Some, too, there had been in which infantry may be said to have settled the fate of an engagement in which both arms had been engaged on both sides. But from the beginning of the fourteenth century we begin to find a logical succession of victories for nations which used the infantry arm unassisted—or almost unassisted—against enemies who relied on their superiority in cavalry. And so great was the moral effect of these battles that a fatal blow was delivered at feudal chivalry—so much so that the knight for over a century abandoned his charger and fought on foot. He sacrificed the advantages of rapid movement and superior impact which his horse gave him, in order that he might try to beat infantry at its own game. There can be no more surprising contrast than that between the tactics on the French side at Creçy and at Poictiers—fights divided by only ten years of unhappy experiment. And this was only a parallel to the contrast in the English tactics at Bannockburn and at Halidon—divided by no more than seventeen years. Yet there was an essential difference between the causes, though the results were the same in each of these pairs of battles. The moral of Bannockburn had been that unaided cavalry could not break a phalanx of spearmen—

which Edward II. might have deduced from his father's experience at Falkirk.   Edward III., more fortunate than his unlucky
sire, and helped by the knowledge of what had happened at
Dupplin Muir, showed that the mere phalanx of spearmen
was helpless against the combination of dismounted knights
and long wings of efficient archery.

The moral of Creçy as it formulated itself, after several
unlucky experiments, in the mind of the French *noblesse*, was
that cavalry was helpless against the combination of archers
and men-at-arms drawn up in a favourable position and with
good flank protection.   Hence came the French tactics at
Poictiers, which—putting aside the unimportant action of the
trifling mounted vanguard—were an attempt to break and
trample down the English line by the solid impact of successive
lines of mailed men-at-arms on foot.   But this, as we have
seen, was no more fortunate than the similar attempts of the
Scots at Dupplin or Halidon, or later French experiments at
Auray and Agincourt.

The moral of Bannockburn had been that the pike-phalanx,
under proper conditions, could defeat mere cavalry : that of
Creçy and Poictiers had been that the combination of bow and
spear could, under proper conditions, beat either cavalry or
the heaviest column of dismounted men-at-arms.   The bow
was the winning weapon in both cases, not the spear : mere
numerical superiority would have destroyed the English knighthood at either Creçy or Poictiers, if their archers had not been
present.

But on the other side of Europe there was going on at the
same time another and a quite separate attack on the supremacy
of feudal cavalry.   The Swiss started on their astonishing
career of infantry triumphs a year after Bannockburn, and
thirty-one years before Creçy.   And they were to maintain
their reputation for fifty years after the English military
supremacy in the West had come to an end.   Formigny and
Castillon had shown the weak points of English tactics long
before the Swiss won their crowning victories at Granson and
Morat.   And the *débâcle* of the Swiss system, which had even
weaker points than the English, was reserved for Marignano
(1515) and Bicocca (1522), when the Middle Ages were well over,
and gunpowder was making an end of all tactical traditions.

The Swiss system was as essentially linked with the pike

as was the English with the bow. When war is reduced to its
simplest elements, there are only two ways in which an enemy
can be met and beaten. Either shock-tactics or missile-tactics
must be employed against him. In the one case the victor
throws himself on his opponent, and worsts him in close combat
by his numbers, the superiority of his weapons, or the greater
strength and skill with which he wields them. In the second
case he wins the day by keeping up such a constant and deadly
rain of missiles that the enemy is destroyed or driven into
demoralised flight before he can come to hand-strokes. Each
of these methods is practicable with very different weapons,
and is susceptible of innumerable variations. The close fighter
may win with the cavalry lance of the Middle Ages, or with
the long pike of the Macedonian phalanx and of the Swiss
" keil," or with the short sword of the Roman legionary and
of the Spanish infantry of Gonzalvo de Cordova, or with the
bayonet charge of Suvaroff's Russian columns, or with the mere
savage rush of superior numbers regardless of losses on the
way, such as that which once destroyed a British battalion at
Isandlwana. And the missile-fighters too may be either on
horse or on foot. In old days they were generally on horse,
like the Parthian archers who shot down in detail the slow-
moving legions of Crassus in the plains of Mesopotamia, or
like their spiritual heirs the Turks of Alp-Arslan and the
Mongols of Genghiz and Batu. Archers on foot were in
general little esteemed in antiquity—the Greek looked upon
them as furtive hoverers on the edge of the fight, not to be
compared in value with the honest hoplite of the line-of-battle.[1]
To the Roman, essentially a close fighter, the bowman was
only an auxiliary—often useful, sometimes necessary. And
so it was in the earlier Middle Age, as we have seen at Hastings
and Arsouf, where the knights gave the decisive blow, but the
missiles of their infantry had made that blow possible. The
new thing in military history in the fourteenth century was to
find the English archer as the actual winner of battles—the
man-at-arms being only his auxiliary. To this there had been
no parallel in earlier centuries.

[1] Cf. not only the *Iliad*, *passim*, but Sophocles, *Ajax*, 1120, for τοξότης used
as a term of contempt by Menelaus to Teucer, "if he boasts like this though only
a bowman, what would his pride be if he were fully armoured?" To which Teucer
answers, that he is as good a man unarmoured as Menelaus fully equipped.

In this aspect, therefore, the archer of Crecy was the ancestor of all modern infantry which breaks down its opponents by the use of missiles. But in actual historical sequence he was not the father of the infantry of modern regular armies, either in England or elsewhere. The bow was officially dropped as an authorised national weapon by an edict of Elizabeth's Privy Council in 1595, while the English regular infantry only goes back to the " New Model " of 1644, some few of whose units were transferred to the permanent standing army of Charles II. in 1660.

The Swiss pikeman, on the other hand, survived long enough to be taken over into the earliest regular armies of the Continent in the sixteenth century ; the pike soon had to be combined with the musket, but remained in constant use till the invention of the bayonet in the very end of the seventeenth century, after which " the musketeer became his own pikeman." It may reasonably be said, therefore, that the Swiss are the lineal ancestors of the modern regiments of continental Europe, where every state began its regular infantry [1] by raising bands of pikemen, who were often actually hired Swiss, and when this was not the case were at any rate trained, like the Emperor Maximilian's *lanzknechts*, entirely in the Swiss fashion and with the Swiss tactics.

It is necessary, therefore, to investigate with some care the rise and development of the military system of the Alpine " Confederates," who from small beginnings made themselves such a notable place in the annals of the Art of War. When the central power of the Holy Roman Empire finally broke down in the thirteenth century, it was not only the great chartered cities which won for themselves a sort of practical independence. There were also non-urban communities, mostly in obscure corners of the realm, which had not been feudalised, or had been feudalised in a perfunctory fashion only, paying a loose and intermittent allegiance to some duke, count, or bishop who had a disputed claim only to their homage. Such were not only the upland valleys which were to form the original nucleus of the Swiss confederacy, but also the marshy lowlands of the Ditmarshians on the North Sea, and the sandy dunes of

[1] I do not call the unmounted members of Charles v.'s *Compagnies d'Ordonnance* " regular infantry," since they were essentially only the hangers-on of the gendarmes. Nor were the *Francs Archers* exactly "regulars."

the Free Frisians a little to the west of them. In quarters
of the Empire, like Swabia or Lower Saxony, where the old
ducal families had gone under, no less than the imperial
authority, it was a matter of local chance what should be the
fate of such abnormally unfeudalised communities. Some of
them fell under the influence of a bishop,[1] or of one of the
hereditary countships which had grown up by imperial grant
out of the old non-hereditary countships of earlier days. Others
kept a greater or less degree of independence, even as the cities
had done, having obtained charters of immunity from one
emperor or another.

Such was the case with the people of the mountain valleys
of Uri and Schwytz, who had obtained, in 1231 and 1240
respectively, *freiheitsbriefe* from Frederic II., exempting them
from all comital authority, and declaring their communities
to be direct vassals of the crown. How Unterwalden, the
third original member of the Confederacy, got its claim to a
similar status is not so clear. But in 1291 the three communities
signed the so-called "Eternal Alliance," which bound them to
support each other, to submit to no external authority, and to
acknowledge no magistrate who was not native born.[2]

The danger to this incipient league was of course the House
of Hapsburg, not so much in its imperial capacity, but as owning
the largest accumulation of feudal territory in the neighbourhood. For beyond their imperial policy the Hapsburgs had
their local ambition in South Swabia, where their original
family holding lay, and where they were continually " adding
field to field." If Rudolf, the founder of their dynasty, had
not succeeded in acquiring the derelict Austrian duchies, his
main object would probably have been to make himself Duke
of Swabia, where his interests were already so predominant.
Hence we find the Alpine confederates consistently striving to
secure themselves against their great feudal neighbours, by
supporting any rival who might arise. They backed the
Luxemburger Henry VII. in 1308, and got further charters
from him, and after his death were strenuous supporters of
Lewis of Bavaria in his struggle for the imperial crown with

[1] The Archbishop of Bremen conquered by force of arms the free Stadings, who
had found the connecting link between Ditmarsh and Frisia.
[2] For all this see Professor Delbrück's interesting summary of the beginnings of
the Swiss in his *Kriegskunst*, iii. 563-570.

Frederic of Hapsburg.   Of course adhesion to Henry or Lewis simply implied opposition to the old enemy, not any particular theory of loyalty to a legitimate emperor ; but civil war being on foot it was natural to take the anti-Austrian side.

It would be wrong to indulge in reminiscences of the legendary William Tell, and to dream of the Confederates as virtuous yeomen merely defending an ancestral liberty against a feudal oppressor.   Gessler's famous hat is as unauthentic as Tell's apple.   The primitive Swiss were a jealous, turbulent, and predatory race—they were already noted for their readiness to serve as the hired soldiery whom emperors took down to their Italian wars, and they were very troublesome neighbours to the rich abbey of Einsiedeln, whose abbots had been complaining of their cattle-lifting propensities for several generations.   In 1314, the Emperor Henry VII. being dead, while a new civil war between the rivals for the crown, Frederic of Austria and Lewis of Bavaria, was impending, the Schwytzers took advantage of the anarchy by descending in force under their Landamman Werner Staufacher on Einsiedeln—which supported the Hapsburg claimant ; they sacked the abbey from cellar to roof, and carried off a number of the monks as hostages to be held to ransom.   After this they then naturally declared themselves loyal partisans of the Bavarian claimant.

After the double election had duly taken place and the war had become general, the counter-emperor Frederic desired his brother Duke Leopold to make an end of this nucleus of Bavarian partisanship in the south, before trouble should spread farther.   The Duke called out the feudal levy of the Hapsburg lands in Swabia, with such other nobles of those regions as adhered to his brother's cause, and added to them infantry from the adjacent towns of Zürich, Winterthur, Zug, and Lucerne. The force cannot have been very large—but no useful estimate of its numbers has been preserved.   Four or five thousand men would be the utmost possible figure.[1]   The month was November, a bad time of the year for Alpine campaigning, but the necessity to chastise the plunderers of Einsiedeln without further delay was urgent.

Duke Leopold mobilised his army at Zug, close at the foot of the enemy's passes.   There were two possible routes of attack on the upland valley of Schwytz—the more obvious and

[1] John of Winterthur gives Leopold 20,000 men, p. 26.

shorter by Arth, at the foot of the lake of Zug, where the St. Gotthard Railway now enters the mountains, the other by the defile of Morgarten, farther east, along the south end of the small lake of Egeri. It seems that the former route had been more or less fortified by the Schwytzers, by means of walls of loose stone (*sungahs*, to use a modern Indian equivalent).[1] This may have been the reason which impelled Duke Leopold to take the longer circuit, and advance by the eastern defile.

But he had obviously neglected the all-important precaution of exploring this road ; he thrust his long narrow column, with the bulk of the cavalry in the vaward division,[2] into the narrow track between the lake of Egeri and the slopes above it, without any preliminary reconnaissance. The Swiss, warned in good time of the fact that the Duke had taken the Morgarten route, were on the spot some time before his vanguard was sighted. To get the very best ground for defence, they had gone forward a little beyond their own territorial boundary, and had blocked the road at its very narrowest by a hastily reared wall of loose stone. While a small force was placed to hold this obstacle, the rest of the confederates hid themselves in a wood and ravine above the road and parallel to it. Their strength is stated in their own (non-contemporary) records at as little as fifteen hundred men, but was probably somewhat more, as Uri had sent its contingent to help Schwytz, though there is no sign that Unterwalden had done so.[3] But two thousand seems a more probable estimate for a levée of the whole military population of the valleys, fighting on the very doorstep of their own land and with everything at stake. Werner Staufacher, who had led the raid on Einsiedeln, was again in command.

Duke Leopold had sent on no fore-riders or scouts, and it was only when his vanguard came up against the newly built

---

[1] For the Letzen, or loose-stone defensive lines of the Swiss, see Delbrück's interesting notes in his *Kriegskunst*, iii. 569–70. John of Winterthur duly mentions them, p. 25.

[2] This is vouched for by John of Winterthur, p. 25.

[3] We are told by the one chronicler who gives a long account of the fight (John of Winterthur) that Leopold had minor forces in motion. One of them is said by the fifteenth-century chronicler Billibald Pirckheimer (i. p. 41), to have been threatening Unterwalden from Interlaken by the way of the Brünnig Pass. This seems plausible : the division was led by Otto of Strassburg, the Austrian *vogt* in the Oberland.

stone barrier, and found it held against them, that he discovered that he was to be brought to action on this particular ground. The van had to halt, while the centre and rear kept coming up, and blocking the road and the narrow grassy slope between it and the wood above. The Duke gave orders that the wall should be stormed—presumably by dismounted knights; for the infantry were in the rear : the force behind it seemed insignificant. But just at this moment a shower of boulders and tree-trunks came rolling down the slope on his right hand, and a moment later the whole main body of the Swiss in dense column burst down from their hiding-place, and charged in flank the vanguard of the Austrians and so much of the head of the Duke's main body as was opposite to them. The disaster was immediate and complete ; the Austrian knights, packed in the road, had no space to turn their horses, and could not charge uphill—below them was the lake, behind them the road jammed by the rest of the army. The thrust of the charging Swiss was too strong to be resisted, since no counter-impetus could be got up against it. The whole head of the Duke's column was trampled down or rolled into the lake. We are told that the bulk of the Swiss were already using on this day the halberd, which was their earliest weapon—effective as a pike by its long point, but still more effective as a smashing weapon—a two-handed axe—for hewing through knightly plate and mail. Those of the Austrians who were at the very rear of the section of the army which had been assailed by the charge saved themselves for a moment, by falling back among their infantry supports in the rear. But this only caused dis-order, and the whole untouched portion of the column made no attempt to resist, went about, and tore away along the road. They were no better than a panic-stricken crowd, and the Swiss, after they had made an end of the vanguard, could pursue without meeting any resistance. " It was not a battle," says John of Winterthur, the one chronicler who gives a full account of the affair, " but a mere butchery of Duke Leopold's men ; for the mountain-folk slew them like sheep in the shambles ; no quarter was given, they cut down all without distinction. So great was the fierceness of the Confederates that scores of the Austrian foot-soldiery, when they saw the bravest knights falling helplessly, threw themselves in panic into the lake, preferring to drown rather than to be hewn

about by the dreadful weapons of their enemies." [1] Duke
Leopold himself escaped as by a miracle, being one of the
few of the main-battle who cut his way back to join the rear.
But fifteen hundred men, and of these the greater proportion
were knights and men-at-arms, had perished. [2]

In short, the Swiss won the day because their leaders, with
considerable tactical skill, had chosen their own ground, and
given the feudal chivalry no opportunity of attacking them at
advantage. " They were masters of the field because it was
they, and not their foe, who settled where the fight should take
place." On a steep and slippery November road, where they
could get no impetus for their charge, the long string of horsemen, penned between hill and lake, was helpless. The crushing
nature of the defeat was due to Leopold's inexcusable careless-
ness in leaving the way unexplored, and walking into a trap.
But he must have been foiled on such ground in any case.
Cavalry cannot operate in mountains—as Edward I. had
discovered in Wales a generation before. This is a simple
and obvious fact—nevertheless the impression made by Morgarten in Central Europe was profound. There had never
before been a case in the Empire of a complete and bloody
defeat of a feudal army by mere peasant infantry.

The knights could comfort themselves—like the French
after Courtrai thirteen years back—by saying that the ground
and the generalship were at fault. But the lesson that feudalism
was doomed in the Alps could hardly be disputed. Cavalry
cannot operate in passes : a feudal supremacy in mountain
lands, when once attacked, was bound to crumble. So it was
that within a few generations the hillmen of Appenzell, Valais,
Glarus, and the Grisons all got rid of the dominance of their
secular or ecclesiastical overlords. The example of Schwytz
was attractive, and was to be followed with success.

But the new Alpine Confederacy was not destined to be a
league of mountain-valleys alone. Less than a generation
after Morgarten it began to develop into a union of city-
republics and peasant-republics, spreading down into the lowlands. All over Germany the imperial cities were fearful of
the possible interference of their feudal neighbours, and linked

---

[1] John of Winterthur, p. 26.
[2] But John of Winterthur tells us that the contingent of his own town, being in
the extreme rear, got off quickly and hardly lost a man (p. 26).

themselves into associations like the various Hanseatic Leagues of the coast and the inland. But in the valleys of the Upper Rhine and the Aar, the special feature of the fourteenth century was that the cities, in their struggle with the *noblesse*, called in the aid of the mountaineers, and ultimately entered into a single association with them, though the local independence of each member was jealously guarded, and quarrels between the confederate units were fierce and frequent.

The extension of the influence of the three original " Forest Cantons " began with their alliance with the small city of Lucerne (1319), but the next move of primary importance was when Bern, the largest and most important urban community south of the Rhine, made up its mind to link its fortunes with the mountaineers. Bern's enemies were not so much the Hapsburgs as the feudal nobles of the west, the small states which represented the ancient kingdom of Lesser Burgundy. This venturesome city-republic, placed among neighbours who were individually of no great strength, had been utilising the anarchy of the long civil wars to extend its boundaries. Having got hold of the towns and regions of Thun and Laupen, which belonged to the Count of Kyburg, the Bernese found themselves in 1339 beset by a league of feudal lords, who all felt themselves threatened. Its members, besides the Count of Kyburg, the most aggrieved personage, were the Counts of Neuchâtel, Gruyères, Nidau, Valengin, Aarburg, and Louis of Savoy the Lord of Vaud ; many smaller barons from the Swabian borderlands co-operated.[1] But what is more surprising is that the considerable city of Freiburg joined in, out of pure jealousy for Bern. On 10th June 1339 these allies laid siege to Laupen, which was held by a garrison of six hundred Bernese.

Dismayed at the strength of the coalition, the Council of Bern sent to ask aid from the Forest Cantons, offering them not only a treaty of alliance but monetary subsidies. The mountain states agreed to come in, moved by the consideration that a successful feudal league would undoubtedly make them its next enemies. Technically they had no interest in the local quarrels of Bern and the counts, and their intervention in this war was purely a matter of high politics or of far-sighted ambition. Each promised its contingent, which was duly

[1] The Bishop of Lausanne also sent a small contingent.

forthcoming. On the night of June 20 the full city-levy of
Bern marched forth, and was joined at Bümplitz—three miles
outside the city—by the Confederates. Covering their march
by the forest, which then extended almost to the gates of
Laupen, they presented themselves before the camp of their
enemies on the afternoon of the 21st. They took up their
position on a hill, the Bramberg, just outside the skirts of the
wood, and waited to be attacked.

The lords of Little Burgundy were surprised by the sudden
appearance of the enemy, but were granted time to array
themselves, because the Swiss had resolved to fight a defensive
battle. On reconnoitring the ground they discovered that the
left front of the enemy was accessible to cavalry, but that the
right was much steeper ; they therefore concentrated all their
mounted men on their own right, and placed their infantry
opposite the less favourable slope. Their total strength is
given as one thousand to twelve hundred men-at-arms, with a
large but not very trustworthy body of infantry [1]—the majority
were the feudal following of the counts—raw and ill-armed
bands ; only the burghers of Freiburg were a well-equipped
and solid body. Whether the commander of the host was
Rudolf of Nidau or Gerard of Valengin seems uncertain.

The Bernese and their allies must undoubtedly have been
much weaker in numbers—the total of six thousand given for
them is probably correct. Their general was Rudolf of Erlach,
a knight of long experience in local wars, who was both a
citizen of Bern and a vassal for some of his lands to the Count
of Nidau. He had been chosen to lead the army by a special
vote of the Council, and consented to take command on condition that the men swore loyalty to him, and undertook to obey
his orders. His task was certainly carried out with great
ability, for it was no small matter to face a formidable
enemy, mustering twelve hundred men-at-arms, not in a defile
like Morgarten, but on an accessible slope. Erlach's tactical
design was to allow the enemy to begin the ascent of the hill,
and, when they were well committed to it, to charge down on
them in dense column. The men of the Forest Cantons were
placed opposite the enemy's cavalry, on the gentler acclivity
upon the left ; they are estimated at one thousand strong,

[1] The contemporary *Conflictus Laupenensis*, giving the Bernese version, speaks
of twenty thousand men, which must be a normal mediæval exaggeration.

and were apparently strengthened with some small contingents of volunteers from other mountain valleys (the Haslithal, etc.). The Bernese, forming the centre and right, had the Freiburgers and the feudal infantry in front of them.

The counts wasted some time before they came forward—they sent a herald with unacceptable propositions for a conference, and when these were rejected, prolonged their halt by the ceremonial of knighting some young squires, and by sending isolated riders forward to taunt and insult the stationary enemy. But at length they moved up the hillside in good order ; when they were well started, Erlach flung his columns at them, risking everything on his confidence in their impetus. At the first moment there was a terrible risk of disaster ; while the front of the Bernese phalanx plunged down in a solid mass, as had been ordered, some of the rear ranks held back, and even recoiled to the edge of the forest just behind them. The contemporary Bernese narrator of the fight confesses that though most of the shirkers were unarmoured men, others were citizens of good military repute. Extraordinary as it may seem, this defection did not lose the battle.[1]

The main mass of the Bernese, who had not looked behind them, completely trampled down the Freiburg contingent, which was immediately opposed to them, and broke it to pieces. Whereupon the feudal infantry on each side was seized with panic and dispersed ; the levies of Vaud are said to have led the flight. Erlach was thus victorious, and able to come to the assistance of his allies of the Forest Cantons, who had been going through trying experiences. They had clashed with the baronial cavalry low down the slope, had been brought to a stand, and were then completely surrounded, and forced to make front in all directions in the formation that the Swiss in after-days called " the hedgehog " (igel). The fight

[1] It is incredible that an incident so little flattering to the *amour propre* of his fellow-citizens should have been narrated by the author of the *Conflictus* unless it had happened. "Fere duo millia territi fugam dederunt versus forestam, inter quos inermes quidam fuerunt, sed quidam qui putabantur etiam validi in pugna et robusti." The chronicler Justinger, writing eighty years after, tries to explain away this panic by a misunderstanding of Erlach's orders—but the contemporary writer must be followed—he could have given excuses if there had been any to give. I cannot follow Dr. Delbrück's ingenious theory that the fugitives were a separate corps, forming the extreme Bernese right. This is in absolute opposition to the authorities, who specially say that there was only one column, "onnes coadunati in unum, quasi unus parvus cuneus se congregantes."

must have been much like Randolph's combat with Clifford on the day before Bannockburn. But the Swiss had not yet adopted the pike, and their halberds, though inflicting the most ghastly wounds, could not keep the cavalry from closing in. There was hand-to-hand fighting of the most furious sort. But the mountaineers stood like a rock, and succeeded in holding their own for the all-important period during which the hostile infantry was being driven off the field.

Presently Erlach came up with his victorious column of Bernese, and charged the knights in flank and rear. Apparently the enemy was already exhausted by his vain attempt to break the men of the Forest Cantons, for after one effort to ride down the Bernese, he turned and rode off the field, not without considerable loss, for many horsemen were forced into the river Sense and drowned. There was no long pursuit, however, for the battle had been fought in the late afternoon, and the dusk covered the flying host. Their casualties, therefore, were not very heavy—fifteen hundred in all according to the contemporary Bernese author of the *Conflictus Laupenensis*, one thousand only if John of Winterthur is to be credited. But the loss was heavy among the knighthood—the Counts of Nidau, Aarburg, and Valengin, and John, the only son of Louis of Savoy, had fallen, with eighty barons and bannerets *insignis militiae*, and several hundreds of their men-at-arms. The infantry had got off lightly in comparison, though the burgomaster and standard-bearer of Freiburg had both been left on the field. The victors displayed in triumph, when they marched home on the 22nd, twenty-seven feudal banners and seventy crested helms. Their own loss had been very moderate, and almost entirely among the men of the Forest Cantons.

Laupen was neither so dramatic nor so bloody a field as Morgarten, but its tactical importance was much greater. The admirers of chivalry could not pretend that here, as at Courtrai or Morgarten, the knights had been beaten entirely because of the impossible ground on which they had fought. In this case infantry had defeated cavalry on a hillside where the latter had no difficulty in forming up and charging. The moral effect, therefore, was very great, and a heavy blow had been given to the supremacy of the horsemen in Central Europe. The feudal horsemen had been proved unable to break a phalanx, even though the men forming it were armed not with the

pike but with the less effective halberd. It boots not to inquire
what would have happened if the counts had brought to the
field one thousand or even five hundred of the bowmen of Falkirk
or Dupplin, and had used them in the fashion which English
leaders had shown to be possible. They had no such tactical
idea in their minds; they merely strove to win by the use of
the charging squadron—and the halberd did at Laupen what
the bow was to do at Crecy six years later.

Sempach, the third of the great victories of the Swiss, is
much more interesting than Laupen, as it displays a tardy
attempt of the *noblesse* to cope with the infantry of the Confederates by new methods. If cavalry charges could not break
the column of halberdiers, perhaps they might be beaten at
their own game by the impact of a column as heavy and better
armoured than their own. Just as the French knighthood
dismounted at Poictiers thirty years back, and with better luck
at Roosebeke in more recent days, so did the Austrian knighthood at Sempach. Though the form of the enemy's tactical
efficiency was so different, a similar method was tried against
it—and with equally disastrous results. It is odd that no
experiment was tried on another line—that of Hastings or
Falkirk, the combination of mounted men and missile-bearing
infantry. But apparently archers were practically unprocur-
able, and crossbowmen were not very numerous or much
esteemed in South Germany. Our surprise is the greater when
we reflect that once in recent years an " English " force, though
one in which born Englishmen were in a minority, had made
a raid into Switzerland, so that the tale of Crecy and Poictiers
and the meaning of the longbow cannot have been unknown.
In 1375 Enguerrand de Coucy, the son-in-law of Edward III.,
had led a great band of free-companies into the valley of the
Aar, nominally in pursuance of a quarrel with the Hapsburgs
concerning the dowry of his mother, a princess of their house.
He wasted Austrian and Confederate regions indifferently,
won many successes, and finally retired for want of provisions
rather than for military reasons. For Duke Leopold and the
Swiss were equally unable to beat him, though they cut off
some of his detachments. The memory of the destruction of
one of them at Büttisholz near Lucerne was long preserved
by the name of the " Englishman's hill " applied to a mound
where a body of the free-companions had made their last stand

and found their grave.[1] At any rate, in the next trial of strength between the Austrians and the mountaineers, we find the former adopting French rather than English tactics.

The Confederacy was now grown stronger, having been formally joined by Zürich in 1351, and by Zug and Glarus in 1352, while Bern turned its alliance into formal adhesion in 1353. The Hapsburg predominance in the lands south of the Rhine was nearing its end, and that of the Swiss League was obviously destined to replace it. The policy of the Confederates was unscrupulous and aggressive, and the final and inevitable conflict was brought about in the winter of 1385–6 by the Lucerners sacking the castle of Rothenburg, and openly taking under their protection the little town of of Sempach, an undoubted Hapsburg possession, into which they threw a garrison. Already often provoked, Duke Leopold the Valiant, nephew of the Leopold of Morgarten, took up the challenge and began to raise an army for operations in the following spring. He himself only ruled " Vorder Österreich," the Hapsburg lands of Swabia and the West, with the county of Tyrol, but he had hired adventurous men-at-arms from every surrounding region from Milan as far as Brabant, for the struggle. It was spread over a long front, since the frontiers of the Hapsburg and the Confederate lands were now continuous from the Aar to the Limmat, and subsidiary operations north and west of Zürich, and eastward toward the Tyrol were on foot, while the main decisive conflict took place only ten miles in front of Lucerne.

On July 9 Duke Leopold, with an army of very moderate strength—it must have been far from representing his whole disposable force—marched from Sursee by the road which passes by the north side of the lake of Sempach. He had with him fourteen hundred men-at-arms and some two thousand five hundred foot, for the best contemporary authorities say. that he had no more than four thousand troops in all. Probably he

---

[1] Enguerrand only went away after he had been ceded the county of Nidau, as compensation for his mother's dowry. For his doings see Pirckheimer's summary (p. 5), which gives the affair in a nutshell : " [Angli] spe praedae magnis adventantes copiis, Bernensem agrum foeda population evastarunt : castella vero et minores vicos diripiebant. Ne tamen usquequaque impune persultavunt, multi a Bernensibus per excursiones et levia proelia caesi sunt : nam ob ingentem multitudinem cum hoste aperto Marte congredi non audebant. Tandem Angli commeatus inopia abire sunt coacti—non minus sociis quam hostibus graves et intolerandi."

left the infantry to beleaguer the revolted town of Sempach, for there is no mention of it in the battle which followed.[1] But he pushed on with the cavalry not on the direct road from Sempach to Lucerne—south-east—but north-east by the minor road which leads to the bridge of Gislikon, obviously to intercept succour coming from Zürich and the north, for the Confederates were in strength at Zürich, which was their base for attacking the Hapsburg lands in the Aargau and Thurgau.[2] He may also have been wishing to avoid fighting with the lake close at his back, which would have been the case if he had remained near Sempach. At any rate he had advanced with his horsemen as far as the hamlet of Hildisrieden, a mile and a half beyond Sempach, where he ran into the vanguard of a Swiss force hastily marching toward him.

Informed betimes of the threatening concentration at Sursee, which implied the Duke's intention either to besiege Sempach or to make a direct march on Lucerne, the Confederate commanders at Zürich had detached all the men that they could spare—there were still operations going on in the north—and had sent them off in haste to get between the Austrian army and its objective. So at least does it seem most easy to interpret their action, though the contemporary chronicles help us little. The detached body, as was natural, consisted of contingents of the four Forest Cantons, whose land was in peril; no Zürichers or other Confederates are spoken of. The force was small, no authority of any value estimates it at over two thousand men,[3] some give figures as low as thirteen hundred or fifteen hundred. Apparently it had not yet been joined by the home-levies which might have come up from Lucerne, or the numbers must have been much greater.

Sempach would seem to have been one of those battles in which two armies, both on the move, mee teach other on the road, neither having had time to chose a position and deploy at leisure. But it was the Duke who took the offensive in the

---

[1] This is definitely stated only by Pirckheimer (p. 5), "Sempach obsidione cingere molitus est . . . omni peditatu in castris relicto." We are told that in passing Sempach some knights called out to the garrison on the wall "to have a dinner ready for them when they should come back from beating their comrades in the field." But this is no less late stuff than the other traditionary tales.

[2] I agree with Dr. Delbrück's ingenious interpretation of the strategical situation in *Kriegskunst*, iii. p. 592.

[3] This is Königshoven's estimate. Justinger gives only thirteen hundred.

first instance. As to the exact course of events, we have all too little contemporary evidence, and far too much non-contemporary garnish from chroniclers of the next century, popular poetry like the *Sempachenlied* of Halbshuter, and garbled tradition. A concrete Sempach-legend was gradually produced by the confluence of many untrustworthy sources, adorned finally with the heroic exploit of the mythical Arnold Winkelried, the man who was said to have broken the Austrian line by throwing himself upon the serried lances of the enemy, and opening a gap at the cost of his life.

Putting all this aside, we seem to see that the armies met, perhaps sooner than either had expected, and certainly before either had time to deploy. The Swiss vanguard, comprised of the contingent of Lucerne, halted and took position on the slope where the Memorial Chapel of 1387 was afterwards built, on a narrow level space in front of the village of Hildisrieden. Apparently the rest of the force was still some way to the rear, Duke Leopold's army, riding up the terraced slopes along which the Sempach-Gislikon road ascends, was marching in three corps, the first with the banner of Austria under the Marshal, John of Ochenstein, the second headed by the Duke himself, the third (consisting mainly of Alsatian, Swabian, and other hired auxiliaries) under the command of the Count of Hohenzollern and the Lord of Oberkirch.

On discovering the enemy Leopold ordered his vaward battle to leave their horses and attack on foot, as the French had done with good success at Roosebeke in 1382, only four years back, against a somewhat similar enemy. This was undoubtedly a tactical experiment made on reasoned premises, and not the consequence of any inaccessibility of the ground, for the Duke kept his second and third corps on horseback. Every knight present must have heard of Laupen, and have known that it was more than doubtful whether cavalry charges would break a Swiss column. But ought not well-armoured fighting-men of excellent courage to be able to bear down less well-equipped peasantry and burghers, on a fair field and with equal weapons? For the knightly lance in a frontal clash should be as effective as the somewhat shorter halberd. The two hinder battles retained their horses; no doubt Leopold intended to use them later for a decisive charge when the Swiss should have given way.

So the Austrian vaward dismounted, handed over their horses to their pages, and went forward on foot " not in too good order, for the lords were angry," and excessively eager to wipe off old scores of which chivalry had evil memories.[1] It seemed at first not impossible that Sempach would prove a repetition of Roosebeke, for when the two columns met front to front, and long and fierce hand-to-hand fighting had lasted for some minutes, the Lucerners were seen to be losing ground, their banner fell, and their casualties were heavy. Indeed it would seem that they were fought out, and the Austrians were hoping for victory when the Swiss main body, obviously only just arriving on the field, suddenly came into action.[2] Allowing the Lucerners to fall away to the flank, they charged in upon the Duke's vaward battle, which was by now almost as exhausted as its original opponents. Three things were ruinous to the Austrians : their enemy came on with a fierce impetus, while they themselves were at a standstill ; they were somewhat outnumbered ; and—most important of all—a long fight on foot in heavy fourteenth-century plate-armour had reduced them to a state of absolute physical prostration : they could barely stand upright and wield their spears when the new clash came.

The fortune of the fight turned at once—the men-at-arms were seen to lose ground, their banner wavered, and a lamentable cry, " Oh succour, Austria, succour ! " ran down their disordered ranks.[3] It reached the ears of the Duke, who a moment before was dreaming of victory almost in his grasp. Without hesitation he flung himself from his horse, and bade his followers copy his example. The second corps went hastily forward in considerable disorder to save the perishing vaward battle. But before it reached the fighting-ground, the enemy had broken through, and the front line had been trampled down. There followed a new hand-to-hand combat, in which the Swiss from the first had the advantage, for the Duke's men

[1] The poor order is insisted on both by Königshofen and the Austrian narrator, Hagen.

[2] Were the Swiss formed in three columns, as was their later custom, or only in two? This cannot be deduced from any of the authorities. It is only known that the contingent of Uri was at the head of the main-battle which delivered the decisive charge.

[3] " Darnach hört der edel Fürst ain chleglicke geschray, ' O retta, Oesterreich, retta,' und sah die Bannyr swehen, gleichsam sie wolbe undergehn. Do ruft er an all sein Ritter und Knecht das sie mit samst tretten von der Rossen, und retteten Ritter und Knecht " (Hagen, 1154-55).

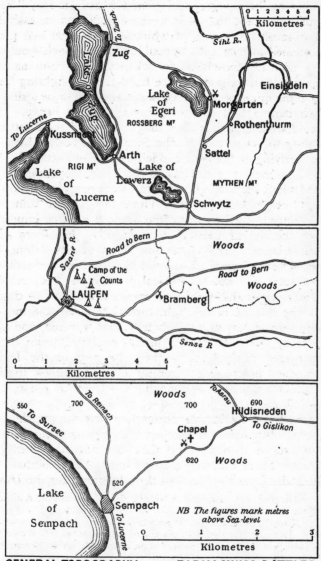

GENERAL TOPOGRAPHY OF THE EARLY SWISS BATTLES
MORGARTEN (Nov.15.1315), LAUPEN (June 21.1339), SEMPACH (July 9.1386)

came up piecemeal and were met and thrown into disarray by the recoiling survivors of the defeated vaward division. Leopold fought like a hero, and was seen for some time holding his own and keeping his men together.

But the battle was lost—so, at least, judged the Count of Hohenzollern and the Baron of Oberkirch, who commanded the mounted reserve of Leopold's army. Instead of coming in, whether on horse or on foot, to make a last attempt to save the day, they turned their bridles and rode off the field followed by all their corps. This ended the affair—the deserted Duke and those who stood by him were hewn down after a desperate resistance.[1] Very few of the knights got away, for their pages had for the most part ridden off in panic with the chargers, when they saw the rear-battle abscond. Lucky was he who had a faithful servant, and who met him in the rout, for to get away on foot in heavy plate-armour from a lost field was no light matter. Yet some must have managed to escape—for when the Swiss counted the corpses next day they found six hundred and seventy-six in all " well-nigh every one a great lord or of noble blood," while the two front divisions of the Duke's army must have numbered over nine hundred spears, since his total force was about fourteen hundred in all.

With Leopold there fell the Margrave of Hochburg, the two counts of Thierstein, and the Count of Fürstenburg, five barons, seven bannerets, twenty-eight knights of Austria, and thirty-five of the Tyrol—not to speak of the hired knights from outside— with over five hundred squires and men-at-arms. He and twenty-six of the more distinguished of his companions were buried together at the Abbey of Königsfeld, where the corpse of his murdered grandfather, the Emperor Albert, already lay.[1] For the Swiss allowed the relatives of the fallen nobles to carry them away under truce on the third day after the battle. The victors had lost, it is said, about one hundred and twenty men, among them the landamman of Uri ; more than half the casualites were in the Lucerne contingent, which had fared so ill at the commencement of the battle.

---

[1] For details see Köhler, *Kriegswesen*, ii. 624, and Dierauer's *Confederation Suisse*, vol. ii. 395, which gives the fullest details as to the casualties. Dierauer mentions that where the abbey was dug up in 1898, the tombs of the fallen of Sempach were opened, and it was found that the skulls were nearly all dreadfully split by halberd-strokes.

This was a sad day for feudal chivalry.   Laupen had proved that the Swiss could beat the knight on his horse—Sempach proved that they could beat him dismounted also—on fair ground and with no great disparity of numbers. From this time forward the Confederates were masters in the Alps, and went forth conquering and to conquer.

CHAPTER II

CHARACTER ARMS AND ORGANISATION OF THE SWISS ARMIES, 1315–1515

THE Swiss of the fourteenth and fifteenth centuries have been compared with good reason to the Romans of the early Republic. In the Swiss, as in the Roman character, we find the most intense patriotism combined with a complete lack of chivalrous feeling or magnanimity, and a certain meanness and pettiness of conception which prevent us from sympathising with either race—however great its achievements. In both, the steadiest courage and the fervour of the noblest self-sacrifice were combined with an appalling ferocity, and a cynical disregard for the rights of all neighbours. Among each the warlike pride, generated by successful wars of independence, led ere long to wars of conquest and plunder. As enemies both were distinguished for their deliberate and cold-blooded cruelty. The resolution to give no quarter, which appears almost pardonable in patriots defending their own native soil, becomes brutal when retained in wars of aggression, but reaches a climax of disgusting inhumanity where the slayer is a mere mercenary, fighting for a cause in which he has no national interest. Repulsive as was the callous blood-thirstiness of the soldiers of Sulla or Cæsar, it was less in moral guilt than the needless ferocity displayed by the hired Swiss soldiery on many a battlefield of the sixteenth century.[1]

In no point do we find a greater resemblance between the histories of the two peoples than in the causes of their success in war. Rome and Switzerland alike are examples of the fact that a good military organisation and a sound system of

[1] After Novara, for example, they put to death several hundred German prisoners —both slayers and slain being mere hired mercenaries.

national tactics are the surest base for a continuous career of conquest.   Provided with these, a vigorous state needs no unbroken series of great commanders.   A succession of experienced veterans of no particular genius suffices to guide the engine of war, which works almost automatically, and seldom fails to cleave its way to success.   The elected consuls of Rome and the elected or nominated " captains " of the Confederates could never have led their troops to victory had it not been for the military system which their predecessors had perfected. The combination of pliability and solid strength in the legion, the powers of rapid movement and irresistible impact which the Swiss column possessed, were competent to win a field without the display of any extraordinary ability by the generals who set them in motion.

The battle-array which the Confederates regularly employed in the fifteenth century—in the fourteenth it was only in process of development—was one whose nearest prototype was the Macedonian phalanx.   They always presented themselves on the field in deep columns, and in the days of their greatest supremacy these columns were furnished with the long pike. At Laupen and Sempach, as we have seen, the pike had not yet become predominant, and the halberd was still the national arm, though some of the men seem to have carried the longer weapon.[1]   The halberd was distinctly inferior to the pike as a means of keeping off cavalry, but was a formidable enough tool of war.   Eight feet in length, with a heavy head ending in a sharp point, it had on its front a blade like a hatchet, and on its back a strong spike or hook.[2]   If the most ponderous, it was the most murderous of weapons.   Swung by strong arms it could cleave helmets and plate-armour as no sword could do. It was the halberd whose edge dashed in the skulls of Duke Leopold's knights at Sempach,[3] and struck down Charles of Burgundy—all his face one gash from temple to teeth—in the frozen ditch by Nancy.

Even after the pike became predominant, the halberd was still retained by some of the Swiss infantry, who had their

[1] At any rate we hear of the pike "spiess" along with the halberd in some of the narratives of Sempach, though not in the strictly contemporary ones.

[2] The halberd differed from the English "brown bill " by having this hook or spike on its back.   The hook is said to have been devised to catch and pull down the reins of charging horses.

[3] See page 251 above, note 1.

regular place in the centre of the column, by the cantonal banner, which was placed under their charge. If the enemy succeeded in bringing the column to a stand, it was their duty to issue out by the side ranks or the rear ranks, which opened to give them egress, and to throw themselves against the hostile flank.

In repelling cavalry charges, however, the halberd, owing to its structure, was a far less useful weapon than the pike. The original adoption of the latter as a national weapon seems to result from the lessons of a disastrous fight near Bellinzona in 1422, when the Swiss, having too many halberdiers and too few pikes in their front, were broken by the men-at-arms of the Duke of Milan. But the halberd was liked by old-fashioned soldiers, and it was not till many years later that it was ruled that the pike must be the normal arm of the cantonal infantry.[1] The older weapon was to be relegated to the reserve and banner-guard. But all through the later fifteenth century, the long pike was supreme with its eighteen-foot ashen shaft and long ten-inch steel head. It was usually grasped with two hands widely extended, and poised to the level of the shoulder, with the point slightly sunk so as to deliver a downward thrust.[2] Before the line projected, not only the pikes of the first rank, but those of the second, third, and fourth, an impenetrable hedge of bristling points. The men in the interior of the column held their weapons upright, till called upon to step forward to take the place of those who had fallen in the front. Thus the pikes, rising twelve feet above the heads of the soldiers, gave to the charging mass the appearance of a moving wood. Above it floated numberless flags, the pennons of districts, towns, and guilds, the banners of the Cantons, sometimes the great standard of " the Ancient League of High Germany "—the white cross on the red field. The long series of quaint sixteenth-century battle-pieces on the famous bridge of Lucerne give some idea of the aspect of such an array.

Next to its solidity the most formidable quality of the

[1] See Von Elgger's *Kriegswesen der Schweizerischen Eidgenossen*, p. 105, for the documents which rehearse the fact that there are still too many halberds, and that "Welcher ein spiess tragen könne, einen spiess tragen sollte."

[2] So Montluc describes it in his commentaries, and so it may be seen in the hands of the Swiss infantry in the large picture of the battle of Pavia in the Ashmolean Museum.

Swiss infantry was its rapidity of movement. " No troops were ever more expeditious on a march, or in forming themselves for battle, because they are not overloaded with armour." [1] When an emergency arrived, a Confederate army could be raised with extraordinary speed : a people who regarded the glory and the profit of war as the main thing which made life worth living, flocked to arms without needing any long summons. The outlying contingents marched day and night in order to reach the mustering-place in good time. There was no need to waste days in the weary work of organisation, when every man stood among his kinsmen and neighbours under the pennon of his own town, valley, or guild. The troops of the democratic cantons elected their officers, those of the larger states received " captains " nominated by their Councils, and then without further delay the army could march. Thus an invader, even though his attack were rather unexpected, might in three or four days find twenty thousand men opposite him. They would often be within a few miles of him before he was aware that a Swiss army was in the field.

In face of such a foe it was hard for the slowly moving feudal or mercenary armies of the fifteenth century to manœuvre—whether strategically in the general campaign, or tactically on the actual battlefield. When once the Confederates were in motion, their enemy was usually forced to fight, not how and where he chose, but according to the desire of his more mobile opponents. The Swiss in their great days always made it their rule to seize the offensive, and not to allow themselves to be attacked. The composition of their various columns was settled at the opening of the campaign, and they marched brigaded as they were to fight. There was no pause needed to draw up an army composed of many small contingents in line of battle—a thing which led to so many quarrels and delays in feudal units. Each phalanx marched on the enemy at a steady but swift pace, which covered the ground in an incredibly short time. Reading the narratives of their enemies, we gather that the advance of a Swiss army had in it something pretentious ; the masses of pikes and halberds came rolling over the brow of some hill or out of the depths of some wood, and a moment later they were drawing

[1] Machiavelli, *Arte della Guerra*, 32.

near, and then—almost before the opponent had time to
realise his position—they were on him, with four rows of pike-
heads projecting in front, and the impetus of file on file surging
up from the rear.

The power of swift movement was, as Machiavelli observed, in no small degree the result of the Confederates'
determination not to overload themselves with armour. Their
light equipment was originally due to poverty alone, but was
deliberately preserved on the discovery that a heavy panoply
was incompatible with their national tactics. How often had
dismounted knights been ruined by their incapacity to bear up
long under the weight of their plate and mail ! Sempach
and Agincourt are only typical examples of a well-known general
phenomenon. Wherefore the normal equipment of a Swiss
pikeman or halberdier consisted of a steel cap and a breastplate
alone, some adding arm-pieces or tassets. Even these were not
in universal employment ; many trusted the defence of their
persons to their weapons, and came out in leather jerkins or
buff coats. The use of closed helms, of gorgets, and of leg-armour
seems to have been confined to leaders alone, who rode on the
march in order to keep up with their lightly-armed followers.
When they arrived in sight of the enemy they dismounted,
to fight on the same terms as the rest. A few of the patricians
of Bern and some of the other large urban cantons were occasionally found equipped as cavalry, but their numbers were
insignificant, and their presence made no difference to the
general tactics of the army.[1]

On the other hand, if cavalry were practically non-existent,
light infantry was by no means unknown in the Swiss organisation. Occasionally it rose to quite a considerable proportion
of the whole host. They were mostly armed with the crossbow, the weapon of the fabulous Tell, but by the middle of the
fifteenth century the " hand-gun " was beginning to prevail—
far earlier than it did in England, where the longbow preserved
to a much later date its superiority over the clumsy firearms
of the day. Indeed it would appear that the earliest Swiss
hand-guns may go back to the last years of the fourteenth
century—there seem to be allusions to " portative firearms "

---

[1] There were eighteen men-at-arms from Soleure with the Bernese at Laupen,
so early as 1339, and there are similar trifling bodies of horse recorded in the
Burgundian wars.

at Zürich in 1388 and 1393.[1] In the fifteenth century, when Swiss tactics had been perfected and standardised, it was the duty of the arbalesters or hand-gun men to precede the phalanx, and to endeavour to draw on themselves the attention of the enemy's light troops and artillery, so that the columns behind them might advance as long as possible without being molested. Thus the true use of a skirmishing line was fully appreciated by the time of Granson and Morat—but we hear nothing of missile weapons (other than casual stones !) at Morgarten, Laupen, or Sempach. When the pikemen had got up to the front, the arbalesters retired between the columns, leaving the decisive blow to be administered by their comrades.

A Swiss army was therefore simple in its elements, and easy to handle. The correlation and subordination of the various arms had few problems. The force was homogeneous and coherent. But there were grave drawbacks nevertheless to its military efficiency. The first was inter-cantonal jealousy: there was a universal prejudice against placing the troops of one canton under the orders of the citizen of another. So strong was this feeling that an extraordinary result followed—the appointment of a real commander-in-chief remained, through the brilliant period of Swiss military history, an exception rather than a rule. The conduct of affairs was in the hands of a council of war, but it was a council which, contrary to the old proverb about such bodies, was always ready and willing to fight. It was composed of the captains of each cantonal contingent, and settled the questions which came before it by discussion and voting. Before a battle it entrusted the command of vanward, rearward, main-battle, and light troops to different officers, but the holders of such posts enjoyed a mere delegated authority, and had not the permanent status of divisional generals. Rudolf of Erlach's position as commander-in-chief at Laupen was quite an exceptional thing; that he felt the difficulties of it was shown by the fact that he got leave to make the troops swear personal obedience to him.

Such a system was, of course, unfavourable to the rise of great generals, or the framing of broad strategical plans. The soldier rested his hope of victory rather on an entire confidence in the fighting power of himself and his comrades than on the skill of his commander. Troops who had proved in a hundred

[1] See Von Elgger's *Kriegswesen der Schweizerischen Eidgenossen*, p. 98.

fields their ability to conquer are comparatively indifferent as
to the personality of their leader, when he is continually being
changed for local political reasons.   There may have been
something more than inter-cantonal jealousy at the bottom of
the aversion of the Swiss to appoint permanent generals—
the councillors of each state must have known something of
Italian history, and have reflected on the frequency with which
the successful general in a city republic blossomed out into a
tyrant.   So there never was any opportunity given for the rise
of a Cæsar or a Sforza or a Bonaparte in Switzerland.

But the Confederates paid for their security from this
sort of danger, by sacrificing the chance of using their victories
as they might have been used by a commander of genius.
Speaking in a general fashion, we may observe that their wars
were directed neither with strategical skill nor with unity of
purpose.   Cantons wished to achieve different ends, often
incompatible ends, and their captains, representing these local
ambitions as delegates, were bound to put forward rival schemes.
The compromise which forms the mean between several plans
of campaign usually combines their faults rather than their
merits.   But, in addition to this, we may suspect that to find
any one Swiss officer capable of working out a large strategical
plan would have been as difficult as to find such a man in a
gathering of feudal barons.   The " captain " was an old soldier
who had won distinction on bygone battlefields, but except
in his wider experience was little different from the men under
his orders.   Of elaborating the more difficult strategical combinations, a Swiss council of war was not much more capable
than a party of veteran sergeant-majors would be to-day.

Hence a long record of wonderful victories leading to
inadequate results ; jealousy between canton and canton lost
many a brilliant chance ; mere narrow lack of political knowledge and petty greed co-operated.   And the Confederacy,
which once and again seemed likely to create a new and
important military state dominating Central Europe, never
rose to its opportunity, and ended in becoming a nursery of
mercenary soldiers for other powers guided by wider conceptions
and wider ambitions.

With tactics as opposed to strategy the case was different.
The best means of adapting the attack in column to the accidents
of the ground or the quality and armament of the enemy's

troops had been learnt in the school of experience. A national tactical system had been developed, whose efficiency was proved again and again in the battles of the fifteenth century. For dealing either with feudal cavalry or with ordinary continental infantry the Swiss method was perfect ; it was only when a new age introduced new conditions into war that it became obsolete in the sixteenth century.

The normal order of battle employed by the Confederates, however small or large their army might be, was an advance in an *échelon* of three divisions. The leading corps (*vorhut*)— that which formed the van while the force was on the march— made for a given point in the enemy's line. The main-battle (*gewaltshaufen*), instead of coming up in line with the first corps, advanced parallel to it, but at a short distance on its right or left rear. The rearward (*nachhut*) advanced still farther back, and often halted until the result of the first shock was seen, in order that it might, if necessary, act as a reserve.[1] This disposition left a clear space behind each column, so that if it were repulsed it could retire without falling back on the next corps and disordering it. Other nations (*e.g.* the French at Creçy and Poictiers), who placed one corps directly behind another, had often to pay the penalty of seeing the repulse of the vaward battle entailing the rout of the whole army— the repulsed front line falling back on the one behind, and carrying it away, or at least spoiling its order and impetus. The Swiss method of attack had another strong point—it was almost impossible for the enemy to wheel inwards and take the leading column in flank—if he did so, he exposed his own flank to the second *échelon* of the Swiss, which was coming up to the support of the first.

It was, of course, possible to attack either with the right column leading, or with the left—the ground settled that point. And occasions were known where the main-battle moved first, with both wings " refused " and coming up later. But this was exceptional. Equally so was an advance by both wings with the main-battle held back at the first. This seems to have been the order at the combat of Frastenz in 1499 against the Tyrolese.[2] And occasionally, in addition to the three normal

---

[1] Machiavelli in the third book of his *Arte della Guerra* has a clear account of this form of advance and its merits.

[2] See Von Elgger's *Kriegswesen*, p. 311, quoting Pirckheimer.

columns, detachments were made, generally of light troops only, to circumvent the enemy's line of battle by a wide sweep, and to threaten his flank or rear by a demonstration or even a serious attack. But the *échelon* of columns was normal, and only abandoned when either the force present was so small that it could not be sub-divided, or so large that it could spare a detachment for subsidiary operations.

If the odds were anything like equal, even small bodies of pikemen could take care of themselves—as was shown in the Swabian War of 1498, when six hundred men of Zürich, caught in the open plain by a thousand Austrian horse, " formed the hedgehog (*igel*) and broke off the enemy with ease and much jesting." On one occasion in 1498, during the operations which preceded the siege of Waldshut, the whole Confederate army, having to offer battle in the plain, went out to meet the imperialist cavalry in three great hollow squares, " geschiklich mit vor- und nachhut," in the midst of which were placed the cantonal banners and their escort of halberdiers. But the enemy would not charge, having old experience of the pikes.

CHAPTER III

THE SWISS BATTLES OF THE FIFTEENTH CENTURY

FOR the first hundred and fifty years of their military career the Swiss were so fortunate as never to meet either with a great master of the Art of War, or with any new form of tactical efficiency which could rival their own phalanx. It was still with the feudal knight or with the motley and undisciplined infantry of the Middle Ages that they had to deal. Their tactics had been framed precisely for successful conflict with such forces, and continued to preserve an ascendancy over them. The burghers and nobles of Swabia, the Austrian noblesse which followed Leopold or Maximilian of Hapsburg, the mercenary bands of the dukes of Milan, and the free-lances of the Armagnacs were none of them exponents of a new system, and served in turn to demonstrate the superiority of that of the Confederates.

In all the fifteenth century, the Swiss only suffered two really decisive defeats, and in each of these the preponderance of numbers was so great against them that the defeat proved nothing. The first was the battle of Arbedo, near Bellinzona, on June 30, 1422. The Confederates had already begun their trespassings across the Alps, and their annexations of " Welsh " territory, as they called the northern valleys of the tributaries of the Po. On this occasion they had provoked Filippo Maria Visconti in no small degree, and he had sent against them his best *condottiere* generals, the famous Carmagnola and Angelo de la Pergola, with—it is said—six thousand mercenary horse [1] and several thousand foot in addition. Carmagnola, who then met the Confederates for the first time, opened the engagement with a cavalry charge. Seeing its entire failure—four hundred horses were piked in the first

[1] The figure is suspiciously large, and ought probably to be reduced by half.

onset [1]—he resorted to another form of attack: he sent his
infantry to outflank the Swiss and annoy them with crossbow
practice, while he dismounted the whole of his men-at-arms [2]
and launched them in deep columns at the enemy's front.
The Confederates, a body of four thousand men from Uri,
Unterwalden, Zug, and Lucerne,[3] were mainly halberdiers, the
pikemen forming only a third of their force. The two masses
met, and engaged in a fair duel between lance and sword on
the one hand, and pike and halberd on the other. The impetus
of the larger force bore down that of the smaller, and, in spite
of the desperate fighting of their enemies, the Milanese began
to gain ground. So hardly were the Confederates now pressed
that the Schultheiss of Lucerne even thought of surrender, and
planted his halberd in the ground in token of submission.
Carmagnola, however, heated with the fight, cried out that
men who gave no quarter should receive none, and continued
his advance.[4] He was driving the broken phalanx before
him, when a new Swiss force suddenly appeared on his flank.
Believing them to be the contingents of Zürich, Schwytz,
Glarus, and Appenzell, which he knew to be at no great
distance, Carmagnola drew off his men and began to reform.
But in reality the newcomers were only a band of six hundred
foragers; they made no attack; while the Swiss main body
took advantage of the relaxation of the pressure to retire as
fast as possible. They had lost four hundred men according
to their own acknowledgment, many more if Italian accounts
are to be received. Carmagnola's loss, though numerically
larger, bore no such proportion to his whole force, and had
indeed been mainly incurred in the unsuccessful cavalry charge
which opened the action.[5]

[1] So Benedetto Giovio in his good account of the battle in his *Chronicon
Novocomense*, i.

[2] For the dismounting, see Benedetto Giovio and the *Rereum Mediolanensium
Historia* in Muratori, xix. Was Carmagnola remembering French tactics at Roosebeke?

[3] Swiss chroniclers allege that they were not much over two thousand.

[4] So Benedetto Giovio, who says that Pergola counselled acceptance of surrender.

[5] Machiavelli, who wrote of course from Italian sources only, calls this the
largest defeat ever suffered by the Swiss, and puts their loss at several thousands.
He is so far from the events he is describing that he is of no more worth than the
later Swiss chroniclers, who understate the defeat and the losses. Contemporary
sources leave no doubt that the casualties must have been much more than four
hundred. The contingent of Lucerne had crossed the Lake of the Four Cantons
in ten large barges: it returned in two. Cf. Etterlein and Diebold Schilling with
Benedetto Giovio for general impressions.

The battle of Arbedo seems to have been, as has already been remarked, the main incident which led to the multiplication of pikes and the diminution of halberds in the Confederate army. By the middle of the century the longer weapon was predominant.

The second defeat of the Confederates, on May 26, 1444, was one which brought them more good than harm in the end ; for the destruction of a small Swiss corps by the " Armagnac " mercenaries of the Dauphin Louis in 1444, was destined to result in the increase of the warlike reputation of such soldiery. The battle of St. Jacob, mad and unnecessary though it was, might serve as an example to deter the boldest enemy from meddling with men who preferred annihilation to retreat. Possessed by the single idea that their phalanx could bear down any obstacle, the Confederates deliberately crossed the Birs in face of an army of fifteen times their strength. They attacked it, broke its centre, and were then surrounded by its overwhelming numbers. Compelled to " form the hedgehog " in order to resist the tremendous cavalry charges directed against them, they held out for some time in the open, and then massed themselves round a ruined Leper-Hospital hard by. The Dauphin launched squadron after squadron at them, but each in its turn was hurled back in disorder. In the intervals between these onsets the French light troops poured in their missiles, but though the clump of pikes and halberds grew smaller it still remained impenetrable. Not until the evening was the fighting ended, and then two thousand Armagnacs lay dead around the heap of Swiss corpses in the centre. Louis saw that a few such victories would destroy his whole army, and turned back into Alsace, leaving Switzerland unmolested.

From that day the Confederates were able to reckon their reputation for obstinate and invincible courage as one of the chief causes which gave them political importance. The generals and armies who afterwards faced them went into battle without full confidence in themselves. It was no light matter to engage with an enemy who would not retire before any superiority in numbers, who was always ready for the fight, who would neither give nor take quarter. The enemies of the Swiss found these considerations the reverse of inspiriting before a combat : it may almost be said that they came into the field expecting a defeat, and therefore earned one. This fact is especially noticeable in the great Burgundian war. If Charles the Rash himself was unawed by the warlike renown of his enemies,[1] the same cannot be said of his troops. A large portion of his motley army could not be trusted in any dangerous crisis. His German, Italian, and Savoyard mercenaries knew too well the horrors of Swiss warfare, against an enemy who gave no quarter, and massacred prisoners in cold blood. The Duke might range his men in order, but he could not be certain that they would fight. At every one of his battles part of his men misbehaved, and they were half beaten before a blow had been struck.

For his great stroke against Switzerland Charles the Rash had endeavoured to secure efficiency for his army by enlisting from every warlike nation of Europe the class of troops for which it was celebrated. Beside his gallant Burgundian knights there marched the hand-gun men of Germany, the light cavalry of Italy, the pikemen of Flanders, and many English archers enlisted from the army which Edward IV. had disbanded after the treaty of Picquigny. But the Duke had forgotten that in assembling so many mercenaries of different races under his banner, he had thrown away the cohesion which is all-important in battle. Without mutual confidence in each other his soldiery would not stand firm. His first battle at Granson was lost merely because the nerve of the infantry failed them at the decisive moment, although they had not yet been engaged.

In that fight the headlong generalship of the Swiss had placed the tactical advantages on the side of Charles : he had both outflanked them and attacked one division of their army before the others came up. He had, however, to learn that an army superior in morale and homogeneity, and thoroughly knowing its weapon, may be victorious in spite of all disadvantages. Owing to their eagerness for battle the Confederate vanguard (*vorhut*), composed of the troops of Bern, Freiburg, Basle, and Schwytz, had far outstripped the remainder of the army. Coming swiftly over the hillside in

---

[1] Yet even the Duke said that "against the Swiss it will never do to march unprepared," to the Milanese ambassador, Panagirola, whose dispatches on the campaign are such a valuable contemporary source. The ambassador himself continually kept informing his master, Filippo Visconti, that the morale of the Burgundians was very poor.

one of their usual deep columns, they found the whole Burgundian host spread out before them in battle-array on the plain in front of the recently-captured Granson.[1]   As they reached the foot of the hill they at once saw that the Duke's cavalry was preparing to attack them.   Old experience had made them callous to such sights : facing outwards the column awaited the onset.   The first charge was made by the cavalry of Charles' left wing : it failed, although the gallant lord of Châteauguyon, who led it, forced his horse among the pikes and died at the foot of the standard of Schwytz.   Next the Duke himself led on the lances of his guard, a force who had long been esteemed the best troops in Europe : they did all that brave men could, but were dashed back in confusion from the steady line of spear-points.   The Swiss now began to move forward into the plain, eager to try the effect of the impact of their phalanx on the Burgundian centre.   To meet this advance Charles tried to shift his line, ordered a movement of his artillery, to bring it better to bear, and intended also to wheel both his wings round, upon the Swiss flank.   The manœuvre appeared feasible, as the remainder of the Confederate army was not yet in sight.   Orders were accordingly sent to the infantry and guns who were immediately facing the approaching column, directing them to retire ; while at the same time the cavalry reserve was sent to strengthen the left wing, the body with which the Duke intended to deliver his most crushing stroke.   The Burgundian army was in fact endeavouring to repeat the movement which had given Hannibal victory at Cannæ : Charles' fortune, however, was very different.   At the moment when the centre had begun to draw back, and when the wings were not yet engaged, the heads of the two Swiss columns, which had not before appeared, came over the slopes of Mont Aubert, moving rapidly towards the battlefield with the usual majestic steadiness of their formation.   This of course would have frustrated Charles' scheme for surrounding the first phalanx, the *échelon* of divisions, which was the normal Swiss array, being now established.   The aspect of the fight, however, was changed even more suddenly than might have been expected.   Connecting the retreat of their centre with the advance of the Swiss, the whole of the infantry

---

[1] Charles had hung its Swiss garrison, thinking to cow the enemy.   It only made them mad with rage.

of the Burgundian wings broke and fled, long before the Confederate masses had come into contact with them.   It was a
sheer panic, caused by the fact that the Duke's army had no
cohesion or confidence in itself ; the various corps in the
moment of danger could not rely on each other's steadiness,
and seeing what they imagined to be the rout of their centre,
had no further thought of endeavouring to turn the fortune of
the day.   It may be said that no general could have foreseen
such a disgraceful flight ; but at the same time the Duke may
be censured for attempting a delicate manœuvre with an army
destitute of homogeneity, and in face of an enterprising
opponent.   " Strategical movements to the rear " have always
a tendency to degenerate into undisguised retreats, unless the
men are perfectly in hand, and should therefore be avoided as
much as possible.   The casualties were few—the Burgundians
fled so early that only one thousand fell — mostly from the
cavalry.   The Swiss loss was only two hundred.[1]

Granson had been a panic rather than a battle, and the Duke's
army had got off lightly, with no appreciable loss in men, though
the whole of his artillery and the riches of his camp fell into
the hands of the enemy.   What was more important was that
the morale of the host, already unsatisfactory, had absolutely
broken down.   But Charles refused to realise this crucial fact ;
and the moment that he had rallied the scattered troops, replaced his lost artillery, and drawn in such reinforcements as
could be scraped together from his more distant dominions,
he resumed his offensive campaign.   It was not without reason
that he earned the name of the Rash—we might rather say
the Fool-hardy !   Granson having been fought in March, he
was again attacking the lands of Bern by June.   And in his
second campaign he was guilty of far more flagrant faults of
generalship than in his first.   Knowing by recent and bitter
experience what the Swiss could do, he placed himself in a
tactical position of the most dangerous sort.   He had set
himself to besiege the little town of Morat, on the lake of the
same name, which was held by a stout Bernese garrison.

---

[1] As to the numbers at Granson, the Swiss muster-rolls chance to have been preserved and show eighteen thousand one hundred and thirteen men of all arms.   The
Burgundians were a trifle less in numbers—perhaps fifteen thousand : but the Duke
had field artillery and horse in great strength—the Swiss practically none : hence
his confidence.

The position which he had chosen and fortified for the covering of his siege operations had the cardinal fault of having a lake at its back—in the event of defeat, there was no possible retreat to the rear, but only one to the extreme flank. And his forces were broken up into three parts, of which two were separated from the third by the besieged town. Moreover, there was thick cover for an approaching enemy along the whole of his front, the wood of Morat extending to within half a mile of the town, and not being occupied, but only watched by outlying piquets. If the enemy should attack and break in his left wing, the right wing might find a decent line of retreat to the south; but if his right wing were beaten, he was in a desperate situation, having to retreat between the fortress and the wood by a dangerous defile along the edge of the lake.

Charles would appear to have got together by June an army rather larger than that which had been scattered at Granson, something like twenty thousand men of the same heterogeneous composition as his earlier host. He had endeavoured to introduce a stricter discipline, and had brigaded the contingents into eight " battles " each consisting of a complement of all arms—horse, " shot," and pikes. Before he started from Lausanne on his campaign he had been exercising the troops in combined movements. All this was well-intentioned, but came too late. It would have taken months, not a few weeks, to produce an army that could manœuvre, with confidence in itself and its leader.[1]

By laying siege to Morat, only thirty miles from Bern, and less from Freiburg, at either of which the Confederates could mobilise, Charles was deliberately challenging them to another fight. There were fifteen hundred Bernese shut up in Morat, and, as both sides had been indulging of late in the disgusting practice of hanging all captured garrisons, it was incredible that the Swiss should not come to the rescue of such a considerable body of their citizens. Charles intended to be attacked in a strong position well garnished with artillery, not, this time, to give battle in the open. He had fortified the long plateau south of Morat, from Courtevon to the knoll of

---

[1] The celebrated " Ordonnance " of Charles the Rash, prescribing new rules of discipline, march, brigading, etc., is dated from Lausanne in May, only a few weeks before the opening of the campaign.

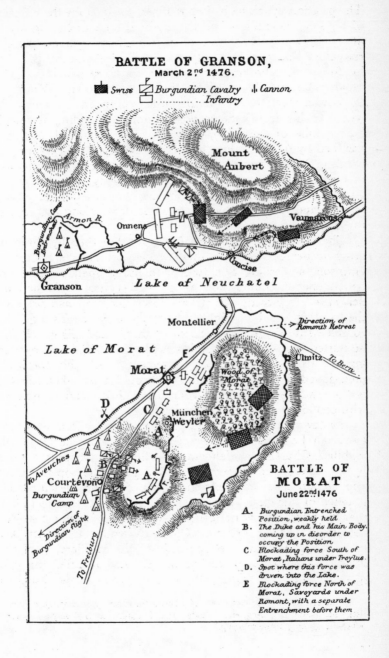

BATTLE OF GRANSON,
March 2nd 1476.

▪ Swiss   ▱ Burgundian Cavalry   ⚑ Cannon
Infantry

Mount
Aubert

Armon R.

Burgundian Camp

Onnens

Vaumarcos

Concise

Granson

Lake of Neuchatel

Montellier

→ Direction of
Romont's Retreat

Lake of Morat

E

Morat

Wood of
Morat

Ulmitz → To Bern

D

C

München
Weyler

To Aveuches

B

A

Courtevon

Burgundian
Camp

Direction of
Burgundian Right

To Freiburg

BATTLE OF
MORAT
June 22nd 1476

A. Burgundian Entrenched
Position, weakly held
B. The Duke and his Main Body,
coming up in disorder to
occupy the Position
C. Blockading force South of
Morat, Italians under Troylus.
D. Spot where this force was
driven into the Lake.
E. Blockading force North of
Morat, Savoyards under
Romont, with a separate
Entrenchment before them

Münchenweyler, with a long line of palisades,[1] with gun-emplacements at frequent intervals, completely covering his camp, which lay behind along the shore of the lake. And another, apparently separate, palisade protected the blockading force north of Morat. This was composed of one of his eight " battles," a Savoyard corps under the Count of Romont; the rest of the army lay south of the beleaguered town, another " battle " under the Sieur de Troylus, mainly composed of Italians, being entrusted with the siege operations on that side; while the main body was charged with the duty of manning the palisades of the entrenched hillside, when the expected army of relief should make its appearance.

The strength of the position, very considerable in itself, was sadly marred by the fact that the wood of Morat, completely screening the movements of an approaching enemy, lay so close in front of it. The Duke is said to have thought of moving farther forward, and entrenching himself on the eastern side of the wood ; but he was deterred by the fact that the ground in this direction, when reconnoitred, was found to be unsuitable for the employment of cavalry. The plateau which was actually occupied had a good glacis of open ground in front of it, giving excellent room for artillery to play on advancing enemies, though (as was afterwards discovered) the lightly moving Swiss came on too fast to be stopped by slow gun-fire. And its slopes were perfectly practicable for the manœuvres of cavalry. Here, then, the Duke hoped to be attacked in position, and to give a good account of himself.

The Confederates only appeared on the tenth day after the siege of Morat had begun, the remoter cantons having been somewhat tardy in sending their help to Bern, of which they were for the most part very jealous—and not without good grounds. But on June 21st they were concentrated in great strength at Ulmitz on the other side of the wood of Morat, less than four miles from the Duke's entrenchments. There were not only twenty-five thousand Swiss pikes, but, what was rare in Confederate warfare, a considerable body—several

---

[1] The length of the palisade is hard to determine with certainty, but surely must have gone as far as the knoll of Münchenweyler, the highest ground, though this is separated by a dip from the main plateau.

hundred lances—of feudal cavalry, brought by Réné of Lorraine and the Austrian nobles of Alsace and Swabia, all of whom were bitter enemies of the ambitious schemes of Duke Charles.

When the enemy had been discovered to be so close at hand, every possible precaution should have been taken to keep touch with him. This was not done. It is most strange that the Burgundian light troops were held back so close to the main body, that the Duke had no accurate knowledge of the movements of his enemies till they appeared in front of his lines. It was thus possible for the Confederate army to march, under cover of the wood of Morat, right across the front of the two corps which virtually composed the centre and left of Charles' array. The Duke on the 22nd waited in battle-order for six hours behind his palisade, without sending out troops to keep touch with the enemy. Moreover it is certain that when the Swiss did not show themselves, he sent back his main body to camp, the day being rainy and dark, and left the carefully entrenched position in the charge of a few thousand men. Hardly had this fault been committed, when the Confederate vanguard appeared on the outskirts of the wood of Morat, and marched straight on the palisade, with its allied horse as a flank guard. ' The utterly inadequate garrison made a bold endeavour to hold their ground, and the first fire of the artillery tore deep holes in the Swiss phalanx and among the Alsatian horse, but in a few minutes the enemy burst in, and the Burgundians were driven down the reverse slope of the hill, into the arms of the troops who were coming up in hot haste from the camp to their succour. The Swiss, following hard in their rear, pushed the disordered mass before them, and crushed in detail each supporting corps as it straggled up to attack them. The greater part of the Burgundian infantry turned and fled,—with far more excuse than at Granson. Many of the cavalry corps endeavoured to change the fortune of the day by desperate but isolated charges, in which they met the usual fate of those who endeavoured to break a Swiss phalanx. The fighting, however, was soon at an end, and mere slaughter took its place. While the van and main body of the Confederates followed the flying crowd, who made off in the direction of Avenches, the rear came down on the infantry, mostly Italians, who had formed the besieging force south of the town of Morat. These unfortunates, whose retreat was cut off by the direction which the flight of the main body had taken, were trodden under foot or pushed into the lake by the impact of the Swiss column, and entirely annihilated, scarcely a single man escaping out of a force of six thousand. The Savoyard corps, under Romont, which had composed the Duke's extreme left, and was posted to the north of Morat, escaped by a hazardous march which took it round the rear of the Confederates.

Though Charles had done his best to prepare a victory for his enemies by the faultiness of his dispositions, the management of the Swiss army at Morat was the cause of the completeness of his overthrow. A successful attack on the Burgundian right would cut off the retreat of the two isolated corps which composed the Duke's centre and left; the Confederate leaders therefore determined to assault this point, although to reach it they had to march straight across their opponent's front.[1] Favoured by his astonishing oversights in leaving their march unobserved, and his palisades ungarrisoned, they were able to surprise him, and destroy his army in detail, before it could manage to form even a rudimentary line of battle.

At Nancy the Swiss commanders again displayed considerable skill in their dispositions, though their game was easy, owing to their superior numbers: the main-battle and the small rear column held back and attracted the attention of the Burgundian army, while the van executed a turning movement through the woods, which brought it out on the enemy's flank, and made his position perfectly untenable. The Duke's troops, assailed in front and on their right at the same moment, outnumbered and demoralised, were not merely defeated but dispersed or destroyed. Charles himself refusing to fly, and fighting desperately to cover the retreat of his scattered forces, was surrounded, and cleft through helmet and skull by the tremendous blow of a Swiss halberd.

The generalship displayed at Nancy and Morat was, however, exceptional among the Confederates. After those battles, just as before, we find that their victories continued to be won

---

[1] "If we attack Romont," said Ulrich Kätzy at the Swiss council of war, "while we are beating him the Duke will have time and opportunity to escape; let us go round the hills against the main body, and when that is routed, we shall have the rest without a stroke." This showed real tactical skill.

by a headlong and desperate onset, rather than by the display of any great strategical ability.   In the Swabian war of 1499 the credit of their successes falls to the troops rather than to their leaders.   The stormings of the fortified camps of Hard and Malsheide were wonderful examples of the power of un-shrinking courage ; but on each occasion the Swiss officers seem to have considered that they were discharging their whole duty, when they led their men straight against the enemy's entrenchments.   At Frastenz the day was won by a desperate charge up the face of a cliff, which the Tyrolese had left un-guarded, as being inaccessible.   Even at Dornach—the last battle fought on Swiss soil against an invader till the eighteenth century—the fortune of the fight turned on the superiority of the Confederate to the Swabian pikemen man for man, and on the fact that the lances of Gueldres could not break the flank column by their most determined onset.   Of manœuvring there appears to have been little, of strategical planning none at all ; it was considered sufficient to launch the phalanx against the enemy, and trust to its power of bearing down every obstacle that came in its way.

CHAPTER IV

CAUSES OF THE DECLINE OF SWISS ASCENDANCY

CANTONAL greed and jealousy leading to political dead-
locks, combined with disregard for the higher and more
delicate problems of military science, was destined to enfeeble
the power and destroy the reputation of the Confederates. At
a time when the great struggle in Italy was serving as a school
for the soldiery of other European nations, they alone refused
to learn. Broad theories, drawn from the newly-discovered
works of the ancients, were being co-ordinated with the modern
experience of professional officers, and were developing into an
art of war far superior to anything known in mediæval times.
Scientific engineers and artillerists had begun to modify the
conditions of warfare, and feudal tradition was everywhere
discarded. New forms of military efficiency, such as the sword-
and-buckler men of Spain, the Stradiot light cavalry, the
German " black bands " of musketeers, were coming to the
front. The improvement of the firearms placed in the hands
of infantry was only less important than the superior mobility
which was given to field artillery.

The Swiss, however, paid no attention to these changes ;
the world around them might alter, but they would hold fast
to the tactics of their ancestors. At first, indeed, their arms
were still crowned with success : they were seen in Italy, as in
more northern lands, to " march with ten or fifteen thousand
pikemen against any number of horse, and to win a general
opinion of their excellence from the many remarkable services
they performed." [1] They enjoyed for a time supreme importance, and left their mark on the military history of every
nation of Central and Southern Europe. But it was impossible
that a single stereotyped tactical method, applied by men

[1] Machiavelli, *Arte della Guerra*, book ii. p. 31.

destitute of any broad and scientific knowledge of the art of war, should continue to assert an undisputed ascendancy. The victories of the Swiss set every officer of capacity and versatile talent searching for an efficient way of dealing with the onset of the phalanx. Such a search was rendered comparatively easy by the fact that the old feudal cavalry and the worthless mediæval infantry were being rapidly replaced by disciplined troops, men capable of keeping cool and collected even before the desperate rush of the Confederate pikemen. The standing army of Charles of Burgundy had been rendered inefficient by its want of homogeneity and cohesion, as well as by the bad generalship of its leader. The standing armies which fought in Italy thirty years later were very different bodies. Although still raised from among various nations, they were united by the bonds of old comradeship, of *esprit de corps*, of professional pride, or of confidence in some favourite general. The Swiss had therefore to face troops of a far higher military value than they had ever before encountered.

The first experiment tried against the Confederates was that of the Emperor Maximilian, who raised in Germany corps of pikemen and halberdiers, trained to act in a manner exactly similar to that of their enemies. The " Landsknechts " soon won for themselves a reputation only second to that of the Swiss, whom they boldly met in many a bloody field. The conflicts between them were rendered obstinate by military as well as national rivalry—the Confederates being indignant that any troops should dare to face them with their own peculiar tactics, while the Germans were determined to show that they were not inferior in courage to their Alpine kinsmen. The shock of the contending columns was therefore tremendous. The two bristling lines of pikes crossed, and the leading files were thrust upon each other's weapons by the irresistible pressure from behind. Often the whole front rank of each phalanx went down in the first onset, but their comrades stepped forward over their bodies to continue the fight.[1] When the masses had been for some time " pushing against each other," their order became confused and their pikes interlocked : then was the time for the halberdiers to act. The

---

[1] Frundsberg, the old captain of Landsknechts, gives a cool and business-like account of these shocks, "Wo unter den langen Wehren etliche Glieder zu grund gehen, werden die Personen, die dahinter stehen, etwas zaghaft," etc.

columns opened out to let them pass, or they rushed round from the rear, and threw themselves into the mêlée. This was the most deadly epoch of the strife : the combatants mowed each other down with fearful rapidity. Their ponderous weapons allowed of little fencing and parrying, and inflicted wounds which were almost invariably mortal. Every one who missed his blow, or stumbled over a fallen comrade, or turned to fly, was a doomed man. Quarter was neither expected nor given. Of course these fearful hand-to-hand combats could not be of great duration ; one party had ere long to give ground, and suffer the most fearful losses in its retreat. It was in a struggle of this kind that the Landsknechts lost a full half of their strength, when the Swiss bore them down at Novara. Even, however, when they were victorious, the Confederates found that their military ascendancy was growing less : they could no longer sweep the enemy from the field by a single unchecked onset, but were confronted by troops who were ready to turn their own weapons against them, and who required the hardest pressure before they would give ground. In spite of their defeats the Landsknechts kept the field, and finally took their revenge when the Swiss recoiled in disorder from the fatal trenches of Bicocca (1522).

There was, however, an enemy even more formidable than the German, who was to appear upon the scene at a slightly later date. The Spanish infantry of Gonsalvo de Cordova displayed once more to the military world the strength of the tactics of old Rome. They were armed, like the men of the ancient legion, with the short thrusting sword and buckler, and wore the steel cap, breast and back plates, and greaves. Thus they were far stronger in their defensive armour than the Swiss whom they were about to encounter. When the pike-man and the swordsman first met in 1502, under the walls of Barletta, the old problem of Pydna and Cynoscephalæ was once more worked out. A phalanx as solid and efficient as that of Philip the Macedonian was met by troops whose tactics were those of the legionaries of Æmilius Paullus. Then, as in an earlier age, the wielders of the shorter weapon prevailed. " When they came to engage, the Swiss at first pressed so hard on their enemy with the pike that they opened out their ranks ; but the Spaniards, under the cover of their bucklers, nimbly rushed in upon them with their swords, and laid about them so furiously that they made a great slaughter of the Swiss, and gained a complete victory." [1]   The vanquished, in fact, suffered at the hands of the Spaniards the treatment which they themselves had inflicted on the Austrians at Sempach.   The bearer of the longer weapon becomes helpless when his opponent has closed with him, whether the arms concerned be lance and halberd or pike and sword.   The moment a breach had been made in a Macedonian or Swiss phalanx the great length of their spears became their ruin.   There was nothing to do but to drop them, and in the combat which then ensued troops using the sword alone, and with little defensive armour, were at a hopeless disadvantage in attacking men furnished with the buckler as well as the sword, and protected by a more complete armour.   Whatever may be the result of a duel between sword and spear alone, it is certain that when a light shield is added to the swordsman's equipment, he at once obtains the ascendancy.   The buckler serves to turn aside the spear-point, and then the thrusting weapon is free to do its work.[2]   It was, therefore, natural that when Spanish and Swiss infantry met, the former should in almost every case obtain success.   The powerlessness of the pike, however, was most strikingly displayed at a battle in which the fortune of the day had not been favourable to Spain.   At the fight of Ravenna, Gaston de Foix had succeeded in driving Don Ramon de Cardona from his entrenchments, and was endeavouring to secure the fruits of victory by a vigorous pursuit.   To intercept the retreat of the Spanish infantry, who were retiring in good order, Gaston sent forward the pikemen of Jacob Empser, then serving as auxiliaries beneath the French banner.   These troops accordingly fell on the retreating column and attempted to arrest its march.   The Spaniards, however, turned at once and fell furiously on the Germans, "rushing at the pikes, or throwing themselves on the ground and slipping below the points, so

---

[1] Machiavelli, *Arte della Guerra*, book ii. p. 34.

[2] It is a curious fact that Chaka, one of Cetywayo's predecessors as king of the Zulus, set himself to solve this problem.   He took a hundred men and armed them with the shield and the "short assegai," a thrusting weapon resembling a sword rather than a spear in its use.   He then set them to fight another hundred furnished with the shield and the "long assegai," the slender javelin which had previously been the weapon of his tribe.   The wielders of the shorter weapon won with ease, and the king thereupon ordered its adoption throughout the Zulu army.   It was this change which originally gave the Zulus their superiority over their neighbours.

that they darted in among the legs of the pikemen "—a manœuvre which reminds us of the conduct of the Soudanese Arabs at El Teb.   In this way they succeeded in closing with their opponents, and " made such good use of their swords that not a German would have escaped, had not the French horse come up to their rescue." [1]   This fight was typical of many more, in which during the first quarter of the sixteenth century the sword and buckler were proved to be able to master the pike.   It may, therefore, be asked why, in the face of these facts, the Swiss weapon remained in use, while the Spanish infantry finally discarded their peculiar tactics.   To this question the answer is found in the consideration that the sword was not suited for repulsing a cavalry charge, while the pike continued to be used for that purpose down to the invention of the bayonet in the end of the seventeenth century.   Machiavelli was, from his studies in Roman antiquity, the most devoted admirer of the Spanish system, which seemed to bring back the days of the ancient legion.   Yet even he conceded that the pike, a weapon which he is on every occasion ready to disparage, must be retained by a considerable portion of those ideal armies for whose guidance he drew up his " Art of War." He could think of no other arm which could resist a charge of cavalry steadily pressed home, and was therefore obliged to combine pikemen with his " velites " and " buckler-men."

The rapid development of the arts of the engineer and artillerist aimed another heavy blow at the Swiss supremacy. The many-sided energy of the Renaissance period not unfrequently made the professional soldier a scholar, and set him to adapt the science of the ancients to the requirements of modern warfare.   The most cursory study of Vegetius Hyginus or Vitruvius, all of them authors much esteemed at the time, would suffice to show the strength of the Roman fortified camp. Accordingly the art of Castramentation revived, and corps of pioneers were attached to every army.   It became common to entrench not merely permanent positions, but camps which were to be held for a few days only.   Advantage was taken of favourable sites, and lines of greater or less strength with emplacements for artillery were constructed for the protection of the army which felt itself inferior in the field.   Many of the greatest battles of the Italian wars were fought in and around

[1] Machiavelli, *Arte della Guerra*, book ii.

such positions ; Ravenna, Bicocca, and Pavia are obvious examples.   Still more frequently a general threw himself with all his forces into a fortified town and covered it with outworks and redoubts till it resembled an entrenched camp rather than a mere fortress.   Such a phase in war was most disadvantageous to the Swiss : even the most desperate courage cannot carry men over stone walls or through flooded ditches, if they neglect the art which teaches them how to approach such obstacles. The Confederates in their earlier days had never displayed much skill in attacking places of strength ; and now, when the enemy's position was as frequently behind defences as in the open plain, they refused to adapt their tactics to the altered circumstances.   Occasionally, as, for example, at the storming of the outworks of Genoa in 1507, they were still able to sweep the enemy before them by the mere vehemence of their onset. But more frequently disaster followed the headlong rush delivered against lines held by an adequate number of steady troops.   Of this the most striking instance was seen in 1522, when the Swiss columns attempted to dislodge the enemy from the fortified park of Bicocca.   Under a severe fire from the Spanish hackbutmen they crossed several hedges and flooded trenches, which covered the main position of the imperialists. But when they came to the last ditch and bank, along which were ranged the Landsknechts of Frundsberg, they found an obstacle which they could not pass.   Leaping into the deep excavation, the front ranks endeavoured to scramble up its farther slope ; but every man who made the attempt fell beneath the pike-thrusts of the Germans, who, standing on a higher level in their serried ranks, kept back the incessant rushes with the greatest steadiness.   Three thousand corpses were left in the ditch before the Swiss would desist from their hopeless undertaking ; it was an attack which, for misplaced daring, rivals the British assault on Ticonderoga in 1758.

The improved artillery of the early sixteenth century worked even more havoc with the Confederates.   Of all formations the phalanx is the easiest at which to aim, and the one which suffers most loss from each cannon ball which strikes it.   A single shot ploughing through its serried ranks might disable twenty men, yet the Swiss persisted in rushing straight for the front of batteries and storming them in spite of their murderous fire.   Such conduct might conceivably have been justifiable in the fifteenth century, when the clumsy guns of the day could seldom deliver more than a single discharge, between the moment at which the enemy came within range and that at which he reached their muzzles. Scientific artillerists, however, such as Pietro Navarro and Alfonso of Este, made cannon a real power in battles, by increasing its mobility and the rapidity of its fire. None the less the Confederates continued to employ the frontal attack, which had become four or five times more dangerous in the space of forty years. A fearful lesson as to the recklessness of such tactics was given them at Marignano, where, in spite of the gallantry of the French gendarmerie, it was the artillery which really won the day. The system which Francis' advisers there employed was to deliver charge after charge of cavalry on the flanks of the Swiss columns, while the artillery played upon them from the front. The onsets of the cavalry, though they never succeeded in breaking the phalanx, forced it to halt and " form the hedgehog." The men-at-arms came on in bodies of about five hundred strong, one taking up the fight when the first had been beaten off. In " this way more than thirty fine charges were delivered, and no one will in future be able to say that cavalry are of no more use than hares in armour," wrote the king to his mother. Of course these attacks would by themselves have been fruitless ; it was the fact that they checked the advance of the Swiss, and obliged them to stand halted under artillery fire, that settled the result of the battle. At last the columns had suffered so severely that they gave up the attempt to advance, and retired in good order, unbroken but diminished by a half in their size.

Last but not least important among the causes of the decline of the military ascendancy of the Confederates was the continual deterioration of their discipline. While among other nations the commanders were becoming more and more masters of the art of war, among the Swiss they were growing more and more the slaves of their own soldiery. The division of their authority had always been detrimental to the development of strategical skill, but it now began to make even tactical arrangements impossible. The army looked upon itself as a democracy entitled to direct the proceedings of its ministry, rather than a body under military discipline. Filled with a blind confidence in the invincibility of their onset, they calmly neglected the orders which appeared to them superfluous.   On several occasions they delivered an attack on the front of a position which it had been intended to turn ; on others they began the conflict, although they had been directed to wait for the arrival of other divisions before giving battle.   If things were not going well, they threw away even the semblance of obedience to their leaders.   Before Bicocca the cry was raised, " Where are the officers, the pensioners, the double-pay men ? Let them come out and earn their money fairly for once : they shall all fight in the front rank to-day."   What was even more astonishing than the arrogance of the demand, was the fact that it was obeyed.   The commanders and captains stepped forward and formed the head of the leading column ; hardly one of them survived the fight, and Winkelried of Unterwalden, the leader of the vanguard, was the first to fall under the lances of Frundsberg's Landsknechts.   What was to be expected from an army in which the men gave the orders and the officers executed them ?   Brute strength and heedless courage were the only qualities now employed by the Swiss, while against them were pitted the scientific generals of the new school of war.   The result was what might have been expected : the pike tactics, which had been the admiration of Europe, were superseded, because they had become stereotyped, and the Swiss lost their proud position as the most formidable infantry in the world.

BOOK XII

ITALY IN THE FOURTEENTH AND FIFTEENTH CENTURIES—THE CONDOTTIERI

CHAPTER I

ITALY IN THE FOURTEENTH CENTURY
THE EARLY CONDOTTIERI

COMPARISONS have often been drawn, and with good reason,[1] between the history of Italy in the fourteenth and fifteenth centuries after Christ, and that of Ancient Greece in the fourth and third centuries before Christ. In each a group of vigorous but quarrelsome city states had in the preceding century beaten off a long-protracted attack by an external power, which they regarded as " barbarous." The Lombard League and the Papacy had finally defeated the attempt of the Hohenstaufen emperors to reduce Italy; the united Greeks had turned back the Persian kings, after the thirty years of threatened invasion, by the victories of Platæa and Mycale. If a further analogy in detail is wanted, Persia had been helped, for reasons of petty inter-state jealousy, by great Greek cities like Thebes, while others (like Argos) had kept out of the game. So in Italy cities like Lodi or Como or Pisa had backed the Emperor consistently, because they hated Milan or Florence just as Thebes hated Athens, and others had failed to give any effective support to the Guelf cause.

When the Persian had been driven back, and all danger from outside was practically at an end, the greater Greek states turned to fierce fighting for hegemony among themselves; hence the Peloponnesian War [431–404 B.C.]—which defeated the ambitions of Athens—and the Corinthian and Bœotian wars [395–71], which made an end of Sparta's attempt to dominate. The wars for hegemony had demoralised and worn out the morale of all the states; and they finally became the prey of Philip and Alexander of Macedon. In Italy the story is more protracted, but essentially the same: the German

[1] See, for example, Freeman's excellent study in his *Historical Essays*, vol. ii.

danger having ceased, after the extinction of the house of Hohenstaufen, we get two centuries of internal strife, caused by the imperialist cravings (if we may use the word for such small ambitions) of states like Venice, Genoa, Florence, and Milan, who wished to devour their neighbours much as did Athens or Sparta in the older world—though hardly ever did any of them rise to the idea of crushing all Italy under their sway. This battle of kites and crows ended in the subjection of the whole peninsula to an external power—the world-empire of Charles V. and the Spanish Hapsburgs—mainly owing to that factiousness and incapacity for honest union, in which the Greeks of the fourth century B.C. were the true antitypes of the Italians of the fifteenth century A.D. Just as Alexander of Macedon did not make a formal annexation of Athens or Sparta, so Charles V. did not make a formal annexation of Venice or Genoa. But as the Macedonian was really, if not technically, the master of all Greece, so was Charles V. of all Italy.

It would be possible to follow out this analogy in half a dozen separate lines of thought—especially in the realm of Art, where nothing can be more suggestive than the parallel between the Greeks' and the Italians' rapid development after the victorious wars against the 'barbarian,' their arrival at the highest excellence in the troublous days of internal strife, and their decadence into commonplace mannerism a generation or so after the loss of liberty. Greek Art in the third century B.C. had got into the state of Italian Art in the days of the Caracci.

But it is the military parallel with which we have to deal in this book, and that is as clear and as interesting as any of the others. The Greek states had defeated the Persian with their own civic levies in the strife by sea and land : the Spartan hoplite at Platæa and the Athenian seaman at Salamis was a citizen, and a loyal one. So were the Milanese infantry and knights at Legnano. The idea that one must fight with one's own arms for one's country continued for some time after the victory over the Great King and the " Holy Roman " emperor. The Athenians still went out πανδημεί—with every citizen in his tribal company—at Delium, as did the Thebans at Leuctra. But perpetual civil strife with neighbours led to moral exhaustion, and the hiring of mercenaries to do the work which the citizen found to be growing intolerable, because it never came to an end. The revolt of the plain man against the perpetual call for active service breathes through every play of Aristophanes. He was asking himself, was the end worth the means— were the Spartans so very unreasonable or hateful—was not peace the best thing of all ? Yet, with a groan, the Athenian fought on to the end of the Peloponnesian War, and saw delusive imperial dreams vanish. He had already begun to hire mercenaries on a large scale in its later years, mainly for sheer want of men to place opposite the greater numbers of his confederated foes. The Spartans' effort to attain the end which Athens had failed to achieve led to the employment of mercenaries on even a larger scale—not because any Lacedæmonian ever shirked military service, but because the full-citizens of Sparta were even fewer than those of Athens. Hence came the immense hired bands which followed Lysander and Agesilaus ; the latter for his campaign in Asia took over *en bloc* the whole of the veteran " Ten Thousand," the corps of mercenaries who had followed Cyrus the Younger to Cunaxa, and had conducted, under the guidance of Xenophon, the famous retreat to the sea. These were the spiritual ancestors of the Almogavars of Roger de Flor, and of the " Angli " of Enguerrand de Coucy and John Hawkwood.

By the middle of the fourth century B.C. every Greek state that could find the money was employing mercenaries by the thousand. Some did it, like the Athenians of the time of Demosthenes, because they had grown sick of continued service in person, and preferred to do their fighting in Thrace or the Ægean by deputy, luring the cosmopolitan bands of Chares, Charidemus, or Diopeithes, and only turning out themselves for the desperate crisis of Cheronæa. Others, like the Phocians in the Sacred War, utterly outnumbered by the enemies whom they had provoked, made head against them by engaging every adventurer who did not fear to touch the gold from the sacrilegious spoil of Delphi. But it was the tyrants, like Dionysius of Syracuse and Jason of Pheræ, who hired mercenaries on the largest scale of all, because a sovereignty won by usurpation could only be maintained by foreign spears. And so things went on, till the Romans finally came across the Adriatic and the Ægean, to make an end of a group of degenerate monarchical states, the Hellenistic kingdoms into which the empire of Alexander the Great had split up—all despotisms resting on mercenary armies of second-rate efficiency.

The military fortunes of mediæval Italy show a complete correspondence with those of ancient Greece. The story of Florence is much like the story of Athens—in this as in so many other respects. Chabrias and Diopeithes were but Carmagnolas and Colleones of an earlier growth. Gian Galeazzo Visconti was no more cruel and unscrupulous than Dionysius the Elder —each the record employer of mercenaries in his own day. The hired bands of the Italian despots and cities crumpled up at the onset of the French gendarmerie of Charles VIII., just as the mercenaries of Athens broke before the " Compassion Cavalry " of Philip of Macedon. And the long-protracted existence of maritime Rhodes may remind us of the surprising survival of maritime Venice, down to the eighteenth century and the advent of Bonaparte.

But to descend to details : Up to the end of the Lombard wars of Frederic II., the Italian states had fought with their own lances, pikes, and arbalests. It was their enemy the Emperor who used mercenary bands, for Frederic II. in his later days did not lead an army of German or Sicilian feudal levies, but long-service troops of various origin, held together by the " cash *nexus* " between employer and employed. His wealth had enabled him to keep together a permanent army, and if the best part of it was German, it was not as their feudal lord that he held his lances in obedience, but as their paymaster. The best part of feudal Germany was intermittently in rebellion against him.

When Frederic *Stupor Mundi* died, the war of Guelf and Ghibelline by no means came to an end, though the Ghibellian party was no longer led by an emperor of genius, and could no longer look for succour from Germany, save indeed on rare occasions like the unfortunate expeditions of Conradin, Henry of Luxemburg, and Lewis of Bavaria. The Imperial theory might survive in the minds of Ghibelline idealists such as Dante, but in reality the wars of the fourteenth century were not, like those of the thirteenth, a struggle between the two rival ideals of the " Holy Roman Empire " and the Papacy. Still less were they a continuance of a national Italian struggle to get rid of the German overlord, or of the contest between a league of free cities and a feudal monarchy. They were waged neither to secure communal independence, nor to chase away the foreigner from beyond the Alps, nor to vindicate the rights of the Church. The break-up of the Holy Roman Empire had let loose particularist ambitions of the narrowest kind—personal ambitions—party ambitions inside each city—civic ambitions of each city against its neighbours. The history of Italy loses the comparative unity that it had possessed so long as the dominating figures of the line of great emperors continued to preside over the struggle. It splits up into regional sections, which only connect themselves when some exceptionally vigorous personality—such as Gian Galeazzo Visconti—trespasses over the normal boundaries and appears as a disturbing element in regions far afield.

In every city there was a Guelf and a Ghibelline party, which cloaked with those old names family hatreds or class hatreds rather than theories or ideals of governance. Frequently one party expelled the leaders of the other from the city, to wander abroad till some conspiracy, or some military success of the enemies of the state, restored the exiles to power or at least to a resumption of civic rights. This was exactly what had happened sixteen hundred years before in ancient Greece, where the " outs," οἱ φευγόντες, were always hovering around to win their way home by a night-surprise or a pact with the national enemy. The history of the Athenian " Thirty Tyrants " of 404–03 B.C., and the rising of the exiled democrats under Thrasybulus, reads exactly like a scrap from Italian history of the later thirteenth or earlier fourteenth century. And just as in ancient Greece, so in mediæval Italy, the exiles were prone to become the mercenary bands of the nearest community where their own party was in power. A Ghibelline city sheltered Ghibelline military fugitives from its next neighbour in order to turn them to military account, quite as much as for reasons of party solidarity. But—also as in ancient Greece—exiles of long standing, who had learned (like Dante) how bitter was the bread of foreign charity, how steep the foreign stairs, became after a time less particular in their conduct, and hired themselves out to any bidder—even a tyrant—who was in need of good men-at-arms.

The rise of the tyrants was as marked a feature of the period after the great wars of independence in Italy as in Greece. They came in many ways—though the basic fact at the bottom of the whole matter was that wholesome civic patriotism and self-reliance was dying. The tyranny might start with a family of high importance, which wormed itself up in several generations to a position that finally gave its chief a position in the state which was inconsistent with republican government—as did the Visconti at Milan and the Medici at Florence. Or it might begin with a successful party leader who executed a *coup d'état*, nominally in the interest of his faction, really in his own, like Mastino della Scala at Verona, or Ludovico Gonzaga at Mantua. But very frequently the tyrant was a successful soldier, who imposed himself on his fellow-citizens, with or without some form of election, in a time of need —like Dionysius of Syracuse in the days of the Carthaginian invasion of Sicily. Such was the case of Castruccio Castracani at Lucca. Or he might be a mere foreign military adventurer, like Francesco Sforza, who started the second tyrant-dynasty at Milan.

But whatever his origin, the tyrant wanted a military force to keep him safe on his throne; and since it could not be a citizen force, for obvious reasons, he had to hire mercenaries. The Medici were the only exception; for several generations they stuck to their power by statecraft alone, and avoided the irritating show of foreign lances. But normally the existence of the tyrant implied the existence of the mercenary guard. The τύραννος, said Plato, must have his ξένοι or δορυφόροι. And when a tyrant grew great, and extended his ambition beyond the bounds of his own locality, like Can Grande della Scala, or Gian Galeazzo Visconti, he wanted not a guard, but a whole army of mercenaries, and became a public danger to all his neighbours, small and great, not merely a terror to his own subjects.

If the tyrant scared his neighbours by raising great bands of trained soldiers of great military efficiency, the only thing that they could do was to hire mercenaries themselves—a dangerous expedient, for the leaders of such bands were prone either to establish themselves as military dictators, or else to sell their men and the city which was employing them to the enemy. Why should a *condottiere* continue to back a losing cause, in which he had no patriotic but only a financial interest, against a foe of overpowering strength ? Leaders there were who kept to their bonds, and won a reputation for complete or comparative loyalty to their employer of the moment. Such were Bartolommeo Colleone and John Hawkwood. But even such men of probity could see no reason why, when they were discharged in October from the pay of one city or tyrant, they should not appear in the next March in the service of their late employer's nearest and bitterest rival.

The cities which did not fall under the rule of tyrants in the fourteenth century employed mercenaries, as freely as did the military despots to whom they were opposed. This came partly from the same cause which had told on the Athenians of the fourth century B.C., the lassitude which falls on a burgher community after many years of war, especially when the war has ceased to be one of life and death, and has become one of mere state ambition. But it was also due in some measure to the recognition of the truth that professional soldiers are superior as fighting material to civic militia intermittently called out, on service for which they see no pressing need. A minor reason was the fact that faction ran so high in most states that the ruling party of the moment did not thoroughly trust all the citizens who would have to be called out for a levy *en masse*. The local noble families were always suspect to democratic governments, the discontented lower classes to oligarchic governments. But perhaps the most obvious cause of all for the hiring of mercenaries was the mere want of numbers—a city state which has embarked on a career of territorial ambition needs something more than its own civic levy, if it intends to build up a little empire by the subjection of its neighbours. It comes to want a standing army, and troops who can be used for garrison duty in conquered but discontented towns and districts, where rebellion is always possible.

This accounts for the large scale on which Venice, the most ambitious of all the republican states, employed mercenaries, when in the fourteenth and fifteenth centuries she had taken in hand the conquest of all the smaller continental neighbour-states. As long as the Venetians confined their ambitions to colonial enterprise in the East, and perpetual commercial wars with Genoa, they could fight out the struggle at sea with their own galleys and their own citizens. It was another matter when they began to encroach on the March of Treviso, the Patriarchate of Aquileia, and the dominions of the tyrants of Padua, Verona, and Milan. The Venetian nobles were resource-

ful admirals and commodores rather than good men-at-arms:
their crews were stout seamen, not line-of-battle pikemen or
arbalesters.   Hence it was practically necessary to hire land-
soldiers, if long land-wars against the trained mercenaries of
the Carraras or the Visconti had become part of the policy of
the state.   Venice became a hirer of *condottieri* on a scale as
large as that of the great lords of Milan themselves.   It was a
dangerous game : to win and hold a land-empire with a non-
national army, commanded by foreign generals, was a veritable
tour de force.   But it was done—not without some unpleasant
crises, when *condottieri* were discovered or suspected of being
in secret touch with the enemy, and plotting treason to their
employers.   The Venetian oligarchy had drastic ways of dealing
with these dangers.   Such was the well-known case of the great
Carmagnola in 1432—when the most famous general of his
age was lured from his camp to Venice by a delusive message,
and suddenly executed for treason suspected rather than proven.
The case of Doge Marino Faliero has similar features : in other
Italian cities, magistrates who had debauched the troops had
often made themselves tyrants.   So had magistrates who had
won themselves popularity with the less privileged classes of
citizens, by attacking a ruling oligarchy.   Faliero, in bitter
strife with the ruling clique of aristocrats, appears to have
conspired—despite of his seventy years—with the leaders of
plebeian discontent and the captains of the galleys.   The combination might have succeeded against a less wary and suspicious
victim than the Venetian oligarchy—it only ended in the detec-
tion and decapitation of the Doge (1355).   Right down to the
days of the League of Cambrai the republic continued to fight
for its land-empire, on both sides of the Adige, with mercenary
armies headed by foreign generals.   And what is most astonishing, it survived, and kept possession of most of its territorial
gains, right through the crisis of the great wars of the sixteenth
century—though only by giving up its old ambitions, and
owning that the Spanish-Hapsburg power had grown too
strong to be challenged.   When Venice ceased to have an
ambitious policy she began to decay, allowed Spanish, Austrian,
and French armies to trespass over her borders in their strife,
and owed her survival to their contemptuous recognition of her
weakness.   The well-remembered Spanish plot for her destruction in 1618 was not a royal enterprise of Philip III., but a

private plan of the Viceroy of Naples and the Ambassador Bedmar.

But we must not stray forward into the sixteenth or the seventeenth century. In the ages with which we have here to deal, Venice was still the most stirring and ambitious of states, and among the greatest of the employers of mercenaries. That she won many lands, but failed to complete her conquest of Lombardy, was due to the fact that the Visconti and Sforza lords of Milan were as wealthy, as unscrupulous, and as capable and ruthless in the handling of *condottieri* and their bands as the Council of Ten itself. What would have happened if Charles VIII. had not crossed the Alps, to make an end of the old purely Italian wars, and to drag the peninsula into the general welter of European politics, it is impossible to say.

Mercenaries had been known for many generations in Italy, but it was not till the fourteenth century that they acquired the complete predominance in war that they were to hold until the advent of Charles VIII. Their energy down to the earliest years of that century had been spent in the service of others— from 1302 onward there came the great change that they began to dream of working for their own ends, rather than for those of their employers. The first vision of this change of purpose came to the renegade Templar, Roger de Flor, the chief captain among the wild bands whom Frederic of Aragon discharged from his service, when in 1302 he made that peace with Charles II. of Naples which marked the end of the great war for the crown of Sicily.[1] The eighteen thousand Catalans, Italians, French, and German outcasts, with whose aid Frederic had been maintaining his claim against the much superior forces of the Angevin king, when thrown upon the world did not disperse. They were persuaded by the half-German, half-Italian adventurer, who had won their admiration by many exploits on sea no less than on land, to try their fortune with him in the Levant, and went off *en masse* to that great expedition which started with the idea of driving the Turk from the gates of Constantinople, but ended in general plunder of the Christian states of the Near East. Roger perished at the hand of an assassin, but his surviving followers ended prosperously, by seizing the Frankish duchy of Athens, dividing it up among themselves, and setting up a duke of their own. Truly it was a

[1] The chronicler Villani calls him the father of all *condottieri*, viii. 51.

tempting lesson to the disbanded mercenaries of the near future.

The adventure of Roger's "Great Company" had not harmed Italy : but the next great dismissal of hired troops was to have serious consequences within the Peninsula. In 1338 Mastino della Scala, Lord of Verona, had gathered many more mercenaries than he could afford to keep in pay, and was forced to get rid of them. Their chief captain, a Swabian knight named Werner of Ürslingen, persuaded them to keep together instead of dispersing, and to offer themselves as an organised unit to the republic of Pisa, then engaged in bitter war with Florence. For three years the Pisans kept them employed, but were forced in the end to make a disadvantageous peace with the Florentines. Werner refused to disband his men, extorted an exorbitant " parting gift " from the Pisans, and then went off to live at large on blackmail. His later employers are said to have given him the hint that there was plenty of money to be got out of the other states of Tuscany. Werner organised his followers into a permanent disciplined unit, which called itself (in imitation of Roger de Flor's horde) the " Great Company," and went forth plundering and to plunder, wasting the countryside, and only moving on when the state in whose territory he was operating consented to give him a large sum, to pass into the lands of their nearest unfriendly neighbour. Werner became a great man—he styled himself " the Duke "—some of his ancestors (he said) had a claim to the duchy of Spoleto by a grant from some emperor— and treated as an equal with cities and princes. In one of his self-revealing moods he called himself " the enemy of God and of compassion." In 1348 he hired himself to Lewis the Great of Hungary, then starting on his expedition of revenge against Joanna of Naples, the murderess of his brother Andrew. Werner did fearful damage in Naples, where he amassed so much treasure that he handed over his company to a successor, and went to enjoy life in his Swabian home, where he died in great prosperity some years later.[1]

Werner's elected heir in command of the " Grand Company " was a Provençal adventurer, Walter of Montreal, whom the Italians called Fra Moriale, because he had once been a Knight of St. John—expelled from the order for good reasons. Main-

[1] He lived till 1354.

taining the cause of Lewis of Hungary in Naples, according to the contract made by his predecessor, Montreal held on to the city and county of Aversa for some time, till he was expelled in 1352 by the armies of Queen Joanna. Driven over the frontier into the States of the Church, he took advantage of the anarchy prevailing there—the Pope was in exile at Avignon—to hire out his band to various employers, all of whom he threw over when it suited him. In 1353 he carried out the greatest enterprise ever accomplished by a free-lance—in a sort of circular tour round Central Italy he extorted by force vast sums from all the states—fifty thousand florins from Malatesta, Lord of Rimini, sixteen thousand from the Sienese, twenty-five thousand from the Florentines, and sixteen thousand from Pisa. Such plunder enabled him to recruit the " Grand Company " up to a strength of seven thousand men-at-arms and two thousand crossbowmen, who were regularly paid, and subjected to a severe discipline. Montreal had a council, secretaries, accountants, camp-judges, a provost-marshal, and a gallows. He was obeyed and feared. In 1354 he hired himself out to the league of the lords of Ferrara, Padua, and Mantua, who were allied to oppose Giovanni Visconti, the archbishop-tyrant of Milan. His troops were on the march for Lombardy, when he paid a flying personal visit to Rome, where he intended to collect some money. He had counted on being too great a personage to be molested, more especially because the Senator and ex-Tribune Rienzi had borrowed funds from the treasure of the " Grand Company " not long before. But shortly after his arrival Rienzi arrested him, tried him for public brigandage and murder, and had him beheaded.

The well-deserved end of its iron-handed chief was a great blow to the " Grand Company," which diminished in importance under the successors elected to replace Montreal—the German, Conrad of Landau, and the Switzer, Bonstetten. It finally broke up, on account of quarrels between the captains of bands ; no one but a man of genius could have kept together such unruly and turbulent masses of adventurers of all nations. Many were Germans—three of Montreal's Council of Eight had been of that race ; many more were Italians—the exiles, outlaws, and bankrupt nobles of fifty petty states ; the balance were Provençals, Catalans, Hungarians, North French, Netherlanders, Castilians, and broken men from lands even more remote.

The story of the fragments of the " Grand Company " becomes complicated with that of a new mercenary invasion of Italy. When Edward III. and John of France disbanded their hired lances, after the treaty of Bretigny, the greatest mass of unemployed soldiers that Europe had yet seen was let loose on the Continent. The majority of them hung together, under captains of approved valour, and in most cases of notorious unscrupulousness. Some drifted into the wars of Charles of Navarre, others into the struggle between Peter the Cruel and Henry of Trastamara in Spain. The largest band, that of the " Archpriest," Arnold of Cervole, which had already black-mailed the Pope at Avignon, and sacked Aix-en-Provence, broke up into fractions : its chief remained north of the Alps to perish by an obscure assassination, but many of its minor leaders drifted across the passes into Italy. Thither also came, along with other captains, Sir John Hawkwood with the wreck of the *Tard Venus*, the second wave of disbanded mercenaries, largely English, who called themselves the " White Company." They appear first in the service of the Marquis of Montferrat, fighting against the Visconti in the spring of 1361. Numerous other bands [1] crossed the Alps in this and the neighbouring years, and though some of them may have wandered back at the general summons of the Black Prince for his Spanish War of 1367, the majority had come to stay.

In the earlier years, therefore, of the fourteenth century, the nucleus of the mercenary bands of Italy had been German, in the later years it was French, and to a lesser extent English. During both periods the nucleus was surrounded by a cosmo-politan accretion of fighting-men of all races and tongues, in which the Italians themselves were well represented : but they never formed the majority of the whole.

Down to the time of the appearance of the disbanded soldiery of Edward III. and John of Valois in 1360–61, the tactics of the Italian wars appear to have remained of the thirteenth-century type, the horsemen being still entirely pre-ponderant over the infantry. An illustrative fact is the pro-portion of horse and foot in Fra Moriale's Grand Company, as given on the last page. There were seven thousand men-at-arms to two thousand crossbowmen—the latter were nothing more than useful auxiliaries, who were expected to

---

[1] With odd names such as the Company of the Star, the Rose, the Bretons, etc.

open the fight, but not to settle it. The English and French soldiery who flocked in after 1361 had of course the lesson of Creçy in their heads—which took effect in inducing the English to utilise their invaluable archers, and both nations to dismount the greater part of their men-at-arms for battle. The English "White Company," in which Hawkwood served in 1363, consisted of two thousand five hundred men-at-arms and two thousand archers—quite a different proportion from that which had prevailed in Montreal's host. This was while he was the employé of the Pisan Republic. Twenty years later, when he was serving the Carraras of Padua, Hawkwood had a much smaller company, and the relation between lance and bow was slightly changed—he showed five hundred horse to six hundred bowmen, the latter all English and all mounted,[1] at the famous battle of Castagnaro, his last and most scientific victory.

From 1360 to the last years of the century Italy was overrun by the Transalpine Free Companies, who only failed to make their domination permanent because they could never combine. Their chiefs were jealous of each other, and no two wished to serve the same Italian employer. The inner constitution of the bands differed in nationality and tradition ; they would not work loyally together. Conceivably an adventurer of real genius might have collected them all under one banner, and have made himself lord of North Italy, as Odoacer the Scyrrian had done a thousand years before, when he combined all the mercenary hordes of A.D. 476 and proclaimed himself king. But the captains of the great bands of 1370 were good soldiers, greedy for gold and ready to accept the fief of a barony, not statesmen of genius. Their ambitions were limited, and they appear to have acted on the homely principle of not killing the goose which laid the golden eggs, i.e. of refraining from destroying the Italian states, because it was by the continued wars of such states that they got their living. Native-born Italian chiefs sometimes aspired to tyrannies ; not so the foreigners, who were, no doubt, conscious that they did not know how to manage a Lombard or Tuscan city, with its complicated intrigues, feuds, and treacheries. Towards the end of the century the bands and their chiefs became less distinctively foreign—apparently the older generation of adventurers, dying out, were not replaced by their countrymen but by Italians

[1] Andrea Gataro's Chronicle, in Muratori, xv. p. 568.

trained in their school. The chroniclers ascribe the commencement of the change to Alberigo da Barbiano, the first native *condottiere* of this period, who formed his "company of St. George" from Italians alone, and justified its existence by defeating the French company of "the Bretons" in 1379. For thirty years he took his band round Italy, serving sometimes Naples and sometimes Milan with great success—he died in 1409, high constable of King Ladislas. In his school were trained the great native *condottieri* of the fifteenth century, such as Braccio de Montone and Sforza Attendolo.[1]

Of the foreign *condottieri* John Hawkwood was not only the most famous but by far the most respectable—"virtuoso" not only in Machiavelli's sense,[2] but according to all military standards of honour in his day. He never broke his oath; he was in 1364 the only captain of the Pisans whom the Florentines could not bribe. He carried out his contracts with rigorous probity, and he never sold his employer of the moment. Nor was he given to assassinations or to intrigues, to cheating his soldiers or to blackmailing neutrals. It is even recorded that he objected to the sanguinary orders of Cardinal Robert of Geneva at the sack of Cesena. Mercenaries of rival bands, who fell into his hands in the course of business, could always count on a quick release and a moderate ransom. It is no wonder that his Florentine patrons regarded him as a paragon of virtue, and placed his figure on horseback over the south-west inner portal of their Duomo.

It may be worth while to give a short account of Hawkwood's greatest battle, a triumph of his old age, in 1387, when he was acting as the general of Francesco de Carrara, Lord of Padua. This prince, engaged in war with the Venetians and with Antonio della Scala of Verona, had hired all the mercenaries that he could afford to pay, and, in particular, Hawkwood, with his five hundred men-at-arms and his six hundred mounted English bowmen, to whom he gave the command, though his son, Francesco the Younger, accompanied the army as its nominal chief. The host is said to have reached the respectable figure of six thousand nine hundred men-at-arms, but had only one thousand six hundred infantry inclusive of Hawkwood's archer-contingent. The Veronese enemy is reckoned at a higher figure—nine thousand men-at-arms, two

[1] Machiavelli, *Principe*, cap. xii. p. 269.   [2] *Ibid.* xii. p. 261.

thousand six hundred crossbowmen and pikemen, not to speak of a civic and countryside general-levy of several thousands of raw and useless foot. Della Scala had prepared for this campaign the vast and extraordinary super-ribaulds, the mitrailleusses firing one hundred and forty-four shots, of which we had occasion to speak in our chapter on Artillery [1]; he had also more than twenty bombards ; all this artillery turned out useless in the battle.

Hawkwood had been blockading Verona for some weeks in February–March 1387, when he was forced by hunger to give up the plan, finding his communications with Padua cut by hostile parties too large to be driven away by mere detachments. He fell back toward Castelbaldo on the Adige, where he had a depot of provisions which the enemy was threatening. The Veronese followed in haste, picking up their outlying forces. They were led by Giovanni dei Ordelaffi, one of the house of the tyrants of Forli, who had taken service with the Della Scalas : he had with him two Italian *condottieri* of note, the brothers Ugolino and Taddeo dal Verme, and a contingent from Ravenna under Ostasio Polenta, lord of that city.

Hawkwood was intending to offer battle as soon as his troops had got into touch with their stores—many were already straggling towards Castelbaldo in search of food. On the night of 10th March he halted near Castagnaro, a few miles in front of Castelbaldo—having caused many waggon-loads of provisions to be sent out to him from the depot, and having hunted up his truants. Every one, including the enemy, had been expecting him to retire across the Adige to Castelbaldo itself, but he had found a position on the near bank, which he thought excellent for a defensive battle in the style of Poictiers—though its strength did not consist in slopes and vineyards like that of the Black Prince's battle-ground of 1356. He had pitched on the line of a small irrigation-drain, one of many such running through the broad space of marshland between the Tartaro river and the Adige. A canal joining the Adige and the Tartaro, into which the drain discharged, gave him flank protection on his right, and marshes were on his left. Here he took up his position, the drain and a rather damp meadow in front of him. There

---

[1] See above, page 222. The figures are those of the Paduan chronicler, Andrea Gataro, in Muratori, xvii., who gives statistics of bands and commanders in great detail, so that it seems hard to reject his figures.

were more water-cuts in the neighbouring plain, all of which
is rather water-logged. The army was drawn up in three lines,
the two front ones composed of six " battles " of dismounted
men-at-arms, while two remaining " battles " on horseback—
one consisting of the whole of Hawkwood's own band—formed
the reserve, and were ranged on each side of the great *carroccio*
of Padua and its banner. The small body of infantry (not
including the English horse-archers) was placed on the bank
of the canal to the extreme right, with the few bombards which
the Paduans possessed: they covered a rather easy passage
across the irrigation drain, where it joins the canal.

Ordelaffi, evidently surprised to find Hawkwood offering
battle on the morning of 11th March, when he had been expected to put himself behind the Adige, took an unconscionable
time in getting his army into line—as might be foreseen with
a mediæval host marching on one single road. But he did not
commit the tactical error of Philip VI. at Creçy, by attacking
with his van before his main-battle or rearward had got into
order. He deployed in two lines across the meadows facing
the Paduan position, dismounting the whole of his men-at-arms
for an attack on foot, and not sending forward any advanced
cavalry like the French at Poictiers or Agincourt. The *carroccio*
of Verona, with a guard of three hundred lances and the whole
of the infantry of the *levée en masse*, was left in reserve. We
hear nothing of the bombards and the big triple-storied ribaulds
during the fight: either they were still trailing behind on the
road, or else Ordelaffi judged that the damp meadow over
which he was about to advance would not bear such heavy
machines. An immovable hostile line behind a water-cut
would have been such a tempting mark for artillery, that it
seems likely that the former hypothesis provides the probable
explanation.[1]

Noon had arrived before the Veronese army moved forward
slowly and in good order, and attacked the Paduan position.
There would appear to have been more honest and continuous
fighting than was usual in these battles of the *condottieri*.
The first line of the assailing party failed to win a passage
across the drain, though it made strenuous efforts to do so.

[1] So suggests Köhler in his account of Castagnaro in *Kriegswesen*, vol. iii. part 3,
p. 364. He thinks that Ordelaffi waited all the morning for the guns to get up, and
finally attacked without them, because the day was wearing on.

All who got over were cast back. Ordelaffi then began to feed his front line with detachments from his second. The ditch was filled in many places with fascines, and the Veronese got across at several points. Hawkwood was obliged to order up his second line to support his first, or the enemy would have broken through. Finally, all the Veronese second line was put into the mêlée by Ordelaffi, who rode about—the only man mounted—supervising each episode of the attack. He even threw in some of his infantry. The Paduans, though still holding together, were beginning to lose ground.

This was the moment for which Hawkwood had been waiting: all the enemy's fighting strength was engaged, save the trifling guard of the *carroccio* and the bulk of the worthless infantry. He took his own English band, lances and archers too, rode with them rapidly to the extreme right, picked up there the arbalesters on the canal bank, and crossed the water-cut unopposed. He then, continuing his circular movement, got completely round the enemy's left flank, and, after some discharge of arrows and bolts, charged in on the back of the Veronese left wing with his horsemen. No troops could have stood such a stroke from the rear: Ordelaffi's flank was ridden down, and the shock ran along the line to the centre. As the Veronese halted and wavered, the Paduans shouted and charged. Hawkwood had left orders with his second in command, Giovanni d' Azzo, that he was to attack at all costs when the enemy felt the blow from behind.

The rest of the battle was an affair of a few minutes. The Veronese broke away everywhere: only one band of two hundred men-at-arms, under Ordelaffi himself, held firm for some time, with the result that every man in it was taken prisoner. All over the meadow the routed men-at-arms were seen running for their horses, which their pages were holding for them. Not half of them were lucky enough to get away.

Hawkwood, when the enemy's left broke, had turned against the mass of infantry in the rear around the *carroccio* of Verona. It made no resistance and broke up: the standard itself was captured, with Giovanni Visconti who had commanded its guard. D' Azzo, with the remnant of the mounted Paduan third line and all of the second who could get to horse, rode through the flying masses, breaking them up and taking prisoners wholesale: he continued the pursuit for some miles along the Legnago road, by which most of the enemy fled.

The victory was absolutely complete. The hostile commander-in-chief, with four thousand six hundred and twenty men-at-arms and eight hundred infantry soldiers, had been captured. The very moderate number of dead on the beaten side was about seven hundred. The great banner of Verona, twenty-four bombards, the three great ribaulds, forty carts of munitions of war, the whole waggon train of the enemy, and his camp fell intact into the hands of the victors, whose own loss is said to have been less than one hundred.

Hawkwood had evidently Poictiers in his head: the task which he took personally in hand was that which the Captal de Buch carried out in the battle of 1356. But a variant on the Black Prince's tactics was necessitated by the fact that bowmen were few: the front-line defended itself by the lance alone, not by the lance and arrow combined. The few archers and crossbowmen available were all reserved for the decisive flank attack. The most notable part of the tactics on both sides is the dismounting of all the men-at-arms, an obvious imitation of the original English tactics of Halidon and Crécy.

CHAPTER II

ITALY IN THE FIFTEENTH CENTURY—
THE LATER CONDOTTIERI

AS the influence of the Transalpine bands of Hawkwood and his contemporaries died down, it is surprising to find that the Italian generals dropped back into the ways of the earlier centuries, and began once more to neglect their infantry, and to rely on cavalry charges as the one potent force in war. A hundred years after, the oddness of this phenomenon struck Machiavelli, who was—alike from his readings in Livy, Cæsar, and Vegetius, and from his personal experience of the Spaniards and the Swiss—a fervent admirer of disciplined infantry. How came the native-born *condottieri* of 1400 to drop the fighting on foot which the French, English, and Burgundian knights, their contemporaries, were still practising at Roosebeke, Agincourt, Verneuil, and Montl'hery? And how did they fail to note, after their early encounters with the Swiss, at Arbedo and elsewhere, that an infantry had arisen which laughed at cavalry charges from behind its serried front of spears? Machiavelli's reply is most interesting, but hardly seems to get to the root of the matter.

"All those who since Alberigo of Romagna [*i.e.* Barbiano] and his disciples, Braccio and Sforza, have been the arbiters of the fate of Italy, down to those who in my own time have allowed Charles VIII. to overrun us, Louis XII. to plunder us, Ferdinand of Spain to deforce us, and the Swiss to insult us, have had one system. Their object has been to increase their personal reputation by destroying the credit of infantry. This they do because, being landless men and living on their gains, they found that a following of a few infantrymen gave them no reputation, while they could not afford to maintain a large body of such troops. And so they restrict themselves to cavalry, finding that with a moderate following of horsemen they can get themselves pay and credit. So things have come to such a pass that in an army of twenty thousand soldiers there will not be more than two thousand infantry. And more than that, they have taken care to relieve themselves and their men of the terrors and fatigues of war. They do not kill each other in their combats, but take each other prisoners without a blow struck. They make no night attacks on fortifications, nor do those inside a fortification ever sally out against the tents of besiegers ; so there is no need to stockade or entrench camps. They do not continue a campaign into the winter. All these customs have got into their military system because they want to avoid both fatigue and danger, and that is the way by which they have brought Italy to slavery and shame." [1]

This, no doubt, was all true so far as it goes. Machiavelli was the most intelligent of observers. No doubt, as Philip de Commines observed in the same generation, infantry is only effective when massed in sufficient numbers, and is rather helpless in tens or twenties. And no doubt a *condottiere*, who came to some tyrant to hire himself out, would look a much less effective tool if he brought thirty draggled crossbow-men rather than ten men-at-arms arrayed *cap-à-pied* and on barded horses.[2] And it is quite true that the infantry often appeared in absurdly small numbers compared to the horse—as we saw at Castagnaro, where the Carraresi had sixteen hundred foot to six thousand nine hundred men-at-arms, or as in Sforza's campaign of 1439, where seven thousand cavalry were accompanied by only two thousand infantry.

But the cause given by Machiavelli for the neglect of infantry is altogether insufficient. If it had been found, as it had been found beyond the Alps, that infantry under certain tactical conditions would repeat the lessons of Bannockburn, Courtrai, Crécy, Laupen, and Navarette, and if the Trans-alpine companies who appeared in 1360 had shown on Italian soil their system of dismounting their men-at-arms for battle with good success, and of utilising missile weapons, why did not the new system perpetuate itself ?

---

[1] *Principe*, cap. xii. pp. 269–72.
[2] The pay of a crossbowman was four florins a month, that of a mounted man twelve florins ; so for the same total sum thrice as many infantrymen as troopers could be kept in service.

The answer is rather intricate. One element in it would certainly appear to be that infantry, being useless in small parties, and only effective in mass—whether as a clump of pikes or as a long line of crossbowmen or archers—requires to be trained to act *en masse*, as were the professional soldiers of England or Switzerland in their prime. Now infantry that acted *en masse*, the communal pikemen and arbalesters of the Lombard League, had been perfectly well known in the thirteenth century—as witness Cortenuova and other fights. But by the fifteenth century the greater part of the Italian cities were in the hands of the Tyrants, who hated to call out the civic levy, because it might turn on them and rend them. They certainly made very little use of it, and in a generation or two it lost its old traditions and efficiency. When, by way of exception, a tyrant did try to employ it—as Antonio della Scala did at Castagnaro—it disgraced itself. And the same was the case in the cities which still kept republican forms, like Florence ; the last desperate efforts to use civic militia in the death-agony of that city in the sixteenth century were deplorable failures.[1] Long disuse had sapped all efficiency, and Machiavelli's sermons in favour of civic infantry were wasted. For long generations the cities which called themselves free had lapsed into that dislike for personal service which we have already noted in the preceding chapter, and the habit could not be shaken off at short notice.

The Italian reluctance to call out the civic levy had fallen upon the states, whether governed by tyrants or not, precisely during the time when infantry was at its lowest valuation, long before the news of Creçy or Poictiers can have been pondered over by thinking men. And the early mercenary-bands were essentially cavalry forces with a small addendum of infantry— the proportion between the two in Fra Moriale's " Great Company " will be remembered. The advent of the disbanded English and French free-lances in 1361 and the following years *might* have led to a complete change of tactics, and seemed likely to do so under the influence of Sir John Hawkwood. It did not, mainly because the bulk of the immigrant bands were not English native soldiery, but French, who had learnt to dismount and to hold the bow in great awe, when

[1] For the worthlessness of Italian sixteenth-century infantry, see Guicciardini, iv. 55 and iii. 123, and Nardis' *Life of Giacomini*. Cf. Ricotti, vol. iii. pp. 249-51.

they were opposed by the armies of Edward III., but who had small respect for their own auxiliary infantry, which had played such an inglorious part at Creçy and elsewhere. When they found themselves involved in the old style of Italian war, as it was going on at the time of their arrival, they gradually dropped back into fighting on horseback. The slow-firing crossbowmen might be practically disregarded by men wearing the heavy plate armour that had recently come in. And the dismounting habit that they had practised in the English battles would be unnecessary against enemies who did not use it, and who possessed no proper infantry of the pike-bearing sort. For the native Italian foot of the fourteenth century were practically all arbalesters—we have heard of the Genoese crossbows at Courtrai and Creçy, but Italian pikemen, civic or mercenary, had long ceased to be seen.

A horseman naturally wishes to use his horse, unless some overruling condition of war forces him to dismount. We have noted that at Castagnaro, the Veronese commander did make his troopers leave their horses, because their opponents (under English influence) had already done so, and had placed themselves behind the obstacle of a water-cut. And Carmagnola at Arbedo, as was shown in the chapter dealing with the Swiss, did the same, when he found that cavalry onsets could not bear down the phalanx of the adversary. But in order to fight an enemy who consisted of a body of horse with some small auxiliary garnish of arbalesters, it was not really necessary to dismount. And this is the main reason why the rather rare pitched battles of the fifteenth century in Italy came to be matters of cavalry manœuvre and successive tilting—such as we see them in the frescoes on the walls of the Siena Palazzo Publico, or the panels of Paulo Uccello.

The man-at-arms, in short, reverted into being a cavalry soldier, because there was in the Italy of 1400–1450 no reason why he should not do so. If Sir John Hawkwood had formed a school of commanders, and if the native English had come down into Italy with their bows in great force, fighting on foot would have become the rule instead of the exception. But, as the chroniclers agree in stating, it was Alberigo da Barbiano who formed the school, and his pupils were fighters on horse-back. They divided into two sects in the next generation— the followers of Sforza Attendolo who believed in massive squadrons few in number, and those of Braccio de Montone, who advocated many and small units.[1] Wherefore it was said that the one displayed more force and the other more skill. But both alike were capable cavalry officers and not innovators in the Art of War.

All these cavalry tactics, as Machiavelli felt, were an abuse and an anomaly in the later fifteenth century. Many parts of Italy are too mountainous for the operations of large bodies of mounted men. Many other parts, such as the marshy lowlands of Lombardy and Southern Venetia, are equally unsuitable—being waterlogged meadows cut up by countless irrigation-canals. There were quite a limited number of regions in which cavalry battles could be fought under favourable conditions. By persisting in using the mounted men alone, the *condottieri* generals tied themselves down to operating in certain limited areas; they must not be entangled in passes, or hampered by sharp slopes, or embogged in marshland. Hence they were restricted to roads and plains, where their heavy horsemen could march in comfort and deploy with good elbow-room. The absurd consequence of this was that a large part of the *condottiere's* Art of War became simply the study of methods for getting the enemy into such positions that he could not attack with advantage. The weaker side manœuvred with the object of placing itself behind obstacles, which large bodies of cavalry could not try to force except under grave disadvantages. The stronger side, resolving not to incur these disadvantages, endeavoured to outflank and dislodge the enemy by circular movements of great length, which avoided the unfavourable terrain. Then the weaker side had to get away in haste and seek for another " blocking " position, from which it would, in due time, be evicted once more. A whole campaign might be a bloodless series of manœuvres for position, with no definite result.

The obvious way of forcing an enemy to fight was to lay siege to a city of such importance that he could not afford to lose it. This would compel him to do something—but it was, of course, possible that instead of trying to drive away the besieging army by attacking it, he might operate against its communications, or carry out a counter-raid into the home-territory of the besiegers. In such a case no general action

[1] See Machiavelli's *Istoria Fiorentina*, v. ii. p. 107.

might take place after all.   This was a very common outline
of a fifteenth-century campaign in Italy : cities could still be
relied upon to make very long resistance, unless there was
treachery within.   For though artillery was improving, it was
not till far on in the century that its action became absolutely
decisive.   While the siege was dragging out its weary length,
the army that wished to raise it would be trying all manner of
circuitous manœuvres around the besiegers' lines and in his
rear.   But if he sat tight, and contrived to keep himself fed,
it was unlikely that the enemy would attack him, unless he had
contrived to scrape together reinforcements which gave him
a large superiority in numbers.

In the centuries that were to come, these situations would
have led to numerous battles, but in the days of the *condottieri*
they did not: for it required some very pressing need to drive
such generals into seeking a pitched battle.   They wanted to
secure ground fit for cavalry action on a large scale, and on
which the enemy had no local advantage, and they were very
cautious unless they had an army which obviously outnumbered
their opponents.   Moreover, they were imbued with the maxim
which Chandos quoted at Auray :

"Est meschief à celui qui assault le premier,"

and preferred to let the enemy take the risk of making the
first move in actual combat.

One of the motives for caution was undoubtedly the fact
that the *condottiere* was not only taking the risks which every
general meets in battle, but was putting his stock-in-trade into
the hazard.   The men-at-arms of his band were his own
private property, so to speak, not national troops ; and if they
were slain or taken his capital had vanished.   His employers
would undoubtedly dismiss a beaten commander, and he would
be thrown penniless on the world, with a broken reputation.
Hence it was wise to take no risks, for the fate of battles is often
settled by luck and not by skill.

And so it came, as Guicciardini says,[1] that " they would
spend the whole of a summer on the siege of one fortified place,
so that the wars were interminable, and the campaigns ended
with little or no loss of life."   When a battle did take place,
there was none of the slaughter of the defeated side which was

[1] *Opere Inedite*, iii. p. 105.

often seen in Transalpine actions.   For the combatants had no
national or religious hatred for each other, and generally not
even personal hatred, though some *condottieri* were jealous of
others, or had old grudges of treachery or insult against them.
But the men-at-arms of each host had probably served half
a dozen times side by side with their enemies of the moment,
since the bands were always passing into the pay of new
employers.   They might often be old friends of the particular
squad against whom they were tilting.   And even if this were
not the case, all mercenaries were more or less brothers in arms,
and despised the tyrant or the *bourgeoisie* which paid them.
Moreover, a prisoner was worth to his captor not only the
value of his horse and armour, but also a ransom, while a dead
man could pay nothing.   Hence victories became ridiculous
—a tactically beaten corps made no great effort to escape,
because surrender meant no more than pecuniary loss.   And
there was a possibility that the victor might offer them the
chance of enlisting in his ranks—in which case the captive
would not even lose horse and arms.   The practice grew up
that prisoners of known status were let go immediately after
their capture, on giving bonds for their ransom.   When in
1428 Carmagnola had captured the better part of the Milanese
army at the battle of Maclodio, he dismissed all the chiefs and
officers on the next day, to the disgust of his employers the
Venetians, who would naturally have liked to shut them up,
and so deprive Duke Filippo Maria of their services for the
rest of the war.   The private profit of the general was made to
outweigh the public interest of his employers, and the war
dragged on once more.

The most constant complaint made by the more philosophical
historians of the fifteenth century is that the *condottieri* deliberately protracted the struggles in which they were engaged,
because the complete victory of one side or the other would bring
peace and the disbandment of armies.   " The Mercenary,"
says Machiavelli, " has no motive of affection or any other sort
to keep him in the field save his bit of pay, and that is not
enough to make him ready to die for your benefit." [1]   He
prefers (very naturally) to live, for his own benefit, drawing
his pay as long as possible—just as a workman engaged by
the month and not by the job will spin out his task for ever,

[1] *Principe*, cap. xii.

And he may have ambitions of his own, entirely different
from those of his employers. "*Condottieri* are either capable
persons or they are not; if they are clever you cannot rely
upon them, for they will be scheming for their own exalta-
tion, either by falling upon you, their employer, or else by
molesting other states, whom you have no interest in pro-
voking. If they are not clever, on the other hand, they will
lose you for a battle and ruin you. And if you say that any
commander, mercenary or no, may do that, the answer is that
both a prince and a republic had better work for themselves.
The prince had better be his own commander-in-chief, and
the republic had better set its own citizens over its army. If
they prove inefficient, they can be changed, and if efficient
they can be prevented by law from getting too much power.
History proves that only princes and warlike republics make
great conquests; mercenary armies have brought nothing but
loss in the end. And it is much harder for an over-great citizen
to master an armed people than a people who have mercenary
soldiers only." [1]

The result of leaving the conduct of war in the hands of
the *condottieri* was that, having no interest in bringing it to a
close, and no particular hatred for the enemy, these generals
came to treat it as a game of chess, played under very strict
rules—a sort of gigantic *Kriegspiel*. The moves interested
them more than the stakes, their employer's profit being indifferent to them. To check a superior army by a well-chosen
position, or an unexpected counter-march, brought them more
satisfaction than the same result achieved by the brutal arbitra-
ment of battle. For in battles anything may happen—panic,
the chance disablement of the commanding officer, unexpected
treachery, a storm or flood which suddenly makes a projected
operation impossible. But in a campaign of manoeuvres the
skill of the player has full scope, and is made less liable to be
hampered by incalculable chances. And so war tended to
become a rather friendly game of chess, generals and armies
being alike destitute of any particular hatred for their opponents.
It was even suspected that, like dishonest pugilists, they sometimes settled beforehand that they would draw the game.
Casualties were few, not so much because of the increased
perfection of fifteenth-century armour, but because the out-

manœuvred party thought it no shame to surrender, and the winning party was out for ransoms and not for slaughter. When we do read of bloodshed, it is generally because one player had been unwise enough to call out some civic militia, whose presence in the field as amateurs the professional soldier resented.   But there was an odd episode in 1439, when the first considerable body of hand-gun men was put into the field by the Bolognese.   Their pellets killed a number of Venetian men-at-arms, shooting through plate and mail ; but when their side was beaten, the victors massacred them all—mercenaries though they were—because their weapon was considered a cruel and cowardly innovation—much like the use of poison-gas in 1916.[1]

But as a rule casualties were absurdly small, and Machia-velli is not far out when he says that the mercenaries did not kill each other in war, giving as his examples the battle of Zagonara (1424) when " in a rout celebrated all over Italy no one died save Ludovico degli Obizzi and two of his men, who were thrown from their horses and smothered in a muddy ditch," and the battle of Molinella (1427) when the Florentines and their enemies " came to a general action which lasted half a day without either party giving way : nevertheless no one was killed, though there were some horses slain and some prisoners taken on each side." [2]   The historian Ammirato, writing a little while after and criticising Machiavelli, says that at Molinella there really was great courage shown by both armies, and that as many as three hundred casualties took place.[3]   But when twenty thousand men meet, and part with a loss of three hundred men between them, we can only say that Machiavelli's sneers are practically, if not literally, justified.   The best commentary on the casualties of these wars is the complaint recorded in 1494 by Guicciardini that the troops of Charles VIII. after their descent across the Apennines shocked Italian public opinion by killing their enemies whole-sale.   This was considered not war but massacre: " Cosa nuova e spaventosa all' Italia, assuefata a vedere guerre quasi simili a spettacoli." [4]

[1] See Marino Sannto in Muratori, xx. p. 1073, and the Chronicle of Bologna, *ibid.* p. 672.   Francesco Sforza also massacred a company of them at Lonigo a little later.
[2] Istoria Fiorentina, IV. i. p. 211, and VII. ii. p. 178.
[3] Ammirato, xxiii. p. 110.   [4] Guicciardini, i. p. 199.

It will be seen easily enough that all these fifteenth-century wars of Italy were unreal—a series of tactical exercises carried out under umpires who enforced certain rules and conventions, rather than a school of true war.   For if it is understood that cavalry alone is to be taken seriously, and that operations must be conducted only on ground where cavalry can move, and that a corps must be " taken off the board " by surrender when it is hopelessly compromised, that such surrender involves no personal discredit to officers or men, that no one is expected to fight to the death, and that broken or retreating troops are not liable to slaughter but only to capture, and that both armies will go into winter quarters in October, all reality has ceased. Troops educated under these principles were quite helpless against an enemy who fought to kill, and who aimed at mere victories won anyhow, perhaps by brutal and unscientific methods.   " Wherefore," says Machiavelli, " in all these wars of the last twenty years [1494–1514], whenever a purely Italian army has taken the field it has made a bad show—as witness first of all the battle on the Taro [Fornovo] and then Alessandria, Capua, Genoa, Vailà [Agnadello], Bologna, Mestre." [1]

There was an immense amount of tactical ability displayed by some of the *condottieri* who worked under the absurd rules summarised above.   But the rules were so cramping, and the conditions so unreal, that their cleverness was rather futile. Above all, their campaigns were a " backwater " in military history, and do not fall into the general scheme of the evolution of the Art of War.   They were a mere prolongation of the old predominance of heavy cavalry, which for most peoples had come to an end at Crécy.   Five thousand English archers or five thousand Swiss pikemen, in the hands of a good general who had already got a few squadrons of men-at-arms, would have upset the military balance of Italy at any moment.   The English never came in sufficient numbers, the Swiss did not descend into the plains in any force till the end of the century, and so the old futile cavalry wars went on down to the advent of Charles VIII. with something like a modern army.   Wherefore it is unnecessary to analyse the operations of Carmagnola, or Francesco Sforza, or any other master of the art of *condottiere* campaigning.   Those who list may study them in the four volumes of Ricotti's *Storia delle Compagnie de Ventura in*

[1] *Principe*, xxvi. pp. 369–70.

Italia, an excellent book full of details.   But the general effect left on the reader's mind is that the whole forms " a tale of little meaning, though the words are strong."   Some of the manœuvring between two masters of the art is as skilful as Wellington's and Marmont's fencing round Salamanca in July 1812 : but the ends and the means are unworthy of the cleverness of the commanders, and there is often a suspicion that they were not doing their best, for some obscure reason or another.   It might not pay the *condottiere* to serve the Venetian Council or the Duke of Milan too well : complete victory might end in the victor's being dismissed with a gratuity that he considered unworthy of his merits.   Conceivably it might even end in his being assassinated, if his employers thought him too clever and too ambitious.   Wherefore it might be better to go on with indecisive campaigns, and draw the highest obtainable salary for the longest possible time.

The real future, as Machiavelli partly saw, was for the army which could combine the action of infantry, cavalry, and artillery.   But the astute Florentine was so intoxicated with his readings in Livy and Vegetius, and so impressed with what he had seen of Swiss pikes and Spanish sword-and-buckler men, that he overvalued the power of infantry as compared with the other two arms.   He wanted to cut down the part of the men-at-arms to something equivalent to that of the part of the *equites* who served along with a Roman legion.   And he does not foresee the rapid development of field artillery.   In the archetypal battle described in his *Arte della Guerra* the guns are allowed to start the fighting with a loud salvo, but do not do overmuch mischief, and have no decisive influence on the result of the action.[1]   It is curious to find that both this military study and the *Prince* were written after Francis I. of France had shown that a judicious combination of cavalry charges and cannon-balls might wreck the Swiss phalanx of pikes.[2]   This does not seem to have struck Machiavelli, who saw hope for the future only in the institution of a new Italian infantry working on the principle of the Roman legion, which should both be able to resist cavalry and to beat other infantry whether armed with the pike or the sword.   He had no conception that in the immediate future the evolution of infantry tactics was to be by the combination of the pike and the hand-gun, nor

[1] *Arte della Guerra,* iii. p. 24.   [2] See above, page 279.

that field artillery was to come to its own, nor that cavalry, when it had become movable by shedding its ridiculous over-weight of armour, was destined to a great future, even down to the days of Gustavus Adolphus, Cromwell, Marlborough, and Frederic the Great.

BOOK XIII

EASTERN EUROPE AND THE NEAR EAST

1230–1500

CHAPTER I

EASTERN EUROPE AND THE TARTARS

WE have already had to deal with two great waves of Eastern invaders who fell upon the rear of Christendom—the Magyars in the tenth century, and the Seljuk Turks in the eleventh. The former, as we have seen, carved out for themselves a kingdom of moderate size in the valley of the Danube, and were within little more than a century absorbed into the general body of European states, though they still showed many traces of their Oriental origin, most of all, perhaps, in their military habits. For they remained all through the Middle Ages a people of horse-bowmen, though their kings and nobles had fallen into the ranks of Christian chivalry, and adopted the arms, armour, and even the heraldry of the West.

The Seljuks cut short the borders of Christendom in Asia only—the westernmost of their conquests were the inland "Themes" of the Byzantine Empire, won at a rush after the disaster of Manzikert (1071). They hewed their way as far as the Sea of Marmora, held Nicæa for a few years, but were driven back from the water by the First Crusaders, and ceased to be a danger, holding no more than the inner plateau of Asia Minor, and none of its coast. That they did no more in the first years of their appearance in the Levant was due to the fact that their central monarchy broke up only a few years after Manzikert, so that the Crusaders and the emperors of the house of Comnenus had not to deal with one great Sultan, but with several small states such as Roum, Damascus, Aleppo, Mosul. The "Great Khans" in Persia, who represented the main branch of the Seljuk horde, were barely in touch with the Christian world, being cut off from it by the dominions of their revolted vassals, the "Atabegs" of Syria and Mesopotamia.

In the thirteenth century Christendom was assailed by a third wave of Oriental invaders, more numerous than the Magyars, and more permanent in their influence than the Seljuks. For the Mongol hosts, who followed the fortunes of Genghiz Khan and his family, not only cut deep into the heart of Europe for a few years, but established a domination over the most numerous of all the Christian races, which was to last for more than two centuries. For if the Mongol power in Persia and in China vanished after a few generations, the " Golden Horde," which had overrun and devastated Russia, profoundly affected all the subsequent history of Eastern Europe. It may be said, indeed, that the Mongol invasion has left effects that work down to this day. For it was the character of that invasion that gave Russian Czardom its peculiar semi-Asiatic shape, and it was mainly in consequence of the workings of Czardom that modern Russian Bolshevism has taken its present detestable aspect.

From the military point of view it is necessary to get some conception of the system of war of the great Mongol armies, and not less necessary to understand the reasons for their success against Eastern Christendom, and their sudden halt and retreat, when it seemed in 1238–41 as if they were about to add the conquest of Central Europe to their exploits. These things cannot be understood without some account of the military organisation of the Russians, Poles, and Hungarians on whom the blow fell.

To commence with the invaders. As every student of history knows, Genghiz Khan's long life extended from 1154 to 1227. Starting as a mere sub-chief among many Mongolian tribal rulers, he spent forty years of fighting in making himself sole leader of his own race, and then in his old age, being at last a respectable military power, started on that astonishing series of campaigns which ruined so many ancient states. He conquered Manchuria, then Northern China, then he turned against Turkestan, and made an end of the old Mohammedan principalities on the Oxus, sweeping all over the Khiva, Bokhara, Samarcand, Merv country, where he did damage that never was repaired to this day, and left deserts where there had been a civilised and thickly peopled group of states. It was for the ill-luck of Asia and Eastern Europe alike that in the first quarter of the thirteenth century there was no existing

first-rate power in either to face such a formidable invasion
as that which Genghiz Khan and his sons led. The Mohammedan states were at the moment weak and disunited : Persia,
which should have been the centre of resistance, was divided
between three or four rival dynasties. The Seljuk Sultanate
of Roum in Asia Minor was also decadent : indeed the only
Mohammedan first-rate power in existence at the moment was
the Eyubite Sultanate of Syria and Egypt—and this was
the only realm in Asia that turned the Mongols back in fair
fighting. Over the rest, Persia, Mesopotamia, Asia Minor,
the Oxus lands, they burst in flood, destroying everything.
And the situation was precisely the same in Eastern Europe—
the first line of Christendom was composed of the group of
Russian duchies, just at the worst of their dynastic quarrels and
endless civil wars—cut up by a dozen cousinly jealousies.
And, behind Russia, Poland, in quite as bad a state of feudal
anarchy, formed the second line.

Both in Europe and in Asia it was against groups of faction-
ridden principalities of no great size or strength that the Mongol
invasion was let loose. And this accounts in great measure
for its appalling success. There had been times, a century
or two before, when united monarchies of considerable strength
had existed in the lands where the descendants of Genghiz
found only weak and secondary states. There had once been
a Caliphate extending from Tangier to Kabul, and later a
Seljuk power which could have stopped any invader from
the remoter Orient. Even Saladin's empire might have held
its own. And Russia had once been a single monarchy and
not a welter of discordant duchies. But in the middle years
of the thirteenth century there was no warder at the eastern
gate of Mohammedan civilisation, any more than at the
eastern gate of Christendom.

We have excellent descriptions of the armies of the Great
Khans, written by intelligent European observers, who had not
only watched their operations from outside, but had penetrated among them, and had dwelt, to their great discomfort,
in their migratory camps. The armies of Genghiz or Oktai or
Batu were strangely combined hosts of vassals and adventurers,
in which the original Mongol tribesmen were but a fraction,
surrounded by Kirghiz, Bashkirs, Turks, and Turcomans of
many sorts, Manchus, and countless other subject tribes.

One wonders how orders were circulated and the words of command passed around, in such heterogeneous hosts. Apparently this was managed by placing native Mongol sub-commanders over every unit of any size.

By far the best account of Mongol warfare is that given by Giovanni de Plan Carpin, the forlorn ambassador whom Innocent IV. sent to Karakorum in 1246. His chapters were afterwards abridged by Vincent of Beauvais:

"By a system starting from Genghiz Khan the army is divided into units of tens. Over each ten horsemen there is a 'decanus' as we should call him, over each ten 'decani' a centurion, over each ten centurions a 'millenarius,' and over the whole body of ten thousand men a commander whom they call a *Tomanbeg*. Over an army of several such bodies there will be two or perhaps three generals, but one of them is obeyed by the others. In this system of tens their discipline resides. For if one or two or three out of the ten fly on the day of battle, all the rest are tried and executed. Unless there is a general retreat ordered, the first to fly are always so punished. And if one or two or three out of a band make a gallant assault, and the rest do not follow them, the laggards are likewise put to death. And if one or more are taken prisoners, and the rest fail to rescue them, then also they are executed.

"The Tartars carry two or three bows (or at least one specially good one) and three quivers, an axe, and a stout rope which can be used to drag vehicles. The better-armed have also scimitars, sharply pointed, curved, and with only one cutting edge. Many have helms and cuirasses of leather. The latter are made of strips about a palm broad, sewn together in threes and stiffened with bitumen : the sewing is so managed that the strips overlap, and when the rider bends himself together they make a double or triple protection for his body. They have bardings of leather for their horses, made in five pieces, which protect them as far as their knees, and iron frontlets are fixed on their foreheads. Their own body-armour of leather strips is in four parts, a long front-piece and back-piece reaching from the neck to the thigh, and joined together on the shoulders by two iron plates fastened by buckles, and two long arm-pieces reaching from the shoulder to the wrist. And on each leg they have cuissarts, which, like the arm-pieces, are joined to the body-armour by straps and buckles. The upper part of the helm is of iron, but the covering for the throat and neck of leather. And all the leather work of the whole suit is made of over-lapping pliable strips, as I described above. But some of them have iron scale-armour, made as follows. They take narrow scales of metal, of a finger-breadth and of the length of a palm. Each scale is pierced with eight small holes, and within they put leather cords or straps, to which they sew the metal scales one over another, in ascending rows, with thin leather laces passed through the little holes. And in the upper rows they have a second lace, for the sake of strength and of holding the scales firmly together. And this scale-armour they can also use for their horses, and they scour it so bright that a man can see his face in it.

"Some of them carry lances, with a hook where the lance head joins the shaft, with which hooks they try to drag an adversary out of his saddle in close combat. The length of their arrows is two feet, plus one palm and two finger-breadths. The heads of the arrows are very sharp, like a two-edged sword: they always carry files with them in their quivers, to sharpen their arrows. Their shields are of wicker: [but, it is added in another place, they do not use them much; and they are seldom seen except in the hands of the guards of the emperor or of generals, for they are not easily managed along with a bow].

"When the Tartar army goes out to war, it has a screen of scouts far out in front of it, who neither plunder, nor burn houses, nor drive off cattle, though they will kill any men that they meet. The host follows behind, which takes all it can, ravages, and slays at large. When they come to a river, the chief men have large round sheets of thin leather, pierced with many eyeholes in their edges. They run a cord through these eyeholes and pull it tight, so making a sort of bag, in which they place their clothes and other gear, and strap their saddles on top, and sometimes sit on top themselves. This float or pontoon they tie to the tail of a horse, who is pushed into the river, with a man swimming at his head to guide him. But they have sometimes been seen to sit on their bag and row it with two short oars. When the leading horse is driven into the water, all the others follow, and so they cross the river. The poorer sort have only a sack of leather, very tightly sewn together, into which they ram their gear, and tie it each to his own horse's tail.

" As to their tactics, when they discover the enemy's host they advance upon it, and each horseman shoots three or four arrows, and if they see that they cannot prevail they retreat, as a snare, in order that they may lure the enemy into ground where they have laid ambushes. Should the enemy follow incautiously, they fall upon both his flanks from the ambush, and so destroy him. But if the foe is very powerful, they will turn aside from him two or three days' march, and burst into another part of his lands and slay and burn there. And if they find that they cannot even accomplish this, they will retreat ten or twelve days' march, and lurk for some time in a safe spot, till they think that the hostile army will have dispersed, and then come out by stealth and ravage again.

" They are most astute in war—as is natural after forty years' continuous campaigning. When they have resolved to fight a general action, their prince or general does not go into the battle-line, but keeps far behind, having with him the camp-followers and even the women, all on horseback, so as to make at a distance the effect of a great reserve : it is even said that they mounted dummy figures on horses, to look like more warriors. They form their central line of vassal and captive tribes, with only a few Tartars among them. The best troops are far out on the wings to right and left, if possible out of sight of the enemy ; and so they close in upon his flanks and attack him on every side. And this encompassing front of battle makes the enemy think them very numerous, even when they are in no great force, because he sees afar off the mounted camp-followers, the women, and even the ' dummies,' whom he thinks are all fighting men, and so grows discouraged. But if the enemy fights well, they will open their circle and let him break through, but set upon him the moment that he scatters, and they will slay more by this sort of flight than in close combat. For you must know that they are not particularly fond of a mêlée, but prefer to shoot and kill from a distance.

" They conduct sieges as follows. When they come to a fortress they surround it, or even circumvallate it, so that no man can issue forth. They shoot strongly both with arrows and with military machines, and keep up the discharge day and night, so as to hold the garrison in a constant state of torment. But they get rest themselves, since one division relieves another every few hours. If they cannot take the town by machines, they will use Greek fire : it is said that they have been known to kill and boil down captives, and project their fat into the town ; for this horrid brew flares fiercely and is almost inextinguishable. And if the place still holds out, they try other devices : if it has a river running through it, they dam it, or cut a new channel, and throw a great head of water against the walls. And if this is impossible, they dig mines and so penetrate into the heart of the place. When they are inside, one part of them sets fire to the houses, while the rest attack the garrison in the rear. If even by mining they cannot prevail, they will build walls completely round the city, and lie there for long months, and so starve it out, unless an army of relief should appear. During such a blockade they will offer the most mild and tempting terms of surrender, but if these are accepted they break their promises, and massacre every one, except perhaps · a few skilled artisans : the nobles and good folk are always exterminated."

Carpin's advice to the princes of Europe as to the method in which a Tartar invasion should be met, shows considerable shrewdness on some points, but is a little deficient in the topographical department—the essential fact that certain types of country are wholly unsuitable for Tartar tactics never emerges in his chapter, " Quomodo resistendum sit eis." His general remarks are sound, but rather obvious. A general league of Christian states, as for a Crusade, is advised : single provinces and small kingdoms are too weak individually to face a Mongol invasion : but all Christendom combined would be amply strong enough. The Russians and Poles were ruined by disunion and local jealousies, as were the Mohammedan states of nearer Asia, which fell one by one. In many things, Carpin observes, we might copy our enemies : it would be far better if Western generals stayed with the reserve and confined themselves to giving orders, as the Tartar Khans do, instead of heading the charge of the " main-battle." All troops should be divided in the Mongol method into permanent bands of hundreds and thousands, instead of working in the usual feudal fashion in " retinues " of countless lords, small and great. Tartar discipline might be copied in punishing the man who leaves the ranks to plunder or to shirk—though the universal Tartar punishment of instant execution is unnecessarily severe. A screen of scouts should always precede the army, and be constantly reporting the slightest touch with the enemy. Especially there should be strong flank-guards kept out, to watch for the habitual encircling attack which he practises. The cavalry should not be in large masses, but in manageable units, which can face any way; and local reserves are wanted, as well as one large general reserve, when the army is drawn out. Infantry should be furnished with the crossbow, which the Tartar specially dislikes, because its bolt easily pierces his leathern armour or the bardings of his horse. On the other hand, the arrows which he shoots cannot pierce the double Western armour (a thing which Boha-ed-din had noted at Arsouf)[1]; wherefore the fully armed knights on barded horses should form the front line, and the ill-protected horsemen keep in their rear, to be used only in a general charge and mêlée, where shooting is impossible. When the enemy gives way, he is probably doing so to lure his pursuer into an ambush; so he must be followed with caution : for this reason a featureless plain, which can hold no snares, is the best fighting ground for a Christian army. [This, as we shall show, is a very disputable generalisation.]

When a raid is known to be coming, the country people should escape into hills, woods, or walled cities, after hiding all food, and burning all grass and standing corn. For a Tartar army lives on the country, and its horses require much fodder. Castles and fortified towns must be provided with many months of rations, " you must see that each man eats by measure a fixed dole, since you know not how long a siege may last." There was one hill fortress in the land of the Alans (in the Caucasus) which the Tartars are said to have besieged for twelve years ! Also a city or castle must have a good provision of balistas and slings (trebuchets), to play on the enemy when they try to set up machines against the besieged place.

All this is quite sensible, if a little obvious. But what Carpin does *not* say is that three sorts of country are impracticable for a host composed entirely of cavalry: dense woodlands, in which horsemen can only move by narrow paths and are at the mercy of missile-bearing light infantry; marshland, where their horses will stick fast, and are confined to narrow tracks on which they can be easily stopped by a cut

[1] See Vol. I. p. 309.

or a barricade, turning movements being impossible ; and, thirdly, precipitous hills and passes, where any intelligent local force can treat an invader, who is tied to his horse, as the Swiss treated the Austrians at Morgarten. The Tartar was essentially a conqueror of the steppe and the plainland, and in Europe it was the lands of the steppes and the plains only that he swept over.

These masses of rapidly-moving horse-archers, when they threw themselves upon Christendom, were confronted by enemies who were of all the Western nations the least suited to resist them. Both in Russia and in Poland there was no central power which could organise resistance. In the latter there was a king indeed, but feudal particularism had reduced his power to nought, and rebellion and civil war were endemic. The nominal sovereign Boleslav V. (1229–79), surnamed " the Chaste," was an exceptionally weak and resourceless person, who never even appeared at the head of an army. In Russia the old monarchy centred at Kief had long broken up, and the titular precedence was being fought for by many dukes, whose claims were equally good, as all alike descended from Rurik, and each had his appanage.

The Russian army at this time was much like that of the Franks in the eighth or ninth century—there was a personal *comitatus* of horsemen who followed each chief (the *droujina* or retinue) clad in chain-mail and bearing lance and shield, and a general levy of infantry from the free peasantry, who were still numerous (*voi*). Rich princes sometimes hired a few mercenaries, who had in the earlier centuries usually been Varangian vikings from the North. The noble cavalry of the *droujina* were the striking force, but very few in numbers compared with the infantry, who were a sort of " fyrd," not particularly well armed, and only able to act in heavy masses. Their weapons were the axe and spear, archery being not overmuch cultivated. The one sound point in their organisation was that they were accustomed to surround their camps with palisades on the eve of an action. The usual tactics were for the army to draw up in front of the palisaded camp (*obos*), with the cavalry in the centre and infantry both on the wings and in the rear as a reserve. The decisive blow was always given by the frontal cavalry charge, the infantry being reckoned capable of defence but not of much

offensive action.   In the case of a check, the army retreated into
its fortified camp, and stood to fight there again.

The bulk of a Russian host consisted of the local levy of
foot; among the Poles, on the other hand, cavalry was the only
arm.   The free yeomanry, which was still numerous in Russia,
had practically disappeared in Poland.   The large majority
of the people had sunk into predial serfdom ; the minority was
composed of a very numerous *noblesse* serving on horseback,
including all landowners, from the poor man owning a few
acres to great barons who could put hundreds of landowning
vassals into the field.   Above these were the numerous dukes of
the royal house of Piast, who, by a system of heritage-partition
lasting over many generations, had acquired appanages with
semi-royal rights, extending over the greater part of the land.
As in eleventh-century France, the king was really master of
nothing but a limited royal domain and a few cities ;   and
urban communities in Poland were few, small, and largely
composed of foreign immigrants, mainly from Germany.   The
Poles, unlike their neighbours the Magyars, were a nation of
lancers : the rich noble served in complete mail on a barded
horse, the poor noble in a leather jerkin on a small nag.   There
were no horse-archers and no infantry—neither pikemen nor
arbalesters.   The only difference was between the light and
the heavy horse.

It is hard to say whether an army consisting of a general
levy of rural infantry unfurnished with missile weapons, and
led by a small body of mailed nobles and princes, or an army
consisting entirely of mounted lancers without either infantry
or bows, was less fitted to face the Tartar horse-archers and
their encircling tactics.   Moreover, both the Russians and the
Poles had few fortified cities, and had not taken to the Western
custom of castle-building.   Their nobles lived in wooden
mansions, protected at the best by a palisade, and most easily
attackable by fire, not in the solid keeps and stone ring-
defences of French, German, or English barons.   And the
towns were no better protected: stone is rare both in Russia
and in Poland, timber plentiful : hence towns with hardly an
exception—Kief was apparently one—if fortified at all, were
girt only with ditch, mound, and stockade.   In a general way
it may be said that the only formidable defences of Russia and
Poland were their forests, into which the whole people could

retire and take refuge, abandoning the open country. But only North Russia is a true forest region, the southern duchies lay in the open lands along the border of the great steppes.

The first irruption of the Mongols into Europe was in 1224, while the old empire-builder, Genghiz Khan, was still alive. One of his armies under two "dukes," Souboudai Bagadour and Jebe Noion, swept round the south side of the Caspian, and after ravaging Mohammedan Aderbaijan and Christian Georgia, reached the open country north of Caucasus through the defile of Baku. The steppes of the Kuban and the Don were in that century held by the Turkish tribe of the Polovtzes,[1] a nomadic horde who had long been the enemies of South Russia, but had never been very formidable to it. Against the rear of the Polovtzes came the Tartar army, which easily beat the Khan Kotiak and his host, who could compete with them neither in numbers nor in fighting efficiency. To escape massacre, the whole tribe fled westward toward the Dnieper, and resolved in their hour of despair to throw themselves at the mercy of the Russians, comparatively civilised foes, with whom they were well acquainted. Kotiak sent his kinsman, Basti, to bear his message to Kief: it ran, as we are told, "To-day the Tartars are taking my country: to-morrow they will take yours," and to show the seriousness of his intentions, the ambassador asked for orthodox priests and had himself and his family baptized, as a sign that the Polovtzes wished to enter the commonwealth of Christendom, as the Magyars — an equally alien race — had done two centuries back.

The news from the steppe, and the desperate and obviously sincere appeal of the Polovtzes had the effect of reconciling for a moment the factious cousins who reigned over the quarrelsome principalities of South Russia. The most powerful of them, Msistislaf of Galicia, took the lead in declaring that old enmities must cease: and in fact seven princes of the South and West joined their arms, and marched to aid the wreck of the Polovtzes on the Lower Dnieper, towards which the Tartars were advancing. But the alliance was incomplete; not a single North-Russian magnate appeared. The Grand Duke of Susdal, who held in the remoter lands much the same predominance as the Grand Duke of Galicia in the nearer ones, had

[1] So named by the Russians: Magyars and Greeks called them Cumars.

not stirred, nor the princes of Riazan, Tver, Pskof or Novgorod. The Russians of the forests betrayed the Russians of the plain-land.

Picking up the Polovtzes on the way, the allied host advanced as far as the river Kalka, a small stream flowing into the Sea of Azof, where they found themselves faced by the Tartars. The chronicles say that the battle which ensued was very badly fought. Like the French nobles at Creçy or Nicopolis, the household cavalry of the Russian princes attacked recklessly, without common tactics or subordination to a leader. The van under the Grand Duke of Galicia charged before the rear had come upon the field, was encircled by the " horns " of the long front of horse-bowmen and shot down helplessly. The Polovtzes gave way in the midst of the battle, and fled through the Russian reserves in their rear, breaking up the infantry. There was a general flight, and while the Prince of Kief and his division threw themselves into the stockaded camp, and stood a siege, the rest retired as best they could. The camp held out for three days, and then surrendered on terms, which were at once violated by the victors, who massacred every man. Six Russian princes had fallen, with seventy of their 'boyars' or great nobles, and not a tithe of the whole army got home.

Yet this awful disaster was not the beginning of the Tartar invasion of Europe, but only a dreadful warning. Genghiz Khan called back his army for his great attack on China, and the Russians had a respite of thirteen years, during which they resumed their old dynastic wars, and forgot the battle of the Kalka. It was not till 1237 that the real definitive attack of the Mongols on the West recommenced. Genghiz had been ten years dead when his son Oktai, the second supreme emperor, having completed the conquest of Northern China, sent his nephew, Batu Khan, to resume the enterprise against Christendom. This time the invasion came not from the South and the side of the Caspian, but from due East, the side of Siberia. Batu came in upon the Upper Volga, where he started by destroying the kingdom of " Great Bulgaria," where dwelt that part of the Bulgar race which had not moved down to the Balkan Peninsula in the seventh century. He then fell upon the rear of the North-Russian duchies, overrunning the easternmost, the state of Riazan, before his arrival was even expected. The next three years, 1238–39–40, saw the most fearful

disasters that Europe had ever suffered from an Asiatic invader
—even Attila and his Huns were less destructive, for they
received an enemy to vassalage, while the Mongols represented
not mere conquest but blind and wilful destruction: they left a
desert behind them, and killed for killing's sake. The North
Russians showed an even greater incapacity to unite for self-
defence than the South Russians had done at the time of the
battle of the Kalka. George, Grand Duke of Susdal, the most
powerful and ambitious prince of the North, found great
difficulty in getting any aid from his neighbours, because of
old grudges. He saw his capital sacked; it never rose again
as a place of any importance. His sons shut themselves up
in Vladimir, his second greatest town, which the Mongols
stormed by the aid of fire, which was fatal to its wooden
walls: the princes and their Archbishop were massacred in
the cathedral where they had taken refuge. George himself,
having collected some reinforcements too late, was defeated
and slain at the battle of the Sita : his corpse was dishonoured
and decapitated. Batu then overran all the open country
between the forests as far as Tver. It was then apparently a
matter of chance whether the victorious horde should continue
its raid westward, towards Great Novgorod, or turn to the
South. But autumn had come, and Novgorod is surrounded
by interminable woods, lakes, and swampy rivers. The
Mongol horsemen hated both marsh and forest, and swerved
aside from the inundation to fall on South Russia, where the
country was more open and food easier to procure.

It thus became the turn of the Southern duchies to face
the storm. They had done nothing to avert it, for they had
failed to aid their Northern brethren. They acquitted themselves badly enough—apparently the memory of the Kalka
lay heavy on their minds. All their fighting was purely local,
the defence of each region by its own prince with his *droujina*
and his peasant levy. There was little combination, and no
help from the nations of inner Europe, who had always been
barred out from Russia by the old feud between the Orthodox
and the Roman Churches. In 1240 fell Kief, the largest city
and the ecclesiastical metropolis of all the Russias, an enormous
place with countless churches and monasteries, and a good
stone wall—a thing almost unknown elsewhere in those regions.
Michael, prince of Kief, was a coward, and fled to Poland

328 THE ART OF WAR IN THE MIDDLE AGES [1241

instead of defending his heritage. His boyars and the citizens, however, made a gallant defence, and held out even after the gates were pierced and the ramparts broken. But the usual end came—the town was fired and conquered street by street— the people massacred, save women and children reserved for slavery (December 6th, 1240). The city had been so great, and its reputation as a holy place so widespread, that its destruction can only be compared to the sack of Jerusalem by Titus, and that of Constantinople by Sultan Mahomet II. During the later months of 1240 the Mongols swept all over Western Russia : its princes fell fighting in a hopeless struggle or fled to Poland, Hungary, and Bohemia. The next year (1241) saw the greatest of all the Mongol successes, and set all Europe in alarm. Batu's objective was Hungary : it is said that he was specially provoked by the reception of the flying Polovtzes by King Bela, who had welcomed them and offered their king lands in the eastern marches of his realm. But the Mongol was aware that if he crossed the Carpathians into Hungary he would have the Poles on his flank and rear. Wherefore he set aside about a fourth of his host, under his cousin Baidar, to serve as a sort of flank guard, and to attack Poland, while he himself with his main body was to cross the central Carpathians, and two smaller divisions were to strike farther east, and distract the attention of King Bela.

Batu was quite justified in treating this offensive towards Poland as a secondary affair, owing to the distracted condition of that country. It was, as has been mentioned above, cursed at this time with a cowardly and incapable king, who was contemned by all the other princes of the house of Piast. At the first alarm, Boleslav fled into Moravia with his wife and his treasures, after turning over the charge of his army to Vladimir, the palatine of Cracow. The latter, unassisted by the appanaged princes, gave battle to the Mongols with the levy of the royal domain alone, and was routed and slain at Chmielnik, thirty miles in front of Cracow (March, 1241). The capital city was found deserted by the Mongols on their approach, all the people having fled into the forests or the Carpathians. They burnt the empty place, and pushed on into Silesia, where they found the princes of Western Poland ready to fight, though they had sent no help to the royal army a few weeks before. They were led by Henry the Pious, Duke

of Breslau; with him was Mitislaf of Oppeln, Boleslav Margrave of Moravia, and Poppo of Osterna, the "Landmaster"
of the Teutonic knights, with a contingent from Prussia and
some other small German succours. The engagement which
followed, the battle of Liegnitz (April 5th, 1241), has won some
fame in history from its marking the westernmost advance of
the Mongols. But we are very ill-informed as to its details.
We only know that the dukes are said to have had twenty
thousand men, mostly Polish light cavalry, but including some
Moravian and German infantry, and that they formed four
battles, in one of which all the foot soldiery were massed. But
they were outflanked by the usual "horns" of the Mongol
array—Baidar is said to have outnumbered them fivefold.
Twice the charge of the Poles broke into the Mongol centre,
but was stopped by troops sent up from the reserve. Finally,
the flank pressure of the archery grew so unbearable that the
Christian army fell into disorder and gave way. There was a
dreadful slaughter in the pursuit, and both Duke Henry and
the Teutonic Landmaster were slain. The victors then spread
their raiding bands all over Silesia, but failed to take Breslau
or the castle of Liegnitz, both of which were well defended.
They then swerved off through Moravia to join Batu, who
was already engaged with the Hungarians. It is said that the
gap made in the population of the Oder valley was so terrible
that the dukes called in thousands of settlers from Saxony and
Thuringia after the war, and that from these immigrants came
the Germanisation of Central Silesia.

The battle of Liegnitz startled all Europe. The West had
paid little heed to the disasters of Russia, for it was remote, and
reckoned alien and heretical. But the complete ruin which
had fallen on the Catholic kingdom of Poland, and the appearance of the unknown and terrible Mongol on the borders of
Germany, sent a shock round the whole of Christendom.
Pope Gregory IX. proclaimed a Crusade, and the Emperor
Frederic II. issued a manifesto of a similar sort from the
secular point of view, calling on all vassals of the Holy Roman
Empire to join his standard. The terror in the West was very
real, but unfortunately the counter-appeals of these old enemies,
the Pope and the Emperor, went far to neutralise each other.
Guelfs could not take the field with an excommunicated
sovereign: Ghibellines would have nothing to do with a

Crusade. Gregory and Frederic did not start their propaganda with a mutual reconciliation, and, failing this, there was much negotiation and general bustle, but no serious effort to " drive the diabolical Tartars back to their own Tartarus."

Meanwhile, before the news of Liegnitz had spread to the outlying realms of Christendom, a yet worse catastrophe had occurred in Hungary. In March the two minor Mongol armies which Batu had detached to his left, had crossed the Eastern Carpathians, and distracted the attention of King Bela by raids on his outlying counties. Somewhat later, Batu himself came over the central passes with his main force, using the " Ruthenian Gates," the defiles which lead down towards Muncacz, Kashau, and Miskolcs. An inadequate force sent to block them, under the Palatine Denis Hedevary, was swept away. When the Mongols reached the river Sajo, they found themselves faced by King Bela and the general levy of Hungary, arrayed on the heath of Mohi, with the Sajo in their front, the broad Theiss covering their right flank, and the hills and woods of Diosgÿor in their left rear. The Magyars were in great force—chroniclers speak of one hundred thousand horse—though still inferior in numbers to the Mongols. They were a host which should have been able to face the enemy with his own tactics, since they were mainly horse-bowmen, though there were numerous contingents of mailed lancers in the retinues of the king and the magnates. Their morale is said to have been not over good—they had heard that the enemy was ravaging far and wide even in their rear ; the news from Liegnitz had been discouraging ; and the King was unpopular. He had been making encroachments upon the feudal rights of his nobles, and was thought too great a friend of the clergy. Two fighting archbishops, Hugolin of Kolocza and Matthias of Gran were among this most trusted generals, and had brought great contingents of their vassals to his camp.[1]

Bela intended to defend the line of the Sajo, which is only fordable in a few places, and had barricaded its only bridge. The fault of his dispositions, as we are told, was that he occupied too short a front, considering the enormous numbers and great mobility of the enemy. His camps were massed on a limited space not far behind the bridge, instead of being drawn back

---

[1] The date of the battle is not certainly known—late April or early May are the limits, April 27 the day favoured by most historians.

and extended to cover all available fords. Batu is said to
have pointed out to his generals this essential mistake. "They
are crowded together," he said, "like a herd of cattle in narrow
stalls, with no room to move about." Tartar tactics being
pretty well known by this time, and the Hungarians having at
their disposal masses of light cavalry, there was no excuse for
the neglect to provide large flank-guards placed far out. Batu,
having studied the position, sent a great body of his men
upstream, with orders to cross the Sajo at unwatched fords
many miles away, under cover of the night. This manoeuvre
was carried out undetected: he then made, even before dawn,
a frontal demonstration with his main body against the Hungarian army. Meeting a strong arrow flight from across the
river, he replied to it, and brought forward seven catapults to
batter the barricades of the bridge, which were presently demolished. Matters were at a deadlock for some time, when
the large detachment which had crossed the upper fords
appeared on the flank of the Magyar army, and almost in
its rear. All King Bela's arrangements were thrown out by
this unexpected development, and while he was trying to
draw back his left wing and to make a new front to his flank,
the attack at the bridge became a real one. One Tartar column
charged over the shattered barricades, and others plunged at
fords, hitherto left unattacked, opposite several points of the
king's line. A furious mêlée followed, but the Magyars were
hopelessly handicapped by the turning of their unprotected
left, and got jammed against the tents of their camp, which
incommoded all manoeuvres. Presently they broke and
scattered. Many, including the king and his brother, got away,
being as well mounted as their pursuers: but the slaughter was
very great. "Fere extinguitur militia totius regni Hungariæ,"
wrote the Emperor Frederic, in a despairing appeal to his
vassals. Both the fighting archbishops, three of their suffragans,
and a great number of magnates were slain: the chroniclers
talk of sixty-five thousand dead—no doubt a vast exaggeration.
But the victory was a decisive one, and there was no rally.

King Bela fled into Austria, but meeting a harsh reception
there, slipped back into the southern part of his own realm,
and took refuge in the mountains of Dalmatia. The Mongols
spread themselves at leisure over the whole of the great Hungarian plain, and ravaged it from end to end, destroying all

its towns. The Danube checked them for a moment, but when it froze in an early and severe winter, they crossed it on the ice, and completed their devastation, making an end of Gran, then the capital of the land, of the royal citadel of Buda, opposite Pesth, and the other cities of the western regions of Hungary, save Stühlweissenberg (Alba Regia) which defended itself behind strong walls. After ravaging the plain, the Mongols even ventured into the mountains of Croatia and Dalmatia, though such a country was not favourable to their tactics. Some of their bands even cut their way through to within sight of the waters of the Adriatic, and approached but did not seriously attack the walls of Spalato, Trau (where King Bela had taken refuge), and even Ragusa. But this enterprise was rather hopeless and very profitless—the Croats and Dalmatians retired up into the Alps, where they could not be followed, cut off the supplies of the invaders, and exterminated many of their detachments in ambushes in defiles, where horsemen were helpless. The Mongol irruption into the Dalmatian Alps was coming to an end from its impossibility of success, when a general evacuation of the Danube countries was caused by external circumstances.

There was arising a danger for the Mongols in the northwest: they had swept through Moravia on their way to Hungary after the battle of Liegnitz, but a threat against their flank was now developing. The Moravian cities of Olmütz and Brunn had resisted successfully behind their walls when the horde went by, and Wenzel, King of Bohemia, was in arms to cover his border early in 1242, with a great national levy, and accompanied by the wrecks of the Poles and many of the German princes of the East, the dukes of Austria, Carinthia, and others. It was hoped that the tardily assembled Crusaders of Western Europe would join. But it is doubtful whether the Mongols knew enough geography to understand the danger that they were incurring on this side, or had sufficient respect for any Western troops to fear defeat. Several more plausible reasons for the drawing back of the Mongol advance may be discerned. The first and most certain is that Batu Khan had just received the news of the death of his uncle Oktai, the second of the Mongol emperors, who had died in China during the previous winter. It was very problematical whether the empire would not break up, since Oktai had

several ambitious and capable relatives, of whom Batu himself
was by no means the least important. He wanted to be at
headquarters with his immediate military following, while the
succession question was being settled. Absent in Hungary, he
did not count as a political factor. He was wanted at Karakorum,
the imperial capital in Mongolia, to watch events.

Other considerations may be pointed out—it is certain that
Batu's army must have decreased in strength during four years
of incessant fighting, even though that fighting had been for
the most part victorious. He was separated from his nearest
base for reinforcements in Turkestan by a thousand miles.
Moreover, his army must have been gorged with plunder, and
no doubt was wanting to get it home, and to visit the paternal
tents for a space. As a parallel we may remember the case of
the discontents of the army of Alexander the Great, when in
a very similar case he had cut his way from Macedonia to the
Punjab in four years. The veterans wanted leave, and were
determined to have it. Thirdly, we note the fact that Batu in
his conquests had swept all over the Europe of the plains,
whose topography was most favourable to the tactics of his
horsemen. He had got all that was to be got out of Russia,
Poland, and Hungary, the three great plain-countries. But
the mountains of Croatia and Dalmatia had already proved
unfavourable to further advance, as had the forest swamps of
Northern Russia. On the one frontier still more or less open
to him, that of Austria and Bohemia, he had run his head
already against one of those districts which (unlike Poland or
Hungary) were full of strongly fortified cities and castles.
Already Olmütz, Stühlweissenberg, and the Dalmatian cities had
successfully resisted him : siegecraft was the weak side of Tartar
tactics, no less than of the tactics of all nations, in those days
when the defensive had the supremacy. The strong towns of
the West with their elaborate enceintes, still more the castles,
with line after line of defence such as thirteenth-century
military engineering had devised, were slow to take, if they
could be taken at all. They were very different from the
wooden Russian cities, with their palisades and earthworks, of
which so many had fallen. Poland and Hungary were lands of
few cities, and not far advanced in the art of fortification, like
Germany or Bohemia. It is hardly doubtful but that Batu
must have understood that further conquests toward the West

would be much slower and less easy than those which he had hitherto carried out with such astonishing celerity.

This much is certain, that the devastating wave of barbarism which had swept so far forward, and had reached the Oder and the Drave, suddenly fell back as suddenly as it had advanced. The Mongols were never seen again west of the Vistula and the Sereth. Western Europe, which had been fearing that it would have to fight for its civilisation and its very existence next year, suddenly found itself freed inexplicably from all danger, and was able to fall back after a couple of winters of intense terror into its old Guelf and Ghibelline wars —the struggle of the Papacy and the Empire. Poland and Hungary found themselves completely evacuated, and their kings were able to emerge from their hiding-places, and their peasants, such as had survived, from the forests or the mountains where they had taken refuge. Neither of these nations were so highly organised as to have suffered a deadly blow from the Tartar devastations : they were not town-dwelling peoples in a high state of civilisation, to whom the burning of their cities would have been ruin—as it would have been to Italy or Germany. The wooden huts of the peasantry could be easily rebuilt—the wooden manors of the nobles were not much more difficult to replace. The loss of life and property had no doubt been dreadful : the strength of both realms was for a time impaired. But when no more Mongol raids came, they could both reconstruct themselves after their fashion. The only lesson learnt was the advantage of fortfication : in Hungary especially we are told that after the Mongol invasion the ruined towns were all rebuilt with good stone walls, and the castles of the nobles multiplied. The great raid of Batu made no permanent landmark in the history of either country. The Poles in two years had resumed their old dynastic strife : the Hungarians recommenced their wars with Austria, and were not unsuccessful in them.

But if the results of the great Tartar raids on Poland and Hungary were almost negligible, with Russia things were far different. For though the invaders left Poland and Hungary for good in 1242, they by no means evacuated Russia. After revisiting his Mongolian home, Batu returned with his horde to the Volga, and set up his palace-tent at Sarai, which soon became a permanent city and the capital of the realm of the

"Golden Horde." In 1260, at the death of the fourth Mongol emperor, Mangu Khan, the princes of the "Golden Horde" declared their independence, and were strong enough to hold down the Russians for two centuries.

In the end the Tartar yoke had one effect for good on the Russians—it taught them to avoid civil strife and seek unity. But unity was only bought by two centuries of servitude. The old Russians had been turbulent, factious, and jealous, but they possessed the feudal virtues, they had their notions of loyalty, even of chivalry : they were reckless in resenting an insult or redeeming a pledged promise. Such mentality disappeared under the exacting Tartar yoke. The princes learnt the precepts of Oriental despotism, and were enabled to practise them because of the abject fear which their subjects felt for the Great Khan. They knew that to assault or expel a sovereign whom the Tartars recognised meant an irruption of the barbarians of the steppe. The whole people contracted, as a consequence of those two centuries of slavery, a blind reverence for authority, which could not be shaken off even when Ivan the Great destroyed the Tartar supremacy in the late fifteenth century.

CHAPTER II

SOUTH-EASTERN EUROPE AND THE OTTOMAN TURKS

WE have already pointed out that the middle years of the thirteenth century, when the Mongol tempest beat upon the Eastern flank alike of the Moslem and the Christian world, were an age of decaying dynasties and of kingdoms that were falling to pieces. This was as true in Western Asia as in Germany, Scandinavia, Russia, Poland, or the Balkan peninsula. And, as we have seen, the successes of the heirs of Genghiz Khan were in no small degree due to the fact that they had to face no first-rate fighting power — with the possible exception of the Mameluke Sultanate in Syria and Egypt, the one state which turned them back with no great difficulty.

Among the decadent realms over which the Mongols swept with ease was the old Seljuk sultanate of Roum, the Turkish holding on the plateau of Asia Minor, which had survived the attack of the Crusaders, but had never recovered its original vigour. When the wave of Tartar conquest retired eastward, the kingdom of Roum was never reconstituted. The last descendants of its royal house only survived as emirs of the trifling state of Sinope on the Black Sea; the rest of Asia Minor broke up into many small principalities. Some of these were formed by tribal chiefs, some by military adventurers; their boundaries were shifting, and they were continually devouring each other. Yet their rulers showed much more energy than had the last sultans of the decadent house of Roum, and they burst into those Byzantine provinces of the Western coastland, which had been retained for Christendom even after the break-up of the Byzantine empire in the Crusade of 1204. Among the least important of the new dynasts was Othman, the son of Ertogrul, who had his dwelling in one of the mountain-valleys which overlooked the Byzantine province of Bithynia. His father had been a petty Turkish chief, the head of four hundred horsemen, one of the countless fractions of vanquished tribes which fled westward before the Tartars of Genghis and Oktai. Wandering into Asia Minor, he served Alaeddin, one of the last sultans of Roum, and was given as a reward a small holding round the village of Soegud on the Kara-Su river, an upland tributary of the Sangarius. He thus became something between a warden of the marches against the Greeks and a tribal chief. Ertogrul died in obscurity ; but he outlived the sultanate of Roum, which seems to have become practically defunct about 1283, and so was one of its numerous heirs—perhaps the most insignificant of them. He died in 1289, if the Turkish chroniclers are right, and was succeeded by his son Othman, who made his small border fief into a state of some little note by his conquests from his Byzantine neighbours in the plain below. The majority of the other emirs, who became independent by the disappearance of the sultanate of Roum, owned lands in the inland, and had no power of expansion save by fighting with each other. But Othman, and three or four of his neighbours to the south, bordered on the decaying empire of the Palæologi, and could increase their strength by encroaching on the Greek. Thus they had the same advantage in Asia Minor that Wessex or Mercia had in Anglo-Saxon England, as compared with Kent or East Anglia—the chance to grow great at the expense of the alien enemy. The whole of Othman's reign of thirty-seven years (1289–1326) was spent in tearing away scrap by scrap from the two wretched emperors, Andronicus II. and Andronicus III., their last Asiatic province, the fertile coastland of Bithynia. Before he died he was master of Broussa, its central city, and the emperor kept nothing save the two famous old towns of Nicomedia and Nicæa. At the same time other emirs, Karasi, Aidin, Saru Khan, and Menteshe, mastered the other coast regions which the Greeks had retained down to 1300, and became rulers respectively of Mysia, Lydia, Ionia, and Caria. The old Turkish inland was divided among many other princes, of whom the emirs of Karaman, who held the ancient Seljuk capital of Iconium, were by far the most powerful.

Under its first independent ruler, the Osmanli state differed in no way from the other emirates, and was distinctly one of the less important of the group. Its prince was but the head of a band of predatory light horse, like any of his Seljuk neighbours. Two things in the main were to be the original causes of the greatness of his house : the first was that it produced a succession of seven generations of able men in direct male descent, a piece of luck that has happened to few families. The second and more important was that it was the one of all the new states of Asia Minor which lay directly opposite Constantinople, with illimitable opportunities of interfering in the detestable politics of the decadent house of the Palæologi. If Othman's little emirate had been in Caria instead of Bithynia, or if any of his three immediate successors had been weaklings, there would never have been an Ottoman Empire.

Othman's one conquest of importance was the town of Broussa, which fell into his hands, apparently after a siege of extraordinary length, only a few months before his death (1326). It seems to have been taken not by storm but by the slow attrition of hunger ; the Turks built two castles opposite to it, barring its approaches by sea and land, and after a blockade, lasting actually for years, the garrison, unsuccoured from Constantinople, finally evacuated the place. It is said that the last governor, Evrenos, became a Moslem in sheer disgust at the way in which he had been abandoned by his imperial master, Andronicus III.

But it was Orkhan, the son of Othman (1326–61), who really made the Ottoman state. He was not a very great territorial conqueror, though in his reign of thirty-five years he more than doubled his father's heritage. He completed, it is true, the conquest of Bithynia by taking the great cities of Nicæa and Nicomedia. And he overran and annexed the neighbouring Turkish state of Karasi, in Mysia, by intervening craftily in the brotherly quarrels of its two sovereigns. Even so, his kingdom remained but a small one. Yet he was a ruler on a very different scale from Othman, who had started his career as the chief of a community of only four hundred lances. A curious note concerning his position occurs in the cosmography of the Damascene geographer, Shehabeddin, an absolute contemporary; he died in 1349. " Orkhan has under his rule fifty cities and a still larger number of castles. He has an army of forty thousand horse and a large force of foot. But

his troops are not particularly effective, nor so formidable as
their numbers would seem to indicate.   He has been peaceful
with his [Mohammedan] neighbours, and has always helped
his allies.   However, he has been engaged in continual wars
. . . he often has twenty-five thousand horsemen in the field
fighting daily with the lord of Constantinople.   The Greek
emperor is eager to buy his goodwill by paying him tribute.
. . . If he has not gained much from his struggles, it is because
his soldiers do not serve him well, and his subjects are ill-
disposed towards him.   I am told that the Osmanlis are a
treacherous crew, whose hearts are full of hatred, and their
heads of base thoughts." [1]

Putting aside Shehabeddin's obvious prejudice against the
Ottomans, and their military efficiency, whose absurdity was
to be shown by the events of the next few years, we have yet
to note that Orkhan is a powerful prince with a large army.
How had the four hundred followers of Othman grown in
fifty years to forty thousand warriors ?   And how came it
that within another fifty years after Shehabeddin's death the
Turkish horse-tail banners were waving on the Danube and
along the Adriatic ?

The answer to these questions would seem to be that
Orkhan, and perhaps also Othman before him, were great
organisers ; and that they built up a military state on newly
won lands in a far more effective fashion than most conquerors
in a similar position, e.g. than the Crusaders in Palestine.
William the Norman was as successful in England—but he
had not, like Orkhan in Bithynia, or the Baldwins in Palestine,
to deal with a subject population alien both in race and in
religion.   It is clear that Othman's four hundred horsemen
cannot have been the actual progenitors of more than a fraction
of Orkhan's forty thousand.   Whence came the rest ?   Some,
no doubt, from the Turks of Karasi, taken over when that
state was annexed ; others, no doubt, from Greek renegades,
of whom we have a few definite instances.   But the great
majority must have been produced by Orkhan's plan for plotting
out conquered Bithynia among military adventurers, lured in
by the gift of land on a sort of feudal system.

[1] Shehabeddin, pp. 129-140, quoted in Gibbons' *Foundation of the Ottoman
Empire*, p. 70. As the author died before Orkhan's European conquests in his last
regnal years, he did not know of the triumphs that were to come.

The peculiar and ingenious variety of feudalism on which the new Ottoman state was based, avoided most of the dangers that were to be seen in the West. When land was conquered it was cut up into holdings, which we may well compare with the old English " knight's fee." The unit was called a " Timar," and was supposed to be of the value of three thousand aspers, nearly £20, for the asper was a very small silver coin, roughly worth about three-halfpence. The holder was called a timariot, and held his fee by the tenure of providing a fully equipped horseman whenever the Sultan called for him. There was none of the Western folly of stipulating for forty days' service only. A timariot might, for good service, be given several fees, and then had to find a new horseman for each of them. If he received more than six such fiefs, he was called a Ziam, and his holding a Ziamet. It much resembled a small barony in France or England.

So far we seem to be dealing with a system much like that of the Christian West. But there was a cardinal difference between Turkish and Frankish feudalism. The Timar-fief was in the good early days of the Ottoman state *non-hereditary*. When the vassal died, his lands returned to the Sultan, and did not go to his sons. And for several generations the strong sultans made it a rule not to give any son his father's identical fief, but to reward him with a grant in some other corner of the empire. This was undoubtedly done of deliberate intention, to avert the great dangers of feudalism in all lands—local particularism and the domination in every valley of some long-established baronial house. The habitual polygamy of the Turk made the Timariot caste multiply very rapidly ; every fief-holder might have half a dozen sons, who at their father's death would like to get land held on military tenure. It could only be obtained by further conquests, since the Timar was a small estate, only capable of supporting one family. Hence there was always a large body of these young men of the military class wanting new soil to be cut up for them. The Sultan could soon count on the service of many thousands of them, all eager for the fiefs that could only be secured by a successful war. The system could only prosper so long as new Christian lands were continually being occupied and parcelled out.

The timariots were the military colonists who flocked into

each newly-subdued region, and held it down by their settlement. It was their existence which mainly explains that rapid
growth of Turkish population in newly-won lands, which
was one of the great features of the fourteenth and fifteenth
centuries. The class was recruited not only from native Turks,
but from all Mohammedan Asia. The Sultan always welcomed
any adventurer from the East who brought a good horse and a
strong lance, and gladly served out a small fief to him. Hence
the whole Moslem world was a recruiting ground for the only
state of that religion which was at this moment a rapidly
growing power. Decay only came when conquests ceased,
and when no new land was available to endow adventurers.
The feudal danger of local particularism appeared in full force
when, because no new conquests were being made, the hereditary owning of land by son after father began to be allowed by
weak sultans.

In the inland of Asia Minor the Timariot system could never
be applied with the same rigour as in European conquests. The
reason was that (after the first acquisition of Bithynia by Orkhan)
the lands won were not taken from Christians, who were liable
to complete expropriation, but from other Moslems—Seljuks
of the minor emirates in the fourteenth and fifteenth centuries,
and afterwards Syrians, Mamelukes, and Arabs, who, being co-
religionists, could not be dealt with in the same drastic fashion.
In subdued districts which submitted without much trouble,
the old Mohammedan landowners could not be evicted relent-
lessly, as Greek or Serbian or Bulgarian nobles habitually were.
For this reason feudal particularism and local baronial influence
remained a real danger to the sultans, especially in Asia Minor,
where the Seljuk " dere beys," or lords of the valleys, remained
an appreciable force, and often gave trouble. In Europe this
trouble did not exist, or at least only existed in one province,
Bosnia, where (in the late fifteenth century) a great faction of
the local nobility apostatised to save their lands, and were
granted leave to continue holding them on their old tenure.
For this reason Bosnia, since it was the one European province
where a local aristocracy was perpetuated, was decidedly the
most unruly region of the empire.

No Oriental sovereign of the more intelligent type depended
on feudal levies alone ; he tried to keep up a personal bodyguard of paid troops as a counterpoise to the landholding class.

Orkhan was wealthy enough to start the corps of Spahis,[1] the mailed horse who rode around his person, and grew to a formidable strength under his successors. They were partly veteran adventurers, partly the sons of late timariots, who were wanting to earn a fief by zealous personal service under the eye of their master.

In addition, Orkhan is credited with the institution of a small body of infantry of the guard, raised in the strangest of fashions, the famous Janissaries,[2] or tribute-children. Recent research seems to discredit the received opinion that they were already a force of importance by 1350, and that as trained foot-soldiery they were intervening with effect in the European wars of Orkhan's immediate successors. The first definite contemporary mention of them only occurs after Orkhan's death, yet Turkish historical tradition is positive in attributing their origin to him. It would appear that in the later fourteenth century they were still nothing but a small corps of personal slave-guards, closely attached to the sovereign's person, and not more than one thousand strong. When we get definite accounts of them in Western authors, we find them still a comparatively small, if a growing, body. Bertrandon de la Broquière, who visited the court of Murad II. in 1433, speaks of them in one place as about three thousand, but in another says that these " Jehannicères," who are the only infantry of any value in the Sultan's army, may be as many as ten thousand.[3] Under Mahomet II. the force seems to be no larger, as Chalkokondulas calls them six thousand to ten thousand in all,[4] and it was not till the time of Soliman the Magnificent that they are spoken of as being twelve thousand strong in the commencement of that long reign, but many more by its end. In the period with which we are now dealing they were a staunch body of fighters, but too few to have a commanding influence in war.[5]

[1] Spahi=Sipahi, and is the same word as the Indian ' Sepoy,' soldier.
[2] Derived, of course, from *yeni-askari*, ' new soldiery,' not any of the fantastic combinations of words given by early European writers.
[3] Broquière, pp. 185 and 268.
[4] Chalkokondulas, v. p. 122.
[5] See, for this compilation of fifteenth-century opinions on the Janissaries, the interesting pages 116–121 in Gibbons' *Foundation of the Ottoman Empire*. But he has missed Francesco Philelfo's letter to the Doge of Venice in 1464, mentioning that Mahomet II. had now twelve thousand of them.

Some short account of them should be given. On all Christian village communities there was imposed the conscription of such boys between the ages of seven and ten as the Sultan's slave-drivers chose to take. Converts to Islam were exempt, and this was a secondary purpose in the institution, since it is clear that, of the Christians who fell away from their faith in the fourteenth and fifteenth centuries, many were influenced by a desire to save their sons from the levy. The young slaves were collected in barracks, where they were brought up under a strict military and conventual discipline. They were the Sultan's private property, and had no rights save what he chose to grant them. They were ruled with an iron hand, and freely flogged or strangled for disobedience. After ten years of this severe training, they were drafted into the Janissary corps. As long as the sultans were strong, the slave-guard were obedient ; in the first two centuries of their existence they gave their masters the immense advantage of a trustworthy military household, unaffected by Turkish family connections or tribal intrigues. It was only when the descendants of Othman became despicable, that the Janissaries became king-makers, like the Prætorians of Ancient Rome. They were all archers, and, thanks to lifelong practice from boyhood, the most efficient wielders of the bow that Eastern Europe knew.

So thorough was the physical and mental discipline to which they were subjected, that it was the rarest of things for one of them to turn back and fly to his father's people, when he got the chance. The great Albanian hero, Scanderbeg, is almost the only quotable instance. To keep the Janissary firm to his allegiance to his master, there was not only the stress of the long discipline to which he had been subjected, but the prospect of the highest rewards. The early sultans made it almost a rule to select their officers, their provincial governors, even their viziers from the ranks of the tribute-children. It has been calculated that two-thirds of the Ottoman grand viziers of the fourteenth, fifteenth, and sixteenth centuries had originally been Christian slaves. The moment that a Janissary was promoted out of the corps, he had no longer to live the celibate semi-monastic life of the barracks, but became one of the favoured few, and enjoyed all the licence that the Mohammedan law allowed. The ambition to become one of the magnates

of the Ottoman state helped to keep the Janissary faithful to
the master who could give him a pashalik, or send him to be
strangled, with equal facility.   The early Janissaries, all picked
men, were something as much like a staff college for the Ottoman army, as a mere archerg uard.   Their brains were quite
as valuable to their master as their bows.

When he had already been reigning for nearly twenty years,
and had got his much enlarged state in good order, Orkhan
was enabled to extend his ambitions to Europe, not so much
of his own intention, but because he was deliberately invited to
intervene in the family quarrels of the Imperial house at Constantinople.   In 1345 the regent John Cantacuzenus, one of the
great mischief-makers of history, was endeavouring to seize
the crown by making himself the colleague, instead of the
mere guardian, of the boy-emperor John VI.   Finding himself
losing ground, he bought the succour of six thousand Ottoman
horse, by sending to Broussa not only a large subsidy, but his
daughter, Theodora, whom Orkhan demanded for his harem.
With the aid of the Turks, Cantacuzenus won his object, and
wore the Imperial crown for eight troubled years.   He was
profoundly unpopular—as he deserved to be—and only maintained himself by hiring Ottoman mercenaries again and again,
generally to hold back the Serbians, who under their great
Emperor, Stephen Dushan, were rapidly making an end of the
Byzantine holding in Macedonïa, Thrace, and Thessaly.   In 1349
as many as twenty thousand of Orkhan's horse were serving in
the Salonica region.   It was in this way that the Turkish riders
got to know the roads of the Balkan peninsula, and to realise
the military bankruptcy of the Greek empire.   They pervaded
all Thrace as the trusted hirelings of the usurping emperor.

In 1353 Soliman, the eldest son of Orkhan, was leading
the mercenaries of Cantacuzenus.   An earthquake chanced to
throw down part of the walls of the city of Gallipoli, the key
of the Thracian Chersonesus, which lies above the since
famous lines of Bulair.   Soliman occupied the place, repaired
the breaches, and refused to move on, when his employer re-
quested him to evacuate this important strategic fortress.
Nor would his father order him to do so, when the emperor
complained of his conduct.

This meant war, and the Turks concentrated at Gallipoli,
and seized the whole peninsula below it.   A popular rising in

Constantinople overthrew Cantacuzenus (1354), but the legitimate emperor, John VI., could not induce the Ottomans to retire.
He could not thrust them out by force, being involved at the
time in a disastrous Serbian war, so he accepted the situation,
and made a peace with Orkhan in 1359, which left the Turks
with a solid *pied à terre* in Europe.

The exploitation of this strategical advantage fell neither
to Orkhan, who was too old to profit by it, nor to his eldest
son, Soliman, who had seized Gallipoli,—he died there by a fall
from his horse only two months before his father expired (1361),
—but to Murad, Soliman's next brother, quite a young man,
but destined to prove the greatest general that the Levant had
seen for many a year. With the resources of his small state in
Asia Minor—only consisting of Bithynia and Mysia—and the
aid of such adventurers as came to his banner from farther
East, Murad conquered two-thirds of the Balkan peninsula,
and destroyed the independence of the Greek empire and the
kingdoms of Serbia and Bulgaria. For though all three survived
him, all had done him homage before his death. The external
circumstances were, of course, exceptionally favourable : the
Byzantine empire was caught in a state of exhaustion from
recent civil war, and engaged in a struggle with Serbia. One
single campaign in 1361 swept away all its continental dominions
up to the very gates of Constantinople. But Serbia might well
have proved a barrier for Christendom against the Turkish
advance ; only six years before it had been an active and
militant power under the great Stephen Dushan, the conqueror
of Macedonia, Thessaly, and Western Thrace, who had also
made the princes of Bosnia, Albania, and Bulgaria his vassals.

Unfortunately Dushan died (1355) just as he was marching
to expel the first Turkish adventurers from the newly-seized
Gallipoli. This was a disaster for all Europe, for such a king
could have turned back the modest invading host with which
Murad started on his career in 1361. On his death, leaving
as his heir his only son, Urosh, a mere boy, his empire, which
had taken a quarter of a century to build up, vanished in a
year. For all his vassals disowned their allegiance, and his
kinsmen and generals, whom he had made governors in
Macedonia and Thessaly, set themselves up as independent
princes. The guardians of Urosh only succeeded in retaining
for him a precarious sovereignty over the old Serbian kingdom

north of the Balkans.   And at this very moment that ambitious
prince Lewis the Great, king of Hungary, delivered a stab
in the back against the Christian kingdoms south of the Danube.
For he invaded Serbia and captured Belgrade from King Urosh
in 1365, and fell upon Bulgaria in 1366, conquered its western
half, and declared it a Hungarian " banate."   If Lewis had
taken up the union of the whole Balkan peninsula as his main
life-work, he might have become the great opponent of the
Turks.   But he appeared as a Crusader and persecutor ; he
bitterly oppressed the Serbs and Bulgarians, in order to force
upon them submission to the Papacy, and, when he had
done all the harm he could, got himself involved in wars in
Poland and Italy, which completely distracted his attention
for the rest of his life.   To Lewis's disastrous irruptions south
of the Danube, Sultan Murad was indebted more than is
generally understood :   Hungary smote and shattered the
Christian powers of the Balkans from the rear, just as the
Turk began to attack them from the front.   The King of
Eastern Bulgaria actually did homage to the Sultan in order
to save the rest of his dominions from the Hungarian.
The usurping Serbian princes in the south fell unaided
before the Ottoman sword, because their kinsmen north
of the Balkans were being harried by perpetual Hungarian
invasions.

This distraction it was which accounted for the comparatively easy way in which Murad conquered Bulgaria and Macedonia, despite of the very moderate force which he could put
into the field in his first campaigns.   But if the Ottoman state
had been as its predecessors in the East, its effort might have
had no permanent result.   It was the astonishing success of
Murad's system of settling every conquered region with
Timariot fief-holders that made the conquest permanent.
By the end of his reign his army at the battle of Kossovo (1389)
had one of its two wings entirely composed of Timariots holding
European land-grants.

The Ottoman army as it stood in the later fourteenth
century had its main bulk composed of this feudal cavalry.
But there was a solid body of regular paid troopers of the
Guard—the Spahis—and a small unit of regular infantry in the
Janissary corps.   In addition there were irregular auxiliaries—
the light infantry, mainly armed with the bow, who served for

plunder (*azabs*),[1] and light cavalry of a similar volunteer sort (*Akindji*), who were neither Spahis nor Timariots, but hoped some day to be admitted among the one or the other.   A successful Oriental prince always gathered about him military hangers-on of this kind, not very efficient for a general action, but formidable plunderers, and sometimes useful scouts, for they pervaded the whole country through which the army moved. It would seem that the Ottoman cavalry were not so universally horse-archers as the Seljuks or Mongols had been.   The Spahis seem to have been mailed lancers, and the Timariots also appear, at least in part, to have carried the horseman's spear ; and if we often hear of their arrows we also find them in close combat, fighting with hand-to-hand weapons, such as the mace and sabre.   Probably an army consisting of mounted archers alone would never have won such successes as the troops of Murad, his son Bajazet, and his great-grandson Murad II. actually achieved.   For Tartar tactics might indeed have prevailed against the Serbs and Bulgarians, whose armies consisted, like those of the old Russians at the Kalka, of a comparatively small body of mailed horsemen—the followings of the king and the princes—and of masses of tribal infantry. But they would have been far less effective against the Hungarians, mainly a race of horse-bowmen, who had only failed before the Mongols on the Sajo for want of numbers and of generalship.   If the Turks had all been horse-archers, the combination of bow and lance among the Magyars would probably have checked them for ever ; for the Ottomans had at first none of that numerical preponderance which the Mongols had enjoyed.

At Kossovo, on St. Vitus's Day, 1389, Murad lost his own life, but discomfited the last rally of the Serbians under their unlucky prince Lazarus and his Bosnian and Albanian allies. From that moment the defence of Europe was thrown upon the Hungarian kingdom, which, for the next hundred and thirty-five years, was destined, with many alternations of success and

---

[1] "Their European ('Greek') foot," writes Bertrandon de la Broquière, "are miserably equipped, some having swords but no bow, others without either sword or bow, many having only staves ('bastons').   It is the same with all this Turkish infantry, one-half of them have only staves : the Asiatic foot is better esteemed than the European ('Greek'), the men being considered better soldiers " (p. 185). "The Sultan has also three thousand slaves of his own, whom he arms well [the Janissaries], among whom are many that were Christians" (*ibid.*).

disaster, to hold the line of the Danube against the Ottoman— till the crash at Mohacs in 1526. The ambitions of Murad's son Bajazet were, unlike those of his father, more Asiatic than European : and though he won much land in the Balkan Peninsula, he won much more from the Seljuk emirs of Asia Minor, most of whom he evicted from their petty principalities.

He was actually absent on an Asiatic campaign when he was called back over the straits by a Hungarian invasion of Bulgaria. This was not so much a Crusade, though it assumed that title, and thereby drew much help from the farther West, as a renewal of the ambitious Balkan schemes of Lewis the Great by his son-in-law and successor, Sigismund of Luxemburg. Before he gained the imperial crown and turned to drafting reforms for the Papacy, this busy, flighty prince, still king of Hungary alone, had taken up his predecessor's schemes for conquest beyond the Danube. In 1392 he had executed a transient and unsuccessful attack on Bulgaria, which only led to the complete annexation of that realm by the Turks in the next year, with the threat of a retaliatory invasion of Hungary to follow. Sigismund cried for aid to the princes of the West— so did Manuel of Constantinople, whose imperial city was being blockaded by Bajazet's troops—and the prophet Philip of Mezières had been for some years working in France and the Netherlands preaching the old crusading propaganda.

Hence came (1396) the unlucky second invasion of Bulgaria and the disaster of Nicopolis—which first introduced the military efficiency of the Ottomans to the notice of Latin Christendom. For the woes of Serbs and other schismatics had not moved the heart of the West more than the woes of Russia had done before the battles of Liegnitz and the Sajo in the preceding century. To Sigismund's aid there had come in many Crusaders from the French-speaking lands, not a few from Germany, and some from Italy and Poland ; even stray English knights joined the muster. The best known leaders were Jean Sans Peur, the son and heir of Philip of Burgundy and Flanders, and two other French princes, Philip of Artois the Constable, and James of Bourbon, also the Admiral Jean de Vienne, and Boucicault the Marshal ; among the Germans were John of Hohenzollern, Burgrave of Nuremberg, and Rupert the Elector Palatine. The numbers of the Crusaders were reckoned at six thousand lances, while Sigismund brought

up the whole national levy of Hungary, and his vassals the
Wallachians, so that the chroniclers who speak of his army as
fifty thousand or sixty thousand strong may not have been
exaggerating to quite such an extent as was usual. Hungary
was a most warlike state, with an immense cavalry-levy; and
with his vassals and allies Sigismund may well have counted
some thirty thousand horse. Of infantry we hear practically
nothing; [1] the Magyars were horsemen, and the Crusaders
were essentially a body of chivalrous adventurers, not a force
of all arms.

Sigismund crossed the Danube, captured Widdin and
Rahova,[2] where he massacred the Turkish garrison, and then
advanced to Nicopolis, the largest city of central Bulgaria.
He had lain fifteen days before it, and was busy both with
bombardment and with a great scheme of mining,[3] when the
near approach of the Sultan was announced to him. Bajazet
had taken some time to call in his Asiatic troops and get them
across the Straits, and had forbidden any partial adventure by
his European contingents till all should be assembled. When
his whole force had been mobilised at Adrianople, he crossed
the Balkans at the Schipka Pass by forced marches, and was
within a long day's march of Nicopolis before the scouts of
Sigismund learnt of his approach.

Bajazet chose to be attacked in position, not to fall on the
Christian camp. He knew the district well, having once besieged Nicopolis himself, and chose his ground on a front of
rolling hillside some four miles south of the city, on both sides
of the Tirnova road, by which he had arrived. The selection
was made in order to utilise ravines on the flank, in which outflanking forces were concealed, and also to allow the Sultan's
third line, or reserve, to be concealed behind the skyline of the
slope on which the army was drawn out. As far as it is possible
to make out a comprehensible plan of Bajazet's array from rather
contradictory sources, he had a screen of his irregular horse in
front, veiling a thick line of stakes, behind which were ranged
his numerous but irregular foot-archery:[4] in the rear of

---

[1] The only mention of them that I find is that Schiltberger (p. 2) states that
when Widdin was captured, Sigismund put into it a good garrison both of horse
and foot.

[2] Not Orsova, as Mr. Gibbons will have it (p. 215).

[3] Boucicault, p. 99.   [4] Not of Janissaries, who were still but few.

these again were solid lines of the feudatory horse. The Spahis of the royal guard and the Sultan himself were out of sight, rather to one flank; and there was apparently another concealed force, consisting of the contingent of the Prince of Serbia, Stephen Lazarevitch, who was serving the conqueror, who had allowed him to retain his father's realm as a vassal. The Serbs hated the Hungarians—naturally enough, considering their provocation—but it was a bitter shame for them to be acting as the tools of the enemy of Christendom. It was Bajazet's plan to sacrifice his irregulars in the forefront of the battle, so as to blunt and disorder the enemy's attack. The feudal horse would then offer him serious resistance, while the reserve would fall upon him from the flank and decide the day. And this, in the main, was the course of the action.

The army of Sigismund was not surprised in its tents, as some Western chroniclers relate. It may have had battle forced upon it earlier than the king expected; but since the Turks had halted four miles away, and did not press in, there was time for some discussion between Sigismund and his allies, and for the whole army to deploy in order. Unfortunately, the discussion was of the most exasperating kind. Sigismund proposed to attack the Turks with swarms of horse-bowmen like their own, and to feel their position, while the heavy squadrons of the Crusaders and of the Hungarian baronage should follow in support. John Mirtcha, the prince of Wallachia, who had been in command of the outlying scouting parties, and had reported the enemy's situation, volunteered to open the attack.[1] This fell in with the king's ideas, and he communicated his intention to the Burgundian and French Crusaders, asking them to take the rearward battle, which would give the decisive blow. In idiotic pride and ignorance the Crusaders refused to listen to the proposal; Jean Sans Peur is said to have objected that he had not come a thousand miles, and spent countless treasure on the expedition, merely to be put into the rearguard. Philip of Artois exclaimed, " The king wants to rob us of the honour of striking the first blow," and cried to the banner-bearer to move on at once without delay. The majority were with him, though the old Sieur de Coucy urged prudence, and a careful reconnaissance of the enemy's

[1] Schiltberger, p. 2. He calls this prince "the Duke of Wallachei, who was called Merter Voivode."

position before any move was made. And so the French corps
moved forward from in front of its camp, deliberately leaving
behind on its flank the king's main army, which was visible,
getting into good array, a mile outside Nicopolis, on the edge of
the plateau which lies above the low-lying town. It is difficult
to say whether the scandalous indiscipline or the tactical ignorance of the French magnates seems the more exasperating
to the commentator.[1]

Leaving the Hungarians and the rest of the army to do
what they might choose, the French knights rode at a slow trot
up the slopes to strike at the Turkish centre, where the front
of irregular horse seemed to be offering them battle. But when
they came within bowshot, the enemy's light cavalry let fly
one or two volleys of arrows, and then sheered off to right and
left, revealing the deep line of stakes and the foot-archers
behind it, deployed in two long "battles" which outflanked
the French corps on each side. The moment that their front
was clear, they opened on the knights with a very effective
salvo, "hail nor rain does not come down in closer shower
than did their shafts."[2] Many riders and more horses went
down at the first volley.

This was the critical moment of the battle, for all depended
on whether the French would charge in before the rest of the
allied army had come upon the field, or whether they would
wait for support, even at the cost of drawing back for the
moment. As Bajazet, so we may suppose, had calculated,
there was no real doubt as to what a body of Western knights,
untrained in Oriental warfare, would do.[3] They charged in
straight upon the stakes, of which there were row on row for
a depth of sixteen feet, all pointed towards the horses' breasts

[1] All that the author of Boucicault's biography finds to say in defence of his
patron's colleagues is that it is not true that they made a *disorderly* advance : on
the contrary, they were well formed up (pp. 101-2). He slurs over the disobedience
as best he can.

[2] Boucicault, p. 103.

[3] General Köhler makes the French dismount at this crisis, pointing out that this
was quite the custom in the West since Poictiers. But the two best authorities,
Schiltberger and Boucicault's biographer, most distinctly state that they did not,
and speak much of the havoc among the horses. It is useless to quote against
them the *Religieux de St. Denis*, who says that the knights dismounted and cut
off the long fashionable points of their steel shoes, or Thwrocz, even though the
latter says that he had spoken with survivors of the fight. I note that Dr. Delbrück,
like myself, disagrees with General Köhler, and keeps the knights mounted.

and acutely sharpened.   Great numbers of the French chargers were spiked, and more shot down by the arrows of the archers, while they were pushing through this mediæval equivalent for modern barbed wire.   Many knights also were disabled, but the mass of them broke through the hindrance, though in great disorder, and got among the archers, many of whom they cut up.   While thus occupied they were charged by the Turkish feudal cavalry, and engaged in a desperate mêlée with them, fighting hand to hand with lance and sword against lance, mace, and scimitar.   They ended by driving back the enemy, but at great loss, and only by a final effort in which they completely exhausted themselves.   Before their ragged line could re-form, they were attacked, somewhat in flank, by the Sultan's mailed Spahis, who came unexpectedly over the skyline in good order, and absolutely rode them down.   The disaster was complete; many of the French fought to the last, and died, among them Philip, Count of Bar, and the most distinguished veteran in the army, the Admiral Jean de Vienne.   But the majority were beaten off their wounded or failing horses, and taken prisoners.   Only a remnant got away.

King Sigismund and the Christian main-battle had no part in this fight, which must have taken but a short time, for a cavalry charge and mêlée is a thing quickly over in all battles. The French chroniclers accuse the Hungarians of deliberately betraying them, and taunt them with flagrant cowardice.[1] That this is unfair would seem to be proved by the fact that the king's corps, the Hungarians and the non-French Crusaders, fought a second engagement of its own on ground nearer the town.   It is possible that Sigismund, righteously indignant at the disobedience of his allies, and washing his hands of the consequences, may have resolved to fight his own battle, and have refrained from hurrying overmuch.   While he was on the march, we are told, a stampede of wounded or riderless horses swept by him, showing that disaster had occurred ahead.[2] But he pushed on and cut up a force of Turkish infantry— apparently the archers, re-formed since the French charge.

[1] There are several angry paragraphs in the biographer of Boucicault, who says that none of the main body fought except the Palatine of Hungary, and the German, Italian, and English strangers.   He disguises the fact that there was any second action, and slurs over the end of the battle in mere abuse of the treachery, felony, jealousy, and cowardice of Hungarians (pp. 104–112).

[2] This detail is from Thwrocz, the Hungarian chronicler.

After this he became engaged with a mass of horsemen—
presumably the Sultan's feudal cavalry—but while contending
with it was suddenly charged in flank by a large body of mailed
men-at-arms, the Serbian contingent under Stephen Lazarevitch, which had been detached by Bajazet and emerged from
an ambush.[1] Sigismund's banner fell, whereupon the Hungarians broke—the Voivode Mirtcha's Wallachians the first—
and raced back for their camp. No defence was made there,
but every one tried to get on board the flotilla of galleys and
provision barges which had attended the army down the Danube.
Sigismund was thrust on board a galley by the Count of Cilly
and the Burgrave of Nuremberg, and made an extraordinary
voyage downstream to the Euxine and Constantinople. Many
others of all ranks put across to the Wallachian bank in the
barges, and fled overland to Transylvania, among them the
Elector Palatine and the Voivode John Mirtcha. But the
majority of the Hungarians were slain, drowned in the river,
or taken prisoners.

Next morning Bajazet, irritated at the very heavy losses
of his army, and still more by the massacres of Turkish prisoners
at Rahova and elsewhere, ordered all his captives to be slain,
reserving only John of Burgundy and about a dozen other
persons of very high rank for ransom.[2] Of the rest, many
thousands were beheaded in the presence of the captive princes,
who were forced to look on. Not till after ten thousand had been
put to death did Bajazet order the slaughter to cease, and
present the survivors—still very numerous—as slaves to his
army.

The prospect for Hungary would have been gloomy, had
not Bajazet preferred Asiatic to European conquests. But
while intermittently blockading Constantinople, and carrying
his arms as far as Athens and the Peloponnese, he was really

---

[1] All this is from Schiltberger's excellent account of the second battle. He says
that his master, Sir Leinhart Richartinger, was dismounted in the mêlée, wherefore
he brought him up his second charger, and rode to the rear again on a Turkish horse
which he had caught. Schiltberger says that the enemy was actually about to fly
when the Serbian charge caught Sigismund in the flank—after which chaos and
panic supervened.

[2] Including Philip of Artois, James of Bourbon, Henry of Bar, the Marshal
Boucicault, with John Strasimir of Widdin, a Bulgarian prince, and Stephen Simon-
tornya of Transylvania. These two last General Köhler makes into Germans, not
recognising that Schiltberger's "Hans of Bodem" means John of Widdin, and that
'Stephen of Sÿnoher' was a Hungarian magnate (*Kriegswesen*, ii. p. 654).

more concerned with keeping down the Seljuk emirates of Asia Minor, of which he had gradually made himself master. It was his Eastern aggressions which ultimately brought him into collision with a greater man than himself—Timur the Tartar, the spiritual heir of Genghiz Khan, a consummate general and a bloodthirsty tyrant, whose atrocities in the way of ingenious torture far exceeded anything that Bajazet ever managed in the line of massacre.[1] Having provoked Timur by sheltering his fugitive enemies, and encroaching on his sphere of action on the Armenian side, Bajazet found his dominions invaded by an army of overwhelming strength in 1402. The battle of Angora was a Tartar action on the largest scale, each side trying to act with the horns of horse-bowmen, and wide-flung manœuvres of innumerable squadrons. Bajazet would probably have lost the game in any case from lack of numbers, but the completeness of his defeat was due to disloyalty in his own army. His covering force, thrown out in front of his main line, consisted of fugitive Turkomans from the East, who had escaped from Timur ; the greater part of the cavalry of his left wing was formed of the Seljuk horse of the newly-annexed emirates of Asia Minor. At the first clash the Turkomans went over *en masse* to the enemy, who had been conducting secret negotiations with their chiefs. Only a little later the Seljuks did the same—five exiled emirs were with Timur, and their old subjects would not fight. The result, of course, was disaster ; though the Ottoman right wing had done well—the Serbian knights of Stephen Lazarevitch particularly distinguished themselves—the left wing had practically disappeared. The Tartars swept round Bajazet's flank and rear ; his victorious right wing got away with some difficulty, but his centre was surrounded and annihilated. He himself made a long stand on a hill, with the wrecks of his Spahis,[2] but was finally beaten down and captured. How he died of a broken spirit in the barred litter to which Timur consigned him is sufficiently well known.

The disaster of Angora ought to have made an end of the Ottoman empire—but did not, owing to the departure of

---

[1] I refer especially to his massacres of children, and his nasty way of burying prisoners of war alive.

[2] Not among his *Janissaries*, as many Western historians have written. Schilt-berger, who was present, particularly notes that the Sultan had a thousand *horsemen* only about him.

Timur to the East, and the blindness of the European powers, who ought to have turned to account the moment of Turkish weakness. The outlying parts of Bajazet's empire fell away —the Seljuk emirates were revived, and Serbia and the South-West of the Balkan Peninsula recovered their independence. There was the best of opportunities for turning the Turk out of Europe altogether—for the sons of Bajazet all proclaimed themselves sultans, and indulged in several years of bitter civil war. But Sigismund of Hungary, after having defended his crown for several years of civil war against his rival, Ladislas of Naples, had become by the deposition of his brother, the Emperor Wenzel, in 1400, so deeply involved in the secular politics of Germany and Bohemia and the religious politics of the Great Schism, that he had no attention to spare for the East. Venice and Genoa, the two naval powers who might easily have cut off Ottoman Europe from Ottoman Asia, refused to combine, and played each their own game. The smaller Christian states were too weak and disunited to do more than win back their own local liberty. So Mahomet the youngest son of Bajazet, who represented the " survival of the fittest," pulled together the fragments of the paternal empire, and Murad II., his heir (1422–51), started once more on that advance against central Christendom, which had been the policy of his namesake and great-grandfather, Murad I.

It was to take another hundred years (1422–1526) before the Ottoman border was advanced beyond the Danube and the Save, though both Murad II. and his son Mahomet II., the conqueror of Constantinople, were generals of first-rate ability. Christendom was blessed in the middle and later years of the fifteenth century with a succession of champions such as she had not before known—John Huniades, the great Hungarian regent (1444–56), and his son, King Matthias Corvinus (1458–90), succeeded in keeping the line of the Danube intact, though they could not prevent Serbia, Bosnia, and the other Trans-Danubian lands from falling again into Turkish servitude. And John Castriot (Scanderbeg), the indomitable Albanian mountaineer, beat off every attack on his upland principality till his death in 1467. It was mainly owing to the personalities of those three great men that the Ottoman power, though guided by sultans of exceptional capacity, was held in check.

The military resources of Hungary, indeed, were exactly

fitted to cope with those of the Ottomans. It was the only European country which possessed a formidable national levy of horse-bowmen, as well as a feudal aristocracy of magnates who had taken to the Western arms and armour. To the Turkish lance and bow they could oppose the Magyar bow and lance. And it was not till far on in the fifteenth century that the Janissaries, originally no more than a bodyguard of the Sultan, became a force large enough to count as a solid infantry corps in war. The Hungarians had no native foot-soldiery of their own, and it is comparatively rarely that we find them hiring German or Bohemian mercenary pikemen, crossbowmen, or hand-gunners.

For this reason the second battle of Kossovo (1448) is one of the most interesting fights from the point of view of the history of tactics. It was not—like Nicopolis or Varna or Mohacs—a wild cavalry attempt to break the Turkish line by a headlong onset. John Huniades, whom long experience had made familiar with the tactics of his enemy, endeavoured to turn against Sultan Murad a scheme of a new sort. To face the Janissaries he drew up in his centre a strong force of German and Bohemian infantry, armed with the hand-guns whose use the Hussites had introduced. The foot on both sides appear to have stockaded themselves. On the wings the chivalry of Hungary were destined to cope with the masses of the Timariot cavalry. In consequence of this arrangement, the two centres faced each other for long hours, neither advancing, but each occupied in thinning the enemy's ranks from behind their stockade, the one with the arrow or crossbow bolt, the other with the bullet. Meanwhile on the wings alternate cavalry charges succeeded each other, till on the second day the Wallachian allies of Huniades gave way before the superior numbers of the Ottomans, and the Christian centre had to draw off and retire. So desperate had the fighting been, that half the Hungarian army and a third of that of Murad are said to have been left upon the field. The tactical meaning of the engagement was plain : good infantry could make a long resistance to the Ottoman arms, even if they could not secure the victory. The lesson, however, was not fully realised, and it was not till the military revolution of the sixteenth century that infantry was destined to take the prominent part in withstanding the Ottoman. The landsknechts and hackbut-men of Charles V. and Ferdinand of Austria proved even more formidable foes to the sultans than the gallant but undisciplined light cavalry [1] of Hungary. This was to a great extent due to the perfection of pike-tactics in the West. The Turks, whose infantry could never be induced to adopt that weapon,[2] relied entirely on their firearms and their sabres, and were checked by the combination of pike and hackbut.

It is noticeable that the Janissaries took to the use of the firelock at a comparatively early date. It may have been in consequence of the effectiveness of Huniades' hand-guns at Kossovo, that we find them discarding the bow and arbalest in favour of the newer weapon. But at any rate the Ottoman had fully accomplished the change long before it had been finally carried out in England, and far over a century earlier than the nations of the farther East, in Persia or India.

In recognising the full importance of cannon the sultans were equally up to date. The capture of Constantinople by Mahomet II. in 1453 was probably the first event of supreme importance whose result was determined by the power of artillery. The lighter guns of previous years had never accomplished any feat comparable in its results to that which was achieved by the siege-train of the Conqueror. For the walls of Constantinople, even in their days of decay under the Palæologi, were still the most formidable system of defences in Europe.[3] Of this Mahomet II. was aware, when he took in hand the reduction of the old fortress, which lay as an anomaly in the midst of his empire: but he was a believer in artillery. Had the story of the exploits of the siege-train of the Bureaus in France, in 1450-51, been brought to him by some wandering Frank? He hired a skilled Hungarian gun-founder, named Urban,[4] who cast him a siege-train of seventy pieces, including one super-bombard, called "Basilica," made of hooped iron, and casting balls of eight hundred pounds weight. It took forty-two days to get this monster from Adrianople to the Bosphorus, and sixty oxen were required to draw it. Eleven other large guns, casting five-hundred-pound stone balls, were

[1] Already, since the middle of the fifteenth century, known as "Hussars."
[2] Montecuculi notes that even in his own day, far into the seventeenth century, the Turk had not taken to the pike.
[3] See above, pages 226-7 of this volume.
[4] Chalcocondylas, p. 204.

prepared, and over fifty of smaller calibre, which threw balls of
two hundred pounds. " Basilica " was a failure, as was generally the case with these very large guns : it showed signs of
cracking on the second day of the siege, and was mended with
many additional hoops, but finally went quite out of order.
The guns of middle calibre, however, successfully carried out
their task ; Mahomet had set up no less than fourteen batteries,
of which nine, intended apparently rather for annoyance than
for serious breaching, contained only four of the smaller bombards each, but the other five were intended for serious work
and had the larger guns—that opposite the gate of St. Romanus,
in the middle of the land-front, containing not only the " Basilica," but three other of the largest pieces. Mahomet had not
been deceived in his idea that the day of artillery had fully
arrived. On the tenth day of bombardment (11th April),
one of the lateral towers of the Gate of St. Romanus fell to pieces,
filling the dry moat, and offering a slope of rubble up which,
as observers said at the time, the outer enceinte could have
been stormed without difficulty if an attacking column had
been ready.[1] By frantic efforts the garrison blocked the gap
with barrels and loose stones. The Turks kept up a continual
fire on the broken wall, and even breached behind it the second
and inner enceinte, though not effectively. The garrison tried
to mount some of their own guns on the adjacent curtain, to
disable the Turkish siege battery, but had to take them away,
because their recoil was found to be shaking the ancient and
rather dilapidated rampart. On 6th May the defences of the
outer breach were demolished beyond the possibility of repair,
and the enemy kept up a fire all the evening on this front, to
prevent the garrison from working at it. An attempt to storm
was made at 11 p.m., under cover of the night, but was beaten
off by heroic hand-to-hand fighting. On 12th May a second
smaller breach was made in the extreme north-west corner of
the walls, in front of the palace of Blachern ; here, too, an assault
was made, but like that on the St. Romanus front, was repelled.
The Turks actually got inside the walls, but were driven out
by a charge headed by the gallant Emperor Constantine in
person. Mines were also tried against several points in this
same direction, but they were detected by the Emperor's competent German engineer, John Grant, and the miners " smoked

[1] Niccolo Barbaro, p. 26.

out." On Tuesday, 29th May, the whole front of both walls beside the Gate of St. Romanus having been battered into a mass of rubble, a decisive assault was made against it, or rather against the precarious line of palisades which the garrison had built upon and behind it, while several minor columns delivered real or simulated attacks on other parts of the wall with ladders, in order to distract the attention of the defenders from the crucial front of action. After many hours of repeated assaults, in which the Turks suffered very heavily, the garrison at the breach of St. Romanus was worn down to a thin line, and the stormers obtained a footing on the second wall. Fighting, however, was still going on, when the fortune of the day was determined by a mere hazard. One of the minor Turkish columns, prowling along the dry moat, came on a low-lying postern near the Kerkoporta—a mile north of St. Romanus— which was badly closed and barely guarded. They burst it open and got inside without difficulty. The noise of the enemy in the streets behind broke down the morale of the much-tried defenders of the great breach, who gave way and were overwhelmed. The emperor, fighting to the last, perished unknown, and was not discovered, under a heap of corpses, till the Sultan had search made for him many hours after.

The power of artillery being thus proved, we read of it employed ere long in battle. Some decades later we find the Janissaries' line of arquebuses supported by the fire of field-pieces, often brought forward in great numbers, and chained together so as to prevent cavalry charging down the intervals between the wheels.[1] This device is said to have been employed with great success against an enemy destitute of guns but superior in the numbers of his horsemen, alike at Dolbek against the Mamelukes,[2] and at Tchaldiran against the Persian cavalry of Shah Ismail.

The ascendancy of the Turkish arms was finally terminated, after our period has come to its end, by the conjunction of several causes. Of these the chief was the rise in central Europe of standing armies composed for the most part of disciplined infantry. But it is no less undoubted that much

---

[1] Richard III. of England is said to have adopted this expedient at Bosworth. His "serpentines" were chained in a row, according to the "Lay of the Lady Bessie."

[2] The arquebus and cannon were novelties to the Mamelukes as late as 1517, if we are to trust the story of Kait Bey.

was due to the fact that the Ottomans, after the reign of Soliman, fell behind their contemporaries in readiness to keep up with the advance of military skill, a change which may be connected with the gradual transformation of the Janissaries from a corps into a caste. It should also be remembered that the frontier of Christendom was now covered not by one isolated fortress of supreme importance, such as Belgrade had been, but by a double and triple line of strong towns along the Austrian-Hungarian frontier, whose existence made it hard for the Turks to advance with rapidity, or to reap any such results from a single battle or siege as had been possible in the fifteenth century. But all this falls outside the Middle Ages, and cannot here be discussed.

CHAPTER III

WHILE the Turks of Murad II. were overrunning the minor Balkan principalities, there was a fierce struggle going on in Central Europe, whose vicissitudes account in great measure for the intermittent attention which the Hungarian state gave to the advance of the Ottomans. It was a public misfortune for Christendom that Sigismund, King of Hungary, was also Sigismund the much-distracted head of the Holy Roman Empire. For while every Magyar's lance and bow should have been turned against the Sultan, half their energies were being employed in the long Bohemian War— no real concern of Hungary—in which their king had got himself involved.

This long struggle (1420–1434) had a military as well as a political importance, since it was marked by a new tactical development, which if less notable and permanent than the influence of the English longbow and the Swiss pike, was yet one of the final blows delivered against feudal chivalry. The system by which the desperate Hussite rebels of Bohemia maintained themselves for so many years against the forces of an Emperor who was also King of Hungary, requires some notice. The Czechs, as every one knows, had risen in arms stirred by two motives, outraged nationalism and spiritual zeal : they were full of a resolve to drive the intruding German beyond the Erzgebirge, but moved even more by the determination to avenge their martyred prophet, and to establish the " kingdom of righteousness " by the sword. If the fate of the struggle had depended on the lances of the Czech nobles, resistance would have been hopeless : they were divided in political feeling, and even if they had been united they could put into the field only tens to oppose to the thousands of German feudalism. It was not apparent to any one, save to fanatics, how the overwhelming strength of the enemy was to be met. The undisciplined masses of burghers and peasants who formed the main bulk of the Bohemian army would, under the old tactical system, have fared no better than the infantry of Flanders had fared at Roosebeke in 1382. They could not emulate the successes of the Swiss, because their land was mainly a rolling upland plateau, not a series of difficult mountain valleys, and still more because they were not, like the men of Sempach, a community long trained to arms, and well skilled with pike and halberd.

The problem of organising the willing but inexperienced bands of the Czechs for successful opposition to the invading German looked hopeless. But it was faced by a man of genius, John Zisca of Trocnow, who had acquired military experience and knowledge of the military habits of his people's national foe, while fighting in the Polish service against the Teutonic Knights. He saw clearly that to lead into the open field men unaccustomed to mass-warfare, and rudely armed with a mixture of spears, flails, scythes fixed to poles, crossbows and hand-guns, would be madness. The Czechs had not in 1420 either a uniform national equipment or a national system of tactics ; their horsemen were few, because a large proportion of the nobility was hostile, or at the best lukewarm in spirit. Their only strength lay in their religious and national enthusiasm, which was real enough to make all differences vanish on the day of battle, though after it they would lapse into bitter sectarian disputes—strife that was inevitable when some were exalted religious fanatics, and others only plain men who hated the Germans. It was evident that the only chance for the Hussites was to start with a simple defensive policy, until they had gauged their enemies' military efficiency and learnt how to handle their own arms. Accordingly, we hear only of entrenchments being thrown up everywhere, and of towns put in a state of defence, during the first months of the war.

But this was not all : in his Eastern campaigning Zisca had become familiar with a system of tactics which he thought might be developed and turned to account by an army of infantry, forced to take the defensive, and unable to face an overwhelming enemy, whose strength lay in a numerous feudal

noblesse. There had now been prevailing in the East for
more than a century the practice of providing against cavalry
attacks by movable trains of waggons, which accompanied an
army on its march, and could be formed into a square or circle
when the approach of an enemy was notified. The idea
seems to have grown up among the Russians, primarily in
their wars of defence against the Tartars ; but they soon applied
it also to their contests with the Poles, another cavalry nation,
though one not so formidable as the old Mongol enemy. We
find it also used in the fourteenth century by the Lithuanians
in their long wars with the Teutonic Knights. The Russians
had been accustomed to fortify their camps of old ; [1] it was a
step forward to provide a movable camp-fortification which
could be set up anywhere at short notice. The structure was
called a *gulaigorod*, or moving town : the essential base of
it was waggons conveying large quantities of stout pavises, or
shields, which could be set up on or between the waggons.
The shields were furnished with loopholes and mounted on
runners, or later on wheels, so that they could be rapidly rolled
out into position.[2] Provided that an army was marching on open
ground, so that the carts could be quickly turned off into a
laager formation, and provided that the enemy was armed with
bows or arbalests only, and not with artillery, the *gulaigorod*
was a good defensive device. It had of course the disadvantage
that it was immovable when once set up, and that if the
enemy refused to attack, and sat down to wait outside, a
deadlock occurred. For troops using such a device could not
take the offensive, and had to wait to be attacked. However,
both Poles and Germans were prone to try the active game,
being full of self-confidence, and given to despise a pedestrian
enemy.

Zisca was not the first of the Czechs to see that waggons
could be used to outline a camp : that was a common idea all
over Europe; *e.g.* Edward III. had shut up his train and baggage in a *laager* of carts behind his line at Creçy, and still
earlier, Bela of Hungary is said to have done the same at the
battle of the Sajo—with no good results. In Bohemia itself,
Hajek of Hodjetin, a general of the Emperor Wenzel, had

[1] See above, p. 326.
[2] I owe some useful notes on the *gulaigorod* to Colonel Alexander Durnow, late
of the Russian Army.

written a booklet on the military art, in which he explained the benefits of utilising the army's carts to strengthen its camp, and of using them as cover for crossbowmen.[1]   But that is not the same thing as the Russian idea of using the *wagenburg* itself as a movable fortification, on which the whole tactics of the army were to be based.   This became the ultimate system of the Hussites, as their war went on.   But undoubtedly the first use of the waggon-square for the salvation of the army was an improvisation in a time of desperate need, not a deliberately thought-out scheme for a far-reaching tactical system.   It was necessary to improvise some means of holding out against an enemy hopelessly superior in cavalry.   Zisca had to use ordinary country or baggage carts for his extemporised fort-resses : and not having the pavises or shields used in Russia to block the gaps between waggon and waggon, he joined them with chains, which gave cohesion, but not cover for the defenders.

The first campaign of the Hussites (1420) was mainly an affair of sieges.   The Emperor Sigismund penetrated as far as Prague, and sat down before it, but owing to the desperate courage of his adversaries could take neither the city nor the hastily fortified hills outside, which the Czechs had entrenched and palisaded.   The fight on the Ziscaberg, half a mile east of the city walls, was not the first victory of the new Bohemian system, but merely the repulse of a detachment which failed to take an outlying earthwork (4th July 1420).   But, largely owing to dissensions in his host, Sigismund broke up from before Prague, and with a much diminished army turned off to relieve the imperialist garrison of Wyschehrad : he was followed by the Hussite army from Prague, surprised, and beaten in the open field.   This was the first real victory of the Czechs, but not—it would seem—one achieved by the tactics which they were about to make famous in their later campaigns.

It was in the respite given by the frustration of the first German invasion of Bohemia that the Czechs gained the leisure to organise their resources, for it was nearly a year before Sigismund found himself strong enough to repeat his attack, in the later months of 1421.   There was much civil strife between the Czech parties, who were already splitting into the two sections of the fanatical Taborites, whom Zisca

[1] See Delbrück's *Kriegskunst*, iii. p. 504.

led, and the more politically minded Calixtines, who only aimed at national independence and religious reform. But in the hour of a German invasion both could be relied upon to co-operate.

The battles of the autumn of 1421 at Luditz and Küttenberg were the first in which the regular *wagenburg* tactics were used in full development, both being victories won over attacking German forces by Hussite armies standing on the strict defensive behind their carts of war, and charging out when their enemies had exhausted themselves by unsuccessful assaults. The essential part of the system was to choose a position which the enemy must attack for some topographical reason, if he wished to attain his strategical end, and then to settle into it thoroughly before the assault was delivered. If there was leisure, not only were carts chained together, but a ditch was dug in front of them, and the earth from it thrown up round the wheels. There was always a broad exit left in the front of the *laager* and another in the rear, to allow of sallies in force. But till the moment of the charge these openings were blocked with posts and chains. The men were told off into waggon-sections, ten according to some accounts, twenty according to others, forming the squad. The half of each squad had long weapons, pikes, halberds or the specially Bohemian war-flails, and was told off for the blocking of the chained gaps between each pair of vehicles. The other half were armed with missile weapons, among which the hand-guns grew more and more numerous as the war went on. For Zisca was the first general in Europe who specialised in the smaller firearms as weapons for large bodies of infantry. For the last thirty years they had been known, but only employed in small quantities, mainly for shooting from walls or trenches during siege operations. Zisca reasoned, as it would seem, that his whole front in a *wagenburg* was the equivalent of a fortress, and that hand-gunners standing in the carts would have good rests for their clumsy tools. Moreover, the pellet of the hand-gun was much more effective than an arrow, and even than an arbalest-bolt, for dealing with the immensely thick double covering of mail and plate now used by men-at-arms : it would go through, where the others glanced off. There was also great moral effect in the flash and thunder of a salvo of many hundred hand-gunners letting fly at once—it was much more terrifying than arbalest volleys. So much were the small firearms valued by Zisca and his successors that by the end of the war it is said that nearly a third of the army were using them. And when the strife was over, and we find disbanded Bohemian soldiers serving as mercenaries, it is usually noted that they were hand-gun men.

It is in accord with this leaning toward firearms that the Bohemians also took to employing a great number of bombards. These were not mere *ribauldequins*, such as were being used farther west in the early fifteenth century, but real cannon, and we may almost call them field-guns, for they were permanently mounted on carts specially made for them. Probably the primitive German field-gun illustrated in Plate XXIX., Fig. 6, may represent an improved form of a Hussite piece. There was still no good method for elevating or depressing such weapons, nor could they be used for flank fire, since there was no means of moving the gun-cart from its fixed place in the line of the *wagenburg*. But against the frontal attack of an enemy moving in mass they would be very effective. And of course the whole system of the *wagenburg* was designed to make the adversary take the offensive, and charge straight forward against the square of carts placed in a good tactical position.

But, however effective the fire of hand-guns and bombards may be, it can only lead to the repulse of an enemy, not to his destruction. The Hussite tactics included a counter-offensive, when the German or Hungarian assault should have been beaten off. This was the object of the large gaps, blocked with movable woodwork and chains, that were left in the front and rear of the *wagenburg*. When the enemy had exhausted himself, it was the duty of the spearmen inside to sally forth and charge him. And cavalry assisted when possible—if (as was often the case) the Hussites had a considerable contingent of horse, they were placed outside and behind the square of waggons at some distance, and ordered to charge round its flank against the enemy, when he should break and begin to fall back. In cases where the numbers of the mounted men were very small, they apparently were taken inside the square and issued out from it along with the pikemen.

All these tactical devices presupposed that the enemy would take the offensive, as he indeed did during the successive

invasions of Bohemia which occupied the earlier years of the
war, and which went on even after Zisca's death in 1424.
They were not so obviously effective when the Hussites themselves crossed their borders, and executed counter-raids against
Germany or Hungary. For it is a different thing to choose
one's own position, with full knowledge of the terrain, in
one's own country, and to challenge the enemy by going
forward into his unsurveyed lands. Yet this the Hussites
often did, especially in the later years of the war. The first
experiment was Zisca's own Hungarian expedition of 1423, a
most perilous business, for he had to conduct his long train of
war-carts through a hostile country infested by bands of light
cavalry, who might have caught it at some ford or defile, when
it would be strung out, and unable to form its square at short
notice. That the column ever got back is a good testimony
to the scouting powers of Zisca's officers, for obviously they
must have had to report the ground clear for many miles around,
before it was safe to break camp and take to the road. We are
told that the moves were accomplished as far as possible by
night.

As the war dragged on, the engagements ever grew more
decisive, as the Czechs fully developed their tactical methods.
Invasion after invasion was a failure, because, when once the
Bohemian *wagenburg* was sighted, the German leaders could
not induce their troops to assail it. The men utterly declined
to face the cannon, hand-guns, and pikes of their enemies,
even when the latter advanced far beyond their rampart of
waggons, and assumed the offensive. The Hussites were
consequently so exalted with the confidence of their own
invincibility, that they undertook, and often successfully
carried out, offensive actions of the most extraordinary temerity.
Relying on the terror which they inspired, small bodies would
attack superior numbers, when every military consideration was
against them, and yet would win the day. Bands only a few
thousand strong sallied forth from the natural fortress formed
by the Bohemian mountains, and wasted Hungary, Bavaria,
Misnia, and Silesia almost without hindrance. They returned
in safety, their war-waggons laden with the spoil of Eastern
Germany, and leaving a broad track of desolation behind them.
Long after Zisca's death the prestige of his tactics remained
undiminished, and his successors were able to accomplish feats

of arms which would have appeared incredible in the first years of the war.

Æneas Sylvius, who during his long stay at the Council of Basle became deeply interested in the military art of the Hussites, no less than in their religious tenets, has left us an account of the manœuvres of their *wagenburgs* which seems to trespass beyond the bounds of possibility. He says that they were sometimes employed not only for the defensive, but for the tactical offensive. " When going into battle they will make two wings of chariots, with their infantry in the middle and their cavalry far out on the flanks beyond the cars. When the time for close attack comes, the waggoners on the wings, at the order of their commanders will turn gradually inward so as to surround some part of the hostile force, and finally join in its rear. The enemy, attacked in front by the Hussite foot and on both sides by the missiles of the men in the cars, are exterminated." This is from his *Bohemian History* ; [1] in his *Commentaries for King Alfonso* [2] he repeats the statement, saying that such manœuvres could only be carried out in a flat country like Bohemia, where ditches and enclosures are rare.

It seems impossible to believe that groups of slow-moving cars, of great weight and filled with men, and drawn by teams of several horses, can possibly have manœuvred in this fashion in face of a hostile army. As Dr. Delbrück very reasonably observes,[3] the wounding of two or three horses in any one of a file of waggons must have thrown the whole group into disorder, and opened gaps in it through which the enemy could penetrate. And the pace must have been so slow—not over two miles an hour with such heavy vehicles—that any enemy with eyes in his head could withdraw from between the circumventing wings. But Æneas Sylvius's story, dressed up with further and more improbable details from seventeenth-century historians,[4] has won itself a place in military history, from which, as Delbrück observes, it has got to be evicted. Such operations are simply impossible. Our modern Tanks executed some such manœuvres in front of Amiens on 8th August 1918 —but no horse-drawn heavy waggon of slow pace could possibly

[1] Chapter xlvii.　　　　　　　　　　[2] IV. chapter xliv.
[3] *Kriegskunst*, iii. 498–501.
[4] Such as the statement that the sections of waggons were drilled so as to form the letters of the alphabet, or geometrical figures !

do so. The cars of the *wagenburg* were essentially defensive, and immovable in action.

The armies of Germany never succeeded in foiling these tactics, and when at last the defeat of the Taborites took place, it resulted from the dissensions of the Bohemians themselves, not from the increased efficiency of their enemies. The battle of Lipan (16th June 1434), where Procopius fell and the extreme party were crushed, was a victory won not by the Germans, but by the more moderate section of the Czech nation, the Calixtines, who had resolved to accept the terms of toleration offered to them by the beaten emperor. The event of the fight indicates at once the weak spot of Hussite tactics, and the tremendous self-confidence of the Taborites. After Procopius had repelled the first assaults on his square of waggons, his men—forgetting that they had to do not with the panic-stricken hosts of their old enemies, but with their own former comrades—left their defences and charged the retreating masses. They were accustomed to see the counter-attack succeed against the terrorised Germans, and forgot that it was only good when turned against adversaries whose spirit was entirely broken. In itself an advance meant the sacrifice of all the benefits of a system of tactics which was essentially defensive. The weakness, in fact, of the device of the waggon-fortress was that, although securing the repulse of the enemy, it gave no opportunity for following up that success, if he was wary and retreated in good order. This, however, was not a reproach to the inventor of the system, for Zisca had originally to seek not for the way to win decisive victories, but for the way to avoid crushing defeats. At Lipan the moderate party had been beaten back but not routed. Accordingly, when the Taborites came out into the open field, the retreating masses turned to fight, while a cavalry reserve which far outnumbered the horsemen of Procopius, rode in between the circle of waggons and the troops which had left it. Thus three-quarters of the Taborite army were caught and surrounded in the plain, where they were cut to pieces by the superior numbers of the enemy. The few thousands who had remained behind within the waggon-fortress were dealt with afterwards. Thus was demonstrated the incompleteness for military purposes of a system which had been devised as a political necessity, not as an infallible recipe for victory.

The moral of the fight of Lipan was indeed rather like the moral of the fight of Hastings. Purely defensive tactics are hopeless, when opposed by a commander of ability and resource, who is provided with steady troops. If the German princes had been generals and the German troops well-disciplined, the careers of Zisca and Procopius would have been impossible. Bad strategy and demoralisation combined to make the Hussites seem invincible. When, however, they were met by rational tactics they were found to be no less liable to the logic of war than other men.

The whole episode is somewhat of a "back-water" in the general history of the Art of War. It could lead to nothing, since the *wagenburg* was only suitable for certain limited conditions, and for dealing with an enemy who showed neither invention nor ingenuity. What would have happened to a Hussite army if the enemy had drawn up a large force of cavalry at a safe distance in front of its *laager*, and then concentrated a powerful enfilading line of cannon against an angle? If the garrison of the *wagenburg* remained immobile, it would be gradually blown to pieces. If it sallied out to charge the guns, it would be cut up in the open by the enemy's superior cavalry. But such tactics seem never to have been tried by the unlucky generals of the Emperor Sigismund.

BOOK XIV

THE FIFTEENTH CENTURY IN WESTERN EUROPE

1400–1485

CHAPTER I

RESUMPTION OF THE HUNDRED YEARS' WAR—
AGINCOURT, AND THE STRATEGY OF HENRY V.

IN the Ninth Book of this volume the history of the
Hundred Years' War has been taken down to its
great central gap, the peace of 1396, between Richard II. and
Charles VI. That peace left England in possession of Bordeaux
and Bayonne, and of the strip of the Gascon *Landes* which lies
between them ; but, save Calais alone, all the rest of the great
holding conceded to Edward III. at the treaty of Bretigny had
been lost—not only his own ephemeral conquests, but also
the greater part of the old Aquitanian heritage, which had
been held by the Plantagenets from Henry II. downwards.
The English had been beaten not in open battle, but by the
clever and cautious policy of Charles V., and the ingenious
battle-avoiding system of tactics which the great Constable
Bertrand du Guesclin had inaugurated.

For nearly twenty years on from the great peace of 1396,
the main threads of the histories of France and England are
not intertwined, as they had been during the long struggle that
engrossed the attention of the last two generations. They
touched, of course, at frequent intervals : the French repeatedly
sent aid of a more or less official kind to Glendower and other
rebels against Henry IV. And that much harassed sovereign,
on his side, sometimes sold the aid of auxiliary bands to one or
other of the great factions, the Burgundians and Armagnacs,
which disputed the control of the person of Charles VI. and the
government of France, after that most unfortunate king had
fallen into the long insanity of his later years. But the main
strength of the two kingdoms was not turned against each
other, and their annals are more filled with internal than
external affairs. The important part of the reign of Henry IV,

is the story of constitutional experiments, of quarrels and negotiation between king and parliament, not the story of foreign wars. And in France, similarly, the governing feature of the time was the strife between feudal particularism, now represented by the great princes of the blood, with their territorial ambitions, and the Crown, rendered for the time almost powerless by the chronic lapses into insanity of the wretched Charles VI.

The opening of the second great section of the Hundred Years' War, after the accession of Henry V., found France and England, from the military point of view, much as they had left each other at the time of the peace of 1396. In the Art of War each party seemed to have learnt nothing and forgotten nothing. The tactics of Agincourt were to be very much those of Poictiers. The fighting in which each nation had been engaged meanwhile had not been very instructive. At Homildon Hill in 1402 the English bowmen had won one more of their typical victories over the Scots—a victory entirely of the type of Dupplin or Halidon. A Scottish army, trying to find its way home after a raid into Northumberland, had been intercepted, and forced to make an endeavour to cut its way through. Formed in the usual heavy columns, by their leader the Earl of Douglas, they had taken up their position high on a hillside, when they found the English archers circling round, and at the same time moving up against their front. When Douglas charged, and his masses rolled down the slope, the archery gave back, more slowly on the wings, more rapidly in the centre, so that the advancing column found itself in a semi-circle of converging arrow-shot. The head of the phalanx melted away, before it could get near the English line of dismounted knights and men-at-arms : the main body broke and retired, losing many prisoners. The fight had never actually come to hand-strokes ; so deadly had been the arrow-shower that the Scots had never been able to close. The disaster was complete—one hundred knights and other gentlemen were slain—five earls and five barons taken prisoners, and there was immense slaughter among the combatants of lower rank. The victors' loss had been inconsiderable, almost negligible.

The battle of Shrewsbury, the other notable fight of the reign of Henry IV., is worth mentioning as being the first

pitched battle fought between Englishmen since the bowman
had become the great power in war.   Both sides formed in the
same array, with wings of bowmen supported by central blocks
of lances.   The rebels—Hotspur's men—had the inferiority
in numbers, but on the other hand the advantage of choosing
their position.   They had taken post on a slope, with tangled
fields of pease, and narrow lanes in front.   Hence the Royalists
suffered severely in getting into action, though, when they did,
their superior numbers gave them the victory.   The battle
was very bloody—one thousand six hundred men fell, out of
armies probably counting together only eight thousand or nine
thousand present.   The whole business was a forecast of the
tactics of the Wars of the Roses.

As to the long Welsh rebellion of Glendower, which fills
up such a large part of the annals of the reign of Henry IV.,
it had its lessons and morals, but they were not those likely
to be useful for continental campaigns.   The first was the
extreme difficulty of dealing with an enemy who fought as
Bruce vainly bid the Scots to do, by ambushes and surprises,
and wisely declined open battles in the field.   When the king
came against him with a royal army, Owen took to the hills,
and disappeared, only making his existence known at intervals
by cutting off stragglers, by attacking badly guarded waggon
trains trailing behind the troops, or occasionally by a night
attack.   In one of these last, King Henry was caught napping ;
his own personal baggage, including his crown and wardrobe,
being captured by the Welsh.   But only one serious engagement
was entered into by Glendower, when at Pilleth, near Knighton,
in 1402, he surprised the levies of Herefordshire and Shropshire
in a pass, routed them and captured their leader, Sir Edmund
Mortimer.   Normally, he refused action with any large body
of enemies, and tried evasive tactics.   His adherents in South
Wales once or twice ventured on open fight, and were beaten for
their pains.   But the net result of this was that, though he
could keep up a rebellion for many years—he had not been fully
subdued even when King Henry died—he was never much more
than a guerilla foe.   The great castles which Edward I. had
built served their destined purpose of bridling the land ; most
of them were never taken, though they were blockaded for
long months on end.   The few that did fall—Aberystwyth and
Harlech were among them—proved snares rather than boons

to Owen, since he was tempted to throw garrisons into them, and then lost castle and garrison together. Especially Harlech, in 1409, was the cause of his worst disaster : the place had seemed so impregnable that he had locked up his family and his treasures in it. But since he was never strong enough to relieve it by force of arms, he had to see it starved out in the end, while he hovered uselessly on neighbouring hills, afraid to commit himself to a general action.

The French, on the other hand, had nothing to learn in the way of the military art from the interminable bickerings of the Orleanists and Burgundians. But they might have drawn unpleasant deductions from the happenings of 1411, when the aid of a very modest contingent of English auxiliary troops enabled the Burgundians to win the fight of St. Cloud, and turned the fate of a whole campaign. The one piece of experience that French soldiers seem to have kept before them was the success of the tactics of the column of dismounted men-at-arms at Roosebeke in 1382. The phalanx of the French chivalry had met and trampled down, in desperate close fighting, the tough pikemen of Ghent : the triumph had been very bloody, because the Flemings had been outflanked by two detached bodies of horse, who charged them on right and left, while the " push of pike " was at a standstill in the centre. The lateral pressure, as we are told, thrust them into a helpless mass, in which more men perished by suffocation than by the point of the lance. It would seem that the receipt for victory for the next quarter of a century was supposed to lie in the combination of a central mass of men-at-arms on foot, with some flanking bodies of horse. This was, at any rate, the scheme tried not only at Agincourt, but at the subsequent fights of Cravant and Verneuil. It was apparently not observed that the triumph of Roosebeke was won over an enemy who had advanced over open ground, with no protection for his flanks, and without any adequate provision of men armed with missile weapons. As to the lesson of Nicopolis—that indiscipline is fatal whether the army fights on horse or on foot—it would seem that the French *noblesse* failed to catch the moral. As after Courtrai, they attributed their disaster to bad generalship and treachery. The alleged cowardice of the Hungarians was made the sole explanation of the lost battle—we have only to read the long account of it in the biography of Boucicault

to see how the typical French knight came to the conclusion
that he had been " betrayed." [1]

The main difference between the armies that fought at
Poictiers in 1356 and at Agincourt in 1415 was in their armour ;
the tactics on both sides remained much the same.   But during
the last two generations the overloading of the man-at-arms
by complicated additional defences had been progressive.   It
was largely caused by the efficiency of the English arrow—
there had been a deliberate attempt to secure safety even at the
cost of mobility.   In the early days of Edward III. the English
knights, as Jean le Bel remarked,[2] had still been wearing
armour mainly consisting of mail, with the padded acton
below and very little plate above.   And they had open helms
without visors, while throat and neck were only protected with
the *camail*, the loose covering of minute chain-mail rings which
hung down from the bascinet.   Shoulders had only been
guarded by the very inadequate device of *aillettes*, a kind of
square epaulettes rising high on each side of the neck, and
intended to catch sword-cuts which glanced from the helm.[3]
The English of 1338 had been notoriously old-fashioned in
their armour, but even their French opponents would have
seemed very inadequately armed to their grandsons of 1415.
The later fourteenth century had seen many changes in armour
—all in direction of " safety first," and all detrimental to
mobility, and tending to secure the early exhaustion of the
wearer.   We have arrived at the time when middle-aged
knights of a stout habit of body died of heart-failure in battle,
without having received any wound, as did Edward of York at
Agincourt, and when, at the end of a long fight on a sultry
day, masters were seen supported by their pages, lest they
should loose their footing and be unable to rise again—a
humorous incident belonging to the forgotten combat of
Dendermonde [4] (1452).

By the later years of Edward III. breast and back plates
of steel had come in, and covered the mail hauberk below ;
while the arms and legs were completely, instead of partially,

---

[1] See above, p. 352.   [2] See above, p. 146.
[3] The knight firing the cannon in Plate XXIX., Fig. 1, is wearing armorial *aillettes*
charged with a lion.   They are typical for 1327, the date of the picture, but were
going out by the beginning of the Hundred Years' War.
[4] Olivier de la Marche, chap. xxv. p. 319.

protected by plate sheathing, accurately shaped to the limbs. But the bascinet with its pendant camail just saw the fourteenth century out, as did the custom of protecting the groin and upper hips by the pendant skirt of the mail hauberk only. The short reign of Henry IV. saw the supersession of both of these survivals by devices of much greater weight and stiffness. The camail disappeared, and the neck and shoulders were for the future guarded by the steel gorget, which met the helmet above and fitted over the upper rim of the breastplate below. Beneath the waist the groin was now covered by a skirt of five or six overlapping steel bands called *taces*, beneath whose lower edge in monuments a slight glimpse of the last rings of the hauberk-skirt can sometimes still be seen. Its mail is also visible occasionally under the armpit—the weak point in the steel breastplate, which had to be shaped away to allow of the movement of the arm from the shoulder. The little gap here, sometimes called *le défaut de la cuirasse*, was sometimes masked by small roundels strapped on externally, which seem to have been called *motons* or *besagues*.[1] They are plainly visible in the figure of Sir John Lysle (*obiit* 1407) in Plate XXXII. They remained in use for some fifty years, till they were rendered unnecessary by an enormous extension of the shoulder-armour into the vast and ugly *pauldron*, illustrated by the brass of Robert Ingylton, shown in the same plate. But this belongs to the time of the Wars of the Roses. At Agincourt, armour, though irrationally ponderous already, had not received the final additions which were to make it absolutely preposterous for practical purposes.

The custom of fighting on foot, now universal among the English knights and usual among the French, had obliged them to take to short and heavy striking weapons for close combat, among which the mace, glaive,[2] axe, and halberd were prominent. Most of these, and particularly the pole-axe, required two hands to yield them effectively, and so the shield had been practically discarded for actual use, and only survived for heraldic display. When we do hear of shields, they are generally pavises, the long heavy protections, more like mantlets than anything else, which were used by arbalesters

---

[1] See Mr. Ffoulkes' *Armour and Weapons*, p. 68 and Lord Dillon in *Archœological Journal*, lxiv. 15–23. Malyns (Plate XXXII.) shows mail in his arm-pits.

[2] A sort of heavy cutting blade fastened to a short, stout staff.

SIR JOHN DE NORTHWOOD
Obiit 1330

REGINALD DE MALVNS
Obiit 1385

SIR JOHN LYSLE
Obiit 1407

ROBERT INGVLTON
Obiit 1472

ARMOUR (FOURTEENTH AND FIFTEENTH CENTURIES)

to cover themselves while loading, and were occasionally employed by men-at-arms in sieges, to keep out arrow-shot. But they were not used in normal battles in the open.

With regard to the personnel of English armies under Henry V. and his successor, we may note that the proportion of archers to men-at-arms was still increasing. In the time of Edward III. it had often been only two to one, seldom more than three or four to one. But in the fifteenth century it rose to six or seven, sometimes even to ten bows to one spear ; at Agincourt, however, it was only five to one, much less than was the proportion twenty years later.

The first campaign of Henry V. in France started with no great promise of achieving anything very momentous. The capture of the single town of Harfleur wasted many weeks of time, though it ended in one of the rare triumphs of artillery in this age—the place having been actually reduced by steady bombardment, though mining co-operated in the result. But this modest success had cost the lives of a fifth of Henry's army—more from camp fever than from casualties in active fighting. And so many more of the besiegers were in a debilitated condition, that an offensive campaign seemed no longer possible.[1] The long march through Northern France, which followed, might have been as useless and disastrous a promenade as those which John of Gaunt had conducted during the Old War, if only the French had kept their heads and refused to attack, as Bertrand du Guesclin would have done under similar conditions.

The circumstances of this march were very odd. After providing a garrison for Harfleur, Henry had not much more than six thousand men left, and the season was far spent, October having arrived. A majority of his council voted for the safe and unenterprising course of taking the army back to England by sea. The king, however, announced that he intended to march to Calais across Picardy. The reasons

---

[1] After sending home the sick, and providing for the garrisoning of Harfleur, we learn from the *Gesta Henrici V.* that there were nine hundred lances and five thousand bowmen left. Walsingham (ii. p. 110) gives the larger figure of eight thousand. The Agincourt Roll, printed by Sir H. Nicholas in his *Agincourt*, accounts for eight hundred and twelve lances and three thousand and seventy-three bows. These figures are incredibly small, and as the details of half the contingents are lost, we cannot trust the sum total, though it purports to include everything. St. Remy, who was present with the English, gives nine hundred lances and ten thousand archers.

which he gave were chivalrous—that he wished to offer the enemy the chance of battle, and would not go home surreptitiously. But Henry was, in fact, a keen professional soldier rather than a knight-errant, and most of his military operations were so well considered, that his true motives on this occasion were probably of a more practical sort. If he could tempt the French to a battle, he hoped to beat them ; if they allowed him to reach Calais unfought, it would add to his prestige, and give him moral ascendancy for the next campaign Probably he thought that his march would be unmolested, since he bade his army prepare to move very lightly equipped, and left all his heavy baggage and guns at Harfleur in charge of a garrison of fifteen hundred men. It was a rash step ; the country was hostile, and the enemy would certainly be in superior numbers, while much depended on weather, which might delay him and make the roads impracticable. It was dangerous to act on the hypothesis that a French feudal army would always do the wrong thing.

As a matter of fact, the whole scheme was nearly wrecked by torrential autumnal rains. The king had intended to cross the lower fords of the Somme, as Edward III. had done in the Creçy campaign. But not only were all the fords found held by the enemy, but the weather was so bad that the Somme was everywhere in flood, and its peat-bogs were one long lake. At every point where there was a road running down to the water's edge, the English vanguard found not only an enemy guarding the causeway, but an impracticable flood between. " There seemed nothing left to expect," says one who marched with the army, " but that when we should have finished our eight days' stock of food, and should have struggled on sixty miles to the head of the Somme, the enemy would set on with superior numbers, and overwhelm a band so small, so wearied with marching, and so weak for want of victuals." [1] The army only succeeded in crossing the river on 19th October, the tenth day of its march, by mounting the Somme almost to its source, where it had grown narrow, and passing it at Béthancourt above Peronne. A party of the enemy's horse came up just too late to hinder the passage.

Meanwhile French contingents of great strength from the

---

[1] *Gesta Henrici V.* in Rolls Series, p. 40. Cf. Juvenal des Ursins and St. Remy for similar notices.

South had been arriving day by day, crossing the Somme at the bridge of Amiens, and joining the Picard levies which had already been in position behind the river. On the 20th an army three or four times as numerous as that of King Henry was concentrated at Bapaume, a centre of roads from which they could cut in and intercept the passage of the English to Calais by any conceivable route that they might take. A capable man in command of the French army might certainly have destroyed the English, even without committing himself to an offensive battle. Having got into a position from which he could block every way between King Henry and the only place where he could find safety, the Constable of France had the power of forcing his enemy to attack him on any favourable ground that he might choose, and on such terms as might suit him best. By placing himself across the Calais road, and sitting still, he could force the English to take the offensive under the worst possible conditions ; there was no need to attack them. But D'Albret was not really a responsible commander in charge of an army which would obey ; there were so many royal counts and dukes present, that he was really only the president of an unruly council of war. The movements of the French army were directed in a haphazard way, after debates in which each magnate urged his own opinion. The Constable, we are told, wished to receive a defensive battle ; the dukes compelled him to deliver an offensive one, because they thought it a shame to allow their manœuvres to be dictated by the movements of an enemy much inferior in numbers and worn out by rain and starvation.

King Henry was in a bad scrape. His army was weary from long marching and was suffering from dysentery ; for three days bread had failed, and the men had been living on meat, eked out by unground corn, nuts, and vegetables from the fields. To stay where he was would be ruin—unless the enemy attacked, his army would perish from sheer starvation and debility. Fortunately the enemy did what the king had hoped, and gave up his advantages.

The strength of the position which Henry had taken up south of the villages of Tramecourt and Agincourt lay in the fact that it was narrow, well guarded on the flanks by orchards and enclosures belonging to those places. It was exactly wide enough—no more than eleven hundred yards across—

to allow an army of six thousand men to develop its full front ; but this being done there was no reserve available. But another fact gave an additional advantage: for near a mile in front the ground was slippery ploughed fields, soaked with the inordinate rain that had fallen in the past week. Henry's line was composed on the old plan of Creçy or Auray: right, centre, and left each consisted of a small body of men-at-arms flanked by two wings of bowmen. These were in each case thrown slightly forward, so that where the archery of the centre met those of the vaward and rereward two projecting angles were formed. Edward Duke of York led the right, the king himself the centre, Lord Camoys the left. The archers were protected with a row of sharp six-foot stakes, their points directed to the front at the height of a horse's breast.

The French exactly repeated the tactics of Poictiers. Once more they dismounted the bulk of their men-at-arms, and sent forward as an advance only two comparatively small bodies of mounted knights, who were directed to charge in, and to endeavour to ride down the archers before the main body should close. One squadron was led by the Count of Vendôme, the other by the Admiral of France, Clugnet de Brabant. Behind them came the first line, the flower of the French *noblesse*, all on foot, commanded by the Constable D'Albret himself, the Dukes of Orleans and Bourbon, and the Counts of Eu and Richemont, with the Marshal Boucicault, a veteran of Nicopolis. A second battle of the same strength followed at an interval, under the charge of the Dukes of Alençon and Bar. There was also a third line under the Counts of Marle, Dammartin, and Fauquembourg, but in this corps the knights were told to retain their horses, being intended for use in the pursuit, when the English should have been broken. It would seem that the comparatively small body of infantry which the French had brought with them, nearly all arbalesters, were relegated partly to the rear of each division, where they could be of no possible use, and partly to the third line.[1]

When the two armies were in presence, at the opposite ends of the open space, 1200 yards long, formed by the orchards of the villages of Tramecourt and Agincourt, there would seem

[1] See St. Remy and Waurin. The *Gesta Henrici V.* says that they were "de post dorsum armatorum."

to have been some ineffectual parleying. It is said that the
Constable offered Henry a free passage to Calais, if he would
surrender his claim to the crown of France, release his prisoners,
and order the evacuation of Harfleur. The king, as might
have been expected, refused the terms. He then waited some
time for the hostile attack, and when it did not come—the
ground was reported almost impracticable by the French
scouts—resolved to provoke it, by going forward far enough
to bring the enemy within long archery range. When he had
advanced, slowly as was necessary in the deep mud, for some
four hundred yards, a shiver was seen to pass along the whole
front of the enemy's first line ; it was the lances coming down
from the perpendicular to the horizontal position for a charge.
At the same moment the two squadrons of horse on the flanks
were seen to be on the move. The Constable, as Henry had
hoped, was about to take the offensive, despite of the condition
of the sodden soil.

Henry at once halted, dressed his line, and ordered the
archers to fix their stakes again. He had obtained the advantage that he desired, by getting the enemy to take the offensive.
The attack was delivered at a funereal pace, for the horses at
once sunk to their fetlocks in the mud, and the knights on
foot to their ankles : to lift the feet required a serious effort
at each step. The cavalry were mostly shot down before they
had struggled to the neighbourhood of the English flanks ;
comparatively few knights were slain outright, but so many
horses were brought down that only a remnant ever reached
the line of stakes, and those that did, while checked by the
obstacle, were shot down at point-blank range by the archers.
This episode occupied but a few minutes, but meanwhile the
first line of the dismounted men-at-arms had got to the front,
though with the greatest difficulty. They lurched forward,
it is said, at the slowest possible pace, all stooping their heads
in order to avoid the chance of an arrow coming through the
visor-slits of their helms. The dense line soon fell into disorder,
partly because some tracts of the fields were more water-logged
than others, partly from having to open the ranks to allow
of the flight of the beaten cavalry, whose remnant came back
helter-skelter against them, accompanied by many riderless
chargers.[1] Moreover, the archers were playing on them for

[1] Monstrelet, p. 375.

the last three hundred yards, and taking no small toll from among them.

But the French vaward, by immense exertions, succeeded in crossing the marshy fields and getting to close action with the English line. At the first " push of lance " there was a great crash, and King Henry's front was borne a few yards backward.[1] But the impetus of the charge died down, and sanguinary hand-to-hand fighting followed, for the French could get no farther forward. We are told that they had not strength to continue the attack, being utterly weary already, and much crowded together. " They were so jammed," like the Flemings at Roosebeke, " that, save those in the front ranks, they could not even raise a hand to strike." [2] Then the English king took the decisive step of bidding his archers throw themselves into the fray for hand-to-hand fighting. His own men-at-arms must have been nearly as tired as the French, though they had the advantage of having walked only four hundred yards in the mud, while the enemy had tramped a much longer distance in the worst of it. We are told that it was the onset of the archers with axe, mallet, and sword that settled the day. That unarmoured men should have prevailed over men cased with mail and plate on plain, open ground was reckoned one of the marvels of war. But prevail they did—the chroniclers speak of the embogged knights as standing helplessly to be hewn down, while the archers " beat upon their armour with mallets, as though they were smiths hammering upon anvils," [3] and rolled them over one on another till the dead and wounded lay three deep. The knightly armour had become a deadly trap when once the wearer was fatigued.

The relics of the first French line were thrown back upon the second, which had now in its turn come up across the puddled ground which had hampered its predecessors. Henry, after re-forming his front as best he could, ordered the advance to continue, for he saw that the newcomers were as fatigued as their comrades, and somewhat shaken and demoralised by what they had seen in front of them. It would appear that

---

[1] *Gesta Henrici V.*, p. 53.

[2] Monstrelet, p. 375, who says that they were much incommoded by the length of their lances, useless in close fight.

[3] *Gesta Henrici V.*, p. 56; Walsingham, ii. 312–13.

the struggle in this part of the action was neither so long nor so fierce as that of the opening phase. It is recorded that many of the French fought gallantly enough—the courage of the Duke of Alençon is especially noted : he felled Humphrey Duke of Gloucester to the ground, and struck off a fleuret from the king's crown before he was beaten down. But few of his comrades showed such vigour, and the French second line broke and lurched to the rear as best it could.

There still remained the third line, including the mounted men-at-arms and a large body of infantry. King Henry was arraying his dreadfully exhausted ranks for a third engagement, when an alarm broke out in his rear. Excited messengers ran up to inform him that a new French force had fallen upon his camp and baggage at Maisoncelles, a mile behind. So great a portion of the English had by this time turned to the task of guarding the prisoners, of whom an enormous number had been taken, that the ranks of the combatants were unduly thinned. Captives, as we know, meant ransoms ; and knights and archers alike had profitable prey under their hands. In the excitement of the moment, Henry gave the hurried order that the prisoners should all be knocked on the head—just as his uncle by marriage John of Portugal had done at Aljubarrota thirty years back. Many soldiers refused to obey—whether from compassion or for financial reasons ; whereupon the king detached some of his personal retinue to carry out the ghastly business. After many unfortunates had been butchered, it became known that the alarm was vain. The attack on the camp had been carried out only by a local squire, Isambard of Agincourt, and a rabble of peasants, who had decamped after killing some chaplains and horse-boys, and appropriating the king's crown, wardrobe, and great seal, with other valuable plunder.

Meanwhile the French third line gave little trouble, the greater part of it melted away ; only the Counts of Marle and Fauquembourg made a partial charge, with the aid of the unlucky Anthony of Brabant, who arrived on the field just in time to be killed. This chivalrous duke had outridden his contingent, which was on the road many miles back, but joined with his body-squires in the last charge, and fell in company with the two counts who had tried to do their duty.[1]

---

[1] Monstrelet (p. 376) says that he joined the *second* line, not the *third*.

So ended this astonishing battle, whose not least astonishing feature was that the victors had lost less than one hundred men in all, though among them were two great nobles, the Duke of York and the Earl of Suffolk. The former, a man of forty-five years and corpulent, died of exhaustion, without having received a wound. Meanwhile the French casualties were appalling—fifteen hundred counts, barons, knights, and nobles, with three thousand men-at-arms, and perhaps a thousand common soldiers. Among the slain were the commander-in-chief, the Constable D'Albret, three dukes— Brabant, Alençon, and Bar—and the Counts of Nevers, Marle, Vaudemont, Blamont, Grandpré, Roussy, and Fauquembourg. Among the prisoners, who would have been much more numerous but for the massacre, but who still amounted to over one thousand in all, were the Dukes of Orleans and Bourbon, the Counts of Eu, Vendôme, and Richemont, and the Marshal Boucicault.[1] The slaughter was far more terrible than that of Poictiers, mainly because flight from a lost battle, comparatively easy in the lighter armour of 1356, was almost impossible in the heavy panoply of 1415. If a knight failed to stagger back to his page and his charger in the rear, he was doomed to death or capture.

The English victory was all the more astonishing because Henry was not able to receive battle in his original position, but had been forced to advance out of it, in order to get the enemy to take the offensive. The fight was on perfectly open, flat ground, not on a hillside or behind hedges—the archers' stakes were useful, but not a decisive item in the causes of victory, for the main struggle ended in a hand-to-hand mêlée. Perhaps the most striking moral of the affair was that armour had become so tiresome that in close contest the archer, with his steel cap and jack or brigandine, had many advantages over a fully equipped man-at-arms. The archer was effective not only with his bow but with his axe or mallet, when once his adversary was tired out and hampered in the mire.

For some years the French feudal *noblesse* was cured of its taste for pitched battles, and the remaining seven years of Henry v.'s reign are full of wars, but singularly lacking in general engagements.

The years 1417–1422 are filled by Henry's long and con-

[1] Walsingham (ii. 313) says seven hundred prisoners only.

tinuous invasion of France, starting with his second landing
in Normandy on 20th September 1417. This long series of
campaigns is of high strategical interest, since it displays a
scheme of conquest entirely contrasting with that of Edward III.
The latter, save as regards the taking of Calais (which stands
by itself), worked by long circular raids, which inflicted an
enormous amount of suffering on France, but had no permanent
effect, because they did not result in the occupation of conquered territory, or the capture of the fortresses by which it
could be held down. Henry's scheme was very different.
The general conditions of France were favourable, since the
civil war between Burgundians and Armagnacs was still raging
fiercely, and neither party paid more than a distracted attention to the foreign enemy. Indeed, both factions showed
themselves on occasion ready to league with him for their
private profit. Henry's plan of campaign was to specialise
on the single duchy of Normandy, the part of France most
accessible from England, and to conquer it town by town, till
he should have taken the whole duchy and established therein
a solid nucleus of conquered territory, as a base for further
operations. This was not a showy programme, but it was a
perfectly feasible one. It was not spectacular or chivalrous in
outward seeming, like Edward III.'s great military progresses
through the heart of France ; but every year a solid block of
territory was subdued. Moreover, Henry was not a raider ;
he made strenuous efforts to preserve the countryside from
devastation. Regarding the Normans as prospective subjects
rather than enemies, he forbade all useless destruction of
public or private property, all arson or sacrilege, all ransoming
or mishandling of non-combatants. French chroniclers confess
that the passing of an English army through a district, though
a sore scourge enough, was not nearly so destructive a business
as the march of an Armagnac or Burgundian host. These
campaigns of Henry, therefore, were restricted within small
limits each year, had a definite purpose, and always ended in
conquest of a block of territory. In 1417 he took Caen, Lisieux,
and Bayeux, with all West-Central Normandy. In 1418 he
got Falaise and the peninsula of the Côtentin from Avranches
to Cherbourg. This involved leaguers of great length, such as
that of Cherbourg, which held out for over six months. In the
autumn of 1418 Henry laid siege to the great city of Rouen,

which, though given no effectual help from Paris, made a
splendid defence, and held out from August 1418 to January
1419, suffering all the horrors of famine before it would yield.
Famine was always Henry's main weapon—he had a good
siege train and used it, but the old method of starvation was
still the most effective means of dealing with a really well-
fortified town.   The rest of 1419 was occupied in finishing off
the remainder of the Norman fortresses—Gisors, Château
Gaillard, Ivry, etc.   By the end of the year the isolated island-
stronghold of Mount St. Michel was the only place left to the
French.   In three years Henry had conquered the whole of
Normandy, and was prepared to stop there ; the offer of
peace which he made to the French during the summer was
that he would take the Treaty of Bretigny boundaries of 1360,
plus the duchy of Normandy, and as a pledge of amity the
hand of the Princess Catherine and a dowry.   He was not
yet aiming at the crown of France, though he always used its
title ; and to resign his claim (a perfectly preposterous one, as
he knew) for a handsome compensation, was one of the offers
which he made during negotiations.

This stage of Henry's campaigning and ambitions came
to an end owing to an event over which he had no control—
the murder of John the Fearless of Burgundy, by his rival the
Dauphin, on 9th September 1419, at the Bridge of Montereau—
a deed of such calculated treachery, for it was done deliberately
at a friendly conference, that the Burgundian party, headed by
the murdered duke's son Philip, threw itself into Henry's arms.
They promised to back his claim to the French throne, in order
to exclude the treacherous Dauphin from the succession.   The
whole strategical situation, no less than the political, was
fundamentally changed, by the fact that a party which controlled great regions of Northern France, and Paris itself,
had adhered to Henry.   But nevertheless we are able to trace
the pursuance of his system, even after he had suddenly become
acknowledged as ruler all over the Isle de France, Champagne,
and Picardy.   Instead of striking by a bold general advance
at the parts of France which still adhered to the Dauphin, he
devoted himself rather to completing the symmetry of the
block of territory which had adhered to him, by besieging and
capturing all the fortresses within it which still were in the
power of the Dauphinois or Armagnac party.   The annals of

1420 and 1421 are filled mainly by interminable sieges—Sens, Melun, and more especially Meaux, which held out from 21st October 1421 till May 1422. It was the fatal dysentery contracted in this last eight months leaguer which killed Henry before his time.

There was only one battle in the period, and at that the king himself was not present. This was Baugé (March 21, 1421), lost by his brother Thomas Duke of Clarence by sheer neglect of the usual English system of battle. The prince was pursuing a large body of Dauphinois horse, who were executing a raid on the southern edge of Normandy in which many Scots auxiliaries had joined. Hearing that they were not far off, he forgot all prudence, refused to wait for his archers, and pursued with the cavalry alone. He caught up the enemy, but they, seeing that his infantry had not come on the scene, and that they outnumbered his horse by two to one, suddenly turned upon him, rode down his squadron by a sudden charge, and drove them into the river Couesnon, which they had just passed. Clarence was killed, and his whole body of men-at-arms slaughtered or taken. The English infantry, coming up after dusk under the Earl of Salisbury, found nought to do save to bury the bodies of the slain. But the battle settled nothing, and did not even lose territory for the English ; it was simply a " regrettable incident "—to use the terms of modern military phraseology. Its only interest is to show that both sides fought on horseback on occasion—if Clarence had dismounted to fight, the enemy would have got away unharmed. But seeing him pressing on, the French and Scots replied by a cavalry charge, in which they were bound to win by their superiority in numbers. In general actions fought on a deliberate plan, both sides, as we shall see, continued to dismount for the next ten years.

CHAPTER II

THE END OF THE HUNDRED YEARS' WAR, 1422-1453—
ORLEANS, FORMIGNY, CASTILLON

THE unwise endeavour to subdue the whole land of France
by force, which started with the Treaty of Troyes, was
destined to continue for many a year. After King Henry's
death (August 31, 1422) the guiding hand was removed, yet
the policy of slow advance by innumerable sieges continued,
and so long as the majority of the Burgundians of Northern
France adhered to the English cause, it could continue. The
regent John of Bedford set himself to extirpate the remaining
Dauphinois garrisons in Northern France, and then to extend
the same system down the line of the Loire. The steady
progress continued till 1428, when the celebrated siege of
Orleans began. It was bound to get slower, as the ground
occupied grew broader, since the military resources of England
were small, and were more and more exhausted in covering
with garrisons the conquered territories. For every town or
fortress left ungarrisoned, and trusted to its own inhabitants,
was liable to fall back by revolt into the hands of the enemy,
save in the purely Burgundian parts of Northern France.
And the friendship of the Burgundians for the English cause
grew progressively cooler as the murder of Montereau was
more and more forgotten, and the friction between English
and Burgundian interests began to develop, owing to the
selfish policy of Humphrey of Gloucester in the main, but
partly also to the growing ambitions of Philip the Good.

These central years of the war are not so destitute of pitched
battles as the later years of Henry v. Such as they were, they
all went in favour of the English. The bloody fights of
Cravant (1423) and Verneuil (1424) were new variations on
the old theme of Agincourt, coming to much the same results,

except as to the mere details of tactics and of the amount of slaughter inflicted on the beaten French.   In each the line was formed with archers and dismounted men-at-arms in the usual style, while the French fought partly with mounted men, though mostly with dismounted.   The effect of the English archery was less marked than at Agincourt, owing to the comparatively small proportion of it present, for both at Cravant and Verneuil there were great masses of Burgundian auxiliaries in the English ranks, and they (of course) did not carry the longbow.   So the archers were not the actual majority of the army, as they had been at Agincourt.   Each of the two fights had its particular characteristics.   At Cravant, which was a comparatively small affair, the English took the offensive, contrary to their wont, after waiting a long time for the French to attack.   At Verneuil, a real pitched battle on a great scale, the French detached a large body of mounted men, Gascons and Milanese for the most part, to turn the English flank by a detour.   While the main armies were fighting in front, all on foot, these turning squadrons fell on the English baggage, which had been *laagered* in the rear under a strong guard of archers. We are told that the horses had been packed three or four deep, haltered firmly by their heads and tails, outside the carts, so that they could not break loose, and that this strange barrier proved impenetrable to the French cavalry, who were meanwhile shot down in numbers by the archers, till they dispersed. The baggage guard then sallied out, and opened fire on one of the French flanks, settling the event of a battle which had hitherto been indecisive, for the two lines of men-at-arms had fought for forty minutes without any advantage to one side or the other.   When the French did break, the slaughter among them was very great, for they were absolutely exhausted, and found that their armour hindered them from making any pace to the rear, when they sought for their chargers and their pages.   Here fell the unlucky Earl of Douglas—the " Tyneman " as he was called from his habitual ill-luck in battle : he had been on the beaten side at Homildon and Shrewsbury and other smaller fights, before he took over a large Scottish contingent to help the Dauphin in 1424.   With him there were slain the Counts of Aumâle, Tonnerre, and Ventadour, with the Earl of Buchan, the second-in-command of the Scottish auxiliaries, and most of his following.   The Duke of Alençon and the Marshal La Fayette were captured alive. The victorious Bedford reported that the enemy had lost seven thousand slain or prisoners, which seems an incredible figure, as it would exceed the casualties of Agincourt, where the French army had been much larger. But there can be no doubt that battles were very costly to the defeated army, when its men-at-arms had dismounted, and were unable to recover their horses.

Rouvray, or the " Battle of the Herrings " (February 12, 1429), the last English victory, was somewhat of a variant on the usual methods of tactics in the Hundred Years' War. A very small force under Sir John Fastolf (ten hundred archers and twelve hundred Paris militia, fighting on the English side) was surprised in the open field by the Count of Clermont and Sir John Stuart, who commanded the remains of the Scottish contingent in the French service. They were escorting a large convoy of salt fish, " lenten stuff "—hence the name of the " Herrings "—to the English army then besieging Orleans. Beset by four times their own number of men-at-arms, they had just time to form a " laager " of their waggons in a rough square. The archers got upon the carts, the French spearmen held the intervals between them. Against this extemporised fortification, the French cavaliers dashed themselves repeatedly, with the usual ineffective result, and had to withdraw with great loss after many had fallen. Had Fastolf, perchance, been studying the reports of the recent successes of the Hussite *wagenburgs* ?

Rouvray ends a long series of victories. The turn of the tide had already started when it was fought, since the long siege of Orleans (October 1428 to May 1429) had begun. The chronicle of the rest of the war was to be one of a very different and a very depressing sort. That turn should have come long before, but the Dauphin and his generals were incapable and demoralised. Otherwise it is impossible to see how English armies of no more than four thousand or five thousand men should have gone on for years nibbling at the edges of the yet unconquered central block of France along the Loire. The slow, painful advance was at last to be checked, by the intervention of a moral power from without—Joan of Arc, the Maid of Orleans.

Stated in the simplest form, the problem set before John of Bedford was to find out whether with a very small English

army, uncertain support from the Burgundian faction, and a
rather meagre supply of money, raised with increasing difficulty
from the reluctant French (for England only supplied a small
proportion of it), he could persevere long enough to capture
one by one, the thousand strongholds of a land which bristled
with castles and fortified towns.　He was able to go on as long
as he did because of the personal incapacity of the French
leaders, and the bitter, though gradually diminishing, hatred of
the Burgundians for the Dauphin.　Clearly the task would
become impossible if the leadership of the enemy got into more
vigorous hands, or if the Burgundians finally threw up their
unpatriotic adherence to the English cause.

The first of these contingencies came about in 1429, with the
appearance of the Maid of Orleans : the second only in 1435,
when Philip of Burgundy made peace and alliance with the
murderer of his father, after fifteen years of hostilities against
him.

That the appearance of Joan of Arc was the turning-
point in the whole matter is clear ; her influence was of course
moral rather than strategic.　Attempts have been made to
show that she was not only a genuine and honest enthusiast
(which most people save M. Anatole France now grant), but
also a Heaven-sent general.　These, I think, are exaggerated.
It cannot be said, as a rule, that she exhibited any great
tactical skill in her operations : her talent was that she inspired
her soldiery to fight with an energy and confidence that had
been unknown before.　That she raised the siege of Orleans
seemed astonishing to her contemporaries, but can hardly
appear so to any one who looks dispassionately upon the
military situation.　An army of five thousand men, which has
strung itself out to the thinnest of lines in order to besiege a
large town, and is divided in halves by a broad river like the
Loire, is in a most desperate condition.　Exit and entrance from
Orleans by French troops had never been entirely prevented—
as the arrival of Joan herself and other leaders sufficiently
proved.　The siege was a badly kept blockade by an inadequate force, only possible because of the demoralisation of the
French.　When they lost that demoralisation, and turned
fiercely to attack the thin chain of redoubts (" bastilles ")
around the city, they were bound to break it, if they showed
ordinary skill.　And the English, it must be confessed, played

into the hands of their enemies : they should have raised the siege long before, instead of hanging on to their untenable lines with a mere " skeleton army."

When the siege lines were broken, Suffolk, a most incapable commander, split up his troops into small detachments, to hold the towns of the Loire which were still in his hands, Jargeau, Meung, Beaugency, and other places. It would have been far better to keep the army together as a field force, till the regent Bedford should send down reinforcements from Paris. But the troops had lost their ancient confidence : the sudden and unexpected energy of the French attacks before Orleans had been such a surprise to them that they had accepted, in all seriousness, the theory that their enemies were inspired by a supernatural fury, due to " that disciple and limb of the fiend called La Pucelle, that used false enchantments and sorcery." [1] To shut up men so cowed in isolated garrisons was a mistake : each party was inclined to panic, when the Maid's white banner appeared before its gates. Hence came a series of disasters— the capture of Jargeau, Meung, and Beaugency in rapid succession, which practically made an end of Suffolk's army. He himself was captured at Jargeau, when his men had flinched from the walls, as he strove to maintain a hopeless resistance in the streets after the gates had been thrown open.

Nor did the destruction of Suffolk's force end the triumphs of the Maid. On the day after the fall of the last of the Loire garrisons (Beaugency), Lord Talbot appeared from Paris with the succours sent to Suffolk by the regent Bedford. On hearing that he was too late, and that the force that he was sent to aid had been crushed, Talbot determined to retreat without delay, to cover Paris. He was surprised near Patay by the Maid, and her captains Lahire and the Duke of Alençon. They came on with such headlong speed that the English had no time to choose one of their usual positions—the archers had not even fixed their stakes when the hostile cavalry hurtled in among them. The combat became a hand-to-hand business, in which the bow could play no part, and the numbers and enthusiasm of the French carried all before them. Talbot was taken prisoner, a third or more of his army was destroyed, and the relics, under Fastolf (the victor of the Battle of the

[1] These are the terms of Bedford himself (Foedera, ix. p. 408).

Herrings), got off to Paris with difficulty. The credit of the
victory must be given directly to the Maid, who bade the men-
at-arms charge straight in, when the English were caught in
disarray before they had formed a line of battle. Whether her
order was inspired by a true military instinct, or by a mere
eagerness to get to handstrokes, it boots not to inquire
(June 17, 1429).

The moral effects of this series of victories were decisive.
Wherever Joan appeared her advance was followed by success.
She chose to march into Champagne, to crown her master
king at Rheims. The towns in this region being of the Burgundian faction, had been mainly trusted to themselves by the
regent Bedford, and were without English garrisons. Whenever Joan appeared before their gates they yielded almost
without fighting—Troyes, Chalons, Rheims, in rapid succession (July 1429). After the triumphant coronation of Charles
VII. at the last-named place, the movement spread into the
Isle de France, where Soissons and Laon adhered to the
national cause. The rising would have spread all down the
Seine and Marne, if Bedford had not at this moment received large reinforcements from England, which enabled him
to take the field, and to defend the line Melun-Senlis. He
dared not take the offensive, fearing the demoralisation of his
army in face of the Maid's miraculous banner, and he could
not prevent many more towns (Compiégne, Senlis, Beauvais,
Creil), from rebelling behind him. Probably Joan was right
when she bade the French captains attack Bedford, doubting
nothing: but La Tremouille and other doubting councillors
persuaded Charles VII. to avoid risks, and to let the national
movement work for itself. Nothing decisive therefore occurred,
and the Maid had her first failure—she induced some of the
French commanders to make a raid on Paris, while Bedford
was drawn off to some distance from it. But Paris could not
have been captured save by panic or treachery; it could not
fall by assault or escalade if its defenders held firm. The
Burgundian burgesses manned their walls, and made ready for
a serious resistance. Joan and her followers after storming
some insignificant outworks tried to escalade the main line of
defences, and were of course repulsed with loss, she herself
being wounded. The wretched councillors of Charles VII.
witnessed the check with malicious joy, more content that the

Maid should have been proved fallible and a false prophet, than grieved that Paris should have proved impregnable.

For the remaining months of her short career Joan was allowed no further part in directing the war. She felt that her influence was waning, but had not lost her belief that she might yet do much for France. On March 1430 she led a small volunteer relieving force to try to raise the siege of Compiégne, then besieged by an Anglo-Burgundian army; she got into the town, but in leading a sortie a few weeks later was cut off and captured. Of the miserable story of her captivity and trial there is no need to speak—it was equally disgraceful to the English, to their French partisans who carried it out, and to her master Charles VII., who made no attempt to save her, by threatening retaliation on his many English prisoners of high rank.

But though Joan was taken and martyred, her work endured; she had not only broken the English advance for good, recovered all the line of the Loire, all Champagne and much of the Isle de France, but had put a permanent moral ascendancy on the side of her countrymen. The actual territorial gain was as nothing compared with this. From henceforth Bedford was fighting for a losing cause. He kept up the impossible game manfully, and so did his successors in command for many a year, but they never had any prospect of ultimate success. For the Burgundian party, without whose aid the claim of Henry VI. to France could not possibly be kept up, gradually drifted over to the national side. There comes a moment when the partisan, who has been bought over to a cause in which he feels nothing but a personal or selfish interest, begins to ask himself whether it is worth while to fight any longer against the inevitable—and in France from 1429 onward that which now seemed inevitable was not the expulsion of Charles VII. from the South, but the expulsion of the English from the North. The men of material interests began to doubt the wisdom of adhering any longer to the losing party. From this time forward they began to drift slowly but steadily across to the king's side. As to the rank and file, whose patriotic sentiments were not restrained by any sordid personal interests, they had been so shamed by the Maid's valiant championship of a cause which they had abandoned as lost, so convinced of her inspiration by the magnificence of her success, that for the future no town in the English sphere of influence could be kept loyal save by the presence of an English garrison. When no such garrison was forthcoming, the gates flew open of their own accord at the first summons made by a French force.

Probably, if Joan had not been handicapped by the luke-warm and doubting spirit of Charles VII. and his councillors, she might have swept the English out of France in her first impetus. The intriguers and jealous courtiers who held her back did Bedford's work for him, and prevented her from achieving her purpose at once. More than twenty years of dismal, weary war were required to complete the expulsion of the stranger, because the first rush of the torrent had been stayed. The English recovered from the panic into which they had been thrown in 1429-30, and became once more the solid and obstinate adversaries that they had been in earlier years. Even after Bedford died in 1435 the game was kept up—there were many capable, hard-fighting veterans like the Earls of Warwick and Huntingdon, the famous Lord Talbot, and captains of lower rank such as John Fastolf and Thomas Kyriel. And among men of the younger generation, Richard Duke of York and his brother-in-law and namesake Richard Neville Earl of Salisbury earned themselves great reputations. A mistaken sense of national pride made the people and parlia-ment persevere in the hopeless struggle, and visit with wrath any statesman who, like the unfortunate Duke of Suffolk, tried to put an end to the war, by surrendering the greater part of the unstable conquests of Henry V., and striving to retain a solid block of territory in Normandy and Guienne, by buying peace with the sacrifice of the rest.

The depressing time between 1435, when the Duke Philip of Burgundy made peace and alliance with his old enemy, Charles VII., at Arras, and the end of the war in 1453 is one of the most dreary periods in English annals. It was impossible that England, when no longer helped by the French faction that had so long served her, could maintain a successful war from her own resources. She was set on accomplishing the impossible—murmured at every tax that became necessary, and grudged every man that was sent across the Channel, yet would not give over the war. Paris was lost in 1436, almost without a fight. The remainder of the garrisons on the Central Seine fell in 1437-8, after a resistance that was in many cases admirably obstinate. Pontoise was four times beleaguered and three times relieved before it fell in 1441. That the war lingered on for yet ten years more was partly due to the exhaustion of the French, and the mediocre character of their generals. They had some dashing adventurers to lead them, but no man of genius like Bertrand du Guesclin in the earlier war. But still more, perhaps, may we attribute it to the vast number of strong fortresses in Normandy and Maine which were still in English hands. If Henry V. and Bedford had taken many laborious years to win them, it now took no less a time for the generals of Charles VII. to win them back. Normandy, already attacked in 1440, was not finally reconquered till 1450, and the defence would have gone on longer but for the exceptional incompetence of the last English viceroy in the duchy, the Duke of Somerset, who was such a favourite of Henry VI., and such an unlucky fighter from his first ventures in France down to his death at St. Albans. His predecessors never lost heart, clung desperately to each outlying fortress such as Le Mans in Maine, which did not fall till 1448, and sometimes won back some place of importance, by a desperate adventure, just when the French thought that they had got everything in their own hands. Pontoise, the frontier fortress towards Paris, was thrice relieved by Lord Talbot and once by Richard of York before it succumbed in 1441. There was always the hope that England might at last send over a great army such as Henry V. had been wont to conduct. Only one such came, in 1443, when Somerset took it for a raid in Maine and Anjou, quite in the style of Edward III., which entirely failed to affect the general progress of the war, and wasted its force to no effect. The fact was that a great military leader was needed, and King Henry VI., when he grew up, was found to be a pious and unwarlike nonentity, incapable of administering a monastery or a school, much more a kingdom. The control of his person was the main object in English politics, and while his councillors quarrelled the war was neglected. There was a party which was bold enough to propose that the war should be given up, on any terms that could be got. But stupid national pride prevented this, the only wise course : and the struggle was fought out to its bitter and inevitable end.

The armies which during these later years of the war followed Somerset or Talbot to defeat were raised by the same

system as those which between 1415 and 1428 had followed
Henry v. and Bedford to victory. The principle of contract
was invariable. The peers or knights who proposed to go to
France undertook to find so many hundred spears and bows on
their own responsibility, while the government took them into
pay. The leaders were recompensed not only by the hard
cash advanced them for levy-money, and by the regular sum
doled out to them per head for their men, but also by the grant
of great lands and titles in France ; the archers and men-at-
arms had high pay and the chance of much plunder. Thrifty
men like Sir John Fastolf made large fortunes out of the war,
even when many of their outstanding bills against the Crown
were never paid. As the years drew on without a peace, there
grew up a whole army of veteran mercenaries of all ranks,
who had spent the greater part of their lives fighting in France.
The return to England, when Normandy and Guienne were
finally lost, of dozens of castellans and governors who had lost
their castles, and thousands of archers and men-at-arms who had
lost their pay and plunder, was not the least of the many causes
which made the outbreak of the Wars of the Roses possible.
For the noble verging towards rebellion, what temptation could
be greater than the presence at his elbow of hundreds of
trained soldiers out of employment ? Every man of wealth
could without trouble procure for himself as many broken
mercenaries as he could afford to pay.

On the whole, the moral considerations give the main explanation of the failure of the English arms in the last years of the
long struggle. But it is well to remember that there were
also purely military considerations to be borne in mind. The
most important one was the inadequacy of the old English
system of tactics, the game of the defensive battle accepted
on an advantageous ground, to fit all the vicissitudes of war.
The commanders who had received the tradition of Agincourt
and Poictiers disliked assuming the offensive. Accustomed
to win success by receiving the attack of an obliging enemy,
who consented to assault well-chosen positions, they frequently
failed when opposed by adversaries who refrained on principle
from assaulting a position, but were continually coming into
action when least expected. In the open field, upon the march,
or while encamped, they were liable to be exposed to sudden
onslaughts. And sometimes the enemy turned their own system

against them, by placing himself on practically unassailable ground, where it would be madness to attack him.   By the end of the war the English officers and men had lost the old confidence, which had distinguished them in the days when the French still persisted in keeping to their former tactics of grand assaults in mass against well-chosen positions.   They were still good soldiers, but they had lost the expectation of inevitable victory.

A fortunate chance has preserved for us, in the pages of Blondel's *Reductio Normanniae*, a full account of the disastrous field of Formigny (April 15, 1450), the last battle but one fought by the English in their attempt to hold down their dominion beyond the Channel.   The narrative is most instructive, as explaining the changes of fortune during the later years of the great war.   The fight itself—though destined to decide the fate of all Normandy—was an engagement on a very small scale.   Some four thousand five hundred English had been collected for a desperate attempt to open the way to Caen.   In that town the Duke of Somerset, commander of all the English armies in France, was threatened by an overwhelming host led by King Charles in person.   To draw together a force, under Sir Matthew Gough, capable of taking the field, all the Norman fortresses had been stripped of their garrisons, and such reinforcements as could be procured, some two thousand five hundred men at most,[1] had been brought across from England under Sir Thomas Kyriel.   The relieving army composed of these two corps, succeeded in taking Valognes and forcing the dangerous fords of the Douve and Vire.   But hard by the village of Formigny it was confronted by a French corps under the Count of Clermont, one of several divisions which had been sent out to arrest the march of the English.   Clermont's troops did not greatly exceed their enemies in number : they appear, as far as conflicting accounts allow us to judge, to have consisted of six hundred *lances garnies* (*i.e.* three thousand combatants), two field-guns, and some local infantry.   The obligation to take the offensive rested with the English, who were bound to force their way to Caen.   Nevertheless Sir Thomas Kyriel and Sir Matthew Gough, the two veterans who commanded the relieving army, refused to assume the initiative.   The old prejudice in favour of

---

[1] To be exact, four hundred and twenty-five men-at-arms and two thousand and eighty bows.

fighting defensive battles was so strong that, forgetting the object of their expedition, they fell back and looked for a position in which to receive the attack of Clermont's troops. Finding behind the village of Formigny a brook lined with many orchards and plantations, which was well calculated to cover their flank and rear, they halted in front of it, and drew up their men in a convex line, the centre projecting, the wings drawn back : the right touched the stream. Three bodies of archers—each seven hundred strong—formed the line of the front; between them were stationed two " battles " of dismounted men-at-arms and billmen,[1] not in a line with the archers but drawn back. The left flank being rather " in the air," a body of men-at-arms, under Gough, were thrown out at some distance from it to serve as a wing-guard. Clermont did not attack immediately,[2] so the archers had ample time to fix their stakes, according to their invariable custom, and the whole force was beginning to cover itself with a trench,[3] when the enemy at last began to move. Through long experience the French had grown too wary to attack an English line of archers from the front : after feeling the position, they tried several partial assaults on the flanks, which were repulsed. Skirmishing had been going on for three hours without any decisive result, when Giraud, " master of the royal ordnance," brought up his two culverins, and placed them in a spot from which they enfiladed the English line. Galled by the fire of these pieces, part of the archers rushed out from behind their stakes, charged the French, seized the culverins, and routed the troops which protected them. If the whole of Kyriel's force had advanced at this moment some thought that the battle would have been won.[4] But the English commander adhered rigidly to his defensive tactics, and while he waited motionless, the fate of the battle was changed. The troops who had charged were attacked by one of the flank " battles " of French men-at-arms, who had dismounted, and advanced to win back the lost cannon: a desperate fight took place, while the English strove to drag the

[1] Billmen are not very often mentioned in these wars, but were here used to strengthen the very small proportion of men-at-arms.

[2] He was waiting for Richemont, to whom he had sent a request for succour.

[3] " Gladio ad usum fossarum verso, et ungue verrente tellurem concavant : et ante se campum equis inadibilem mira hostium astucia efficiebat " (Blondel, iv. 6).

[4] " Et si Anglici, incaepto conflictu praestantes, Gallos retrogressos insequi ausi fuissent," etc. (Blondel, iv. 7).

pieces towards their lines, and the enemy to recapture them. At last the French prevailed, and pushing the retreating body before them, reached the English position. The archers were unable to use their arrows, so closely were friend and foe intermixed in the crowd of combatants which slowly rolled back towards them. Thus the two armies met all along the line in a hand-to-hand combat, and a sanguinary mêlée began. The fate of the battle was still doubtful when a new French force arrived in the field. The Counts of Richemont and Laval, coming up from St. Lô, appeared on the flank of the English position with three hundred *lances garnies, i.e.* twelve hundred men. All Kyriel's troops were engaged, and he was unable to meet this new attack. His men recoiled to the brook at their backs, and were at once broken into several isolated corps. Gough cut his way through the French, and reached Bayeux with the troops who had formed the flank guard. But Kyriel and the infantry were surrounded, and the whole " main-battle " was annihilated. A few hundred archers escaped, and their commander, with some hundreds more, was taken captive, but the French gave little quarter,[1] and their heralds counted next day three thousand seven hundred and seventy-four English corpses lying on the field. Seldom has an army suffered a more complete disaster : of Kyriel's small force not less than five-sixths was destroyed. What number of the French fell we are unable to ascertain : their annalists speak of the death of twelve men-at-arms, none of them of note, but make no further mention of their losses. " They declare what number they slew," sarcastically observes an English chronicler,[2] " but they write not how many of themselves were slain and destroyed. This was well-nigh the first foughten field they gat on the English, wherefore I blame them not ; though they of a little make much, and set forth all, and hide nothing that may sound to their glory."

There still remained unsubdued the old Plantagenet hold-ing in the south of France, the remnant of the duchy of Aqui-taine, around Bordeaux and Bayonne, which had remained free

---

[1] " Fusis enim Anglorum bellis robusti quingenti sagittarii in hortum sentibus conseptum prosiliunt . . . ac inexorabili Gallorum ferocitate, ut quisque genu flexo arcum traderet, [in sign of surrender] omnes (nec unus evasit) gladio con-fodiuntur " (Blondel, iv. 8).

[2] Grafton, *Henry VI.*, year xxvii.

because the spirit of the inhabitants was Gascon, not French, and their loyalty still clung to the house which had ruled them from time immemorial. The strength of the attachment of the Bordelais to England was strongly shown in 1451–52. The main French army was turned against Guienne and over-ran it in the former year, no succour at all being forthcoming from beyond the seas, as the first troubles of the Wars of the Roses were just breaking out in England. The Gascons had to surrender town after town. It looked as if the struggle was over when Bordeaux fell in August 1451. But the moment that the French army had withdrawn, Gascon nobles and burgesses appeared in London to pledge themselves that they would rise again at the first appearance of help from King Henry. And the pledge was well kept. Putting aside civil troubles for a moment, the English government sent the veteran Lord Talbot with a very small army, less than three thousand men, to make the last venture. He landed in October 1452 at the mouth of the Garonne, and at once the whole country-side rose and joined him, Bordeaux throwing open its gates and driving out the French garrison. In a few weeks much had been won back, and a considerable Anglo-Gascon force was in the field.

Castillon, the last battle of the great French war, was unlike Formigny, in that the English attacked, instead of waiting in position to receive the enemy in the old style. But, indeed, an offensive policy was forced upon them. The veteran Lord Talbot, like Gough and Kyriel at Formigny, was trying to relieve a besieged friendly garrison, Castillon town being held for the English. The French besiegers had fortified lines of circumvallation all around the place, and had lined them (it is said) with more than a hundred pieces of artillery. They remained quiet in their lines, and would not come out, defying Talbot to break through and relieve the place. Determined not to give up the game, Talbot, like Dagworth at Roche Derien, formed men-at-arms and archers in a phalanx, and dashed at what he thought the weakest point in the line of palisades. The attempt was hopeless, the column of attack was blown to pieces by the French artillery, and though the charge was pressed home, and a few men got within the French lines, the result of the battle was never for a moment doubtful. When the attack had failed the French came out of their entrenchments, and swept the remnants away.   Talbot, who had been mortally wounded by a cannon-ball, was killed, and so were his son and most of the other English commanders.

Such was the end of the English attempt to hold Guienne, the only part of the French possessions of Henry VI. which was still loyal in spirit, and where the people sided with their old suzerain, and took the field freely, up to the last, under the English banner.   A great part of Talbot's army at Castillon had been Guiennois and not English.   We may sum up the moral of Formigny and Castillon by saying that the form of tactics of which Edward III. and Henry V. had given the classical examples at Creçy and Agincourt lost its efficiency when the enemy refused to attack, and forced the English to take the offensive, against artillery or prepared positions. Under such conditions the old tactics proved comparatively ineffective.   They presupposed a defensive battle.

We have seen that cannon were being employed freely throughout the last stage of the great French war, and latterly in the field as well as in sieges.   In the dreary annals of the last twenty years of the war, when the limits of the English territory were always receding, the French siege-train did its work as a rule with success.   The campaigns which drove the English out of their last strongholds both in Normandy and Guienne were both notable for the large amount of cannon employed, and for the efficiency with which Jean and Gaspard Bureau used them.   As has been noted above, these two brothers conducted sixty successful siege operations in the single year 1449–50.[1]   Cannon had improved at such a rate during the last twenty years that tedious operations like the battering of Rouen, Meaux, or Orleans were no longer the rule.   It is not unnatural, therefore, that in the war on English soil which followed immediately on the disasters in Normandy and Guienne, we shall find guns playing a more visible part from that which they had taken in the last civil strife in the days of Hotspur and Owen Glendower.

[1] See above, p. 226.

CHAPTER III

THE WARS OF THE ROSES (1455–1485)

IT might perhaps have been expected that the disasters of the final stage of the Hundred Years' War would have taught English generals that the time-honoured tactics of Crecy and Agincourt were not infallible. That they were good for dealing with an enemy who consented to attack an English army ranged in a position which it had chosen at its leisure, was still true. In such a case it did not much matter if the enemy were horse or foot, or both combined. But problems had been raised to which the old receipt for victory gave no adequate answer—what was to be done with an enemy who altogether declined to take the offensive, or who stockaded himself and used artillery in profusion, or who delivered unexpected assaults against an English army on the march ? Was the employment of mounted, in conjunction with dismounted, men-at-arms a complete mistake ? If that device had been a failure at Agincourt and Verneuil, it had been of some effect at Patay and Formigny. Could artillery be employed to advantage in the field, as well as behind earthworks ? Had the development of the hand-gun to be taken into consideration as a new force in war ?

On the whole, we must decide that these questions, if asked, were met in the main with a reply in the negative. When the English, driven home to their own soil, plunged into thirty years of civil strife, they fell back on the tactics of Shrewsbury Field. Towton and Barnet and Tewkesbury were fought with the old combination of bow and spear, with no complications of mounted squadrons, and with no decisive employment of artillery. At the two last-named battles, as at Northampton and 'Lose-Coat Field,' there were guns used, but they rarely affected the fate of the day. Normally the men-at-arms dismounted, and threw out the archers on their flanks, and settled down to an old-fashioned battle, starting with a bitter archery-contest and ending with a hand-to-hand mêlée.

In the main the cause of this resumption of old tactics was the continued supremacy of the bow. Though the English had been driven out of France, it was not because the archer had been superseded as the most effective infantryman either by the pikeman, the arbalester, or the hand-gunner. Despite of the recent disasters, the testimony of all Europe was given in favour of the longbow. Charles of Burgundy considered a corps of six hundred English bowmen the flower of his infantry. Charles of France, a few years earlier, had made the " archer " the basis of his new militia, in a vain attempt to naturalise the weapon of his enemies beyond the Channel. James of Scotland, after a similar endeavour, had resigned himself to ill success, and turned the archery of his subjects to ridicule in verse.

There are few periods which appear more likely to present to the inquirer a series of interesting military problems, than the years of the great struggle, in which the national weapons and national tactics of the English were turned against each other. The Wars of the Roses were, however, unfortunate in their historians. The dearth of exact information concerning the various engagements is remarkable, when we consider the ample materials which are to be found for the history of the preceding periods. The meagre annals of William of Worcester, Warkworth, Gregory, and the continuer of the *Croyland Chronicle*, the single good monograph by the author of the *Arrival of King Edward IV.*, and the ignorant generalities of Whethamstede, are insufficiently supplemented by the later works of Grafton and Hall. When all has been collated, we still fail to grasp the details of many of the battles. Not in one single instance can we reconstruct the exact array of a Yorkist or a Lancastrian army. Enough, however, survives to enable us to draw some conclusions, if we regret the scantiness of the sources of our information.

Nothing is more extraordinary than the way in which England, which had found the greatest difficulty in providing expeditions of three thousand or four thousand men for the French war, was able to put really considerable armies, which sometimes reached ten thousand men a side, into the field in the

fratricidal civil wars which followed.[1]   But the explanation of
the phenomenon is not very hard. The national government
from 1422 to 1453, in raising men for the long strife overseas,
took them into pay for long periods, at high rates, and had to
maintain them far from home.   On the other hand, the armies
of the Wars of the Roses were not regular forces embodied for
long service, but casual and tumultuary, hurriedly raised and
suddenly disbanded, often after only a few days of fighting.
These armies were mustered and kept together by the personal
efforts of the lords and knights who had taken sides, and knew
that their own heads and estates depended on their being able
to put as many men as possible into line at the crisis. A
typical army of this time consisted of three elements.

First came the " household men " of each lord, the nucleus
of professional fighters whom he always kept about his person
—largely veterans of the French war.

Secondly came the armed levies whom both sides raised
from time to time by the old system of " commissions of array,"
from the shires.   But we must remember that when two
committees of partisans were striving to call out the shire
levies in the cause of the rival kings, the wise gave heed to
neither summons, and waited for the ordeal of battle to determine which sovereign they should acknowledge. The towns
in particular preserved a most Gallio-like attitude, and permitted the adversaries to tear each other to their hearts' content
before the judgment seat, before giving their decision as to
which was their lawful lord. The only occasion when a
general shire-levy seems to have turned out in great strength
was before the rout of Ludford, in October 1459, when the
troops assembled in King Henry's name were so numerous
that nothing was left for the Duke of York but to fly in haste.
This was an altogether exceptional incident.

But the really important element in the hosts of the Wars
of the Roses were the men gathered under the system of
" Livery and Maintenance."   This pernicious practice recalled
the fashion of pre-Conquest feudalism. The knights and
squires of a district bound themselves, by written agreement,
to some great neighbouring lord, to espouse his quarrels in every
place from the law-court to the battlefield, in return for his

---

[1] Despite of all exaggeration by chroniclers, we cannot put the armies of Towton
and Barnet at less.

protection and assistance in all troubles of their own. The Magnate gave his adherents his " livery," that is, he allowed them to wear his badge—the Bear and Ragged Staff, the Stafford Knot, the Fiery Cresset, or whatever it might be— and engaged to "maintain" them, *i.e.* to champion all their rights and claims. They, on the other hand, had to take the field under his banner with all the tenants and retainers that they could raise.

How large the forces collected in this fashion might be, can be guessed from the content of one indenture which has chanced to survive. In 1452 Walter Strickland, a Westmoreland squire of wide estates, contracts with Richard, Earl of Salisbury, to follow him with all his tenants, viz. " bowmen horsed and harnessed, 69 ; billmen horsed and harnessed, 74 ; bowmen without horses, 71 ; billmen without horses, 76 "— a compact little body of nearly three hundred men. There is a saving clause in the indenture that the call to arms must not be detrimental to Strickland's loyalty to the King. But this was a hypocritical formality : in the early days of the war the Yorkists always pleaded that they were the King's true subjects, anxious to deliver him from evil councillors.

We can easily see how a great peer, who had gained a few such adherents, could bring to his party gathering a contingent numbering many hundreds. It is clear that when the system had spread far, the power to issue Commissions of Array became comparatively otiose, since most of the men who should have served in the shire-levy would already be under arms in some great lord's livery.

With these facts before us it is easy to understand how a considerable force could be collected for a short campaign, without there being any great need for preparation, or for a regular supply of pay. Every knight had his armour in his closet, every bowman or billman his weapon in his chimney corner. A campaign abroad was a thing which required long notice and much money. But a campaign in the next shire was a thing easy to begin and easy to finish : all armies of this time were quickly gathered and as quickly dispersed.

As to tactics, the full supply of archery on both sides made the fighting very bloody : but as the masses of bowmen neutralised each other, it was not necessarily they who won the field. Both sides found the arrow-shower too hard to bear, and were forced to close in the end, and to settle the matter by hand-to-hand fighting.   There was only one considerable engagement in which archery was all-important, and this was because one side in it happened to be much more fully provided with it than the other.   This was Edgecote Field, near Banbury (July 26, 1469), where the Yorkist army under the Earl of Pembroke, being mainly Welsh levies from the March (not from the bow-using South Wales), had a comparatively small number of archers among them, and were beaten off the field in the interchange of missiles by the Northern Rebels of " Robin of Redesdale," who were much better provided with that arm. Amid the snowstorm of Towton there was a curious stratagem employed by Lord Fauconberg which gave the Yorkists the advantage in the preliminary interchange of missiles ; [1] but as the armies erelong closed and got to prolonged hand-to-hand fighting, we cannot say that the arrow actually settled the day—it was the bill and sword which were the decisive weapons.

Of some of these great and bloody battles the chronicles have left us such a scanty record of details that it is hard to make out their tactical importance.   We practically know nothing of Mortimer's Cross or Hexham, Hedgely Moor or Wakefield.   Northampton was a battle in which one side, borrowing a leaf from the French in the late war, stockaded itself behind a line of entrenchments from water to water, lavishly garnished with artillery.   This device did not, as might have been expected, discomfit the Yorkists, because a sudden heavy rainstorm drenched the powder of the Lancastrians, and hardly a gun went off when their opponents charged their palisades.   There was some treachery too ; at one point of the line a contingent admitted the Yorkists into the entrenchments with little or no fighting.   Both the first and the second battles of St. Albans were street fights, the former on a very small scale—the taking of a barricaded town—the latter on a larger one, where the fighting in the streets was only a part of the whole game, which ranged over the adjoining heaths.

---

[1] Blinding snow having set in, Fauconberg threw out a skirmishing line which opened upon the Lancastrians, and retired after loosing a few flights.   The enemy, finding himself within range, replied heavily ; but as the Yorkists had fallen back many yards, all the Lancastrian arrows fell into empty ground, till their stock was nearly exhausted.

410 THE ART OF WAR IN THE MIDDLE AGES [1461

The great regular battles were Towton, Barnet, and Tewkesbury. In all three of them considerable armies were in the field, and in all three regular lines of battle in the old style were formed. Barnet and Tewkesbury form part of one complicated piece of strategy—Edward IV.'s greatest achievement—with which we must deal as the crises of a campaign, and not as two isolated battles.

A few points more are worth noticing in regard to the Wars of the Roses from a general point of view. The first is the excessive loss of life among the leaders compared with the led throughout the war. Two causes may be given for this. The first was the inordinate heaviness that knightly armour had attained at this time, which (as has been said before)[1] made flight very difficult at the moment when the line had been broken. The second was deliberate policy on the part of the conquerors in some cases: Edward IV. in particular habitually directed his men to let the commons go, and to strike down without quarter every one of gentle blood,[2] and Warwick sometimes did the same. This embittered spirit had not been seen in the earlier years of the war, when at the first St. Albans prisoners were freely taken. It was only in 1460 that deliberate and systematic executions of prisoners came in, first practised by the Lancastrians after Wakefield, and second St. Albans, and later, in revenge, by the Yorkists on a larger and more ruthless scale, so that after Hexham and Tewkesbury there was a very large set of executions in cold blood. In ordinary wars prisoners of high rank were valuable assets, representing so much ransom a head. But when each side had attainted the other, and distributed its estates among new owners, there was little use in pardoning, since the spoils of the prisoner had already been discounted.

That this cruelty was deliberate, and did not result from mere lust for blood, is sufficiently shown by the careful way in which both sides avoided indiscriminate sack and slaughter of non-combatants. Though the towns were constantly being taken by one side or the other, there is hardly a mention of pillage on a large scale, still less of massacre. Almost the only case in which we find widespread complaints of the chroniclers as to misbehaviour by an army, was that of Queen

---

[1] See above, p. 377.

[2] This he told Philip de Commines, who mentions it in book iii. § 5.

Margaret's northern host, in its march from York to St. Albans in 1461; and then it is only reckless plunder along the road, not slaughter, that is laid to their charge. Indeed, the victorious Lancastrians lost their chance of capturing London on the day after the victory of St. Albans by reason of their chiefs refusing to allow the army to enter the gates till it had got into order again—a piece of policy which ruined Henry VI., since the defeated Yorkists rallied and reoccupied the city, while the Lancastrians and the Corporation of London were arguing about terms of quiet and peaceable entry. That both parties showed wisdom in their self-restraint seems to be indicated by the fact that in all cases during these campaigns the cities and the countryside, with few exceptions, yielded quietly to the victor, because they knew that they had nothing much to fear from him. He would behead peers and knights, but would do no harm to merchants and burgesses, however often they might have sworn their allegiance to one side or the other. This tended to make the wars far less of a curse than might have been expected to the nation; despite of the many arbitrary transferences of landed property from owners on one side to owners on the other, the prosperity of the nation as a whole does not seem to have been impaired to any serious extent—as witness many a fine church and manor house dating from the years 1450 to 1490.

It is a curious fact that the whole of these long wars only brought to the front one general of the first class—King Edward IV. Warwick, the King-Maker, though the most prominent fighting-man of the first ten years of the period, was only a capable leader after the fashion of many of the English generals in the old French war—such as Bedford or Talbot. He introduced no new ideas into the military art—nor could he boast, like King Edward, that he had never been beaten in any battle in which he was engaged. One of his great fights, the second St. Albans, was distinctly lost by bad tactical disposition of his army, on a front that was too long for his numbers, and had no compensating local strength. At Barnet, however, his final failure, he seems to have committed no special military error, and to have been discomfited merely by the superior tactical power of his opponent, backed by a certain amount of bad luck. On the whole it was as statesman and an organiser rather than as a general that he made his mark on history.

The Yorkist king, on the other hand, never failed in any task that he undertook, from his first appearance in the field at Northampton down to his final victory at Tewkesbury.   Nor is the reason far to seek : he was not only a good tactician, a hard fighter, and a genial leader of men, much loved by his troops, but he was one of the first mediæval generals who showed a complete appreciation of the value of time in war. His marches were even more remarkable than his battles. This came out equally in the campaign of 1461, when he was acting as a commander-in-chief at the age of twenty, and in his Barnet-Tewkesbury campaign, when he was ten years older, and in the full vigour of age and experience.

On December 30, 1460, the army raised by Queen Margaret and the Lancastrian lords of the north had defeated and slain Richard of York at Wakefield.   The victors knew so little the value of time, that they were only facing Warwick and the rallied forces of the Yorkists at St. Albans on February 17, seven weeks after their first victory.   In the second fight, too, they won the day—our blurred narratives of this battle only allow us to judge that Warwick's tactics were not over-good, and that some of his troops were not over-loyal.

All now turned on the relative appreciation of the value of time shown by the victorious Lancastrians and by the Yorkists. St. Albans is but one short march from London ; but the Queen and her generals allowed themselves to be persuaded by that worthy but misguided person, Henry VI., that it would be better to enter the capital peacefully under terms of surrender, than to rush it, with high probabilities of misbehaviour on the part of the Northern moss-troopers, on the day after the victorious battle.   The negotiations went on for nine days, and then came to an unexpected end.

Edward of York was at this time in the far west, with a small army, making head against the Lancastrians of Wales and the Marches.   On February 2, he had inflicted a crushing defeat upon them at Mortimer's Cross, near Wigmore, and had pursued them far into the mountains.   The news of the Lancastrians' march on London having reached him, he turned back, and was at Gloucester on February 20, when he received the news of the disaster of St. Albans from his cousin Warwick, who had retired westward into Oxfordshire after his defeat.

Now came the test of his intelligence and activity. On February 22 he was already at Burford, where he was joined by Warwick and the wrecks of his army. From the Earl he got news that London had not yet fallen, and that the Corporation were spinning out time in negotiations. Edward resolved to dash in by a forced march, and save the capital, if the thing were possible. This move was made at a splendid pace, and with complete success : starting from Burford on February 23, he entered London unopposed on the afternoon of February 26, just in time to stop the capitulation. On the next morning Edward was proclaimed King, amid unwonted enthusiasm on the part of the Londoners, who considered that he had saved them from ruinous exactions on the part of the Lancastrians. The Northern Army, cheated of its expected money-contribution from the City, showed great discontent. Many men went off homeward, deserting the royal standard, and a day later a retreat to York was ordered for the whole army (February 27).

The enemy having disappeared from his front, Edward thought it possible to spend a few days in organising the administrative and constitutional foundations of his new government, and in picking up as many men from the scattered Yorkists of the South as he could collect. But when he had once started from London (March 16), he pushed matters on with his accustomed celerity, and by March 29 brought the enemy to action at Towton, a few miles south of York, where he and Warwick utterly discomfited them, in a battle of the old type fought with bow and lance in a blinding blizzard of snow.

This was the first campaign in which Edward showed his appreciation of the value of time, and his power of moving troops with great rapidity. But the Barnet-Tewkesbury campaign was still more creditable to him as a general.

The preliminaries of this daring strategical adventure may be given in a few words. In October 1470, Edward had lost his crown, and had been driven ignominiously out of England, surprised by the sudden rising of the partisans of Warwick, who had thrown off his allegiance, hurried to France, and leagued himself with his old enemy Queen Margaret of Anjou. Edward had been caught unprepared, before he could mobilise that predominant part of the Yorkists' faction which was personally attached to him. He thought, and quite correctly, that he had not been fairly beaten, and from abroad entered into secret negotiations with his partisans.[1] Meeting much encouragement from them, he started (March 1471), only six months after his expulsion, to invade England. With some twelve hundred followers he sailed from Flushing, his place of exile and shelter in the dominions of his brother-in-law, Charles of Burgundy, who had lent him fifty thousand crowns and a few German mercenaries to help the venture.

Warwick had been apprised of the coming invasion, and had taken his precautions against it. He had a fleet watching the Flemish coast, under his nephew, the Bastard of Fauconberg. The Earl of Oxford, a stalwart old Lancastrian, had been sent into Norfolk to arrest suspected Yorkists (who were many) in that direction. Warwick's brother, Lord Montagu, was in charge of Yorkshire, and had called out the Neville vassals in the North Riding, where their interest was over-powering. But a storm drove Fauconberg's squadron into harbour, and in the thick of it Edward set sail from Flushing. He touched at Cromer in Norfolk, only to find that Oxford was guarding the coast of East Anglia too carefully to make it advisable to land there. Edward then took a bold resolve—driving before the gale he made for the Spurn Head, having resolved to come ashore in Holderness, a region which he thought would have been left unguarded because it had never been Yorkist in sympathy. He was right; he disembarked quite unopposed at Ravenspur, within the estuary of the Humber. The countryside was hostile, but before bands had begun to gather against him, Edward had made a forced march through it, and presented himself before the gates of York on March 18, almost before his landing was generally known. Towns never fought in the Wars of the Roses, as we have already seen, and Edward disarmed the opposition of the citizens by declaring that he came not to claim the crown, but simply to ask for his paternal inheritance, the Duchy of York. The town let him in, and fed and entertained his troops. But at this moment Lord Montagu appeared with the Neville levies of the North Riding, and placed himself at Tadcaster,

---

[1] The narrative of this campaign comes mainly from the anonymous but invaluable *Arrival of King Edward*, the one good military narrative written by a contemporary during the whole of the thirty years of the Wars of the Roses.

across the path from York to London. Edward dared not
fight him, being still far too weak, but made a flank march
through Wakefield and Doncaster (March 21) by which he got
completely round his opponent's left wing, and again placed
himself on the London road. Montagu, whose generalship
had been so bad as to cause him to be suspected of disloyalty
to the Lancastrian cause, could only set out in pursuit of him—
a day too late. In the West Riding Edward had picked up
quite a number of followers, Stanleys, Harringtons, Parrs,
and other old Yorkists, and was now three or four thousand
strong. Still, when he reached Nottingham on March 23,
his position was a very dangerous one. Montagu was pursuing
him : Warwick, the moment he had received news of the
invasion, had marched from London northward on the 22nd,
and was making for Coventry. He had sent orders for Oxford
to join him, with the Lancastrians of the eastern counties, while
Clarence, his son-in-law (of whose treachery he was ignorant),
had received a commission to mobilise Gloucestershire and
Wiltshire. Somerset, the head of the old Lancastrian party,
had gone to his own county to raise troops there and in Dorset.

Edward at Nottingham would, as he advanced south,
have all these forces converging upon him. But they were
scattered, and he was in the central position. The nearest
enemy to him was Oxford, who had now reached Newark.
Edward marched straight at him, and forced him to retire
eastward into Lincolnshire—but instead of pursuing he made
for Leicester, the centre of a strong Yorkist district, where he
is said to have been joined by several thousand retainers of
his friend Lord Hastings (March 27). By his rapid movement he had outmarched Montagu, who was now two days
behind him.

The next foe in front was Warwick himself, who had reached
Coventry, and was raising his own Midland forces there.
But he had not as yet an army fit to face Edward, and shut
himself up in the town (March 29) to wait till Montagu and
Clarence should come up. The King at once moved round
Coventry, and placed himself to the south of it, so as to get in
between the King-Maker and his coming supports, and at
the same time to block the London road, and cut off Warwick
from the capital. There was more than a strategic object
in this : he knew that his brother Clarence was a traitor,

and was coming to reinforce him, not to help his father-in-law.
On April 3 the treacherous Duke led his forces into the midst
of Edward's army, and joined him near Banbury.

But on the same day, Montagu united with Warwick at
Coventry, and Oxford also came up, so that the King-Maker
was in a position to fight, even in spite of the defection of
Clarence. He started to seek Edward, but the latter had
moved on steadily, making straight for London, and out-
marching his pursuers reached Daventry on April 7, and St.
Albans on April 10. Next day he was before the gates of
London, where, the Lancastrian partisans having gone out
with Warwick ten days before, the Yorkist faction opened the
gates. On seeing Edward in possession of London, his old
adherents in Essex and Kent joined him in great strength.
When Warwick reached Dunstable on April 11, he heard that
London had surrendered that very morning. He slowed down
in order to pick up Edmund of Somerset, who joined him with
contingents from the west on the 13th, and then resumed his
march upon the capital. On the evening of that same day
he lay across the great North Road, camping apparently at
Monken Hadley, a short mile from Barnet. Edward marched
out that same afternoon, and at nightfall they lay opposite each
other in the dark, the one on the high ground across the London
road, the other a little lower down, just outside the village of
Barnet. Between them lay the open heath then known as
Gladsmoor, but now as Hadley Green. Their scouts got into
touch, and Warwick, aware of an enemy near at hand, ordered
his guns to play on the spot where he judged that the Yorkists
were lying. We are told that they overshot the mark, as did
Edward's artillery when it tried to retaliate, the armies being
nearer than either had calculated.

But at sunrise they were no more visible to each other than
in the night, for a dense fog had come on, and lasted all the
forenoon. The opponents groped their way toward each other
by sound rather than by sight, and as it chanced each outflanked the other's left wing unconsciously.[1] The order of
array was that in the King's army his youngest brother,
Richard Duke of Gloucester, had the vaward, Edward and his
elder brother Clarence the main-battle, and Lord Hastings

---

[1] I can see no justification for Sir James Ramsay's view that the armies faced east
and west, not north and south, in his *York and Lancaster*, ii. pp. 370–71.

the left or rearward wing. Among their opponents Warwick took the left, yielding the posts of greater honour to Lancastrians ; the Duke of Somerset had the centre, and the Earl of Oxford the right. Archery being ineffective in the thick fog, the opponents soon came to hand-strokes. The Lancastrian right under Oxford found itself completely outflanking Hastings, who was turned, rolled up, and driven off the field. Some of his men fled as far as London, and reported there that all was lost. With inexcusable heedlessness Oxford did not keep his men together nor turn upon the Yorkist centre, but allowed them to pursue the fugitives far into the fog, where they got scattered and lost their bearings.

Meanwhile, on the other flank, Richard of Gloucester turned Warwick's exposed flank, and forced him to throw it back *en potence* and to lose much ground. But the earl kept his men together, and they did not break up, as the Yorkist left had done. King Edward and Somerset appear to have fought a hard but even fight with their respective main-battles. The turning movement of Gloucester would probably have settled the battle in the end—but it was, by complete chance, closed in another fashion. The Earl of Oxford, having collected eight hundred of his men, started to feel his way back to the battle, guided by its clamour alone. He had lost his way so entirely, that he appeared not in King Edward's rear, where his presence would have been fatal, but behind Somerset's line. Mistaking his banner with the star of De Vere for the King's device of the " Sun in Splendour," Somerset's archers took the newcomers for Yorkists and began to shoot at them. Presently each recognised the others, but drew the false deduction that their comrades had deserted to King Edward—there had been so much treachery of late that the idea was not wholly unnatural. The cry of " Treason " burst out on both sides, and Oxford's and Somerset's men made off through the fog in different directions, leaving Warwick and his wing deserted on the field. They were soon surrounded and exterminated : the great Earl was slain " somewhat flying " as he tried to get back to his horse in the skirts of Wrotham Park. We are told by Commines that he had been wont to keep mounted in battle, for the better direction of his line, but had on this occasion been persuaded to dismount, by his brother the Marquis of Montagu, lest his Lancastrian allies should accuse him of

being too loth to risk his person.[1] Montagu fell with him,
but no other peer or knight of great note.[2] King Edward's
casualties were probably as numerous as those of the enemy—
he lost the lords Cromwell and Say, and the heirs to the
titles of Berners and Montjoy. In his routed left wing there
had been considerable slaughter, while the fog allowed an
easy escape to the main body of his opponents, pursuit being
practically impossible.

That after such a decisive victory as Barnet there should
have been another pitched battle fought within three weeks was
due to the indomitable and misdirected energy of the ever-
unlucky Margaret of Anjou. She had been lingering in
France with her son Edward Prince of Wales, unwilling,
apparently, to put herself in the power of her new ally, Warwick.
Only the news of the Yorkist landing at Ravenspur determined
her to cross the Channel. Adverse winds kept her in the
Seine mouth till April 12, and it was only on the very day of
Warwick's death that she came ashore at Weymouth, with
no armed force save a few French mercenaries lent her by
Louis XI. On the 16th she got the news of Barnet : there were
the strongest reasons for turning back at once to France, but
she had come ashore in the West Country, which was devoted
to her cause, and only a part of the knighthood of Devon and
Somerset had been in time for Barnet. The Duke of Somerset
himself came to join her in a few days, with the wreck of the
Lancastrian army from the recent battle. Either she persuaded him, or he persuaded her, to continue the struggle.
King Edward was far off, enjoying the fruits of victory ; before
he could move there would be time for her to raise all the
West. Moreover, news had come that Jasper Tudor, Earl of
Pembroke, had collected a considerable force in Wales, and
that the Bastard of Fauconberg, who commanded Warwick's
fleet, was off the mouth of the Thames and threatening London.
It was resolved to strike for the lower Severn, join with the
Welsh levies, and try once more the fortune of war.

By April 22, Margaret and Somerset had reached Taunton,
being joined every day by small succours from Devon and
Cornwall. King Edward had dismissed part of his Barnet

---

[1] Commines, book iii. chap. vii.
[2] Though the Duke of Exeter was left for dead on the field. He was, however,
found by his friends to be still alive, and hurried into sanctuary.

army at once, and even when he got the news of the Queen's landing had naturally supposed that she would set sail for France on hearing of Warwick's end.   But when she showed no signs of doing so, and was reported to be marching inland, he had at once to take his measures.   It was obviously necessary to mobilise again without delay, and then both to keep between her and London, and to prevent her from joining the Welsh army of Jasper of Pembroke.   If she desired to meet the Earl, the natural place for their junction would be on the lower Severn, and presumably she would make for Gloucester Bridge, the shortest route to Wales.   Accordingly Edward marched from Windsor, the spot which he had chosen for his mobilisa-tion, for Cirencester, a place on which all the Roman roads of Western England converge : for it has direct communication with Gloucester, with Bath, and also with the eastern road which runs through Berkshire to Speen and London.   To go farther west than Cirencester would be hazardous, since the Queen might take the bold, if risky, step of marching on London direct ;   and if Edward had moved westward to Gloucester, or some other locality suitable for blocking her road northward, she would gain several marches on him if she struck for the capital.   On April 29, the day on which Edward reached Cirencester, Margaret and her army were at Bath—from which she could move either on the London road, on the Bristol road alongside of the Severn estuary, or on the Cirencester road if she were courting a prompt battle.

On April 30, on learning that the Lancastrians were certainly not on the London road, Edward moved against them to Malmesbury.   But on getting there he found that the enemy, having news of his approach, had taken the Bristol road, the one farthest from him, obviously intending to coast up the estuary of the Severn towards Gloucester.   Edward at once swerved north, and on May 1 was at Sodbury, where he discovered that by rapid marching the Queen had just got past him, and was but a few miles away, moving on Berkeley. If she should reach Gloucester before her pursuer, there was a strong possibility that the citizens (acting as all townsmen did in those days) would open their gates, to avoid the chance of a sack.   And if the Lancastrians got off over Gloucester Bridge into Wales, the campaign might be indefinitely pro-longed.   The King therefore sent swift riders to Richard

Beauchamp, Constable of Gloucester Castle, bidding him keep the gates closed at all costs for a few hours, as he was so close on the heels of the enemy that they would not be able to undertake even the shortest of attacks on the city.

Edward then, instead of descending into the valley-road which the Lancastrians had taken, cut across by a parallel road along the crest of Cotswold, which was a trifle shorter than that in the plain of Berkeley. This day (May 2) was one of tremendous exertion for both armies, and each of them covered nearly forty miles—a fact which suggests that in both of them billmen and bowmen no less than men-at-arms, must have been " horsed and harnessed," for the feat would have been impossible for true infantry. During great part of the march the Yorkists on the heights could make out the march of the enemy in the lower road. When the Lancastrians reached the gates of Gloucester in the afternoon they summoned the place, and the Constable had considerable difficulty in preventing the Corporation from admitting them. He succeeded however, and Somerset and the Queen, seeing that the shortest way to Wales was barred, and that the Yorkists were only a few miles off, ordered their weary army to continue their march along the Severn. They struggled on nine miles more to Tewkesbury, the point where the Avon falls into the Severn : but were then so dead beat that they could not push on for the seven or eight miles more which would have taken them to a point of safety—Upton Bridge, which was unguarded, and where passage toward Wales would have been possible. Probably the halt was made because there were two defiles before the weary army—that through the town of Tewkesbury, and then that over the Avon bridge beyond. The army and its train would have got jammed in them, and would have taken many hours to get through. So they halted in the field outside Tewkesbury and encamped there.

Edward, after an equally fatiguing march, descended from Cotswold, passed through Cheltenham, and forced his men on for five miles more, till they encamped at Tredington, so close to the enemy that it was impossible for him to get away without fighting. The Lancastrians, however, had no intention of further retreat—they considered, like General Smith-Dorien at Le Cateau, that to deliver battle in a strong position gave a weary army a better chance than to continue its retreat for

another day, with an active enemy immediately upon its heels.
The position was a tempting one, from the tactical point of
view.   The rolling ground outside Tewkesbury to the south
was covered (as the writer of the *Arrival of King Edward* tells
us) with " evil lanes, and deep dykes, hedges, trees, and bushes."
Somerset arrayed his army in the normal three divisions along a
rising ground a mile outside the town, in front of a farm called
Gupshill, with the Swillgate stream covering his left, and a
smaller brook his right.   Somerset himself had the " vaward
battle " or right wing—in the centre was the young Prince
Edward under the charge of Lord Wenlock, one of the few
surviving followers of Warwick and Sir John Langstrother, the
Prior of the Knights of St. John.   The Earl of Devon had
the " rearward " or left wing.   Excellent though the ground
was for actual defence, it had the dreadful defect of a stream
and a defile to its rear, so that there was little chance of retreat
if a disaster should take place.

King Edward had an ugly piece of fighting in front of
him, owing to the strength of the Lancastrian position, but he
was determined to force on battle, because he had got his
enemies at bay.   He drew up his army in the same order and
under the same commanders as at Barnet—Lord Hastings on
the left or rearward wing, himself and his brother Clarence
in the centre, Richard of Gloucester on the right.   He detached an ambush or flank guard of two hundred spears to
his extreme left beyond Hastings' line, fearing lest it might
be turned under cover of the trees of Tewkesbury Park—this
precaution turned out to be useful for offence, though it had
been intended mainly for defence.

On arriving in front of the Lancastrian line, Edward found
the position so strong that he would not attack at once, but
sent forward his archers and (what is noticeable) certain
bombards, to gall the front of the enemy by fire at long range.
After the interchange of missiles had gone on for some time,
Somerset, either because the artillery was hitting him too hard,
or because he thought he had the Yorkists at a disadvantage
at the bottom of the slope, left his position behind his line of
hedges, and charged furiously down upon Hastings, in the
meadow in part of Gupshill farm, now known (from the slaughter
that took place there) as the " Red Piece."   Somerset's charge
was not supported along the line ; both Wenlock and Devon

refused to leave their vantage-ground and to go downhill into
the dip.   Hence the Duke's sally had ruinous consequences ;
he was held by Hastings, and taken in flank and rear both by
the ambush in the Park to the west, and by detachments from
the King's main-battle.   He was driven uphill again after a
hard tussle, and the Yorkists, following on his heels, scrambled
into the Lancastrian position along with him.   Edward, seeing
that he had got his enemy turned, ordered the whole line to
advance.   The Lancastrian centre, attacked on two sides,
was driven back towards Tewkesbury, and then Devon and
the left wing also gave way before Richard of Gloucester.
As a mark of the temper of the time we may mention that
Somerset's first act when he got back to the position, was to
seek out Lord Wenlock, the commander of the centre, furiously
accuse him of treachery for not joining in a general charge,
and then to beat out his brains with his battle-axe.   This
summary removal of a divisional general seems, however, to
have had no actual effect on the fate of the battle, though it
must surely have had some discouraging results on the morale
of actual spectators.   The Lancastrians, driven back on the
fords of the Swillgate and Severn, and jammed in the defile,
suffered dreadful slaughter.   Devon and Prince Edward were
" slain in the field," no quarter being given to leaders.   Somerset scrambled through and took sanctuary in Tewkesbury
Abbey, but was dragged out and beheaded next day, in
company with some twelve or fifteen knights of note.[1]

So ended the main struggle of the Wars of the Roses, for
within less than a month of the battle of Tewkesbury the last
outlying Lancastrian partisans were crushed.   And here also
ended the military career of that very capable general, King
Edward IV., for he never fought another battle, though he once
took over an expedition to France, which ended at Picquigny
(1475) in a bloodless meeting with King Louis and a profitable
peace.   He was a standing puzzle to his contemporaries—
careless, easy-going, and pleasure-loving in quiet times, but
a very thunderbolt of war when once he took the field.   The
shrewd Philip de Commines, who knew him well, summed
him up as " not a schemer, nor a man of foresight, but of an
invincible courage, and withal the most handsome prince that

[1] I owe much to Canon Bazeley's *Tewkesbury* (Gloucestershire Archæological
Society, 1903).

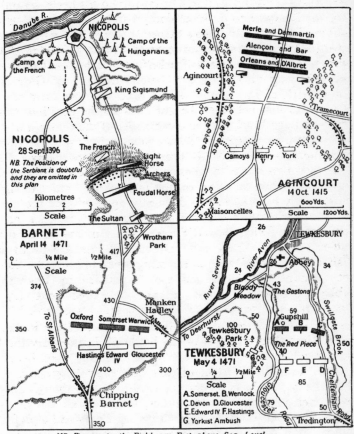

NB Figures in the Field are Feet above Sea-Level

ever my eyes did behold.　Most fortunate was he in his battles, for he fought nine general actions,[1] all on foot, and was always the conqueror."[2]　To talk of fortune in such a context is, of course, absurd ; if Edward had some luck, he deserved it by his keen strategical eye, and his admirable sense of the value of time.　To study his campaigns on the map, and with the calendar, is to become convinced that we have to deal with a modern general, not with one of the normal conductors of fifteenth-century war.

There was one more campaign in the Wars of the Roses, that of Bosworth Field (1485).　But this can hardly be taken for serious military study—since it was not settled by strategy or tactics, but by mere treachery.　Bosworth was not an honestly fought field, like Towton or Tewkesbury.　It was useless for Richard III. to bring his enemy to action, having against him a superiority of numbers of ten to three and the advantage of position, if his own troops refused to fight.　At the moment of collision on Ambion Hill, one-third of the royal army disobeyed the order to advance, and another third, on drawing near the field, joined the enemy.　Richard must have won, if his men had been ready to serve him.　But save certain desperate personal adherents, whose fortunes were tied up with his own, they refused to strike a blow.　It was no use for the King to charge himself, if the large majority of his army refused to follow.　Realising that he was doomed to ruin by his well-deserved unpopularity, he saw that there was no future for him, and deliberately threw away his life.　He could not hope for a turn of the tide and a restoration, such as his brother got in 1471, simply because he had earned the hatred of his whole realm.　Wherefore it was better to perish.　The rhymer of the " Lay of the Lady Bessie " grasped the situation, when he made the King reply to the knight who urged him to fly :[3]

> " ' Nay, give me my battle-axe in my hand : set the crown of England on my
> helm so high :
> For by God that shaped the sea and land, King of England this day I must
> die :
> One foot I will never flee while the breath is my breast within.'
> As he said so did it be : if he lost his life he died a king."

---

[1] Northampton, Mortimer's Cross, Towton, Barnet, Tewkesbury, are obvious. But what are the other four ? Perhaps Ferrybridge (the day before Towton) and ' Lose-Coat Field ' (March 1470) may count.　But I cannot make out the last two.
　　[2] Commines, book iii. chap. vii.　　　　[3] Percy Folio MS., iii. 257 and 362.

The strife of the Roses had for a whole generation kept England out of continental wars. There was no relation between the archaic English system of bow- and spear-tactics inherited from Edward III., and the general trend of military evolution over the sea. And when Bosworth had been fought and won, Henry VII., emerging from the welter to be the occupant of a most rickety throne, was averse to having anything to do with foreign campaigns. He reigned for twenty-four years of an epoch when the whole Art of War was in the melting-pot, when the great Italian campaigns were displaying all manner of new problems and experiments. But he kept out of the strife so far as he was able, sending, when pressed, one or two negligible contingents to foreign allies, and taking care that the one considerable force which he ever dispatched overseas—the Boulogne expedition of 1492—should not be involved in any serious fighting. Hence it is not too much to say that for over fifty years, from 1455 to 1509, England was completely out of touch with the modern developments of the Art of War. It was not till the reign of Henry VIII. began that the military problems of the Renaissance began to be studied on this side of the Channel. Wherefore, since this book deals with the Middle Ages alone, the story of English strategy and tactics must stop at 1485.

CONCLUSION

THE ART OF WAR AT THE END OF THE MIDDLE AGES

IT has long been recognised that it is impossible to cut up history into definite and precise periods, more especially when we have to deal with the history of many countries surveyed together, and not with the annals of a single state or nation. Nothing could be more futile than to endeavour to fix on some particular year or event as marking the end of the Middle Ages. Even if some date could be chosen which served fairly well for Italy, France, or Germany, it would be an unsatisfactory date for England, Russia, or Scandinavia. It is not practicable to divide history into water-tight compartments. And this is as true for the history of the Art of War as for the history of economic or religious or constitutional developments in Christendom at large.

But it is necessary to choose some halting-place, or the writer will find himself involved in one of those interminable " Universal Histories " which earlier and bolder generations did not fear to take in hand. I have ventured, therefore, to close this book with the year 1485, so as to exclude the great . ...an wars, which opened with the march of Charles VIII. across the Alps in 1494. An English writer may be pardoned for stopping at 1485, the end of the Wars of the Roses, because 1494 is in his own national history a date of no particular importance ; while when he has once begun to comment on the reign of Henry VII. he can no longer say that he is in the Middle Ages. For continental history 1485 is almost as good a point at which to break off as 1494—the last war of Granada being the only event of importance in the nine intervening years. But if once the date 1494 is passed, a new period in the world's military annals has begun, and there is no practicable halting-place till the end of the seventeenth century.

During the later chapters of this volume we have been working up to the conditions which made the experiments of the sixteenth century possible. The supremacy of feudal cavalry is long gone by; it had ended at Creçy and Laupen and Aljubarotta, if not at Courtrai and Bannockburn. There had followed on it the abnormal century in which the horseman forsook his horse—as the tale of Dupplin Muir, Poictiers, Sempach, Agincourt, and Arbedo has shown us. This unnatural experiment was caused by disasters suffered by the old-fashioned charging squadron at Bannockburn, Creçy, and Laupen, where it had failed when it tried its own unaided strength against the bow or the pike. For more than four generations Western commanders dismounted their men-at-arms, or at least the greater part of them, when they found themselves confronted with an army arrayed in the English style with the bow supported by the spear, or in the Swiss and Flemish style with the massive column of pikes. The experiment was seldom happy: at Roosebeke and Arbedo successes were scored by the dismounted man-at-arms against the pikeman. But there is a dismal list of failures—against the bow as at Mauron, Poictiers, Auray, Agincourt, Verneuil; and against the pike as at Sempach and several other more obscure Swiss victories.

This did not mean that the tactics of either the English or the Swiss were really invincible, but merely that their adversaries did not for a long time discover how to deal with them. The English system was essentially fitted for defensive battles only; for an army settled down in a position with well-covered flanks, and attacked in front by an obliging enemy—whether horse or foot—it was certainly admirable. But it was not easy to apply against an enemy who caught an English army on the march—as at Patay; or who defied it to attack an entrenched position—as at Castillon; or who assailed it by long range artillery fire, and forced it to choose between taking the offensive or being slowly shot down—as at Formigny. And similarly, the Swiss system was even more fallible than the English, though no one for a long time discovered how to deal with it. A Swiss column could run down ordinary mediæval infantry, or pike off even the best mediæval cavalry. But it was terribly vulnerable to every form of missile, from the cannon-ball down to the arrow, and if once stopped in its career, and forced to halt and face outward, it was the easiest of marks. Charles of Burgundy was not wrong in his theory but in his detailed application of it, when he tried at Granson to deal with the Swiss column, by forcing it to halt in order to receive successive cavalry charges, while artillery was being brought up to play upon its flank. Nor was he wrong in theory either at Morat, where he thought that an entrenched position lavishly garnished with cannon would stop the " steam-roller " tactics of the enemy. But at Granson he was so badly informed of the enemy's force and movements that he acted as if the Swiss vanguard was the whole Swiss army, and was completely discomfited by the successive arrivals of the rear *échelons* of the adversary. While at Morat the entrenched camp was sound enough, but was so badly guarded that not a fourth of the army was in it, when the Swiss delivered the frontal assault that might have ruined them if the position had been properly manned. The justification of the unlucky Duke's theory, but not of his practice, was seen forty years later when Marignano was a Granson which " came off," and fifty years later when the most arrogant of Swiss armies dashed itself in vain against the bloody trenches of Bicocca.[1]

We have seen that beside the English and the Swiss systems there were two other schemes of tactics tried during the fifteenth century—those of the Italian *condottieri* and of the Hussites. The first was a thoroughly unreal business, as we have shown at some length in the Twelfth Book of this volume. The survival of heavy cavalry tactics in Italy, as an almost bloodless game, played by professionals under strict rules, lasted down to the French invasion of 1494. With the intervention of a barbarous enemy, who fought to kill, and did not see that he was beaten if he were tactically out-manœuvred, the whole absurd system was swept away. As to the Hussites, their *wagenburg* device reminds the commentator somewhat of the English order of battle, in that it was good only for the defensive, and against adversaries who consented to make frontal attacks. But it was far clumsier than the English method, since waggons are slow to move, and the hand-gun never attained to the rapidity of fire of the longbow. Against resourceful generals, and troops which started the action in a state of good morale, the *wagenburg* system ought to have failed at an early stage of the war, because of its inherent inadaptability to a campaign of movement. It achieved some astounding successes, but

[1] See above, pp. 279, 280.

the best proof of its limitations is the fact that no one even thought of continuing it after 1434—except, indeed, the Russians in their very special sort of campaigning against Tartars and Poles. With them it remained in use even down to the seventeenth century.

To sum up the lessons of the fifteenth century, we may say that the systems of the English and the Hussites had been proved inadaptable to many conditions of war : that the tactics of the dismounted man-at-arms, whether employed against the bow or against the pike, had secured few victories, and those of an unconvincing sort. The fame of the Swiss column was at its height since Granson and Morat ; its essential drawbacks were beginning to be guessed at by acute observers, but it was reserved for the sixteenth century to demonstrate them. The condottiere wars of Italy were a solemn farce.

Meanwhile professional soldiers were groping about for the moral of what they had seen and heard. One tendency of the later fifteenth century was a decided recrudescence of the idea that cavalry must be more used—not as the only force in war, but in combination with missile-bearing infantry and with field artillery. There was a lively controversy going on during the last period of the Hundred Years' War between those who favoured the English system of dismounting the man-at-arms and using him as a support for infantry—whether armed with bow, crossbow, or hand-gun—and those who thought that mounted men might be as effective as dismounted for that purpose. We hear of cavalry charges at Baugé—where the English knights had outstripped their infantry, and the French, seeing them unaccompanied by the formidable bow, tried with success an assault on horseback.[1] At the considerable combat of St. Riquier (August 31, 1421) between French and Burgundians, no English being present, both sides indulged (having little infantry), in a genuine tilting match, " with a grand clattering of arms, and horses thrown to the ground in horrible fashion on both sides." [2] Yet the opposite theory was still predominant : at Cravant not only did the Burgundians dismount like the English, but the Dauphinois also. And the same was the case at Verneuil, save that the French made a large flanking detachment of Gascon and Italian horse to fall on the English archers—an experiment which failed completely

[1] See above, p. 389.   [2] Monstrelet, i. chap. 246.

of its purpose.[1] At Patay, as has been mentioned before, the French surprised the English on the march, and beat them by charging in before " the archers had time to fix their stakes." But that it was the surprise that settled the day, not any failure in the old English defensive tactics, was shown at the combat of Clermont-en-Beauvoisis (January 1430), by Sir Thomas Kyriel's little victory over the Count of Clermont, where the English, being " on foot, with a wood in their rear and sharp stakes in their front," repulsed an assault of double numbers. "*As they were on horseback*," remarks Monstrelet,[2] " they were soon repulsed by the arrows of the archers and thrown into confusion"—a remark which shows how strongly the chronicler was impressed with the idea that the bowman in position was invincible.

In the next year (1431) at the considerable battle of Boulegn-ville, where the Duke of Bar was beaten by Anthony of Vaudemont and the Burgundians, the latter are said to have been drawn up in the English style. " The Burgundian men-at-arms wished to remain on horseback, but the Picards and English would not suffer them ; and at last it was ordered that every man, whatever his rank, should dismount ; and he that disobeyed should be put to death." [3] They stood, their flanks covered by archery and stakes, to receive battle. Where-upon Réné of Bar dismounted the greater part of his men-at-arms also, before delivering his attack, which was completely repulsed, mainly by arrow-shot. The Duke himself was wounded and taken prisoner, along with the Bishop of Metz and some two hundred combatants more.

Even after the English had retired across the Channel, to continue the practice of their national tactics in the Wars of the Roses, the influence of their teaching was still felt on the Continent. An interesting passage in Commines gives us an account of the debate before the battle of Montl'hery, where Charles the Rash and Louis the Wily met for the only occasion in open battle. The chronicler was with the Burgundian count. " Our first orders were that every man should alight without any exception : but that was countermanded, and nearly all the men-at-arms mounted again. However, some good knights and squires were ordered to remain on foot, among the rest the Lord of Cordes and his brother ; and the Lord

---

[1] See above, p. 391.   [2] Book ii. chap. 76.   [3] *Ibid.* ii. chap. 108.

Philip of Lalain was likewise on foot, for at that time among the Burgundians it was held more honourable to fight in that fashion along with the archers. This custom they had learnt from the English, when Duke Philip was making war on France, during his youth, for thirty-two years together without any truce." [1]

That the English style was on the wane is sufficiently shown by the fact that Charles ended by mounting his knights, and trusting everything to a cavalry charge, in which he won considerable advantage, but exposed the flank of his own infantry, who were fallen upon by a body of French horse and badly cut up. This fight of Montl'hery was a most confused affair, each side having routed one of the enemy's wings, but having failed to get any decisive advantage thereby. Charles was held to have been victorious because he was in possession of the battlefield next morning. But it was a very technical victory. " Never was there a greater rout on both sides," says Commines ; " but what was remarkable, the two princes themselves both kept on the field to the last. But on the king's side there was a personage of note who fled as far as Lusignan in Poitou without stopping ; and on the Count's side another who ran as far as Le Quesnoy in Hainault— which two cavaliers certainly had no intention or desire to molest each other." [2] There would seem no doubt that the fact that two masses of very undisciplined gentry were both taking the offensive, on horseback, was the cause of their wild scattering, and of the inconclusive result of the day. For if either side had been dismounted and taking the defensive, it might conceivably have been annihilated, but it would not have been dispersed over ten square miles, partly in pursuit and partly in headlong flight, before the day was two hours older. But with untrained cavalry this is quite possible— as witness the event of Edgehill in our own annals, when two large bodies of raw English horse met each other in the first clash of the great Civil War.

But after Montl'hery Charles of Burgundy stuck to the system of using cavalry as cavalry, and only detailed a few officers of note to stay on foot and steady his archer-line. At his victory of St. Troud in 1467, he made a centre of infantry— mostly archers, but with a few men-at-arms—with two heavy

---

[1] Commines, i. chap. iii.   [2] *Ibid.* chap. iv.

wings of horse.[1]   At Granson he had horse and foot in each of
the divisions of his army.   In his reorganisation of his beaten
host at Lausanne, as has been mentioned above, each of his
eight brigades was a mixed force.[2]   These were all moves in
the right direction—the future lay with the tactician who should
be able to combine all arms—horse, foot, and artillery—instead
of trusting entirely to one.   But Charles the Rash was not the
man to bring any system to perfection : and he lost his life and his
military reputation fighting against an enemy whose sole tactical
expedient was the ponderous rush of the column of pikes.

Two other characteristics of the fifteenth-century Art of
War have still to be mentioned.   The first was the increasing use
of field artillery, which we have noted in dealing with the
tactics of the Hussites, with the fields of Formigny and Castillon
on French soil, and those of Northampton, Barnet, and Tewkesbury on our own side of the Channel.   But the rate of fire
was so slow, and the equipment of the field-gun so inefficient
for prompt movement, that we find ourselves still only at the
beginning of the development of artillery tactics.   Guns were
hardly effective as yet, except in defensive battles, and behind
entrenchments.   Machiavelli, well after the end of the fifteenth
century, will only allow them a salvo or two before the " real
fight " of infantry and cavalry commences.   It was reserved
for the great artillerists of the sixteenth century to make the
gun more movable and more effective.

There remains only one more point on which stress must
be laid upon fifteenth-century foreshadowings of changes
which were to become all-important in the next period—this
was the age when a real standing army first began to be seen.
Many kings had kept personal guards permanently on foot,
and the Italian despots of the fourteenth and fifteenth centuries had developed such corps to a considerable size.   The
Janissaries of the Turkish sultans, though they had grown by
the end of our period to the respectable figure of ten thousand
bowmen, were not a regular army, but a vast extension of the
slave-guard which the caliphs of Bagdad and the Eyubite
rulers of Egypt had maintained in earlier days.   They were
familia regis, in an even more correct sense than were the
modest body of knights and constables whom Edward I.
designated by that name.

[1] See Commines, II. chap. ii.   [2] See above, p. 268.

The first real standing army, as opposed to the personal guard of the king, was undoubtedly that composed of the twenty *Compagnies d' Ordonnance*—fifteen for Langue d'Oil and five for Languedoc—which Charles VII. of France organised and kept permanently on foot, after he had concluded his long truce with the English in 1444. They were not attached to the king's person, but quartered in strategical positions all over France : Charles kept only the two companies of his Scottish archers for actual escort-duty or palace-watch. The " Companies " were not bodies of mercenaries hired from *condottieri*, for the king nominated all officers, paid the men individually, and dismissed old and recruited new gendarmes at his pleasure. Moreover, he had a staff of inspectors who reviewed the companies at reasonable intervals.[1] The original purpose of this organisation was to keep peace in a land which for thirty years had been suffering under the brigandage bred by civil and foreign war. For the regions from which the English had recently been driven were in a state of absolute anarchy, and those to which they had never penetrated were in little better case. The ill-paid bands which had been levying war in the king's name were hardly to be distinguished by their conduct from those which were frankly robber gangs working for their own profit. All " Écorcheurs " were enemies of the peasant, the wayfaring merchant, or the bourgeois of small unwalled towns. Charles selected from the mass of his disorderly adherents a score of captains, most of whom were French nobles, but some professional mercenaries both of native and of foreign blood.[2] They were chosen not entirely for military skill, but as trustworthy and hard-handed personages who could keep their men in order. And to them was given the task of selecting a limited number of steady troopers and archers who were to form the twenty companies. All the rest of the king's forces, a heterogenous and most disreputable crew, were disbanded with a high hand, and the majority of them had already been induced to join the great expedition which the Dauphin Louis took off to his enterprise against Switzerland and Alsace.

[1] For a full account of the of the *Compagnies d'Ordonnance*, see De Beaucourt's *Histoire de Charles VII.*, vol. iv. pp. 387–400, and Susane's *Histoire de la Cavalaire Française*, chap. i.

[2] Such as the Italian Bonifazio de Valperga. Gaspard Bureau, the great artillerist, and Tristan L'Hermite, the notorious confidant of Louis XI., seem to have had companies a little later.

These were the " Armagnacs " whom we have found fighting the Swiss at the battle of St. Jacob-on-Birs, and getting small profit from their adventure.[1]

The picked men who were retained in the king's service were organised in companies, each officered by a captain, lieutenant, ' guidon ' and ensign, and consisting of one hundred *lances fournies*. The " lance " consisted of one man-at-arms, a *coutiller* who acted as his squire, a page, two archers, and a *valet de guerre*, all furnished with horses. Thus the companies were a mixed force of light and heavy horse and mounted archers, running up to six hundred men apiece. The units were organised in 1445, and received regular pay from January 1, 1446, onward, the man-at-arms getting ten *livres tournois* a month, out of which he had to keep his horses and the page, while the other members of the lance got four or five livres apiece. In addition, liberal rations were provided. Those companies which were not placed as garrisons in royal castles, but in towns and cities, were billeted on the inhabitants: but the latter had no responsibility beyond that of finding a bed, a table, and linen for both. No food was to be extorted from them, as the rations were reckoned ample for man and horse.

The *Compagnies d'Ordonnance* were kept permanently on foot—after the English war recommenced in 1449 they were of course more needed than ever. And when Louis XI. succeeded his father he found to his hand a force without which he could never have made head against the leagues of his unruly relatives and vassals. If that most unpopular prince had been forced to rely on feudal levies alone, he would have succumbed in the struggle. But he had in the companies a solid nucleus of veteran troops, uninfluenced by local or personal ties to rebel lords, and kept loyal to their paymaster by the regularity with which he served out their stipulated *livres tournois* month by month. For, however great the drain on his exchequer, Louis XI. regarded his invaluable standing army as having the first call on it. These companies were undoubtedly the model on which all later permanent forces were modelled, such, for example, as the six hundred *lances garnies* which Charles the Rash levied in 1471, and kept on foot till the end of his life.[2]

[1] See above, p. 264.   [2] Commines, III. chap. iv.

Charles VII. did not raise any regular infantry, unless the archers of the *lance fournie* may be called mounted infantry. But to supply himself in time of war with foot soldiery somewhat better than the rabble of his earlier days, he instituted the *Francs Archers*, a sort of territorial militia only called out in time of actual war. The system by which they were raised was that in each parish, or similar unit, an able-bodied man was designated, who received permanent immunity from much taxation, and personal freedom from the feudal rights of his local lord when on the king's service, as also regular pay of four francs a month—the same as that of the archers of the *Compagnies*—when actually called out to the field. In return he was bound to provide himself with light armour—a steel cap and a brigandine or jack—and with a bow or crossbow.[1] Arrangements were made by which all the *Francs Archers* of a district were occasionally assembled for a muster by royal inspectors, and they were directed to keep themselves in constant efficiency by regular attendance at the butts. Various authorities speak of the total of this sedentary militia as rising to eight thousand men under Charles VII., and to a much higher figure under Louis XI. ; but it is evident that they were, if much better than peasants, a body of only mediocre efficiency. For on their first assembly at the outbreak of a war, they were but a mass of individuals, needing to be enregimented, and to be trained to act in mass. They could have nothing of the cohesion caused by constant embodiment, which was to be found in the *Compagnies d'Ordonnance*. These reasons, no doubt, explain the fact that the corps fell out of use, and cannot be called the real progenitors of the French regular infantry, since they were essentially a militia like the " selected bands " of an English county in the time of the Tudors. The real origin of regular foot-soldiery in France, as in the other states of the sixteenth century, is to be found in the Swiss mercenaries whom Louis XI. first hired, and Charles VIII. and his successors kept permanently on foot.

By 1485, then, standing armies were beginning to appear, and since they were the tools of kings, and in no wise the property of their captains, like the bands of the Italian *condottieri*, nor of their feudal lords, like ordinary mediæval troops,

---

[1] There were *Francs Arbalêtiers* as well as *Francs Archers*, see note in Beaufort, iv. 403, though the latter term is the one almost invariably used.

their political was even greater than their military significance, in a period when absolute monarchy was gaining ground, and feudalism was dying. But a book dealing with the Middle Ages is not one which can be expected to trace the development of this new phenomenon.

Having summed up the state of the Art of War at the end of the fifteenth century, we leave it at the commencement of a new epoch, which was destined to last for a couple of centuries. The next really important date in military history is that of the invention of the bayonet, which changed the face of war and " made every musketeer his own pikeman "—for essentially the period between 1494 and 1690 is the period of " pike and musket." We have seen the first hints of what the character of the new epoch was to be in studying the history of the Swiss, and the first triumphs of the pike have been detailed, down to the two astounding victories at Granson and Morat (1476), which first taught Europe that a new period in tactics had arrived. But the pike alone was not wholly self-sufficient, as Machiavelli saw, before most of his contemporaries had discovered the fact. It required to be well supported by other arms, as was sufficiently shown by its failures at Marignano and Bicocca.[1] And the final development of the lessons of the great Italian wars was the supplementing of the pike by the musket—the child of that once despised hand-gun, which had first become a serious weapon in the hands of Zisca's Hussites.[2] When pike and musket have combined into the sixteenth-century " regiment," we are in the midst of the new period of the Art of War. But it was a period in which pike and musket, though predominant, did not settle everything, for the field-gun was beginning to grow important, and the horseman, when once he began to strip himself of his absurd load of defensive armour, and regained an ever-growing mobility, was destined for a great future. The man-at-arms became a *demi-lance* by 1560, when he had freed his lower limbs from the encumbering weight of cuissarts and greaves. And later, as a mere " cuirassier," with breast and back plate alone, he became still more masterful. In the seventeenth century, under Gustavus Adolphus and Cromwell, he had regained a position such as he had not held since Creçy, and became so formidable to the composite pike-and-

[1] See above, pp. 278–9.   [2] See above, p. 365.

436 THE ART OF WAR IN THE MIDDLE AGES [1485

musket regiment that it required the invention of the socket-bayonet to re-establish the balance between the two arms.

Here we leave the tale of the transformations of the Art of War, which we have followed for a thousand years and one century more, from Adrianople to Bosworth Field. We quit it at a time when efficiency in war had ceased to be the attribute of a class, and was becoming the attribute of a profession. War was no longer an occupation in which feudal chivalry found its glory and the rest of society its ruin. It was becoming by the end of our period a subject of much study, a matter not of tradition, but of experiment, and the vigorous sixteenth century was to add to it many new forms and variations. The Middle Ages were over, and the stirring and scientific spirit of the Renaissance was to work changes destined to make the methods of mediæval war seem farther removed from the strategy and tactics of the modern world than were those of the great days of Ancient Greece and Rome.

INDEX—I

CHRONOLOGICAL INDEX OF BATTLES DESCRIBED IN THESE
TWO VOLUMES

437

INDEX—II

INDEX

458 THE ART OF WAR IN THE MIDDLE AGES

Turma, Byzantine military unit, i. 184.

Turmarch, Byzantine officer, i. 184, 211.

Twenge, Sir Marmaduke, at Stirling Bridge, ii. 77.

Tyrants, in ancient Greece and mediæval Italy, ii. 285, 287–288.

Ufford, Thomas, son of Earl of Suffolk, present at Navarette, ii. 186. *See also* Suffolk.

Unstrut, battle on the, i. 121.

Urban, the gun-founder, ii. 357.

Urbicius, tactical suggestions of, i. 23.

Ürslingen, Werner of, *condottiere*, ii. 292.

Uzès, Raymond Bishop of, i. 458.

Valens, Emperor, slain at Adrianople, i. 13.

Valerian, Emperor, defeated by the Persians, i. 6.

Valery, St. *See* St. Valery.

Valois, Philip of. *See* Philip vi. of France.

Vandals, conquered by Belisarius, i. 29, 30.

Varangians, the, at battle of Dyrrhachium, i. 166.

Vassi, the Frankish, i. 102.

Vegetius, his description of the Roman army, i. 17, 18.

Venice, naval power of, i. 232; conquers Syrian seaports, i. 254; land conquests of, ii. 289–290.

Verneuil, battle of, ii. 392.

Vienne, John de, Admiral, defeats the English fleet, ii. 200; slain at Nicopolis, ii. 352.

Vikings, their origin and character, i. 89–91; their war-vessels, i. 91; their armour, i. 92; their tactics, i. 96–97; checked by the Franks, i. 106–107; checked by Alfred and Edward, i. 111, 112.

Vilani, Matteo, on guns at Creçy, ii. 218, 219.

Visconti, Gian Galeazzo, ii. 286–288.

Visigoths, political and military weakness of the, i. 445; their military customs, i. 45; their arms, i. 46.

Vittoria, the Black Prince at, ii. 183.

Wace, his account of Hastings, i. 153 *et seq.*

Wagenburg, the, used by Russians and Hussites, ii. 363–365.

Wakefield, battle of, ii. 412.

Walcourt, Thierry of, present at Steppes, i. 451.

Waldric, captures Robert of Normandy, i. 383.

Wales, Princes of. *See* Llewellyn and Edward. *See also under* Welsh.

Wallace, Sir William, his victory at Stirling Bridge, ii. 75–76; ravages Northumberland, ii. 77; defeated at Falkirk, ii. 78–80; his execution, ii. 82.

Wamba, Visigothic king, military legislation of, i. 45.

Wareham, sacked by the Danes, i. 90.

Warrenne, John Earl of, present at Lewes, i. 423–430; defeated at Stirling Bridge, ii. 75–76.

Warrenne, William ii. Earl of, present at Tenchebrai, i. 381; at Bremûle, i. 387.

Warrenne, William iii. Earl of, at Lincoln, i. 397.

Warwick, Richard Neville Earl of, ii. 411; defeated at St. Albans, ii. 412; rebels against Edward iv., ii. 413; his last campaign, ii. 414–416; slain at Barnet, ii. 417.

Warwick, Thomas Beauchamp Earl of, Marshal of Edward iii., ii. 133; present at Creçy, ii. 138.

Warwick, William Beauchamp Earl of, victorious in battle near Conway, ii. 70.

Weald, the, archery in, ii. 60–61.

Wearmouth, sacked by the Danes, i. 90.

Wedmore, the Peace of, i. 112.

Weland, Viking king, i. 106.

Welsh, strife of the Anglo-Saxons with, i. 65, 66; early arms of the, i. 68; present at Lincoln, i. 396; archery of the, i. 404; ii. 59–60; present at Lewis, i. 423; at Evesham, i. 439–440; at Falkirk, ii. 60, 80; at Creçy, ii. 129, 136, 146.

Welsh March, castles of the, ii. 22–23.

Wenlock, John Lord, slain at Tewkesbury, ii. 422.

"Weregeld Document," the, importance of, i. 109–110.

Wessex, early organisation of, i. 67; the "Burgal Hidage" of, i. 111, 112.

White Company, the, ii. 294–295.

William i. the Conqueror, his invasion of England, i. 149; wins battle of Hastings, i. 150–166; captures Exeter, i. 134; employs movable towers, i. 135; institutes knight-service, i. 361; his castles, ii. 13, 15; builds the Tower of London, ii. 15–16.

William ii., Rufus, employs the fyrd, i. 359–360; enlarges the Tower of London, ii. 16; his castle-building, ii. 16.

William Clito, present at Bremûle, i. 385; victorious at Thielt, i. 443–445; dies, i. 445.

William Crispin, his exploits at Bremûle, i. 387–388.

William the Lion, King of Scotland, captured at Alnwick, i. 400.

William Longsword. *See* Salisbury.

William of Nevers, Count, his unfortunate Crusade, i. 240, 241.

William of Poictiers, Duke of Aquitaine, his unfortunate Crusade, i. 233.

Winchester, Saher de Quincey Earl of, present at Lincoln, i. 413–418.